Lecture Notes in Information Systems and Organisation

Volume 23

More information about this series at http://www.springer.com/series/11237

Cecilia Rossignoli · Francesco Virili
Stefano Za

Editors

Digital Technology and Organizational Change

Reshaping Technology, People, and Organizations Towards a Global Society

Springer

Editors
Cecilia Rossignoli
Department of Business Administration
University of Verona
Verona
Italy

Stefano Za
Department of Business and Management
LUISS University
Rome
Italy

Francesco Virili
Department of Economics and Management
University of Sassari
Sassari
Italy

ISSN 2195-4968   ISSN 2195-4976   (electronic)
Lecture Notes in Information Systems and Organisation
ISBN 978-3-319-62050-3   ISBN 978-3-319-62051-0   (eBook)
https://doi.org/10.1007/978-3-319-62051-0

Library of Congress Control Number: 2017946623

Printed on acid-free paper

This Springer imprint is published by Springer Nature
The registered company is Springer International Publishing AG
The registered company address is: Gewerbestrasse 11, 6330 Cham, Switzerland

Contents

Contents

Introduction

Cecilia Rossignoli, Francesco Virili and Stefano Za

We are glad to propose in this volume, according to an enduring tradition, a selection of the papers presented at the XIII conference of ItAIS, the Italian Chapter of AIS (Association for Information Systems), held at University of Verona on October 7–8, 2016. The conference theme: "ICT and innovation: a step forward to a global society" suggests a composite, inclusive, and rich view over the multiple dimensions of innovation, along the technical, organizational, and social perspectives, encouraging an open dialogue within our evolving community of research and practice. The interconnections of the technical, organizational, and social dimensions have been outlined in several studies [e.g. 1–4]. Indeed, IT-driven innovation is happening at the same time at all the levels of analysis (i.e. individuals, organizations, and society) and blurring internal and external organizational environment boundaries [5]. In its entirety, the research work presented in this volume, can be seen as a mosaic of different approaches and views, offering in its complexity and richness a fresh answer to recent research calls [6], underlining the limitations of traditional studies too often exclusively focused on a rigorous and detailed analysis of a single micro or macro phenomenon. Our perspective, instead, underlining heterogeneity, interactions and variety in multiple socio-technical

C. Rossignoli (✉)
Department of Business Administration, University of Verona, Via Cantarane 24, 37129
Verona, Italy
e-mail: cecilia.rossignoli@univr.it

F. Virili
Department of Economics and Business Administration, University of Sassari, Via Muroni
25, 07100 Sassari, Italy
e-mail: fvirili@uniss.it

S. Za
Department of Business and Management, LUISS University, Rome, Italy
e-mail: sza@luiss.it

© Springer International Publishing AG 2018
C. Rossignoli et al. (eds.), *Digital Technology and Organizational Change*,
Lecture Notes in Information Systems and Organisation 23,
https://doi.org/10.1007/978-3-319-62051-0_1

1

aspects, aims to shed some new light on our more urgent contemporary challenges, as recently outlined by European and other International Institutions [7].

With the idea of spanning across levels and across organizational boundaries, the volume collects 21 contributions, selected from the ItAIS Conference papers. All the selected papers have been evaluated through a standard blind review process in order to ensure theoretical and methodological rigor. The threefold structure of the volume reflects three main pillars that have been explored by the included papers. The first part is focused on how ICT innovation is transforming information systems design and software development practices, with its related challenges. The second part opens the view on the organizational world and its evolution enabled and driven by the Information Systems world depicted above. The third part is devoted to some of the corresponding transformation and challenges towards a global society.

This publication is the result of a team work where many people have actively contributed. We are grateful to the Authors, the Conference Chairs and Committee members, to the members of the Editorial Board, and to the Reviewers for their competence and commitment.

1   Part I: IS Design Innovation and Challenges

The contributions grouped in this section are devoted to software development and information systems design practices, as innovative waves in our Information Systems world are often at the very roots of the organizational and societal evolution taken into account in the rest of the book.

De Michelis opens this debate focusing on the role of business designers and organizational networks within innovative companies competing in the globalized market. He proposes some first hints on how business designers promote or should promote networks and suggest that organizational networks are necessary for doing business design. Moreover, he focuses on how Information and Communication Technology can support the effectiveness of networks, suggesting the technological innovation that should foster the raise of business designers.

In her exploratory research study, Khalil aims at understanding, through different expert perspectives, the challenges and success factors encountered in distinct types of ICT projects (agile vs. plan driven approaches), using a qualitative research approach based on semi-structured interviews with senior project management consultants. In their research-in-progress, Chaves, Scornavacca, and Fowler aim to address the complex phenomenon of knowledge sharing within the context of social media. The objective of the paper is to examine how the affordances of social media impact knowledge sharing dynamics in intra-organizational Information Technology (IT) projects. This paper adopts Design Science Research (DSR) as research paradigm and the Technical Action Research (TAR) as validation method.

In her contribution, Simone discusses on systems (re-)design in the light of the socio-technical (ST) design approach and by considering how (re-)design can be made more manageable by looking at the work practices that mitigates the limits of the current ST systems. On the same argument, Bednar and Sadok report upon some results of an empirical study involving employees from 32 SMEs in the UK on how they approach socio-technical principles in the design of their work systems. They are particularly interested in what extent employees are engaged with decision making, change in work practices and job satisfaction. Finally, Cabitza and Varanini introduce a new concept, namely "cybork", to account for the dynamic nature of socio-technical systems and make this nature a primary concern of systems thinking to understand and intervene on this kind of systems.

As conclusion of this section, Melonio describes an interesting example of participatory game design. It is a complex interaction design process, taking various design tasks and demands different cognitive skills. This project has been conducted with children for eliciting their expectations for games for them.

2   Part II: Organizational Innovation and Challenges

In this section research interest shifts from IS design innovation in itself to its enabling effects, evolving forces and business transformation pressures in the organizational world. Firms experiment both opportunities and competitive pressures to evolve their business models and organizational processes thanks to the IS innovation forces taken into account in the preceding section. The first paper in this series takes into account the increasing organizational relevance of IT managers. Ricciardi, Zardini and Bonomi argue, based on their analysis and integration of different theoretical frameworks, that positive and strong IT managers' relations within their organization have a positive influence on organizational life and performance in several intertwining ways. Scholars investigating the importance of effective IT managers' relations tend to rely on two mainstream theoretical approaches: the resource-based view (RBV) and sister theories, on the one hand; and the business-IT alignment view, on the other hand. Ricciardi et al. propose that these two theories, although very effective in explaining several aspects of the importance of IT managers' relationships, are not sufficient, and could be usefully complemented by at least two further important theories: Lawrence and Lorsch's view of organizational differentiation and integration, and the cyclical model of organizational learning proposed by Zollo and Winter. Therefore, their study presents the contribution of these four theoretical approaches to explaining the importance of IT managers' relationships.

De Nicola and Villani present a methodology to support innovation processes in business contexts. The methodology consists of three phases. First, an innovation team composed of stakeholders, domain experts and knowledge engineers collects domain knowledge. In the second phase of the methodology, creative sparks are identified to ignite a collaborative activity by the innovation team, which may lead to identification of new innovative ideas. In the third phase, selected ideas are elaborated and validated in the specific business context. In their contribution, they focus on the first two phases and present an innovation management system to support them. Although the proposed methodology is general purpose, they describe an application in the business intelligence sector.

Focusing still on innovation, the contribution provided by Lazazzara and Galanaki builds on diffusion of innovation (DOI) and institutional theories to address the current lack of cross-national studies on e-HRM adoption and usage. The core research question asks about the factors influencing e-HRM adoption and usage for HRM. As result, the economic sector of activity, size, global competition and educational level were associated with e-HRM adoption and usage at the organizational level. Moreover, a strategic orientation of the HR function seems to be a prerequisite for e-HRM adoption and usage.

The following two contributions are devoted to emerging and evolving challenges in relatively mature areas of digitalization for contemporary businesses: customer satisfaction for e-tailers and data mining in the banking industry. Russo, Confente, and Borghesi focus on e-commerce and customer relationships, with a special interest on a quite new phenomenon in a consolidated field: the impact of return policies on customer satisfaction. Return policies are particularly relevant in cloths and shoes e-markets: almost one third of all online-ordered clothes are returned by customers. It is increasingly important for e-tailers to offer the appropriate return policy as this will attract online customers. The aim of their paper is to better explore the impact of return policy and other drivers in enhancing the satisfaction and loyalty perceived by customer when purchasing online in a B2C context.

Diniz, Luvizan, Hino, and Ferreira investigate the adoption of big data in the banking sector. Besides requiring huge investments, big data implementation also demands an articulation between the many centers of power within a bank and a re-definition of concepts once dominant in the organization. This study describes the process of big data adoption in three major Brazilian banks and unveils the process of implementing a new technology platform in the "pluralistic context" that characterizes bank organizations. The Actor-Network Theory is used for describing and understanding the initial phases of the big data adoption journey in these banks. The authors aim to understand how some bank managers became aware of the relevance of big data to its incorporation to the bank's corporative strategy.

Digital platforms play often a relevant role in fostering organizational learning process [8]. The last three papers close this section exploring this challenging and relevant area. E-learning is pervading higher education, being a convenient training opportunity in a busy and demanding society. Despite being a popular phenomenon both in research and in practice, e-learning is however far from being successfully implemented in any context. This is a matter of both inadequate exploration of the learners' perspective and insufficient reflection about the implications for the instructors. Caporarello, Manzoni, and Bigi focus on the first aspect, surveying 277 university students about their opinion and experience of e-learning. Based on their findings (that were partially unexpected and expected), they develop some managerial implications for instructors and educational organizations. Crombie, Mersch, Dulskaia, and Bellini present early results of the first European applied game-jam network called JamToday. The paper presents the work achieved by the JamToday Network in the first two years and very concrete and practical tools and methodologies developed by the JamToday Network to support game-design approaches for learning environments from design to transfer and evaluation. Caporarello, Magni, and Pennarola describe the results of an interesting business case experiment. They analyze individual learning in a computer-based simulation setting (business game). In particular, the study points out the importance of the team environment in stimulating individual states that may foster individual learning. By taking into account 402 individuals who participated in a computer-based simulation, they underscore that individual perception of integration climate foster individual curiosity and decreases individual aggressiveness. Moreover, they outline that individual curiosity does have an impact on individual learning.

3   Part III: Societal Innovation and Challenges

This section concerns societal innovation challenges at large. The first four chapters show how different generations are responding in different ways to ICT innovation phenomena like Internet usage, knowledge intensive processes, knowledge work, and digital employee experiences. The last two chapters are focused on societal issues regarding two specific digital artifacts, Electronic Medical Record, discussing the opportunities and challenges of sharing health information, and Time Accounting System, disclosing interesting opportunities for time banks and similar parallel non-monetary economies in the developing countries.

Hussain, Ross, and Bednar investigate on the Internet usage by elderly people, born from the mid 1920s to the early 1940s. In this case Internet could be a challenging technology for them due to their experience and knowledge in using the computer and Internet. At the same time, elderly people are anxious about Internet security, as they believe they can be victimized, hence the reason why the generation avoids the technology as much as possible. Participants also believed there was no need to use the Internet, as they have managed without the technology throughout their career. The paper also discusses the key elements by outlining the benefits and drawbacks relating to age-related disabilities, affordability, and privacy/security issues.

Modern organizations, increasingly adopt knowledge Intensive Processes (KIPs) and use work teams to perform knowledge intensive tasks and coordination activities. The chapter of Aloini, Covucci, and Stefanini offers a methodological support towards a more quantitative and systematic analysis of knowledge workers and their collaboration dynamics. Focusing on generation X, Sarti and Torre aim to demonstrate the positive impact of the use of ICT and knowledge work content on employees' wellbeing. Their results offer interesting stimuli for a debate between scholars and practitioners in the management of employees, calling for attention to the controversial effect of ICT usage and particular attention to this mid-generation.

Even though, organizations face the co-presence of three generations of workers ("baby boomers", Xers and Yers), another generation will join the workforce in the next years: the generation Z. Accordingly, companies must be able to understand their characteristics and expectations, in order to manage their generation mix. The contribution of Meret, Fioravanti, Iannotta, and Gatti, firstly reviews the extant literature, afterwards analyzes and discusses the results of a survey among 298 young people, belonging to the generation Z. The findings reveal both a universal profile of the future generation of workers, together with their digital behaviors.

Badr provides a literature review on Electronic Medical Record (HER) and summarizes a few persistent challenges that EHR systems should address relating to security and safety of patients. In particular, in his position paper, two major initiatives are revealed: (1) The premise of patient engagement and (2) the guidelines. As conclusion of this section, Sultana, Locoro and Corrêa da Silva describe the first validation steps of the prototype of a Time Accounting System (TAS), which has been designed and developed to investigate how a technology that facilitates service exchanges using local currency can be accepted in a developing country, namely in Bangladesh.

References

1. Brass, D. J., Galaskiewicz, J., Greve, H. R., & Tsai, W. (2004). Taking stock of networks and organizations: A multilevel perspective. *Academy of Management Journal, 47*(6), 795–817.
2. Sasidharan, S., Santhanam, R., Brass, D. J., & Sambamurthy, V. (2012). The effects of social network structure on enterprise systems success: A longitudinal multilevel analysis. *Information Systems Research, 23*(3), 658–678.
3. Venkatesh, V., Rai, A., Sykes, T. A., & Aljafari, R. (forthcoming). Combating infant mortality in rural India: Evidence from a field study of eHealth Kiosk Implementations. *MIS Quarterly.*
4. Ahuja, M. K., Chudoba, K. M., Kacmar, C. J., McKnight, D. H., & George, J. F. (2007). IT road warriors: Balancing work-family conflict, job autonomy, and work overload to mitigate turnover intentions. *Mis Quarterly, 31*, 1–17.
5. Markus, M. L., & Robey, D. (1988). Information technology and organizational change: Causal structure in theory and research. *Management Science, 34*(5), 583–598.
6. Johns, G. (2006). The essential impact of context on organizational behavior. *Academy of Management Review, 31*(2), 386–408.
7. Venkatesh, V., & Sykes, T. A. (2013). Digital divide initiative success in developing countries: A longitudinal field study in a village in India. *Information Systems Research, 24*(2), 239–260.
8. Za, S., Spagnoletti, P., & North-Samardzic, A. (2014). Organisational learning as an emerging process: The generative role of digital tools in informal learning practices. *British Journal of Educational Technology, 45*, 1023–1035.

Part I
IS Design Innovation and Challenges

Business Designers, Organizational Networks and ICT

Giorgio De Michelis

Abstract Within innovative companies competing in the globalized market we can observe two distinct phenomena characterizing their changes with respect to the past: the proliferation of organizational networks and the raise of a new profile of top manager/entrepreneur that has been called business designer. Scholars and practitioners are paying great attention to these two phenomena in order to characterize them and to improve their reproducibility. Since business designers are characterized mostly for their way to design and develop innovation at the level of products, services and customers relationships, while organizational networks are seen as transformers of the organization of innovative companies, there has been little or no attention to the mutual relations binding the two phenomena. In this paper I propose some first hints on how business designers promote or should promote networks and suggest that organizational networks are necessary for doing business design. The last sections discuss how Information and Communication Technology can support the effectiveness of networks and suggest the technological innovation that should accompany the raise of business designers.

Keywords Organizational network · Business designer · Design thinking · Situated computing

1 Introduction

Globalization, with its consequences on markets and societies, is provoking deep transformations in organizations, from every viewpoint: customer relations, marketing strategies, production's organization and product design are widely changing and only those companies that change trying to become flexible and proactive actors will survive and, sometimes, grow. This claim, for whose rough generalization I apologize with my readers, is particularly true for all enterprises

G. De Michelis (✉)
Università degli Studi di Milano-Bicocca, Viale Sarca 336, 20126 Milan, Italy
e-mail: gdemich@disco.unimib.it

© Springer International Publishing AG 2018
C. Rossignoli et al. (eds.), *Digital Technology and Organizational Change*,
Lecture Notes in Information Systems and Organisation 23,
https://doi.org/10.1007/978-3-319-62051-0_2

competing in markets where innovation is a major success factor, like high-tech, but not only there. Scholars and practitioners of several disciplines (work sociology, industrial economics, organizational science, information systems, etc.) are observing and studying from different viewpoints the changes undergoing in organizations. Two issues raised in those studies seem to me particularly important, since they offer two complementary views on new organizations.

On the one hand, the growing presence of *network* structures in organizations [5, 6, 15]: from enterprise networks and networked enterprises, to collaborative networks. Networks appear, as first, as new structures mitigating and circumventing the rigidity of hierarchical organizational systems: networks allow to negotiate forms of cooperation without being obliged to fix rules and roles, trespassing organizational boundaries and constituting flexible aggregates where people not only coordinate themselves but also co-create knowledge. This is the reason for which, in these years, we have seen the growth of two types of organizational networks: institutional, inter-organizational and intra-organizational, networks, on one side, and collaborative networks, on the other side. While the former aim at creating flexible settings for putting together resources and capabilities, the other let people, from different organizational units and/or with different expertise, work together in the design and/or development of new products/services. For its variety, the concept of organizational network has been occasion of a large set of studies and of some specific analytical tools like the Actor Network Theory (ANT; [25]), becoming one of the most relevant issues in the debate on organizations.

On the other hand, the emergence of a new entrepreneur/top manager profile, that has been called *business designer*, to indicate that, at the beginning of the third millennium, business needs not to be administered but designed. Business design has been studied and practiced by a growing number of scholars and managers/consultants/entrepreneurs, with the aim to understand how innovative companies operate in the global market being able to bring innovation to economic success and to create strong companies [9, 20, 21, 28]. Research on this subject has coupled direct observation of the behaviour of the leaders of radically innovative companies with the aim to understand their distinctive features, and the development of a conceptual framework capturing the main factors influencing the success of radical innovation and allowing its repeatability in time. At the basis of all the efforts along this perspective, there is the shared recognition that, like its name underlines, coupling business and design thinking is its first necessary step, since design allows to look at business from a viewpoint where innovation is not immediately subsumed to economic discourse and opens the minds to accepting multi-disciplinary collaboration. The outcomes of this research have been also highly influential in defining the programs of new courses aiming to educate those who want to become business designers (Rotman School of Business in Toronto [28], D-School at Stanford University [http://dschool.stanford.edu], Domus Academy in Milano [www.landing.domusacademy.com/master-programs/business-design] are some examples of schools moving along this direction).

Even from this very short survey, it emerges that networks and business designers, share a focus on opening organizations to a greater flexibility in their practice and in continuously reinventing themselves, but their originating factors are quite diverse, since networks are sustained by the growth of (ICT based) systems supporting them in always more effective and varied ways and by project orientation, while business designers are singular and, in some sense, exceptional outcomes of a combination of entrepreneurship and design thinking. Moreover, networks are emerging social aggregates and binds within and among organizations, integrating and/or substituting traditional organizational structures, while business design connotes a new entrepreneurial style adopted by people who are capable to play the business game innovating it from several diverse viewpoints. Finally, even if they are global phenomena, they have a particular relevance in the Italian industry [7, 10], connoting its (best) enterprises from decades. Their combination is, therefore, an interesting puzzle. The questions that arise from the above considerations are: do organizational networks and business designers have anything in common? If yes, can we study how business designers can improve their effectiveness curing their organizational networks? Can they develop the ICT infrastructure of their company as the main, or, at least, one of the main, supports of their business?

In order to give some preliminary answers to the above questions, it is necessary to survey, at the conceptual level -networks and business design- and to discover their mutual connections, taking into account that, on the one hand, there are diverse types of organizational networks, on the other, we have several examples but only a vague and incomplete definition of 'business designers'. In trying to do what announced above, this paper, first, discusses the new managerial profile of 'business designer' and surveys two examples of business designers, then, resumes what we know about organizational networks. In this work, we try to find a good equilibrium between conceptual clarity and adhesion to what we see in the reality. The second part of the paper discusses how business designers and organizational networks are interrelated and how, discovering these interrelations, allows to define innovative plans for the development of ICT platforms. A short conclusion terminates the paper.

2 A New Managerial Profile

At the beginning of this century, I designed, with my friends of Domus Academy, the design school of Milano, a new Master for creative top managers and entrepreneurs (we were looking at the people leading Made in Italy companies). This Master was called Master in Business Design (MBD) to distinguish it from standard MBA (Masters in Business Administration) courses: it continues to be offered and delivered in these years, even if I don't have anything to do with it from years [www.landing.domusacademy.com/master-programs/business-design]. Our MBD was a quite ambitious school willing to banish Business Administrators in the loft, substituting them with a new figure, having a culture strongly influenced by design thinking. The inspiration moving us had multiple and heterogeneous sources: on the one hand, the multi-disciplinary experience we did collaborating (technologists and designers) in the design of innovative interactive systems; on the other hand, the observation of new entrepreneurs trying to invent simultaneously new products/services, new companies, and, even, new markets in the diverse sectors where Italian industry has a leading position, like mechanics, furniture and fashion [7, 10]; and, finally, the intuition that the crisis of the hierarchical model required also to reinvent the profile of the managers guiding the non-hierarchical companies, dismissing it.

   We were not the only ones moving in that direction. As we have already mentioned in the Introduction, in the same years Roger Martin uses, at the Rotman School of Management of the Toronto University, 'business design' to give a name to the new perspective [28] on which he is addressing its courses, including MBA itself; similar experiences are ongoing at several other, often very prestigious, schools, like Stanford University, where D-School (formally, the 'Hasso Plattner Institute for Design') is created, as a center for experimenting new educational programs, where computer scientists, designers and business experts work together developing design thinking [http://dschool.stanford.edu]: innovative design studios transform themselves in a new type of strategic consultancy companies capable to help companies to use design thinking to become change makers (one name for all: IDEO [21]). And research and educational experience are still ongoing on the necessary meeting between management and design culture: few months ago, it has appeared a collective book on the subject [20].

   The unrest characterizing all these experiences does not allow to fix the concepts characterizing the field. In order to make some clarity, we need, therefore, to characterize the meaning of the terms appearing in 'business design'. We do it looking at their etymologies 'business' derives from 'busy'. The business has not, originally, an economic connotation, but indicates something happening, that engages us. Even if its not difficult to explain why, quickly, it narrowed to characterize work and economic activities, it is useful in this context keeping in mind its original meaning, since, today, the distinction between work and 'free' time is always more fuzzy and we make, frequently, reference to things that we do out of our working context or for pleasure, as voluntary performances, as part of our business. In particular, it seems to me interesting that the separation between economic and non economic business is, essentially, impossible when the activity is 'statu nascenti': a group of friends, like the creators of the Noah Guitars, [www. noahguitars.com], can start an activity for purely pleasure reasons (creating a new innovative rock guitar), discovering later that it has become always more engaging, that it has a strong potential, needing therefore for a well defined business model (foreseeing also an economic return). Many start-ups follow the inverse path: they begin with the aim to make money, but they never reach their objective, even if their creators have fun working at them.

   For what regards design, Klaus Krippendorff opens his paper *On the Essential Context of Artifacts or on the Proposition that "Design is Making Sense of (Things)"* [22, p. 9] with this claim: "The etymology of *design* goes back to the Latin *de* + *signare* and means making something, distinguishing it by a sign, giving it significance, designating its relation to other things, owners, users, or gods. Based on this original meaning, one could say: design is making sense (of things)" 'design' originates, therefore, from the sign through which human beings make a thing distinguishable to become, progressively, the sign through which we make sense of it. Rather, design allows to reach the thing of which is made sense: in this way we can better understand its elongation in time.

Together with 'business', therefore, 'design' means 'making sense of what is engaging us'. It has to do, not only with granting the optimal performance of an economic activity, like requested by the role of a business administrator, but also, and mostly, with doing anything may be necessary and/or possible for bringing what we do, with other people, to a temporary completion. It is clear that, for business designers, making sense means covering all the relevant dimensions of their business: from their different performances and practices to the objects and/or service performances deriving from them and to their aesthetic and functional qualities; from the conditions where the business is performed to those of its participants; from the communication with its stakeholders to the relationships with its potential customers and beneficiaries; from its environmental impact to its profitability. I call the innovation of the business designer 'design driven innovation' [9] to distinguish it from the more traditional 'market pulled' and 'technology pushed' innovations: while traditional innovation forms are centered on one principal element sustaining it (the market, the technology), design driven innovation has at its center the stake holders and is, intrinsically multi-dimensional. Even if we should not imagine that the business designer must, perforce, bring again all of those issues into question, there is no aspect of his/her business that she cannot reinvent or redefine.

The emergence of business designers, in fact, is not due to their innovative education: rather it is grounded in the changes ongoing in the market. When the market is steady, business designers are needed only for pushing a new product/service in the market. All companies competing in steady markets may be satisfied with having a good administrator managing them, But when, as it happens now, the social and economic context is highly turbulent and unforeseeable, and breakdowns (both negative, menacing their position, or positive, opening new possibilities of business) are frequent inside and outside the organizations, undermining their conduct, their leader must be able to transform these breakdowns into occasions, rather than considering them as obstacles. This will be possible if their organizations will be able of reshaping themselves so that their efforts re-focus on new targets. In all these cases, in fact, administering is no more sufficient. Aligning activities to the planned objectives, absorbing the breakdowns, is not enough: rather it is necessary to redefine plans and, if needed, to re-design the business itself. There are several examples of companies, that have been able to perform radical changes in order to re-gain a strong economic profitability (for example, Nokia did it twice in these last thirty years), as well as there are also several examples of companies who have not been able to do it, and begun to decline (Yahoo and Benetton may be analyzed from this viewpoint).

For this reason, from the last years of the twentieth century, business design [9, 10, 20, 28] has become a widely discussed concept. This couple of words are used, generally, to characterize the growing contamination of managerial with design culture and to outline how design thinking can strengthen those who lead innovative companies. Generally, business design is characterized for its way of approaching the market: from putting the emphasis on products and/or services to creating a dialogue with the customers and the stakeholders, from improving the reach of commercial channels, to caring customers and their needs and desires. The business designer has a radically different style in guiding a business with respect to the business administrator: while the second must grant the efficiency and effectiveness of the performances of the organization, whose nature is assumed to be almost stable and well known, the business designer is continuously redefining the business in all its components, without assuming anything as fixed, even the market where his/her organization will compete. When a car maker was searching, some years ago, a new manager, it looked for a profile capable to run at best an established business because it needed a business administrator (things are changing also in the automotive sector, today, and car makers are no more sure that their market is stable); quite differently, an entrepreneur like Steve Jobs [19], probably the 'champion' of business designers, has continuously reinvented the business, the market and the customer relationships of Apple, without paying too much attention to typical economic and financial indicators.

3   Examples of Business Designers

As I said in the Introduction, I want to outline the profile of business designers, taking into account that the concept has its routs in existing entrepreneurs and top managers who have been able to create and develop innovative companies. Moreover, I have also claimed that Italian successful companies, those that are frequently collected under the header of "Made in Italy", have as their charismatic leaders, persons who can, generally, be considered business designers, or, more interestingly, who inspired the new profile of the business designer.

It is not possible, within the limits of a conference paper, to survey adequately an adequate number of 'business designer' candidates, but we can try, surveying some well chosen examples, to let emerge, in few lines, some elements characterizing them and some problems that their analysis currently leaves open.

First of all, even if business design is something that became of topical interest in the last twenty years, we can find even in the previous century, some precursors who were adopting an entrepreneurial style anticipating many of its characteristic features. A name comes to my mind with this respect: Adriano Olivetti [4, 30], who lead Olivetti, but for a short period during the fascism, in the years between 1932 and 1960, when he died unexpectedly at the age of 59. Olivetti, founded by Adriano's father Camillo at the beginning of the twentieth century, was, when Adriano became its CEO, a mechanical manufacturer specialized in typewriters and selling them mostly in Italy. During Adriano's leadership, Olivetti added mechanical computing machines to typewriters, entered in the electronic sector, with a Laboratory designing computers, and became a multi-national company selling its systems all over the world, and buying, one year before the death of Adriano, an important American maker of typewriters, Underwood.

In the years when Adriano lead Olivetti, in particular between 1945 and 1960, companies were facing completely different problems with respect to today. At a planetary level, Taylorism was just beginning its diffusion; globalization was not yet a real problem; instruments were mostly mechanical and only from the end of the fifties electronics became a real industrial opportunity; ... At the national level, Italy was a dramatically poor country trying to recover from the second world war that left it defeated and destroyed; it was mostly an agricultural country with few industrial companies and almost no multi-nationals; there were few laureates; the reconstruction of the cities was going on slowly. In those years, when most of the Italian entrepreneurs were dealing with the problems of re-launching production, looking almost exclusively to the Italian market and to mature non-technological products, Adriano transformed Olivetti in a completely new type of company changing it from many viewpoints: he innovated its products from the technological and aesthetic viewpoints, calling some of the best Italian industrial designers to collaborate with Olivetti and having some of its products exhibited in Museums like New York's Museum of Modern Art; he adopted a new communication style, from journals, books, diaries and calendars, etc. to shops, advertising and packaging, of a unique level of quality; he innovated the production processes adopting Taylorism, without loosing attention of the working conditions, selecting the best students of the Italian Universities for its management, promoting cultural programs from sociology and psychology to planning and architecture; he developed innovative social services for his workers and created a special relationship between Olivetti and its territory (Canavese; he was also elected Major of its main city, Ivrea); he commissioned the buildings of Olivetti (factories, offices and services) to the best Italian (and to some foreign) architects; he established a laboratory for the design of computers at their dawning, that brought Olivetti in the most innovative sector of electronic technology. The complexity of the figure of Adriano Olivetti is too high for trying to capture him in a simple formula: let me recall that he was also a prominent political figure in Italy (he created the "Movimento Comunità" with which he was not only elected major of Ivrea but also a member of the Italian Parliament), but we can not avoid to underline that the mixture of the interests he expressed in the years when he was managing Olivetti prefigure some of the characteristics of the business designer. It is not, therefore, by chance, that several observers have associated to Adriano Olivetti the figure of Steve Jobs, who can be considered its prototype.

Steve Jobs, in fact, has been a unique case among the CEOs of the High-Tech companies emerging, between the sixties and today, in the United States of America [11, 19]. Both during his first period leading Apple, and even more during the second one, as well as when he acted as CEO of Pixar, the famous computer animation film studio, he acted quite differently from the large majority of the managers of High-Tech companies. His companies were focused in creating new unique products/services offering to their customers new unique experiences rather than in improving their position in the market; he was directly involved in the design of new

products and services, like the Mac, the iPod, the iPhone and the iPad, in the creation
and design of the Apple Stores and of the Pixar and Apple Campuses, in the design
of the communication of his companies; he was neither a technologist nor a designer,
but he played a major role in defining the new products/services that made Apple the
leading innovative company in the last thirty years. With respect to this last theme,
iPod was a tremendous success because it was a beautiful, perfectly working, tool for
managing and listening digital music, but also and mainly because it was accompanied by iTunes, that revolutionized the music market; iPhone not only was a better
smart phone that those offered by its competitors, but also it redefined, once for all,
what a Smart phone was, and all competitors had to modify their products in order to
adhere to the new standard. Every new Apple product aims to be unique and final. In
particular, Steve Jobs played a major role in designing this combination of new
systems with new services.

With the above claims, I don't want to say that what Jobs did is unquestionable:
there are many aspects of how Apple works that merit to be discussed like its
refusal to adopt open source technology, its remaining a close system where
everything is done internally, its outsourcing production to large, slavist factories in
the Far East, etc. What I want to stress is that Jobs managed Apple quite differently
from its competitors in the digital sector, guiding it to create new products and
services aiming to change the markets where they were placed and, also, to change
the lives of its customers.

As I mentioned in the previous sections, Italian industry has several hundreds of
entrepreneurs that can be considered business designers, whose companies compete
for the leadership in global market sectors of various dimensions (sometimes very
small), creating products combining aesthetic and functional excellence, augmenting them with services enriching customer experience, enhancing their roots in
the territory and contributing to increase its quality, and distributing their products
in a growing number of countries [7, 10]. Also Italian business designers are not, up
to now, the outcome of schools, capable to educate people aspiring to become
entrepreneurs towards an effective management of innovation, and, therefore, they
correspond only partially and incompletely to the profile of business designers, but
their relevance in the Italian industry qualifies them as a reference for all those who
want to deepen their knowledge about business design. Moreover, if we compare
the Italian case with the loneliness of Steve Jobs in the ICT industry, it appears
quite clearly that business design fits at best with innovation but not specifically
with technological innovation.

4 Organizational Networks

What is a *network*? The etymology of the term can be helpful, since its meaning had
a strong evolution, accompanying the transformations of our means of moving and
communicating. Network, is the combination of *net* + *work* and its sense has moved
from any "any complex, interlocking system", that reflected the growth of transport

systems, to "a broadcasting system of multiple transmitters" and "interconnected group of people" taking into account the emergence and evolution of mass-media. It is more interesting to look, at a more detailed level, at the etymology of *net*: it derives from the high-German verb *najan*, whose meaning is "to sew". In the same vein, the Italian word *rete*, in accordance with the German glottologist and philologist Georg Curtius, stays for SRET-E, formed, through metathesis, on SERT-US, the past of SERERE, "to weave".

A 'net' is, in brief, something that has been sewed or weaved: as any sewed or weaved artefact, it connects with threads several points/knots, leaving empty spaces between knot and knot, as well as between thread and thread. The term has been used, for example, to give a name to a widely used fishing tool, that is constituted by a, more or less, thick texture of, knotted each-other, strings. In the metaphorical use we do in this context, a net is any structure, constituted by knots and connections.

Finally, a network is something made as a net and, therefore, its use has grown to name nets that have been built by human beings. We have, therefore, computer-, organizational-, human-, institutional networks. In all these cases, knots are entities (humans or human aggregates, with or without a juridical personality), while connections may be of different types: signals, communications, commitments, but also, economic transactions, material or human exchanges, etc.

Networks of this type are always more frequent in several situations and their conceptualization allows to analyze and understand the behaviour of collective subjects, whose members have complex mutual interrelationships, and how net-worked relations influence the behaviour of individual actors. We can claim, without fear of exaggerating, that the network concept is today inescapable by any person who wants to analyze and understand any type of social phenomena, and not only those.

It is not surprising, therefore, that, within sociological and anthropological disciplines, Bruno Latour and colleagues developed Actor Network Theory (ANT; [24, 25]) where any object or individual is observed within the social networks it is part of. ANT is widely used in situated studies of social aggregates and, always more, in the analysis of dynamic changing socio-technical systems.

If we give a closer look at *organizational networks*, we see that there are, both, networks of organizational units, inside one organization or connecting several organizations [5, 6, 15], and networks of people, who collaborate on a common endeavour [12, 13, 16, 31, 32]. In the first case, network links are, generally, service relations or shared resources, so that hierarchical structures are substituted by light, focalized, mutual relationships, suiting better the evolving nature of the interplay between the involved organizational units, since they can be continuously re-negotiated with a clear responsibility distribution. In the second case, links define forms of collaboration, whose main texture is knowledge [13, 16, 29]: collaborative networks, in fact, constitute social aggregates, from work-teams to communities of practice [13, 33] allowing people with different experiences and competencies to understand each-other and make things together, and this is impossible without they create and share the necessary knowledge. It is interesting that networks of orga-nizational units and networks of people are always more often emerging together within innovative companies, since, on the one hand, collaborative networks are a necessary mean to make effective enterprise networks and network enterprises, and on the other hand, collaborative networks need to be supported by adequate resources, in particular repositories and data bases where explicit knowledge generated within the collaboration can be easily stored and accessed. Beyond the complexity that any network has, due to its need to put together different subjects, organizational networks exhibit also (and this has not been remarked adequately, in my opinion) the need to harmonize institutional and collaborative networks.

Innovative organizations create networks precisely to improve collaboration, so that they can get the resources and competencies they need, whenever they need them. Collaboration, in fact, is beneficial for its putting together subjects with different competencies and resources so that better and more effective performances are possible or, even, new performances individual participants are not capable of. On the other side, collaboration is not easy: first, it needs specific artefacts for coordination aiding the integration of individual performances [33]; second, it requires knowledge sharing and understanding each-other, that can be aided by mechanisms for collective knowledge [16]; finally, interests of all the involved stakeholders must be taken into account, avoiding to forget or penalize any of them [17], and harmonized solving conflicts in a positive sum game approach [2].

It is well known that cooperation problems become more acute when participants are not co-located, when they have diverse cultures and/or competencies, and, finally, when the objective of the cooperation is radically innovative so that it can not be related with any previously existing experience, thing or concept.

The context within which organizations live today is, for all its observers and protagonists, one of the most heavy crisis the industrial world has faced. For many of them, therefore, what companies do, is a response to it. Also the growth of organizational networks is part of this response. It is reasonable, therefore, to ask what will happen, when the crisis will finish. There are several reasons, inside and outside companies, that the hope that things will return to the order preceding the crisis will not come true. The current crisis is not a transitory turbulence, rather, it is the new order that emerges. On the one hand, globalization has nothing of transient, rather we start to see today some of the elements characterizing it (new forms of economic exchange, like sharing economy [18], redefinition of market sectors, under the pressure of technological innovation, social changes all over the globe); and the list could continue); on the other, most of the companies where networks have become an important organizational arrangement, can not divest themselves of networks: the latter have become an integral part of their organization.

5 Organizational Networks and Business Designers

As Isaacson recalls, Steve Jobs claimed frequently that he wanted to "build a real company, which is the hardest work in business [...]. That's how you really make a contribution and add to the legacy of those who went before. You build a company that will still stand for something a generation or two from now". That's what Walt Disney did, and Hewlett and Packard, and the people who built Intel. They created a company to last, not just to make money. That's what I want Apple to be" [19, p. 279]. In the same vein, Adriano Olivetti wanted to innovate the company that he inherited from his father, without affecting its robustness as well as its being a good place to work. So, even if it seems that business designers do not pay great attention to the organizational level, its champions contradict this belief. Surely, they deal with the organization of their companies, in a peculiar way: they are not aiming to build a new type of rational organization, rather, they want only to grant that the management of innovation is effective, without loosing the capability of administering the business. Their companies, therefore, are frequently strange combinations of old-fashioned organizational structures and innovative ways of designing the business.

The relationship between institutional and collaborative networks merits some more words. Collaborative networks are where things are done within organizations: they are not social aggregates that organizations promote or create in order to improve the performances of their organizational units and to facilitate their integration; rather, organizational units are created to grant to networks the best conditions for their action and interaction. The fact that, always more frequently, networks capable of complex performances involve people of different units and, sometimes, of different organizations, requires not only that their organizational units support them but also that they establish among each other institutional links so that their diversities remain a richness without becoming an obstacle.

The collaboration between designers, engineers (sometimes engineers with different specializations), marketing professionals and communicators, that is needed in order to create new products in industries like furniture and mechanics, etc., is made possible by the collaborative networks they create in order to work together, and by the support they get by the network links that are established between their organizational units. Design departments (and sometimes independent design agencies) are needed in order to grow teams of designers who share a work practice, a style and the capability to invent new things that not only have aesthetic qualities but are capable to give form to products and/or services enriching the experience of their users, but, within any project, they need to create network where they can share their experience and co-create those products and/or services. We can interpret what happens within a collaborative network as the intertwining of several, diverse service relations, but these service relations are not standardized and their quality depends strongly on the knowledge co-created and shared by participants. Collaboration, therefore, is mainly grounded on knowledge creation and sharing: and this involves both tacit and explicit knowledge [29]. While collaborative networks are where participants socialize co-creating and sharing tacit knowledge, sharing explicit knowledge, internalizing and externalizing it require trespassing organizational boundaries and therefore collaboration must be supported by institutional links among the involved organizational units. Effective organizational networks are well-managed and well-behaving combinations of collaborative and institutional networks. This is not something organizations can achieve defining good rules, neither it is something that can be administered: whenever networks become something where rules play an important role, then they are at risk of being annihilated by bureaucracy. Organizational networks require that the management of the organization takes responsibility of avoiding that rules inhibit collaboration and of granting that institutional and collaborative networks are coherently ruled towards their objective. This requires a careful design of the business.

Despite the fact that business designers are generally characterized for what they do changing the way their company presents itself to its stakeholders (customers, suppliers, investors, public authorities, etc.), it appears clear that they need to reinvent their organization, building it around their organizational networks. It is not by chance, therefore, that the pioneer of business design, Adriano Olivetti, and its champion, Steve Jobs, shared during their lives not only the passion for the aesthetic and functional qualities of their products and of their packaging, for the elegance of the communication of their company, but also the care for the spaces where their collaborators did their job and for the way their company was organized.

If, as Krippendorff claims [22], design is 'giving sense' (to things), then a business designer is constantly renovating the sense of his/her business, or better of the businesses of his/her collaborators. This means that his/her care is dedicated to the fact that collaboration works well giving raise to well designed products and services, i.e. that thy listen and understand each-other, that they co-create new products/services and new knowledge. If you try to orchestrate specialized departments and collaborative networks by means of rules and roles, then it is probable that, despite your intentions, the outcome will be frictions and conflicts; business designers do it through conversations, knowledge flows and repositories, so that any network manages the knowledge wrapping its activities, that is the glue allowing to its participants to collaborate effectively, and any department updates the specialized knowledge characterizing the professional practice of its members, and explicit knowledge continuously flows from departments to networks for being internalized, and from networks to departments for being externalized [29].

6   ICT and Business Designers

As I have sketched above, knowledge is a key concept in the interplay between business designers and organizational networks, it is natural therefore to investigate how this fact may impact the design of information systems. The design of information repositories and data bases is not neutral with respect to organizational structures: abandoning monolithic corporate information systems networked organizations need for distributed systems, managed with great autonomy by networks and departments and for effective information flows among them. Networks, in fact, need explicit knowledge (digitalized information) mostly as a support for internalizing it within their practice, while departments need it for granting its accessibility to any interested party, within the company and its partners.

Business designers, therefore, should pay always more attention to provide to their collaborators the access to the knowledge they need as well as ways for creating repositories where they can store all what they do collaborating in the networks they participate in. The standard functions of corporate information systems, should not be neglected, but they should be considered some of the services that knowledge basis is able to provide efficiently. Current information systems like ERPs are not ready for this change of perspective, but they are moving to create better 'business intelligence' services [23].

But something more relevant is moving in the ICT sector. I make reference to the growing attention that scholars and professionals, vendors and users, are paying to data. Open data [3], as well as big data [26, 27], together with cloud computing infrastructures [1], bring to the attention of the public the relevance that data stored in the net may have for the knowledge of people and organizations and make possible to build adequate and efficient services for the access to knowledge. For what regards us, moreover, it supports the move from the traditional concept of information system, to a new idea, where data are taken first, as basis for the knowledge of the organization. So the emergence of data as crucial issue for ICT applications, may be supportive to the development of systems for the innovative organizations, for the organizational networks and for the business designers.

Innovative organizations, therefore, should make one step further, going beyond the mere idea of adopting the ICT services offered in the market augmenting their efficiency and increasing their business intelligence, to become exigent customers requesting the technology capable of making their networks effective. This will become, I think, one of the most relevant duties of business designers.

7 Conclusion

As said in the previous section, innovative companies lead by business designers and including several, frequently changing, organizational networks need systems allowing to each of its networks, and to each of its collaborators, an easy access to the knowledge they need as well as a repository where what they generate day by day is stored and organized. Open and big data, together with cloud computing infrastructures, constitute the necessary basis for services of this type and make them possible today. But open and big data, with the sophisticated algorithms they use, are not sufficient: what innovative companies need is a system providing knowledge access to its users on the basis of the knowledge creation processes engaging them [8]: every network has its own continuously changing context, every person participates in several networks and transfers knowledge among the networks in which she participates, and the list of the elements characterizing the intrinsic complexity of the knowledge creation process supporting innovation could continue. A static idea of data and of their relations with knowledge cannot give adequate answers to it. The construction of systems of this type, requires a radical paradigm shift in information system design: I call the new paradigm 'situated computing' [14], to indicate that, in this new perspective, ICT applications need to reflect the situatednes of human condition in the way they process data. Bu this is a different story.

Acknowledgements The origin of this paper has been a Seminar I gave in April 2016 within the Master in World Natural Heritage Management (WNHM-Master) in Trento. There I presented, for the first time, my reflections about the business designer as a manager of an organization. My long lasting collaboration with Federico Butera has been of paramount importance in the development of the ideas presented here about organizational networks. I studied collaborative networks doing research in CSCW (Computer Supported Cooperative Work). It was, finally, with Emilio Genovesi, Giovanni Lanzone and Giulio Ceppi that I designed the Master in Business Design at Domus Academy at the beginning of this century. To all the people I have nominated, and to the many more that contributed to my work with suggestions and discussions, goes my sincere appreciation. The responsibility of what is written in these pages is only mine.

References

1. Armbrust, M. et al. (2010). A view of cloud computing. *Communications of the ACM, 53*(4), 50–58.
2. Aoki, M. (1984). *The cooperative game theory of the firm*. Oxford: Oxford University Press.
3. Bizer, C., Heath, T., & Berners-Lee, T. (2011). Linked data-the story so far. *Semantic services, interoperability and web applications: Emerging concepts* (pp. 205–227). IGI Global: Hershey PA.
4. Bricco, P. (2005). *Olivetti, prima e dopo Adriano*. Napoli: L'ancora del Mediterraneo Editrice.
5. Butera, F. (1999). *Il campo di fragole: reti di imprese e reti di persone nelle imprese sociali italiane*. Milano: Angeli.
6. Butera, F. (2005). *Il castello e la rete. Impresa, organizzazioni e professioni nell'Europa degli anni '90*. Milano: Angeli.
7. Butera, F., & De Michelis, G. (Eds.). (2011). *L'Italia che compete: L'Italian Way of Doing Industry*. Milano: Angeli.
8. Crabtree, A., & Mortier, R. (2015). Human data interaction: Historical lessons from social studies and CSCW. *Proceedings of ECSCW 2015* (pp. 3–21). Berlin: Springer.
9. De Michelis, G. (2001). La creazione di conoscenza e l'innovazione design-driven nei distretti allargati. *Studi Organizzativi, 3*(1), 121–136.
10. De Michelis, G. (2011a). L'ipotesi di una Italian way of doing industry. In Butera & De Michelis, 2011, 47–67.
11. De Michelis, G. (2011). La lezione di Steve Jobs. *Studi Organizzativi, 13*(2), 201–214.
12. De Michelis, G. (2012). Communities of practice from a phenomenological stance: Lessons learned for IS design. In G. Viscusi, G. M. Campagnolo, & Y. Curzi (Eds.), *Phenomenology, organizational politics and IT design: The social study of information systems* (pp. 57–67). IGI Global: Hershey PA.
13. De Michelis, G. (2014). La geometria variabile dell'Intelligenza Collettiva. *Sistemi Intelligenti, 26*(3), 521–532.
14. De Michelis, G. (2015). Situated computing. In V. Wulf, K. Schmidt, & D. Randall (Eds.), *Designing socially embedded technologies in the real world* (pp. 63–73). London: Springer.
15. Dioguardi, G. (2007). *Le imprese rete*. Torino: Bollati Boringhieri.
16. Grasso, A., & Convertino, G. (2012). Collective intelligence: Tools and studies. *Computer Supported Cooperative Work (CSCW), 21*(4), 357–369.

17. Grudin, J. (1988). Why CSCW applications fail: Problems in the design and evaluation of organizational interfaces. In *Proceedings of CSCW 1988* (pp. 85–93). New York, NY: ACM Press.
18. Hamari, J., Sjöklint, M., & Ukkonen, A. (2015). The sharing economy: Why people participate in collaborative consumption. *Journal of the Association for Information Science and Technology*, published online, http://onlinelibrary.wiley.com/doi/10.1002/asi.23552/full
19. Isaacson, W. (2011). *Steve jobs*. New York, NY: Simon & Schuster.
20. Junginger, S., & Faust, J. (Eds.). (2016). *Designing business and management*. London: Bloomsbury.
21. Kelley, T. (2001). *The art of innovation: Lessons in creativity from IDEO, America's leading design firm*. New York, NY: Doubleday.
22. Krippendorff, K. (1989). On the essential contexts of artifacts or on the proposition that "design is making sense (of things)". *Design Issues, 5*(2), 9–39.
23. Kumar, K., & Hillergersberg, J. (2000). ERP experiences and evolution. *Communications of the ACM, 43*(4), 23–26.
24. Latour, B. (1993). *We have never been modern*. Cambridge, MA: Harvard University Press.
25. Latour, B. (2005). *Reassembling the social—An Introduction to actor network theory*. Oxford: Oxford University Press.
26. Madden, S. (2012). From databases to big data. *IEEE Internet Computing, 16*(3), 4–6.
27. McAfee, A., & Brynjolfsson, E. (2012). Big data. The management revolution. *Harvard Business Review, 90*(10), 61–68.
28. Martin, R. (2009). *The design of business: Why design thinking is the next competitive advantage*. Boston MA: Harvard Business School Press.
29. Nonaka, I., & Takeuchi, H. (1995). *The knowledge creating company*. Oxford: Oxford University Press.
30. Occhetto, V. (1985). *Adriano Olivetti*. Milano: Mondadori Editore.
31. Schmidt, K., & Bannon, L. (1992). Taking CSCW seriously: Supporting articulation work. *Computer Supported Cooperative Work (CSCW), 1*(1), 7–40.
32. Schmidt, K., & Simone, C. (1996). Coordination mechanisms: Towards a conceptual foundation of CSCW systems design. *Computer Supported Cooperative Work (CSCW), 5*(2), 155–200.
33. Wenger, E. (1998). *Communities of practice: Learning, meaning, and identity*. Cambridge: Cambridge University Press.

The State of the Practice of Agile and Plan-Driven Approaches in ICT Development Projects: An Exploratory Research Study

Carine Khalil

Abstract The number of research studies and surveys on software project management is constantly growing. However, the state of the practice of software project management methodologies is still disparate and confusing. Therefore, project teams are often confused by whether or not they should adopt agile methodologies, or keep on working in a "traditional" way. Given this focus, this research aims at understanding, through different expert perspectives, the challenges and success factors encountered in different types of ICT projects. We adopted a qualitative research approach based on semi-structured interviews with senior project management consultants. Consultants are involved in different kinds of ICT projects: agile and plan-driven projects. The research paper has important implications for practitioners and academics. Findings show that the nature of the reported problems varies depending on whether the teams are working in an agile or in a traditional environment.

Keywords ICT projects · Agile methodologies · Plan-driven methodologies · State of the practice

1 Introduction

Software and information system projects are managed in complex and unpredictable environments. Given the increasing competition in the IT field, IT organizations and services must deploy effective project management methodologies that enable them to deliver, on time and budget, a product that meets customers changing needs.

Different project management principles, processes, and techniques have emerged and gained attention, through time, among practitioners. The last two decades have witnessed the rise of new methodologies called "agile" methodologies.

C. Khalil (✉)
Paris Descartes University, Paris, France
e-mail: carine.khalil@parisdescartes.fr

© Springer International Publishing AG 2018
C. Rossignoli et al. (eds.), *Digital Technology and Organizational Change*,
Lecture Notes in Information Systems and Organisation 23,
https://doi.org/10.1007/978-3-319-62051-0_3

Agile methodologies rely on a set of principles, practices, and tools, that enable software teams to develop their product iteratively and constantly integrate, at lower cost, customer feedback and changing requirements. These methodologies are viewed as a way that helps project teams overcome the limitations of plan-driven approaches such as waterfall and "V" cycle models [1–3].

Many case studies, systematic literature reviews, and surveys have been conducted on agile methodologies and project management in general [4–8]. While surveys generally focused on gathering quantitative data on challenges and success factors in agile and traditional projects, case studies examined, more deeply, these challenges and factors of success. They also studied and compared the impact of different project management methodologies (agile and waterfall methodologies) on teams' performance and client satisfaction. Even though the related work covers different project management topics (challenges and factors of success in software development projects, agile adoption success factors, agile and waterfall project outcomes, distributed agile development, limitations of waterfall methodologies), major findings result from systematic literature reviews or case studies that are related to one specific context, which, in this latter case, constrains their generalization to other contexts. Therefore, the state of the practice of traditional and agile project management approaches is still disparate and confusing. In this respect, our research project aims at exploring, through expert perspectives, the way agile and plan-driven approaches affect ICT project outcomes. It highlights success factors and limitations of both agile and plan-driven approaches and reports the lessons learned from using both approaches.

Given this focus, we adopted a qualitative approach based on semi-structured interviews with senior project management consultants. The consultants included in our study are involved in agile and traditional ICT development projects and have both agile and plan-driven project management expertise. They intervene, as service providers and under consultancy contracts, in several industries and projects types. They help software teams getting their product delivered on time and within budget.

Our research goal is to explore the "best" practices and challenges associated with both traditional and agile IT project management approaches. We aim at categorizing the reported limitations and success factors related to each of these two methodologies.

We structure the following paper as follows: Sect. 1 reviews the related work on waterfall and agile methodologies in software development. In this section, we will focus on the challenges and factors of success reported in the traditional and agile project management literature. Section 2 describes the research methodology. Section 3 presents the major findings of our qualitative research study. We conclude this work with the major limitations and contributions of this work.

2 Plan-Driven and Agile Methodologies: Challenges and Success Factors

In traditional approaches, IT projects proceed according to clearly defined phases and the product deliverable is produced at the end of the process. Extensive planning and documentation are valued throughout the whole process. The requirements are defined up-front in order to minimize uncertainty and therefore better manage risks [9]. In this respect, the development team and the customers agree on what will be delivered early in the development process. As the scope of the work is defined in advance, project progress is easily monitored [9]. For [10, 11], traditional approaches seem more appropriate for stable ICT projects with clear initial user requirements and goals. Up-front planning gives support for people who are sponsoring the project [12]. However, many practitioners have criticized plan-driven approaches. They consider them as rigid, unable to adapt to inevitable changing demands and requirements [13–15]. In addition, excessively specified plans and extensive documentation are viewed as wastes as they become obsolete and necessitate rework [1, 14, 16]. In this respect, a set of methodologies called agile methodologies emerged in order to respond to these limitations and handle innovative IT projects.

Many agile methodologies exist. The most popular ones are scrum project management and extreme programming [6]. Agile approaches emphasize short and iterative development lifecycles, constant collaboration between the development team and the client as well as continuous integration. These values and principles are materialized with a set of ceremonies (retrospective meetings, daily meetings, weekly meetings with the client), practices (iterative development, pair programming, collective code-ownership, continuous code integration, unit-testing...) and tools (product backlog where requirements are prioritized by the client at the beginning of each iteration, sprint backlog where requirements are estimated by the development team, burn down chart that measures the work progress...).

Different empirical studies have examined the impact of agile practices, ceremonies and tools on development team performance and clients' satisfaction. Daily meetings valued by agile methodologies seem to enhance communication between team members [2, 17–20]. They help teams better controlling their project towards its goals [21]. Iterative development adds agility to the development process by providing continuous feedback on the incremental product deliverable [12]. It facilitates the monitoring of the project progress [22]. It also enhances the collaboration with the clients and improves organizational learning by incorporating their feedback into future iterations [13, 23]. The organization can rapidly see if it is creating value or wastes and therefore improve its actions [24]. Besides, agile collaboration tools such as storyboards and virtual whiteboards reinforce information exchange between team members. These tools create an informative workspace and improve the common vision of the project [20]. Moreover, involving the customer to frequently collaborate with the team fosters the shared vision between the counterparts [2, 25–27].

However different challenges have been reported in the literature regarding the use and implementation of agile practices in ICT development projects. Frequent and informal communication is difficult to achieve in distributed environments, which affects the collaboration between team members [28], and the pursuit of a common goal [3, 22, 29]. Large-scale projects are also viewed as a challenge for implementing collaboration practices such as daily meetings, pair programming, retrospective meetings and reviews with the client. In addition, team's composition can constrain knowledge sharing between team members [25]. Plus, unstable team members that intervene in different projects in parallel have more difficulties to create an agile environment where knowledge sharing and collective problems solving are valued. In fact, the implementation of agile practices in matrix organizations is not easy to achieve. In such organizational structures, the lack of authority of the project manager can be a real problem [30].

Even though agile practices are beneficial in high-changing environments, the implementation of these practices is still perceived as difficult. In this respect, top management and project teams are often confused with whether or not they should adopt agile methodologies. Given this focus, we decided to conduct a qualitative research study with project management consultants involved in different types of projects and organizations. The aim of this research is to explore and understand, from their perspectives, when agile approaches can be beneficial to project teams and, eventually, if these methodologies can be combined with plan-driven ones.

3 Research Methodology

The research study has been carried with the collaboration of a French consulting firm specialized in project management. The exploratory study lasted three months, from September 2015 to December 2015 (Table 1). A qualitative approach has been adopted in order to examine the state of the practice of project management methodologies in different industries. Eighteen semi-structured interviews were conducted, each lasting a minimum of one hour and half. The panel was composed of project management consultants with agile and traditional background. These consultants are attached to the same consultancy firm. They work, as a service provider, for different industrial clients. Thus, they are involved in ICT projects characterized with different technical, organizational, human and security constraints.

The aim of these interviews is to examine the existing management practices and the way these practices can be improved in order to meet project needs. Our interviewees worked as consultants for large groups such as Airbus, EDF, SNCF.

Table 1 Research methodology

Phases	Period of time
Elaborating the interview guide based on our research objectives	September 2015
Conducting and transcribing the interviews	November 2015
Synthetizing and analyzing the collected data	December 2015

The respondents were informed about the purpose of this study. Invitations to participate in the study were sent to them by the technical director of the consultancy firm. They were asked to think of projects they have been involved with and select two of them: one project where agile methods were "successful" and another one where plan-driven methodology was "successful".

For analyzing the collected data, we adopted an interpretive approach. We began with multiple readings of the transcribed interviews to better understand the context and projects in which respondents were involved. Our research objectives and interview guide have guided us in identifying key concepts stated in each transcribed paragraph. A set of inductive categories emerged and were subsequently defined and justified with verbatim [31]. Among these categories: characteristics of agile projects, characteristics of plan-driven projects, reported wastes in traditional projects, limitations of traditional methodologies, advantages of traditional methodologies, challenges in implementing agile practices, benefits of agile projects...

4 Findings

A set of problems and issues has been reported in the projects in which the respondents were involved. The nature of these problems varies depending on the way projects are managed.

In plan-driven ICT projects, team members usually participate in the phase in which they are specialized (requirements definition phase, design phase, development phase, test phase, or maintenance phase). However, this seems to decrease the global vision of the project and leads to misunderstandings between different team members *"the development team has only a partial view of the product they are building... the maintenance team is in the same case"*. This linear way of decomposing the project encourages team members to work in an isolated way, which decreases the common vision of the product and leads to rework and delays. Another reported issue in traditional projects is the lack of communication between development teams and the customer. The latter is mainly involved in the requirements definition phase at the beginning of the project. This seems to enhance the gap between what has been planned in the beginning of the project and delivered at the end of it *"in our "V" cycle projects, they often accuse us of being completely mistaken regarding the project needs"*. The gap is even more accentuated where projects are large. In addition, retrospective meetings, organized between team members and the customer, are considered as insufficient. This also increases the risk of delivering a product that doesn't meet customer needs. Moreover, data analysis shows that up-front estimation and planning are difficult in large traditional projects. Teams are incapable to define the whole business requirements and estimate accurately the budget and the product delivery date *"software projects are rarely identical. It is really difficult to have an accurate estimation regarding the time and the work load"*; *"it often occurs that we have to stop the project because we underestimated the required resources"*. Moreover, the "rigidity" of the sequential process seems to constrain the integration of changes during the project *"people are not okay to integrate changes or unplanned specifications"*. Most of the outlined issues have been already highlighted in previous studies as well as in surveys and have been confirmed in this study. Nevertheless, waterfall lifecycles seem useful for small projects (two or three-months projects for example). According to the interviewees, such projects do not require different release lifecycles. They can be planned and estimated up-front. Unlike what previous studies may imply, traditional methodologies fit small projects rather than big projects *"small projects can be run through "V" cycle model ...it is pointless to have different releases in a three-months project"*. This statement is even more accurate when projects are critical necessitating documentation and high traceability.

Compared to traditional ICT projects, fewer problems have been reported in agile project outcomes. According to the interviewees, agile practices such as iterative development, client-on-site and requirements prioritization improve teams' performance and better respond to customers' needs. This statement can also be found in the Standish Group's recent survey (Standish Group, 2015). In fact, in agile environments, the nature of the reported problems isn't the same as in traditional ones. In traditional environments, problems mostly result from the application of traditional principles and processes and consequently affect the project outcomes. However, in agile environments, the reported problems are mostly related to the early stage of adoption of agile practices.

Many contextual factors have been cited as affecting the adoption of agile practices in ICT projects. Unstable teams and matrix organizational structures constrain the creation of an agile environment. Implementing agile practices and principles such as daily meetings, retrospective meetings, auto-organization and auto-management is not easy in such contexts. Plus, the lack of project manager's authority has been also reported as a problem in such organizations. These challenges have been mentioned in previous studies [25, 30] and verified in this research paper. In addition, project managers can be reticent regarding the implementation of agile practices where teams' auto-organization and management are emphasized. In transitioning to agile, project managers are afraid of losing their actual position and power over their team *"Project managers have no idea about how their job description will evolve while transitioning to agile"*. In this respect, the lack of interest and involvement of project managers can limit the adoption of agile methodologies. Another reported barrier that has been discussed in previous research work and found in this study is the organizational culture [25]. In organizations where oral culture and mutual adjustments are emphasized, the implementation of practices that enhance knowledge sharing and creation is facilitated. However, in formal organizations, based on procedures and documentation, tacit knowledge sharing supported by agile practices, is harder to achieve. Another important issue that has been frequently evoked by our respondents is the impact of normative constraints. Projects with high security and technical levels drive project managers to rely on plan-driven approaches based on detailed documentation and planning *"the quality of the product is measured according to the delivered documentation and not to the product itself... we need to have a struc-tured process with precise deliverables*". The respondents also stated other types of barriers. The unavailability of the customer affects the quality of the product requirements definition and prioritization. Retrospective meetings with the cus-tomer are therefore difficult to set up. In addition, the lack of mutual trust between the customer and the development team seems to constrain the creation of an agile environment *"if the customer insists on signing a contract with hundred pages and clauses, this customer isn't ready for working in an agile mode"*.

Unlike what has been reported in some research studies, our respondents don't perceive the geographical distribution as a challenge *"the distribution of project teams is not a problem... Information and communication technologies enable us to communicate over long distances"*. And according to the interviewees, team size should not exceed twenty persons.

Data analysis shows that when agile practices are correctly adopted, they result in more successful projects. However, many contextual challenges can constrain their adoption and affect the project progress and outcomes.

In fact, the respondents are aware of the respective limitations of both agile and plan-driven approaches. Accordingly, they stressed on the need of combining both approaches even though they have no clear idea about how to mix them. Until now, there is no defined hybrid methodology that can be deployed for managing projects that necessitate both approaches *"we don't have any recipe for combining different methodologies and improving our project performance. We proceed case-by-case"*.

5 Discussion and Concluding Remarks

The analyzed data accentuates the problems faced by traditional and agile teams involved in the development of ICT projects. In fact, depending on whether the projects are running in a traditional or agile way, the nature of the reported prob-lems will not be the same. Even though traditional approaches provide a structured and disciplined way for managing high-level critical ICT projects, they produce many types of waste such as rework, obsolete documentation, partially done work and errors in the developed system. These wastes increase project delays, and cost. Therefore, there is a real need for responding to the highlighted traditional limi-tations. Accordingly, agile practices can be viewed as part of the solution. Through iterative development, retrospectives with a customer representative and product backlog reprioritization, development teams can decrease the "tunnel effect" resulted in traditional software development methodologies. The gap between what has been planned and delivered will be smaller if release cycles are shorter and the client is more involved. Therefore the product has higher chances of meeting the customer's needs. Moreover, sharing an informative workspace (physical or virtual) would enhance project's common goal and the team's visibility regarding the project progress. As a result, rework and waiting can be decreased. Nevertheless, implementing agile collaboration practices can be challenging. As previously mentioned, many contextual barriers can constrain their adoption. While human, cultural, and organizational barriers imply a change management program, normative constraints require a structured project management approach that can be close to traditional approaches. In this case, it seems useful to build a hybrid methodology that deals with waterfall limitations through agile practices. This can constitute an up-coming research goal.

The involvement of consultants with both agile and traditional backgrounds increases the legitimacy of the collected data and reported statements. It helped us better understand why agile methodologies are useful and if they can replace or be combined with traditional methodologies.

This research paper has important implications for both researchers and practitioners. It highlights, through senior consultant perspectives, the types of challenges and advantages encountered in both agile and traditional environments. It also stresses on how agile practices can respond to traditional limitations and also shows when plan-driven approaches are necessary in the development of ICT projects. Therefore, it sheds light on the need of combining both agile and plan-driven methodologies in order to overcome the challenges faced in both environments. Nonetheless, more interviews could have been conducted with consultants from different firms in order to increase the generalization of our findings.

References

1. Sutherland, J., Viktorov, A, Blount, J. & Puntikov, N. (2007). Distributed scrum: Agile project management with outsourced development. In *Proceedings of the 40th Annual Hawaii International Conference on System Sciences*, 247a.
2. Svensson, H. & Host, M. (2005). Views from an organization on how agile development affects its collaboration with software development team. In *International Conference on Product Focused Software Process Improvement, Lecture Notes in Computer Science* (Vol. 3547, pp. 487–501). Springer, Finland.
3. Paasivaara, M., Durasiewicz, S. & Lassenius, C. (2008). Distributed agile development: Using scrum in a large project. In *3rd International Conference on Global Software Engineering* (pp. 87–95). IEEE.
4. https://www.standishgroup.com/sample_research_files/chaos_report_1994.pdf.
5. http://www.infoq.com/articles/standish-chaos-2015.
6. http://stateofagile.versionone.com.
7. http://www.wellingtone.co.uk.
8. Chow, T., & Cao, D. B. (2008). A survey study of critical success factors in agile software projects. *The Journal of Systems and Software, 81*, 961–971.
9. Cooper, R. G. & Sommer, A. F. (2016). The Agile–Stage-Gate hybrid model: A promising new approach and a new research opportunity. *Journal of Product Innovation Management, 33*(5), 513–526.
10. Coram, M., Boehm, S. (2005). The impact of agile methods on software project management. In *12th IEEE International Conference and Workshops on Engineering of Computer-Based Systems, IEEE Computer Society* (pp. 363–370). Washington, DC, USA.
11. Fernandez, D. J., & Fernandez, J. D. (2008). Agile project management—Agilism versus traditional approaches. *Journal of Computer Information System, 49*(2), 10–17.

12. Karlström, D., & Runeson, P. (2005). Combining agile methods with stage-gate project management. *Software IEEE, 22*(3), 43–49.
13. Highsmith, J., & Cockburn, A. (2001). Agile software development: the business of innovation. *Computer, 34*(9), 120–122.
14. Poppendieck, M., & Poppendieck, T. (2006). Implementing lean software development: from concept to cash. Addison-Wesley.
15. Petersen, K., & Wohlin, C. (2009). A comparison of issues and advantages in agile and incremental development between state of the art and an industrial case. *Journal of Systems and Software, 82*(9), 1479–1490.
16. Boehm, B. (2002). Get ready for agile methods with care. *Computer Publications, 35*(1), 64–69.
17. Chong, J. (2005). Social behaviors on XP and non XP: A comparative study. In *The Agile Development Conference, IEEE Computer Society* (pp. 39–48).
18. Melnik, G., & Maurer, F. (2005). Perceptions of agile practices: A student survey. In *2nd XP Universe and First Agile Universe Conference on Extreme Programming and Agile Methods* (pp. 241–250).
19. Robinson, H. & Sharp, H. (2004). The characteristics of XP Teams. In *Extreme Programming and Agile processes in software engineering* (pp. 139–147). LNCS, Vol. 3092. Springer.
20. Sharp, H., & Robinson, H. (2008). Collaboration and co-ordination in mature extreme programming teams. *International Journal of Human Computer Studies, 66*(7), 506–518.
21. Paasivaara, M., Durasiewicz, S. & Lassenius C. (2009). Using scrum in distributed agile development: A multiple case study. In *4th International Conference on Global Software Engineering* (pp. 195–204). IEEE.
22. Begel, A. & Nagappan., N. (2007). Usage and perceptions of agile software development in an industrial context: An exploratory study. In *1st International Symposium on Empirical Software Engineering and Measurement* (pp. 255–264). IEEE Computer Society.
23. Middleton, P., Flaxel, A. & Cookson, A. (2006). Lean software management case study: Timberline Inc. In *6th International Conference on Extreme Programming and Agile Processes in Software Engineering* (pp. 1–9).
24. Poole, J. (2004). Distributed product development using extreme programming. *Lecture Notes in Computer Science* (Vol. 3092, pp. 60–67). Springer.
25. Khalil, C., Fernandez, V. & Houy, T. (2013). Can agile collaboration practices enhance knowledge creation between cross-functional teams? *DSDM* (Vol. 205, pp. 123–133), Springer.
26. Koskela, J., & Abrahamsson, P. (2004). On site customer in an XP project: empirical results from a case study. Software process improvement. In *11th European Conference, Lecture Notes in Computer Science* (Vol 3281, pp. 1–11). Berlin: Springer.
27. Mann, C., & Maurer, F. (2005). A case study on the impact of scrum on overtime and customer satisfaction. *Proceedings of the Agile Development Conference* (pp. 70–79). Washington: IEEE Computer Society.
28. Simons M. (2002). Internationally Agile. InformIT.
29. Yap. M. (2005). Follow the sun: Distributed extreme programming development. In *Proceedings of Agile Conference* (pp. 218–224). Kirkland.
30. Khalil, C., Fernandez, V., & Houy, T. (2013). *Les méthodes agiles en développement informatique*. Presse des Mines, Paris.
31. Gibson, W. J., & Brown, A. (2009). *Working with qualitative data*. UK: Sage Publications.

Affordances of Social Media in Knowledge Sharing in Intra-Organizational Information Technology Projects

Marcirio Silveira Chaves, Eusébio Scornavacca and Danielle Fowler

Abstract This research-in-progress aims to address the complex phenomenon of knowledge sharing within the context of social media. The objective of this paper is to examine how the affordances of social media impact knowledge sharing dynamics in intra-organizational Information Technology (IT) projects. This paper adopts Design Science Research (DSR) as research paradigm and the Technical Action Research (TAR) as validation method. One social media artifact will be designed and investigated within the context of an IT project. The expected contributions of this work will be twofold: (1) The results of this research should add to the literature on empirically tested theory of social media affordances on knowledge sharing dynamics in IT projects; (2) The instantiation of the TAR study will characterize a contribution of the type 'situated implementation of artifact'. This research should have implications for both the Project Management and Knowledge Management communities. Practitioners should be directly benefited by this work with an in-depth understanding of social media affordances on knowledge sharing dynamics.

Keywords Knowledge management · Project management · Affordance lens · Social media · Design science research (DSR) · Technical action research (TAR)

M.S. Chaves (✉)
Business School, Pontifical Catholic University of Rio Grande do Sul,
Porto Alegre, Brazil
e-mail: marcirio.chaves@pucrs.br

E. Scornavacca · D. Fowler
Merrick School of Business, University of Baltimore, Maryland, MD, USA
e-mail: escornavaca@ubalt.edu

D. Fowler
e-mail: dfowler@ubalt.edu

1 Introduction

Knowledge sharing from an individual-level perspective is a more complex phenomenon than is often portrayed in the literature [1]. Barriers to knowledge sharing include lack of resources to capture knowledge [2], usefulness of captured knowledge [3, 4], lack of purpose [5], unwillingness to share and seek knowledge from other colleagues [6], and lack of management to knowledge sharing initiatives [7]. Together, these barriers compose the class of problems for which this research proposes to deal, using the affordance lens [8].

The concept of an affordance refers to the possibility or potential for an action that can be taken on an object or environment [9]. In technology related research fields such as HCI and interaction design, the affordance is taken to mean the action potential that can be taken given a particular technology [8, 10].

This concept can provide a powerful lens for studying the relations between technology and people in organizations, and also a better language for describing how particular practices are shaped and patterned by structure and setting [11]. The notion of affordance describes the linkage between the capabilities afforded by the materiality of technological artifacts and actors' intentions and goals.

The contradictory effect of technology affordances on online knowledge sharing [10] suggests value in examining the role that social media affordances play in knowledge sharing [8]. This paper describes such a research project in progress that will examine the argument that social media affordances facilitate knowledge sharing in intra-organizational projects. Baxter and Connolly [12] found that there is a lack of evidence to suggest that social media have been adequately tested, empirically. In this same vein, Yeo and Arazy [13] call for further research on social media (e.g. wikis) across various industries (e.g. business, education, government) and geographical regions.

The objective of this research is to verify how the affordances of social media impact knowledge sharing dynamics in one intra-organizational IT project. The central research question is "how do the affordances of social media impact knowledge sharing dynamics in intra-organizational IT projects?"

2 Theoretical Background

2.1 Knowledge Management and Knowledge Sharing

Although knowledge, knowledge sharing and knowledge management are complex and multifaceted concepts, this study adopts the classical definition of knowledge inspired in Nonaka [14], Huber [15] and Alavi and Leidner [16]. Knowledge is a justified belief that increases an entity's capacity for effective action, and is embodied in both explicit (e.g. documents, recorded solutions, and formal analysis) and tacit (e.g. insights, intuitions, and assumptions) forms. Explicit or codified knowledge refers to "knowledge that is transmittable in formal, systematic language" [14, p. 16]. Tacit knowledge is personal, undocumented, context-sensitive, dynamically created and derived, internalized, and experience-based [17]. Both tacit and explicit knowledge are pervasive in project-based organizations and need different approaches to be managed. Gomes et al. [18] report on explicit and tacit knowledge sharing in project management process groups.

Nonaka, Toyama, and Konno [19] present a unified model of dynamic knowledge creation on which this research is based. Their model unifies the Socialization, Externalization, Combination, and Internalization—SECI model, shared context (ba) and leadership. SECI is a well-known model proposed by Nonaka [14], where explicit and tacit knowledge interact with each other in a continuous process. Ba roughly means place and is defined as a "shared context in which knowledge is shared, created and used" [19, p. 14], since knowledge needs a context in order to exist. The main objective of ba is interaction and it needs to be 'energized' (stimulated) to become active and build meaning into a workspace. Considering that knowledge needs a physical context to be created, ba offers such a context for action and interaction. Nonaka, Toyama and Konno's unified model allows dynamic interactions among organizational members, and between organizational members and the environment. These features make this model suitable for the context of project management. In addition, ba is appropriate to the dynamic Web 2.0 environment, since it is an open place where project members with their own contexts can come and go, and the shared context (ba) can constantly evolve.

The main benefits from using Web 2.0 tools in organizations is the sharing of ideas and the access to organizational knowledge [20]. As regards to the knowledge management processes, Westbrook [21] stresses that the robust data collection about projects conducted within a department is the most significant advantage of the usage of Web 2.0 tools. A Web 2.0 platform is a propitious way of developing dynamic and collective learning [22–24] and promotes continuous interaction between tacit and explicit knowledge [23]. For this reason, social media make the process of knowledge creation easier—as the process of knowledge creation proposed by Nonaka [14].

Shang et al. [23] designed a model of knowledge creation, combining Nonaka's SECI model [14] and social media. This model combines the SECI model and social media with the objective to propose an effective, modern and dynamic model of knowledge management. This model is composed of four types of knowledge creation, as follows:

Socialization (from tacit knowledge to tacit knowledge): the suggestion is interaction through Web 2.0 platform and communication via videoconferencing, teleconference or VoIP—Voice over Internet Protocol.

Externalization (from tacit knowledge to explicit knowledge): knowledge and information sharing via instant messaging (chat services), e-mails and also recording of the conversations realized via VoIP, videoconferencing and teleconference.

Combination (from explicit to explicit): utilization of RSS, mashups, social bookmarking, and tag collaborative management using folksonomy.

Internalization (from explicit to tacit): this is learning in practice focused on giving feedback to users that learn through trial and error and execution of software that is updated via Web 2.0 interface.

From this knowledge-creating cycle, Shang et al. [23] categorized Web 2.0 services into four distinct service models:

Exchanger: this platform allows users to socialize and externalize knowledge with a low control mechanism. On this platform, Web 2.0 services permit users to exchange written or voice messages—e.g. VoIP communication, instant messaging, and tagging. The content of the information is unorganized and has no quality assurance.

Aggregator: this platform enables the socialization, externalization and combination of knowledge, also with a low control mechanism. On these sites, individuals can share audio, text and video, allowing them to enrich the process of sharing knowledge with others. Examples of services are blogs, RSS, mashups, folk-sonomies and social networks.

Collaborator: in this service model, users can go through the whole cycle of knowledge creation. Individuals can organize, review, edit and reuse information on these services. Besides this, participants can also develop new code and improve the tools of use, stimulating the collective creativity. In order to ensure the quality and reliability of the content, services of this platform type have high control mechanisms. Web 2.0 services such as RSS, wikis and mashups are instances of collaborative services.

Liberator: as the collaborator platform, this service model allows participants to share knowledge through the complete SECI cycle with low control mechanisms. Services of this model allow users to access, revise and change the code for continuous quality improvement. Examples of open-source applications are Firefox and Linux. Due to this openness and lack of review process, systems errors and information mismatching can occur.

2.2 Web 2.0 Technologies in Organizations

The study of social media use in projects and organizations is arguably still in its infancy. Considering their use for knowledge sharing, Paroutis and Al Saleh [25] found four key determinants: history or "the old/established way of doing things", outcome expectations or perceived benefits and rewards, perceived organizational or management support, and trust (i.e. the quality/accuracy of the information being shared and whether bloggers and wiki contributors "knew what they were talking about.").

The main social media uses in organizations comprise:

Wikis. A wiki is a web-based collaborative authoring system for creating and editing content [26]. In addition to facilitating the collaborative creation of content both as a teaching tool [27] and in projects, Stocker et al. [28] reports other benefits of wiki usage from a literature review: enhancing reputation, making work easier, helping the organization to improve its processes, facilitating knowledge sharing and creativity, reducing information overload within the enterprise, and the ability to make knowledge work and its output more visible and transparent. Grace [29] highlights other advantages in the usage of wikis, including ease of use, central repository for information, tracking and revision feature, collaboration between organizations and solving information overload by e-mail. Majchrzak, Wagner, and Yates [30] conducted a survey with 168 corporate wiki users and they found three main types of benefits from corporate wikis: enhanced reputation, work made easier, and helping the organization to improve its processes.

Stocker et al. [50, p. 1] recommend that before implementing corporate wikis, companies should be "aware of usage potential, the need for additional managerial support, and clear communication strategies to promote wiki usage." Stocker et al. [28] describe relevant aspects of wiki projects, e.g. different viewpoints of managers and users, an investigation of other sources containing business-relevant information, and perceived obstacles to wiki projects.

In sum, little information is available about the success of the usage of wikis in projects, in term of user satisfaction, impact on the job and impact on the organization [31]. Related work on enterprise wikis is still at a rather experimental level [31]. To date, the same is true for wiki appropriation and usage in projects, where very little has yet been reported [28]. While Rosa et al. [32] propose a collaborative model based on social media to support lessons learned, Chaves et al. [33] report the usage of wiki pages to support the management of lessons learned in projects.

Weblogs (blogs, henceforward) have become popular because they are easy to manage, create, use and maintain. A blog is a discussion or informational site published on the Web, consisting of entries typically displayed in reverse chronological order. Most blogs are interactive (i.e. open to comments by visitors) and have a set of characteristics that allow them to gain popularity. The technical and behavioral characteristics of project blogs are very lightweight, chronologically sequenced, easily skimmed, with entries easily accessed [34]. Baxter, Connolly and Stansfield [35] identified five types of blogs: employee blogs, group blogs, executive blogs (e.g. CEO blogs), promotional blogs, and newsletter blogs. Group blogs are mostly used for project-related purposes of both an internal and external nature.

Other Web 2.0 tools could be explored in this study depending on the interests of the IS project managers, which include microblogging, VoIP, Rich Site Summary (RSS) and social bookmarking.

Microblogging "allow[s] users to exchange small elements of content such as short sentences, individual images, or video links" [36]. It is a broadcast medium in the form of blogging that allows users to write brief text updates (usually less than 200 characters) and publish them, either to be viewed by anyone or by a restricted group which can be chosen by the user. Notable active microblogging services are Twitter (twitter.com), Identi.ca, Tout (www.tout.com), Yammer (www.yammer.com) and Communote (www.communote.com).

Westbrook [21] uses skype to conduct orientation, training sessions and meetings with interns who work remotely. In addition to voice, videos can be managed to support the registration of complex tasks in IT projects. Such videos will help the retention of knowledge in projects.

Rich Site Summary (**RSS**) is a set of web feed formats used to publish frequently updated works such as wiki and blog entries, audio and video in a standardized format. Using this technology, project members can be automatically notified of updates in a wiki or a blog being used in a project, eliminating the need for periodic visits to search for updates in these sites.

A social bookmarking service is a centralized online service that enables users to add, annotate, edit, and share bookmarks of web documents [37]. In the context of PM, the use of a platform of bookmarking by members of a project is crucial to capture and share knowledge from an external environment. Technical problems are often discussed in specialized forums and blogs, which store and describe a set of recurring problems and solutions. Once a project member finds some useful knowledge in a forum or blog, he/she can bookmark the web site or page and share it with co-workers. Moreover, the search process is facilitated by the use of tags. For instance, relevant knowledge about the planning phase of a project can be bookmarked with the tag "planning", which can help further searches on this topic. These usage examples of social media also make the process of knowledge sharing easier.

2.3   Affordance Lens

Research on affordances usually follows the principles proposed by Gibson [9] or Norman [38]. Gibson's affordances feature offerings or action possibilities in the environment in relation to the action capabilities of an actor; they are independent of the actor's experience, knowledge, culture, or ability to perceive; and their existence is binary—an affordance exists or it does not exist. On the other hand, in the Norman's affordances the perceived properties may or may not actually exist; suggestions or clues as to how to use the properties; they can be dependent on the experience, knowledge, or culture of the actor; and they can make an action difficult or easy.

A set of social media affordances has been proposed in the literature. In this study, we focus on affordances that enable capture of the interaction between the actor and the object (the relational perspective at the ontological level). In addition, we consider that organizational affordances emerge from social practices involving technology and are related to the experience, skills, and cultural understanding of the user [39, 40].

Majchrzak et al. [10] theorize the following affordances: metavoicing, triggered attending, network-informed associating, and generative role-taking. Treem and Leonardi [8] describe editability, visibility, persistence and association. Considering only Wikis, Mansour, Askenäs and Ghazawneh [41] found additional affordances: commenting, accessibility, viewability and validation.

From these combined works we will focus on the following affordances:

Metavoicing: means engaging in the ongoing online knowledge conversation by reacting online to others' presence, profiles, content and activities [10]. Individuals add meta-knowledge to the content that is already online. Examples of metavoicing include retweeting, voting on a posting, commenting on someone's post, voting on the comment, "liking" a profile.

Triggered attending is engaging in the online knowledge conversation by remaining uninvolved in content production or the conversation until a timely automated alert informs the individual of a change to the specific content of interest [10].

Network-informed associating is engaging in the online knowledge conversation informed by relational and content ties [10].

Generative role-taking is engaging in the online knowledge conversation by enacting patterned actions and taking on community-sustaining roles in order to maintain a productive dialogue among participants [10]. Participants argue, complain, and share frustrations publicly in these conversations [8].

Editability refers to the fact the individuals can spend a good deal of time and effort crafting and recrafting a communicative act before it is viewed by others [42]. It is a function of two aspects of an interaction: communication formed in isolation from others, and asynchronicity. The affordance of editability is used in three ways to shape behavior:

1. Regulating personal expressions: users to strategically manipulate the ways that personal information is shared with others. E.g. "About You" feature; many users patterned contributions in a way that would increase recognition from others and garner rewards; organizational members used the ability to dictate labels as a form of impression management;
2. Targeting content: users of social media often tailor messages for specific audiences; Although social media can share information widely, the editability afforded by technology provides users with greater control of how content is viewed by others;
3. Improving information quality: "change control" and the ability to review and edit content.

Visibility is tied to the amount of effort people must expend to locate information. If social media enable people to easily and effortlessly see information about someone else, we say that the technology was used to make that person's knowledge. Visibility "refers to the means, methods, and opportunities for presentation; in our usage it primarily addresses the speakers" concerns with the presentation of self" [43, p. 5]. Three types of information or actions that are made visible using social media in organizations:

1. Work behavior: One of the most common and basic features of social media is that they present content communally, which means contributions can be easily located and viewed by other employees. E.g. "In employee weblogs, ideas that were previously unarticulated or hidden in personal archives become visible, interlinked, and searchable" [44, p. 11]. "The very act of creating a bookmark is

an explicit indicator of the utility or value of the internet and intranet information resource" [45, p. 9].

2. Metaknowledge: Profile pages—employees used the visible information contributed to learn more about the backgrounds, interests, and activities of coworkers [46].

3. Organizational Activity Streams: social media afford individuals the ability to see information related to the status of ongoing activities in the organization. Zhao and Rosson [47] interviewed 11 Twitter users at a large IT company and asked how microblogging might influence organizational communication. Respondents felt microblogging could assist in "keeping a pulse on what is going on in others' minds" by providing access to streams of comments from individuals across the organization (p. 249). Yardi, Golder and Brzozowski [48] analyzed a year of log data on an internal blog server at a global technology company and interviewed 96 employee bloggers of various activity levels. Employees expected posting material to social media to provide increased social recognition in the organization, and lack of recognition deterred continued participation.

The affordance of *persistence* has also been referred to as reviewability [49], recordability [50], and permanence [51]. Communication is persistent if it remains accessible in the same form as the original display after the actor has finished his or her presentation [43, 52]. "Persistence opens the door to a variety of new uses and practices: persistent conversations may be searched, browsed, replayed, annotated, visualized, restructured, and recontextualized, with what are likely to be profound impacts on personal, social, and institutional practices" [53, p. 68]. Examples of persistence are when a poster to a blog or SNS logs out, that information remains available to users and does not expire or disappear; If tasks are assigned via a team wiki, a communal record persists that is difficult to discount.

Three ways in which the literature shows how the affordance of persistence affects organizational action are: Sustaining knowledge over time; creating robust forms of communication (i.e. how difficult it is to destroy, compromise, or abandon content); growing content (the nearly limitless space afforded by social media such as blogs and wikis facilitates the growth of communication through the addition of posts and pages.)

The last affordance to be researched in this study is *associations*, which are established connections between individuals, between individuals and content, or between an actor and a presentation. The association of a person to another individual is most commonly referred to as a social tie. A social tie is best expressed through one's friends on a social networks service such as facebook, following a microblogger, or subscribing to another's tags. On the other hand, there is the association of an individual to a piece of information. Exemplars of this form of association are a wiki contribution, a blog contribution, or the tagging of an article. Baxter, Connolly and Stansfield [12] verified the association between blogs and organizational learning in the context of software project environments.

3 Research Design

This study will be conducted in the Design Science Research (DSR) paradigm [54–56] which is rigorous and systematic, yet also permits flexibility and freedom. DSR is currently highly recommended as a research approach by editors of top tier journals, e.g. Goes [57]. It focuses on the creation and evaluation of artifacts to solve identified organizational problems. The DSR paradigm addresses "unsolved problems in unique or innovative ways or solved problems in more effective and efficient ways" [55, p. 81]. In the following, we explain how the DSR seven guidelines fit this study.

(1) Design as an artifact: This study will produce one instantiation as an artifact for every organization studied. This instantiation will be implemented by introducing social media (the IT artifact) to support knowledge sharing in intra-organizational IT projects. This artifact will be chosen by the organizations and it can be a wiki, a social network or a blog among others.

(2) Problem relevance: As stressed by Baskerville [58, p. 442], "it is a fundamental premise that a design is problem-driven, and leads to an artifact that solves the problem when the artifact is introduced into nature". Hevner et al. [55, p. 85] highlight that the relevance of any DSR effort is with respect to "practitioners who plan, manage, design, implement, operate, and evaluate information systems and those who plan, manage, design, implement, operate, and evaluate the technologies that enable their development and implementation." Dealing with the insertion of new technologies to support knowledge sharing in intra-organizational IT projects remains a challenge for project managers.

(3) Design evaluation: The artifact will be evaluated using Technical Action Research (TAR) in IT projects, since the aim is study the artifact in depth in a business environment. Wieringa [59] recommends TAR as a rigorous method to evaluate or validate artifacts in DSR. TAR is 'the use of an experimental artifact to help a client and to learn about its effects in practice' [59, p. 269]. In TAR, the researcher has three roles [59]: As a technical researcher, he designs a treatment intended to solve a class of problems; as an empirical researcher, he answers some validation knowledge questions about the treatment; and as a helper, he applies a client-specific version of the treatment to help a client.

As regards to the data collection, two different sources of evidence will be used in this study. Semi-structured, in-depth interviews with open questions will be carried out in order to generate in-depth knowledge of the project. The choice of semi-structured rather than structured interviews will be employed because they offers sufficient flexibility to approach each respondent differently, while still covering the same areas of data collection. They will follow a pre-designed interview protocol to provide adequate coverage for the purpose of the research. Questions in the interview protocol will be developed based on a detailed literature review. The questions will be piloted with IT project managers and project members. An adjusted interview protocol will be used with practitioners having different roles in the management of projects being examined to investigate their point of view about social media. Focus groups will be also used to refine the artifact [60]. The interviews and focus groups will be recorded to secure an accurate account of the conversations and prevent the loss of data. A content analysis of the interviews will be carried out following the recommendations of Bardin [61], using MAXQDAplus.

Finally, the objective of the design evaluation is to collect evidence that the instantiation is useful in addressing criteria such as validity, usefulness and utility.

(4) Research contributions: The instantiation developed as an artifact in this study will improve the design science knowledge base. The results of this study should add to the literature an empirically tested theory of social media affordances on knowledge sharing dynamics in intra-organizational IT projects; In addition, the instantiation of the TAR study characterizes a contribution of the type 'situated implementation of artifact' [54].

(5) Research rigor: Rigorous methods in both the construction and evaluation of the design artifact should be applied. This study adopts the DSR paradigm using TAR studies to evaluate the artifact proposed. The TAR studies will be evaluated using criteria such as validity, utility, reusability, efficacy and maintainability.

(6) Design as a search process: Due to the iterative nature of design science, the artifact should mature as the technical action researches are being carried out. At the end of this study, it is expected to have a more fully-realized artifact.

(7) Communication of research: This study will disseminate its results through the publication of articles in conferences and top-tier journals.

4 Conclusion and Further Developments

This research-in-progress paper proposes an investigation into how the affordances of social media impact knowledge sharing dynamics in intra-organizational IT projects. Research on the usage of an affordance lens to study issues on IT project management is rare, if it exists. The test of this theory in a project management setting can be considered an original scientific contribution of this work.

This research adopts the Design Science Research (DSR) as paradigm and Technical Action Research (TAR) as method. DSR is a problem-solving approach, which is in line with the needs of the Knowledge Management and Project Management fields. As a result, the cooperation between the university and organizations is encouraged, through the discussion of the topic in the reality of organizations.

The expected contributions of this work will be twofold: (1) The results of this research in progress should add to the literature an empirically tested theory of social media affordances on knowledge sharing dynamics in intra-organizational IT projects; (2) The instantiation of the TAR study will characterize a contribution of the type 'situated implementation of artifact.'

This research should have implications for both Knowledge Management and Project Management communities. Practitioners should be directly benefited by this work with an in-depth understanding of social media affordances on knowledge sharing dynamics. In addition, the interaction between researchers and project stakeholders can change organizational processes and, as a result, reduces costs. Moreover, the adoption of free social media can reduce costs in the organizations where the action research will be carried out.

References

1. Schauer, A., Vasconcelos, A. C., & Sen, B. (2015). The ShaRInK framework: A holistic perspective on key categories of influences shaping individual perceptions of knowledge sharing. *Journal of Knowledge Management, 19*(4).
2. Shokri-Ghasabeh, M., & Chileshe, N. (2013). Knowledge management: Barriers to capturing lessons learned from Australian construction contractors perspective. *Construction Innovation, 14*(1), 108–134.
3. Chua, A., & Lam, W. (2005). Why KM projects fail: A multi-case analysis. *Journal of Knowledge Management, 9*(3), 6–17.
4. Newell, S., Bresnen, M., Edelman, L., Scarbrough, H., & Swan, J. (2006). Sharing knowledge across projects limits to ICT-led project review practices. *Management Learning, 37*(2), 167–185.
5. Ruikar, K., Anumba, C. J., & Egbu, C. (2007). Integrated use of technologies and techniques for construction knowledge management. *Knowledge Management Research & Practice, 5* (4), 297–311.
6. Pemsel, S., & Wiewiora, A. (2013). Project management office a knowledge broker in project-based organisations. *International Journal of Project Management, 31*(1), 31–42.
7. Williams, T. (2008). How do organizations learn lessons from projects—And do they? *Engineering Management, IEEE Transactions on, 55*(2), 248–266.
8. Treem, J., & Leonardi, P. (2012). Social media use in organizations—Exploring the affordances of visibility. *Editability, Persistence, and Association, Communication Yearbook, 36*, 143–189.
9. Gibson, J. J. (1979). *The ecological approach to visual perception*. Boston: Houghton Mifflin.
10. Majchrzak, A., Faraj, S., Kane, G. C., & Azad, B. (2013). The contradictory influence of social media affordances on online communal knowledge sharing. *Journal of Computer-Mediated Communication, 19*(1), 38–55.
11. Fayard, A. L., & Weeks, J. (2014). Affordances for practice. *Information and Organization, 24*(4), 236–249.
12. Baxter, G. J., & Connolly, T. M. (2014). Implementing Web 2.0 tools in organisations: Feasibility of a systematic approach. *The Learning Organization, 21*(1), 6–25.
13. Yeo, M. L., & Arazy, O. (2012). What makes corporate wikis work? Wiki affordances and their suitability for corporate knowledge work. In *Design science research in information systems. Advances in theory and practice* (pp. 174–190). Springer Berlin Heidelberg.
14. Nonaka, I. (1994). A dynamic theory of organizational knowledge creation. *Organization Science, 5*(1), 14–37.
15. Huber, G. P. (1991). Organizational learning: The contributing processes and the literatures. *Organization Science, 2*(1), 88–115.

16. Alavi, M., & Leidner, D. E. (2001). Review: Knowledge management and knowledge management systems: Conceptual foundations and research issues. MIS Quarterly, 107–136.
17. Duffy, J. (2000). Knowledge management: To be or not to be? *Information Management Journal, 34*(1), 64–67.
18. Gomes, F., Oliveira, M., & Chaves, M. (2016). Knowledge sharing in project management process groups. In *17th European Conference on Knowledge Management* (pp. 1–2). Northern Ireland, UK, September, 307–315.
19. Nonaka, I., Toyama, R., & Konno, N. (2000). SECI, Ba and leadership: A unified model of dynamic knowledge creation. *Long Range Planning, 33*(1), 5–34.
20. Bughin, J., Chui, M., & Miller, A. (2009). How companies are benefiting from Web 2.0. McKinsey Quarterly, 9.
21. Westbrook, R. N. (2012). Online management system: Wielding Web 2.0 tools to collaboratively manage and track projects. *Journal of Library Innovation, 3*(1), 86–100.
22. Murugesan, S. (2007). Understanding Web 2.0. *IT professional, 9*(4), 34–41.
23. Shang, S. S. C., Li, E. Y., Wu, Y.-L., & Hou, O. C. L. (2011). Understanding Web 2.0 service models: A knowledge-creating perspective. *Information & Management, 48*(4–5), 178–184.
24. Thomas, C., & Sheth, A. (2011). Web Wisdom: An essay on how Web 2.0 and Semantic Web can foster a global knowledge society. *Computers in Human Behavior, 27*(4), 1285–1293.
25. Paroutis, S., & Al Saleh, A. (2009). Determinants of knowledge sharing using Web 2.0 technologies. *Journal of Knowledge Management, 13*(4), 52–63.
26. Gholami, B., & Murugesan, S. (2011). Global IT project management using Web 2.0. *International Journal of Information Technology Project Management, 2*(3), 30–52.
27. Parker, K., & Chao, J. (2007). Wiki as a Teaching Tool. *Interdisciplinary Journal of E-Learning and Learning Objects (IJELLO), 3*(1), 57–72.
28. Stocker, A., Richter, A., Hoefler, P., & Tochtermann, K. (2012). Exploring appropriation of enterprise wikis. *Computer Supported Cooperative Work (CSCW), 21*(2–3), 317–356.
29. Grace, T. P. L. (2009). Wikis as a knowledge management tool. *Journal of Knowledge Management, 13*(4), 64–74.
30. Majchrzak, A., Wagner, C., & Yates, D. (2006). Corporate wiki users: results of a survey. In Proc. of the International Symposium on Wikis (pp. 99–104). Odense, Denmark: ACM Press.
31. Arazy, O., Gellatly, I., Soobaek, J., & Patterson, R. (2009). Wiki deployment in corporate settings. *IEEE Technology and Society Magazine, 28*(2), 57–64.
32. Rosa, D. V., Chaves, M. S., Oliveira, M., & Pedron, C. (2016). Target: A collaborative model based on social media to support the management of lessons learned in projects. *International Journal of Managing Projects in Business, 9*(3), 654–681.
33. Chaves, M., Tessi, M., Winter, & Damasceno, J., Jr. (2016) Validating a Collaborative Lessons Learned Model: A Multiple Cases Analysis. XL Encontro da ANPAD—EnANPAD, Costa do Sauípe, Bahia, Brazil, September pp. 25–28.
34. Grudin, J. (2006). Enterprise knowledge management and emerging technologies. In *Proc. of the 39th Hawaii International Conference on System Sciences* (pp. 57a–57a), IEEE.
35. Baxter, G. J., Connolly, T. M., & Stansfield, M. H. (2010). Organisational blogs: benefits and challenges of implementation. *The Learning Organization, 17*(6), 515–528.
36. Kaplan, A. M., & Haenlein, M. (2010). Users of the world, unite! The challenges and opportunities of Social Media. *Business Horizons, 53*(1), 59–68.
37. Noll, M. G., & Meinel, C. (2007). Web search personalization via social bookmarking and tagging (pp. 367–380). Springer Berlin Heidelberg.
38. Norman, D. A. (1988). *The psychology of everyday things*. New York: Basic Books.
39. Kemp, J. W., Livingstone, D., & Bloomfield, P. (2009). R: SLOODLE: Connecting VLE tools with emergent teaching practice in second life. *British Journal of Educational Technology, 40*(3), 551–555.
40. Zheng, Y., & Yu, A. (2016). Affordances of social media in collective action: The case of free lunch for children in China. *Information Systems Journal, 26*(3), 289–313.

41. Mansour, O., Askenäs, L., & Ghazawneh, A. (2013). Social media and organizing: An empirical analysis of the role of wiki affordances in organizing practices. In *Reshaping Society Through Information Systems Design (ICIS)*, December 15–18, Milan.
42. Walther, J. B. (1993). Impression development in computer-mediated interaction. *Western Journal of Communication, 57,* 381–398.
43. Bregman, A., & Haythornthwaite, C. (2001). Radicals of presentation in persistent conversation. In *Proceedings of the 34th Annual Hawaii International Conference on System Sciences*. Los Alamitos, CA: IEEE Computer Society Press.
44. Efimova, L., & Grudin, J. (2008). Crossing boundaries: Digital literacy in enterprises. In C. Lankshear & M. Knobel (Eds.), *Digital literacies* (pp. 203–226). New York: Peter Lang.
45. Pan, Y. X., & Millen, D. R. (2008). Information sharing and patterns of social interaction in an enterprise social bookmarking service. In *Proceedings of the 41st Annual Hawaii International Conference on System Sciences*. Los Alamitos, CA: IEEE Computer Society Press.
46. DiMicco, J., Millen, D. R., Geyer, W., Dugan, C., Brownholtz, B., & Muller, M. (2008). Motivations for social networking at work. In *Proceedings of the 2008 ACM Conference on Computer Supported Cooperative Work* (pp. 711–720).
47. Zhao, D. & Rosson, M. B. (2009). How and why people Twitter: the role that micro-blogging plays in informal communication at work. In *Proceedings of the ACM 2009 International Conference on Supporting Group Work* (pp. 243–252).
48. Yardi, S., Golder, S. A., & Brzozowski, M. J. (2009). Blogging at work and the corporate attention economy. In *Proceedings of the SIGCHI Conference on Human Factors in Computing Systems* (pp. 2071–2080). ACM.
49. Clark, H. H., & Brennan, S. E. (1991). Grounding in communication. *Perspectives on socially shared cognition, 13,* 127–149.
50. Hancock, J. T., Toma, C., & Ellison, N. (2007). The truth about lying in online dating profiles. In *Proc. of the SIGCHI conference on Human factors in computing systems* (pp. 449–452). ACM.
51. Whittaker, S. (2003). Theories and methods in mediated communication. In A. C. Graesser, M. A. Gernsbacher & S. R. Goldman (Eds.), *Handbook of discourse processes* (pp. 243–286). Mahwah, NJ: Erlbaum.
52. Donath, J., Karahalios, K., & Viegas, F. (1999). Visualizing conversation. *Journal of Computer-Mediated Communication, 4*(4).
53. Erickson, T., & Kellogg, W. (2000). Social translucence: An approach to designing systems that support social processes. *ACM Transactions on Computer-Human Interaction, 7,* 59–83.
54. Gregor, S., & Hevner, A. R. (2013). Positioning and presenting design science research for maximum impact. *MIS Quarterly, 37*(2), 337–355.
55. Hevner, A. R., March, S. T., Park, J., & Ram, S. (2004). Design science in information systems research. *MIS Quarterly, 28*(1), 75–105.
56. March, S. T., & Smith, G. F. (1995). Design and natural science research on information technology. *Decision Support Systems, 15*(4), 251–266.
57. Goes, P. B.: Design science research in top information systems journals. MIS Quarterly 38 (1), iii-viii/March (2014).
58. Baskerville, R. (2008). What design science is not. *European Journal of Information Systems, 17*(5), 441–443.
59. Wieringa, R. J.: Technical Action Research. In Design Science Methodology for Information Systems and Software Engineering (pp. 269–293). Berlin: Springer (2014).
60. Tremblay, M. C., Hevner, A. R., Berndt, D. J. (2010). Focus Groups for Artifact Refinement and Evaluation in Design Research, Communications of the Association for Information Systems: Vol. 26, Article 27.
61. Bardin, L. (1977). *L'analyse de contenu* (Vol. 69). Paris: Presses universitaires de France.

Everything Is Permitted Unless Stated Otherwise: Models and Representations in Socio-technical (Re)Design

Carla Simone

Abstract Systems (re-)design is discussed in the light of the socio-technical (ST) design approach and by considering how (re-)design can be made more manageable by looking at the work practices that mitigates the limits of the current ST systems. The conclusion is that ST re-design requires reconsidering how ST systems are designed, for the benefit of whom and how control is exercised.

Keywords Models · Representations · Conviviality · End-user empowerment

1 Motivations and Background

When a term becomes popular, it is usual to notice a drift of its meaning, possibly forgetting to appreciate the value of its original connotation. This is the case of the term *socio-technical* that is used in combination with terms such as system, design or approach. Too often in the last years it is sufficient for something to be socio-technical to acknowledge that the target reality is made of social and technological components: this connotation is nowadays obvious and simply tells us that the target technology is directly accessible by the end-users though a suitable interface to accomplish their tasks, and in this way the technology and the organization have a mutual influence and have somehow to be jointly designed. There is a lack of recent conceptualizations of the interplay of the social and technical components from which we can derive hints on how this interplay can be supported. Looking back into the literature we find much richer connotations that—despite the evolution of the technology and its influence on the organizations—are still inspiring.

C. Simone (✉)
University of Siegen, Siegen, Germany
e-mail: simone@disco.unimib.it

© Springer International Publishing AG 2018
C. Rossignoli et al. (eds.), *Digital Technology and Organizational Change*,
Lecture Notes in Information Systems and Organisation 23,
https://doi.org/10.1007/978-3-319-62051-0_5

49

As reported in [1], there are many ways in which this interplay can be managed in relation to the different underlying perspectives and related disciplines: the ICT designers and the management perspective that are focused on construction and control, respectively; or the economic perspective that offers an alternative view based on the concept of 'cultivation of the installed base', thus focusing more on the technological components, and looks for the definition of suitable standards; or a more integrated perspective that sees human, technological and social elements linked together by indissoluble and ever negotiated relations (as in Actor Network Theory [2]); or finally, the philosophical perspective offered by the Heidegger's definition of the essence of the technology, that opens to 'a new sense of responsibility that is based on what is largely beyond our control'.

As each of the above perspectives (and possibly others ones) has deep consequences on how socio-technical (re)design is conceived, it is necessary to take a specific position and to motivate this choice. We like to do so by starting from the basic tenets of the socio-technical design approach as identified from the very beginning of its conception [3]: they include the goal to increase the quality of the working life within organizations. This general concept was associated with a set of principles [4][1] that are still valid and almost neglected by those of the above perspectives that are more widely adopted. By the way, the same concept has been formulated and promoted in terms of conviviality [5] and more recently of hedonomics [6]. However expressed, this concept includes the *quality of the interactions* between the social and the technical agents: a quality that has to go beyond usability, efficiency and effectiveness and encompass the pleasure of a joyful interaction of the social agents with the technology itself and among themselves through it. This implies that ST design should aim at achieving the harmony of this interplay by profitably leveraging the positive features of the two kinds of agents and avoiding the risk that their combination exacerbates the negative ones. Social agents are characterized by positive features such as flexibility and improvisation when they have to cope with unforeseen situations; interpretation and sense making in presence of uncertain and ambiguous information; tailoring of their tools to better fit their needs and attitudes; creation of the conditions to make the cooperation with other social agents smooth and productive in concrete contexts. Technical agents afford persistency, distributedness, pervasiveness, rich and multimodal interaction; the organization of the management of huge amounts of data, the regularity of processes execution, the verification of predefined properties of data and processes; the speed of elaboration and communication.

---

[1]We recall here the more relevant ones to our discourse. *Minimal Critical Specification*: No more should be specified than is absolutely essential but the essential must be specified. *The Socio-technical Criterion*: Variances, if they cannot be eliminated, must be controlled as close to their point of origin as possible. *Boundary Location*: Boundaries should facilitate the sharing of knowledge and experience. *Information* must go, in the first place, to the place where it is needed for action. *Design and Human Values*: High quality work requires jobs to be reasonably demanding; opportunity to learn and an area of decision-making. *Incompletion*: The recognition that design is an iterative process.

These two sets of capabilities point to opposite goals that are however to be pursued to make an Information System, interpreted as a socio-technical (ST) system, viable: variability versus stability, light connections versus robustness, creativity versus reliability, improvisation versus accountability. This is the challenge of ST design: to reach an optimal compromise between these opposites.

Moreover, the context where social and technical agents operate evolves in consequence of social, economic and technological changes. This commonly recognized fact implies that the interactions between the social and technical agents evolve too in order to cope with the possible misalignments emerging from those changes: this is what calls for ST systems continuous re-design.

Re-design can be performed at two distinct, although mutually influencing, levels. At the first one re-design is due to the fact that social agents appropriate and transform the functions of the technical agents during their use, and symmetrically technical agents modify the practices of the social agents using them. Here redesign usually involves circumscribed changes to allow for unanticipated usages of the technology, or to extend its capabilities to respond to new needs that can emerge from an increased appropriation of the technology by the users themselves: existing routines and technical functionalities remain substantially unmodified and re-design usually involves a local community[2] (of practice [7]) where collaboration tones down individualism. At the second level re-design is due to the fact that the organization needs to change its strategies in consequence of internal or external factors or innovative technologies become available, and accordingly has to change the constraints that it imposes to the lower level. Here re-design happens at the organization level, can be more or less dramatic and surely percolate from the top to reach the more local social agents: these are called to modify their routines and/or the technology in use, accordingly.

To sum up, the overall socio-technical system needs to be continuously re-designed to cope with different requirements and constraints, and must then be malleable at both the community and organizational levels. According to any good engineering approach, to make continuous re-design of (ST) systems effective we have to take *design for malleability* at any level as a basic and unavoidable principle for the construction of (ST) systems.

This challenge requires a critical view of some current interpretations of ST system design and the identification of a possible alternative: the next sections aim to give a contribution in this direction by taking the technical standpoint and considering its implications on the social side in the aim to preserve the harmony hinted above. The argumentation is empirically based on field studies derived form the literature (especially in the ambit of Computer Supported Cooperative Work [8]) and from our empirical research, e.g. [9, 10].[3]

---

[2]We use the term community to avoid any reference to any specific organization structure.

[3]This work was done when the author was with the University of Milano Bicocca.

2   Issues Hindering Malleability

How to manage *control* is a central issue to keep the organization alive in a context that is complex either because the target organization is big and distributed, or because it is a smaller organization living in a network of allies and competitors, or because of both reasons. Companies face this problem in different ways depending on their different organizational culture: however a still diffused approach, beyond any official statement, is to base control on a normative approach whose aim is to prescribe behaviors that can be more easily monitored and checked in a centralized way. This is especially true for the technical agents of the ST systems, we would say, independently of the kind of organization in which they operate. As an exemplar case, consider the cloud technology that was proposed to make applications more flexible and more easily manageable. This is surely true for the individual users or communities and their own ICT applications, but the real adoption of this innovation in the organizations mostly interprets flexibility and manageability in terms of standardization and top-down handling of any technological change and evolution. The consequence is that the harmony that should be the goal of ST (re-)design is seriously compromised because the social and the technical agents are, in a way by definition, misaligned.

To sustain the above claim in more general terms we propose to consider the pervasive role that models play in the mainstream, and therefore widely applied, approaches to the design of the technical component of an IS (hereafter denoted as IT-IS). Sooner or later in the IT-IS lifecycle the designers (that is the professionals involved in the process irrespective of their specific role in design) build or make use of *models of the business processes* and *models of the data* these access and manipulate, and try to achieve the efficiency and effectiveness of the overall IT-IS on the basis of *models of the quality* of the to above basic components.[4] The various formalisms that are used to construct such models are not in question: we can generically refer to the standard BPMN [11] for processes, ER [12] for data and some basic indicators such as completeness, consistency, correctness and the like for their quality [13]. Here we want to discuss the more substantial issue of how these models are constructed and for which purpose.

Processes and data models are constructed by the designers in the aim to capture the mechanisms governing the target (portion of) organization and then build the related IT-IS on their basis by using the most appropriate technology. For what concerns the processes important are the activities and their sequences, the loops and the decision points, the roles of the involved actors with the related rights, the exchange of information across the processes, etc. For what concerns the data

---

[4]We purposely omit in our argumentation any consideration about the infrastructural components of an IT-IS that are almost used as black-boxes within an organization, and therefore are not objects of re-design, although they can be one of its causes.

important are their constituents and structure, the filters that establish the access conditions, the elaboration modalities for each activity and process, and so on. Ideally, the more the model is rich and detailed the more it serves its purpose; in practice, this can be too costly and the actual models can be less accurate. However, the goal of the experienced modeler is to capture the most significant (frequent, crucial) cases in order to circumscribe within the IT-IS the need to handle exceptions to those cases that are rare and require an ad hoc treatment. Now, what are the problems with this pervasive and potentially highly detailed modeling?

A first problem is self-evident: wiring the models into the IT-IS reduces its malleability and makes changes much more difficult and expensive as any modification requires the effort (time and competence) of the pertinent designers even if the change regards a circumscribed feature. This extends the period needed to implement it and forces the people who would take advantage from this change to manage the source problems for a longer period or to find a workaround that may be undesirable or in the worst case sanctionable [14].

But the real issue is more substantial. The processes and data models are built by the designers of the IT-IS with the involvement of the management and possibly of the people that will be the direct users (the so called end-users) of the technology. This involvement takes various forms depending on the adopted methodological approach: from a series of interactions with some selected stakeholders typically in the initial phases of the re-design, to a more systematic involvement of the end-users as in the User Centered (UC) [15] approach, and finally to a more active involvement of these latter in the re-design activities as in Participatory Design [16] and in some of its derivate approaches that fall under the umbrella of End-Used Development (EUD) [17]. We can say that all these approaches, irrespective of the specific terminology used, can be viewed as complying with the ST design tenet to focus on the organization and the end-users, and can be recognized along the history of ST design evolution [18]. Regardless of the differences characterizing them, in these approaches the tools used to build the models are basically those proposed by the designers and reflect their intentions since they have a predominant role in the interaction with the users. In other words, the aim to empower the users (in the more mature interpretation of ST design in the wild) equals making them more able to understand and use those tools, and in so doing influence some aspects of the final IT-IS.

At this point, the main question is: is this interpretation of user empowerment profitable to reach the harmony mentioned in the previous section? Moreover, does the predominant form of top-down control go in this desirable direction? The answer can be found in the empirical research conducted to understand the needs of the end-users in various application domains and the impacts of IT-IS constructed according to the approaches described above. There is no room here to account for this research in any systematic and exhaustive way. We only point to a practice that is widespread and might shed light on where a possible answer can be sought for the above questions.

3   Lessons from the Field

The dream of a paperless working place proved to be an illusion. It is a common experience that paper still pervades the offices, the hospital wards, the professional studios, the research labs irrespective of the kind of technology that is deployed there. This amount of paper has been more recently flanked, and in some cases reduced, by the appearance of IT applications that are able to mimic the properties of the paper and enrich them with the typical properties of the ICT technology. The paradigmatic applications observed in this phenomenon are the spreadsheets that combine the possibility to build forms within a sheet, to inscribe them and to make them active through appropriate functions, to link information located in different sheets, to make sheets sharable across cooperating actors and information sharable with other productivity tools. The main motivation of success of spreadsheets is that they can be bent to serve different purposes: from mere information repositories, to folders of interconnected and/or computed forms, up to simple databases with the related basic functionalities.

These applications used in presence of official IT-IS have been named *shadow tools* [19] for their capability to be autonomously and collaboratively constructed and used by people "in the shadow" of the big systems and in a way that is protected from any external influence. Shadow tools are needed because the official IT-IS are often too prescriptive in the way procedures and data policies govern the various activities: to contrast this negative aspect the actual work (or part of it) is performed using shadow tools and its outcomes are then uploaded in the official IT-IS so as to comply with the organization constraints. For example, the official IT-IS does not allow for the management of temporary information that has however to be recorded and made persistent after an additional elaboration; or does not allow users to add temporary or unofficial information to the standard data model for sake of monitoring crucial situations; or the logic by which forms unfold in the interface forces a sequence of operations that sometimes are not doable in that order or the presented information is optimized for the current task and some contextual information is missing or hard to find. This level of flexibility is difficult to anticipate at design time and is instead easy to achieve on paper and via lightweight applications. A similar phenomenon is reported in [1] in the case of a more complex shadow tool. A centralized Costumer Relation Management application was flanked by applications with the same aim that were constructed in various departments owning the needed resources: these distributed solutions fit the local practices and information needs, still maintaining some links with the centralized solution. In this case the management accepted this autonomous behavior and recognized its undoubtably improved effectiveness: this example shows that a different attitude of the management toward redesign and innovation is possible.

Shadows tools point to a bottom-up phenomenon that tells us several lessons: first, current IT-IS generate a double and invisible work [20] that surely negatively influence the quality of the people's working life, unless suitably recognized; second, this additional work testifies that end-users are able to construct technologies that fit their needs and to modify them at run-time when needed; third, the construction of these technologies is not based on any sort of explicit model, rather it is based on the practices end-users have developed to reach their working objectives and that they are able to trans-late in the technology, effectively enough to take into account the local conditions and to cope with their variability; fourth, that this can happen since end-users can reasonably appropriate the underlying technology (e.g., the spreadsheets), possibly along a progressive and collaborative learning process allowing them to increasingly exploit its affordances.

4 Design for Malleability

The lessons derived from the shadow tools phenomenon can inspire an operational interpretation of the goal to design for malleability. Indeed, this goal can be translated in the goal to avoid the waste of the invisible work performed by the end-users and the knowledge that they mobilize: both of tem are invaluable resources for the organization upon which the harmony between the social and technical agents can be constructed. Making shadow tools emerge from the shadow means to rethink the way IS are conceived in a more radical way in comparison to the agenda proposed in [21] although we share its concerns about the difficulties to introduce a new perspective in the managerial practices. However, without this radical reflection any attempt to make ST (re)design coherent with the tenets of the ST approach is likely to have only a partial success, if not a failure. This reflection in turn requires rethinking the top-down approach to control and the role of the designers in this game. We propose a way to discuss this rethinking along the levels of re-design mentioned in the introduction.

The community layer of re-design is obviously the one closer to the argumentation of the previous section. Here a natural solution is to make the hidden tools exit the shadow and become the official way to operate. This would obviously require the smooth integration of their outcomes in the ST-IS. To this aim it seems necessary to interpret the control that the management has to exercise not as the prescription of how activities are to be performed, rather as the check of the quality of the outcomes that these activities have to make available to the overall ST-IS system: the minimum data sets to be exchanged, by whom, when, in which format, in which progression and so on. In other words, it is necessary to recognize that the (same) information can have different pragmatic meanings and quality requirements at the community and at the organization level: for example, the data useful for the administration of a hospital or those useful for health research do not coincide with those that support the everyday care at the patient bed and might require a different quality, and vice versa [22].

The action of control should also promote the awareness of what has to be delivered according to the established quality indicators, in order to anticipate possible problems and to start the renegotiation of the related terms, if deemed necessary. In other words let what already happens in the shadow of the IT-IS (at both the technical and social level) and therefore with a negative connotation, become the norm and then be supported to improve its effectiveness.

This strategy also indicates how the role of the designers should be redefined: they should provide the end-users with "a better spreadsheet", that is an open platform that offers basic building blocks and composition rules that end-users can apply to build and modify their tools in a more agile way [23].[5] This platform and the possible sharing of building blocks of general interest across communities is what has to be maintained under a centralized control, not the local tools built on top of it. To this aim, designers could, if and when necessary, assist the end-users to make their usage of the platform optimal and implement new basic building blocks when they require to do so. This is a different, more radical way to empower end-users: first because they are in full control of their tools construction and second because they interact with the designers speaking the 'language of their practices' (not the one of some exogenous model) during that tools construction and usage. Notice that this approach also applies to more recent technologies that are apparently more malleable, such as web based technologies. Indeed, the problem is not about technical issues rather it is about the 'semantic level' of the components that are made available [25]: the primitives they afford should be based on end-users work practices and not on a mere general purpose or engineering perspective.

With this scenario at the community level, ST re-design at the organization level coherently becomes the redefinition of the contracts that each community is committed to, in the spirit of [26]. The organization can then be viewed as a network of contracts[6] that bind information producers and consumers (and no more as a set of interconnected processes producing and exchanging data). Any change at this level requires a redefinition of the contracts and, at the lower level, the adaptation of the ways the contractors fulfill them accordingly. This idea is drawn from the widespread view of a complex technical system as a set of components with interfaces connecting them: the interfaces have the main role to encapsulate the components internal behavior and to circumscribe the effects of more global changes in order to make the overall system more resilient. Strange enough, this idea is not usually applied to ST systems as if the presence of a social component would require a more pervasive and prescriptive form of control that is exercised by a compliant technology and specifically by the prescriptive models it incorporates, sometimes for sake of introducing some form of standardization [27].

5 From Models to Representations

The critical view of the role of models in ST system (re-)design does not mean that modeling as such has to be banned. Models are problematic when they are constructed in the aim to incorporate them in a technology because they hinder its

---

[5]A prototype of this kind of platforms for document based applications is described in [24].

[6]We prefer to speak of 'contracts' instead of 'commitments' as these latter somehow imply a procedural way to deal with them (i.e., the famous and widely criticized negotiation loop).

effectiveness and malleability, as discussed in the previous sections. Instead, modeling can play a useful role when its outcomes are used for different purposes: to make the distinction clear we call these artifacts *representations*. The main difference between models and representations is that the latter are not required to own the typical properties of the former: they can be incomplete, contain ambiguities, can use not standardized notations and so on. In fact their role is not to govern the activities of the people, rather to play as a scaffold that can support their mutual understanding when they interact and collaborate. As such representations can be as formal, complete and ambiguous as the actors˙deem necessary to make their interaction and collaboration effective: in other words their quality is relative to a context and not expressed in terms of absolute properties [22]. In this view, representations become *resources for situated actions* [28] and as such under the control of who performs them.

In the design for malleability hinted above representations can (and often actually) support *negotiation, documentation* and the current *work practices*. Negotiations occur at both levels of re-design, although under different conditions. At the community level representations can help its members to negotiate meanings and reach a mutual understanding of the ways in which activities can be performed to fulfill the organization constraints, to highlight possible conflicting proposals and the possible confluence on a reconciled view that will guide their collaboration: they become part of the community 'repertoire' [7]. In this context, these representations can be augmented with special representations (that is various kinds of annotations) that document the recurrence of problematic situations that would require an adaptation of the current work practices as well as the effectiveness of the latter in specific circumstances [9]. At the organization level, representations can help the contractors to better document the contract itself that has to be expressed in a unambiguous language that is usually different from the community and organization jargons: for example representations can add information about the context in which the exchanged information will be used, by highlighting and motivating the crucial role of some piece of information, the consequences to miss the stated deadlines and the negotiated level of quality, and so on.

What can be noticed is that this additional invisible work—that is in any case performed to make what is going on possible and to give it a meaning—is not supported by the traditional IT-IS because it is out of the scope of attention of the management and of the designers that define its requirements and specifications. When this work is somehow recognized under the perspective (if not the fashion) of Knowledge Management, the typical solution is based on the so called Enterprise Social Networks (ESN): ESN offer standard communication and sharing functionalities that should magically make people exchange their work experiences irrespective of the loose integration of the ESN with the IS-ST through which the activities are expected to be performed [10]. Then, ESN generate another kind of double work that in this case is promoted and appreciated by the management that invested in these technologies: indeed, the additional work to keep the information updated in the ESN becomes a stereotypical sign of their usefulness.

6 Conclusions

The approach to ST continuous redesign outlined in this paper has some implications: on the technical side, the proposed and empirically based design for malleability asks to focus on functionalities and technologies that are usually outside the IS-IT or at least poorly integrated with them, and give the communities of end-users the active role of bricoleurs of the tools they need [23, 29]. On the other hand, innovation that is one of the causes of continuous redesign can be interpreted as the result of the interplay between a top-down and a bottom-up process that meet at the interface of local creativity and organization strategies. In this game the consequences of innovation [30] that can be hardly anticipated outside the real practices can be continuously monitored and managed in a less disruptive way. This is a way to seek for the quality of the working life and to make change management a collaborative process where conflicts can be dealt with on the basis not only of power relations but also of the concrete dimension of the work practices. The currently available technological infrastructures allow the construction of malleable IS beyond what the management and the designers are used, if not equipped, to construct: seriously focusing on work practices is a fruitful way to better exploit this space of possibility.

References

1. Ciborra, C. U., & Hanseth, O. (1998). From tool to Gestell: Agendas for managing the information infrastructure. *Information Technology & People, 11*(4), 305–327.
2. Latour, B. (1991). Technology is society made durable. In J. Law (Ed.), *A Sociology of monsters.essays on power, technology and domination* (pp. 103–31). New York: Routledge.
3. Trist, E. (1981). The evolution of socio-technical systems. *Occasional paper 2*.
4. Mumford, E. (2003). *Redesigning human systems*. IGI Global.
5. Illich, I. (1973). *Tools for conviviality*. New York, USA: Harper and Row.
6. Hancock, P. A., Pepe, A. A., & Murphy, L. L. (2005). Hedonomics: The power of positive and pleasurable Ergonomics. *Ergonomics in Design, 3*(1), 8–14.
7. Wenger, E. (1998). *Communities of practice: Learning, meaning, and identity*. Cambridge University Press.
8. Schmidt, K., & Bannon, L. (2013). Constructing CSCW: the first quarter century. *Computer Supported Cooperative Work, 22*(4–6), 345–372.
9. Cabitza, F., Colombo, G., & Simone, C. (2013). Leveraging underspecification in knowledge artifacts to foster collaborative activities in professional communities. *International Journal of Human–Computer Studies, 71*(1), 24–45.
10. Cabitza, F., Simone, C., & Cornetta, D. (2015). Sensitizing concepts for the next community-oriented technologies: Shifting focus from social networking to convivial artifacts. *The Journal of Community Informatics, 11*(2). http://ci-journal.net/index.php/ciej/article/view/1155/1151.
11. Chinosi, M., & Trombetta, A. (2012). BPMN: An introduction to the standard. *Computer Standards & Interfaces, 34*(1), 124–134.
12. Thalheim, B. (2013). *Entity-relationship modeling: Foundations of database technology*. Springer Science & Business Media.

13. Batini, C., Cappiello, C., Francalanci, C., & Maurino, A. (2009). Methodologies for data quality assessment and improvement. *ACM Computing Surveys, 41*(3), 16.
14. Alter, S. (2015). A workaround design system for anticipating, designing, and/or preventing workarounds. In Enterprise, Business-Process and Information Systems Modeling (pp. 489–498). Springer International Publishing.
15. Norman, D. A., & Draper, S. W. (1986). *User centered system design.* NJ: Hillsdale.
16. Bratteteig, T., & Wagner, I. (2014). *Disentangling participation: Power and decision-making in participatory design* (pp. 1–118). CSCW Series-Springer.
17. Lieberman, H., Paternò, F., Klann, M., & Wulf, V. (2006). End-user development: An emerging paradigm. In *End-User Development* (pp. 1–8). Netherlands: Springer.
18. Mumford, E. (2006). The story of socio-technical design: Reflections on its successes, failures and potential. *Information Systems Journal, 16*(4), 317–342.
19. Handel, M. J., & Poltrock, S. E. (2011). Working around official applications: Experiences from a large engineering project. In *2011 CSCW ACM Conference* (pp. 309—312).
20. Suchman, L. (1995). Making work visible. *Communications of the ACM, 38*(9), 56–44.
21. Baxter, G., & Sommerville, I. (2011). Socio-technical systems: From design methods to systems engineering. *Interacting with Computers, 23*(1), 4–17.
22. Cabitza, F., & Simone, C. (2012). "Whatever Works": Making sense of information quality on information system artifacts. In G. Viscusi, G. M. Campagnolo, & Y. Curzi (Eds.), *Phenomenology, Organizational politics, and IT design* (pp. 79–110). The Social Study of Information Systems: IG Global.
23. Cabitza, F., & Simone, C. (2015). Building socially embedded technologies: Implications about design. In V. Wulf, K. Schmidt, & D. Randall (Eds.), *Designing socially embedded technologies in the real-world* (pp. 217–270). London: Springer.
24. Cabitza, F., & Simone, C. (2010). WOAD: A framework to enable the end-user development of coordination-oriented functionalities. *Journal of Organizational and End User Computing (JOEUC), 22*(2), 1–20.
25. Cabitza, F., & Simone, C., (to appear). Malleability in the hand of end-users. In F. Paterno & V. Wulf (Eds.), *End-User Development* 2nd (ed). Netherlands: Springer.
26. Winograd, T., & Flores, F. (1986). *Understanding computers and cognition: A new foundation for design.* Intellect Books.
27. Christensen, B., & Ellingsen, G. (2016). Evaluating model-driven development for large-scale EHRs through the openEHR approach. *International Journal of Medical Informatics, 89,* 43–54.
28. Suchman, L. (1987). *Plans and situated actions: The problem of human-machine communication.* Cambridge: Cambridge University Press.
29. Ciborra, C. U. (1992). From thinking to tinkering. *Information Society, 8,* 297–309.
30. Silver, M. S., & Markus, M. L. (2013). Conceptualizing the SocioTechnical (ST) artifact. *Systems, Signs & Actions, 7*(1), 82–89.

Design of Socio-technical Systems: What Does the Practice Tell Us?

Peter Bednar and Moufida Sadok

Abstract In this paper we report upon some results of an empirical study involving employees from 32 SMEs in the UK on how they approach socio-technical principles in the design of their work systems. We are particularly interested in what extent employees are engaged with decision making, change in work practices and job satisfaction. Our findings reveal that employees would prefer more responsibilities, more involvement in the decision making and in change of work practices. Additionally, it seems that recognition and appreciation by management are the most valuable job satisfaction criteria. Therefore, our findings further support the conclusion that socio-technical principles are not outdated. From a socio-technical lens, the debate on the productivity issues should not only consider buying more technology as a crucial part of the design of a work process but additional effort is required to connect it with employees' capabilities.

Keywords Socio-technical analysis · SME · Organizational change · Design of organizational system

1 Introduction

At any particular time, organizational behavior subsists as an accommodation between differing perspectives of stakeholders [1]. So when it comes to real world organizational activity this is the consequence of the actions of individual employees. This in turn is not the same thing as an abstract model of activities,

P. Bednar (✉)
School of Computing, University of Portsmouth, Portsmouth PO1 2UP, UK
e-mail: peter.bednar@port.ac.uk

P. Bednar
Department of Informatics, Lund University, Lund, Sweden

M. Sadok
Institute of Criminal Justice Studies, University of Portsmouth, Portsmouth, UK
e-mail: moufida.sadok@port.ac.uk

© Springer International Publishing AG 2018   61
C. Rossignoli et al. (eds.), *Digital Technology and Organizational Change*,
Lecture Notes in Information Systems and Organisation 23,
https://doi.org/10.1007/978-3-319-62051-0_6

but instead the result (intended and unintended consequences) of purposeful actions. These actions are at best influenced by the decisions made by employees in the context of their job situation (professional problem space). The complexity of the real world means that in everyday life an employee need to deal with exception handling to overcome contextual deviations. This is why people need professional skills, ability, willingness and possibility to make appropriate decisions as part of their job activities. However, it is not always the case that organizational practices allow or support contextual adaptation and flexibility by managerial delegation of professional decision making. Without adaptation to context any work activity will suffer from not being optimal and thus not achieve excellence.

In this paper, we describe some of the results of an empirical study involving employees from 32 SMEs in the UK on what extent Socio-Technical (ST) principles (Table 1) are implemented. The interviews described here were done over a period of approximately six months. Each interview was done face to face, consisting of one researcher and one employee at a time, usually within the compound of each company. Interviews typically would take ½ an hour. We purposefully have chosen to focus on questions that are related to three main themes. They are: decision making process, change in work practices and job satisfaction factors. Our main focus was to explore the current practices related to these questions in order to identify gaps in regard with ST perspective. The interviews were guided with the socio-technical questionnaire included in Mumford's book [2]. The SMEs are ranged from very small shops with only two employees and owner/manager, to business entities with more than 200 employees which are part of large franchises. The activities of these companies cover a wide variety of sectors, such as manufacturing industry, restaurants, consultancy, education and retail. The dependency on IT to do the job varies from medium to high levels. In most companies we successfully interviewed 2 or 3 employees, while in few we managed to interview only one employee. In total we collected and analyzed 75 questionnaires. Our interviewees are drawn from a range of positions within their respective organizations some senior, some more junior, some experienced, some manager and some less so. They are all concerned with change in work practices, and the questions are organized in such a way as to give equal consideration to the technical and social sides of systems change. We have selected

Table 1 Socio-technical principles for work design [17]

Principles	Descriptions
1. Responsible autonomy 2. Adaptability and agility 3. Focus on whole tasks 4. Maintaining meaningfulness of tasks	1. Work is organized in teams/groups with internal supervision and leadership, while maintaining holistic co-ordination between teams 2. Work teams organized to be agile and adaptable to deal with complexity and solve local problems 3. Tasks designed specifying the objective to be completed, without prescribing a method to be followed 4. Tasks designed so that each has total significance and dynamic closure for participants

to interpret both open-ended and closed-ended questions to assess the engagement in implementing ST principles.

The following section introduces the theoretical background of this research. The key findings of the empirical study are then discussed in Sect. 3. Conclusions are drawn in Sect. 4.

2 Background

ST methods advocate a human-focus analysis that reflects on social and technical factors in the design of organizational systems. The underlying principles of ST practices (Table 1) lies in the active participation of stakeholders, the co-creation, the co-development [1–8]. Consequently, the implementation of ST principles is expected to create the conditions for job enrichment, to support development of good will from the different communities of practices through constructive conversation and interaction between different stakeholders giving the opportunity to develop high level of efficiency and performance.

A wide range of Socio-Technical (ST) methods have been developed and implemented [7, 9]. Particularly, In Effective Technical and Human Implementation of Computer supported Systems (ETHICS) analysts have support mechanisms and descriptions with advice, comments and examples for over twenty different but related analyses [2, 3]. By way of a narrative and storytelling that draws on the author's own experiences applying ETHICS in many companies in Europe and the United States, [Mumford, 2003] discussed how her research perspective in relation to ST philosophy can be applied in managing change with the introduction of a new work systems or a new technology as a part of the change process. The case studies described in her book offer examples of organizational design activities and assessments to illustrate how the suggested method, based on a participative design, can provide support to problem solving and change process management.

It follows that it is desirable for managers to engage in a dialogue in which they can explore the values, goals and preferences of relevant stakeholders in context during the change process. Such a dialogue, supported by appropriate tools and techniques, can help an organization to avoid a rush to premature consensus on change, e.g. to invest in new technologies when change in work practices without changing technologies could be an option—reorganization and improvement of work practices can sometimes remove the need for technological investment [10].

However, participation at all levels in work system design is an important socio-technical principle that is not always realised (or realisable) in practice. The use of ST methods in professional practice continues to pose a number of challenges [9] and is not always adequately supported. Limitations to participation may be damaging to the usefulness of any designed system, because the contextually-dependent knowledge of unique individuals will be lost in the design process. Individuals must be empowered to join in co-creation of their system, surfacing their contextual understandings and participating fully in ownership and control of their project [11].

A major contribution of ETHICS is that it incorporates several stakeholder analyses and also explores different types of participation and empowerment, which allows reflection over engagement and involves stakeholders in their own definition of desirable change practices and system boundaries. Mumford and Beekman [12] reflected upon the engagement of employees as follows: *"If a technical system is created at the expense of a social system, the results obtained will be sub-optimal."*

3 Analysis of Findings

Bednar and Welch [13] looked at the nature of professional commitment and how transcendence value systems, professional 'pride' and the exercise of judgment are important in creation of beneficial organizational developments. A professional must be allowed to make decisions as part of their employment or their possibility to do their job with excellence will be severely inhibited and any pursuit of organizational excellence will be in vain. The first topic of our exploration is therefore related to decision making process. Particularly, we asked our interviewees about the possibilities of taking initiatives or making decisions, they expressed a kind of frustration when it comes to decide or judge what kind of changes or adjustments should be achieved to effectively do their job. As noted in Fig. 1, 28% of our interviewees said that there is little scope for initiative while almost 40% said that there is some scope for initiative. Additionally, just above 40% of survey respondents said that their job provides them with an opportunity to make decisions and use their own judgment. 28% cited that they do not have at all such opportunities. It was clear from the interviews that the vast majority of employees did not experience much managerial enthusiasm in support for employees taking initiatives and make decisions on their own.

We asked what information employees wanted but were not given. Our interviewees mainly mentioned information related to news tasks and changes in work practices. The conversations about this topic were especially interesting topic as lack of information about changes in work practices and thus involvement in those change processes are key aspects of the ST principles (Table 1). Thus not only did many employees feel they were not engaged, but it was obvious that they felt they were not even informed about the most fundamental aspects of the ST principles. Table 2 provides examples of verbatim related to this question.

It is widely recognized that ST change perspective is beneficial in supporting design of useful and usable work systems [14]. The second topic explored in our research was the involvement of employees in change in work practices. In Fig. 2, almost two thirds of our interviewees are consulted when major changes are made to their job or to the work of the department. Interestingly, this also confirms that most of the interviewees would like to participate in the decisions that affect their department.

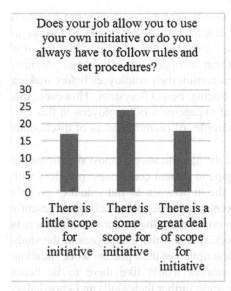

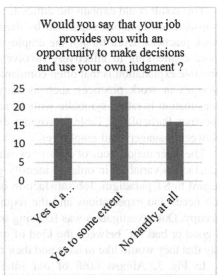

Fig. 1 Decision making practices

Table 2 Decision making and required information

Question	Verbatim
What information would you like to have that you are not given?	"Future changes that might happen in the company" "How and what changes are affecting my work" "Full information about new tasks and training"

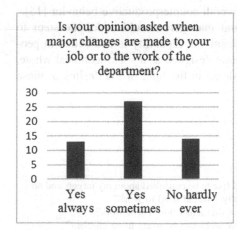

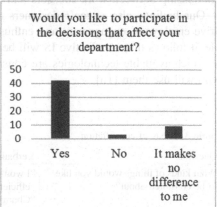

Fig. 2 Involvement in change in work practices

This result could explain the difficulties experienced by companies in taking into consideration opinions expressed by their employees when it comes to change in work practices. Even though the employees' opinions are asked it seems that it is more challenging to effectively involve them in organisational change. Another possible explanation is that often companies consult their employees before making changes in work practices such as introducing new IT system. However, this consultation is rather symbolic without real engagement of employees in this perspective. Particularly, Table 3 provides examples of preferred areas of discussions between managers and employees.

The other major focus of our survey was the identification of most significant job satisfaction variables in order to identify gaps in current companies' practices with regard to ST paradigm. Job satisfaction is the fit between an individual or group's job needs and expectations and the requirements of the job which they presently occupy. Our investigation was focusing on considering the extent to which there is a good or bad 'fit' between the kind of work situation that employees in the study say that they would like to have and their description of their present work situation.

In Fig. 3, Almost 60% of our interviewees would like there to be better opportunities than there are at present to develop further their skills and knowledge.

This important percentage is quite alarming as SMEs experience productivity problems and face resources shortage. When skills and knowledge are not fully used to do their job, employees could engage in counter productive work behavior. Additionally, three quarters of our interviewees perceive their work tedious as they have few problems to solve and their work requires little skill and knowledge. In such a situation it does not help if employees are not allowed to influence or make decisions on changes to their work practices in real terms.

When asked what gives our interviewees most sense of achievement in work, they said that recognition and appreciation of their efforts are very significant as motivational factors. This result (see Table 4) is coherent with the finding of a previous study that showed the role of the recognition as a mediator factor in the relationship between work stressors and overall counterproductive behavior [15].

Our findings also suggest designers and managers should undertake steps to drive employees' engagement and enthusiasm. As capability is embedded in people, it follows that an effective IS will be one designed as a socio-technical whole, in which available technologies are considered in the light of the desires of those who will use them [16].

Table 3 Areas of consultation

Question	Verbatim
What kinds of things would you like to be consulted about?	"I would like to be consulted about my targets and how efficiently I would need to work" "Changes that affect how I will work" "How my work can be made more efficient" "Detailed changes in the job role" "Changes that affect my working practices"

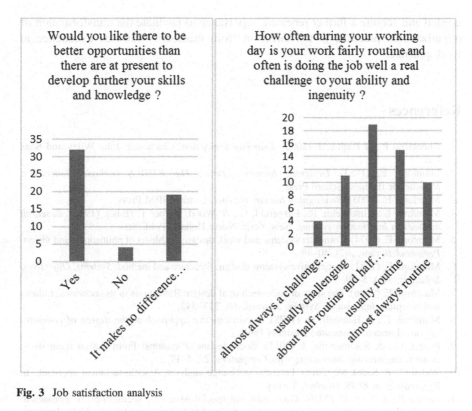

Fig. 3 Job satisfaction analysis

Table 4 Examples of job satisfaction analysis

Question	Verbatim
What gives you most sense of achievement in work?	"Being recognized, after being able to do an improvement or a new idea in my job" "When I come in under budget because of new ideas and changes to the standard routine. I also appreciate how my assistant works with me as well as challenges me to new concepts" "When work is recognized and appreciated"

4   Conclusion

The main objective of this paper was to explore the implementation in practice of ST principles. Our results show clearly that there continue to be large opportunity for SME's to potentially benefit from involving ST principles more pro-actively when it comes to their business development practices. As improving productivity at work is a crucial issue not only for larger businesses but also for SMEs it is probable that work design methodologies such as ETHICS will continue to be needed and acquire a further renewed importance to facilitate the transformation of organizational practices in the direction from mediocrity towards excellence in work practice.

References

1. Checkland P., & Poulter, J. (2006). *Learning for Action*. Chichester: John Wiley and Sons Ltd.
2. Mumford, E. (1983). *Designing human systems: The ETHICS method*. Manchester: Manchester Business School Press.
3. Mumford, E. (2003). *Redesigning human systems*. London: IRM Press.
4. Mumford, E., Hirschheim, R., Fitzgerald, G., & Wood, Harper T. (Eds.). (1985). *Research methods in information systems*. New York: North Holland Publishers.
5. Mumford, E. (1974). Computer systems and work design: Problems of philosophy and vision. *Personnel Review, 3*(2), 40–49.
6. Mumford, E. (1981). Participative systems design: Structure and method. *Systems, Objectives, Solutions, 1*(1), 5–19.
7. Mumford, E. (2006). The story of socio-technical design: Reflections in its successes, failures and potential. *Information Systems Journal, 16*, 317–342.
8. Mumford, E., & Henshall, D. (1978). *A participative approach to the design of computer systems*. London: Associated Business Press.
9. Baxter, G., & Sommerville, I. (2011). Socio-technical systems: From design methods to systems engineering. *Interacting with Computers, 23*, 4–17.
10. Welch C., & Sadok M. (2016). Potential is change analysis: A socio-technical approach. In *Proceedings of ECIS*, Istanbul, Turkey.
11. Bednar P., & Wech C. (2016). Guest editorial special issue on a sociotechnical approach to organizational transformation. *International Journal of Systems and Society*, (3:1), January–June.
12. Mumford, E., & Beekman, G. (1994). *Tools for change & Progress*. The Netherlands: CSG Publications, ISBN 90-75198-01-9.
13. Bednar, P., & Welch C. (2016). Learning for professional competence in an IS context. In U. Lundh Snis (Ed.), *Nordic contributions in IS research. Vol. 259, Lecture Notes in Business Information Processing* (pp 163–175). Switzerland: Springer International.
14. Bednar, P., & Welch C. (2016). Special issue: On a sociotechnical approach to organizational transformation. (Editorial). *International Journal of Society Systems Science. 3*(1), vii–xi. January 2016.
15. Roxana, A.-C. (2013). Antecedents and mediators of employees' counterproductive work behavior and Intentions to Quit. *Procedia—Social and Behavioral Sciences, 84*, 219–224.
16. Bednar, P. (2016). *Complex methods of inquiry: Structuring uncertainty*. Lund University Press, ISBN: 978-91-977186-8-4.
17. Emery, M. (2000). The current version of Emery's open systems theory. *Systemic Practice and Action Research, 13*(5), 623–643.

Going Beyond the System in Systems Thinking: The Cybork

Federico Cabitza and Francesco Varanini

Abstract In this paper we make the point of the need to introduce a new concept, and the related term, to account for the dynamic nature of socio-technical systems and make this nature a primary concern of systems thinking to understand and intervene on this kind of systems: the cybork.

Keywords Systems thinking · Socio-technical systems · Gestell · Bildung · Cyborg · Cybork

1 Motivations and Background

The cybork is a concept that we do not draw from the void, nor we have coined just as a result of a free association of ideas and words. All the opposite, we propose it as a term that condenses different flows of thinking in itself and yet adds something to all of them, right in virtue of its synthetic nature. These converging traditions are: cybernetics, socio-technical system theory, and systems thinking. Far from having the ambition to summarize the main tenets of these disciplines and schools of thought, or better mindsets, in what follows we will outline the elements that justify our proposal, or at least motivated us in introducing it.

As quite clear, the first part of the term Cybork comes from cybernetics. As widely known, Cybernetics is the name that Norbert Wiener in 1948 gave to a multi-form and trans-disciplinary approach to the study of any complex system from the perspective of the self-regulatory and feedback processes that keep it together, if not thrive. Wiener chose this term from the Greek *kybernetiké*, the craftsmanship of the *kybernan*, i.e., the steersman, a term that in its turn the Latin

F. Cabitza (✉)
Università degli Studi di Milano-Bicocca, 20126 Milano, Italy
e-mail: cabitza@disco.unimib.it

F. Varanini
Università degli Studi di Udine, Via Palladio, 8, Udine, Italy
e-mail: fvaranini@gmail.com

© Springer International Publishing AG 2018
C. Rossignoli et al. (eds.), *Digital Technology and Organizational Change*,
Lecture Notes in Information Systems and Organisation 23,
https://doi.org/10.1007/978-3-319-62051-0_7

translated into *gubernator*, which acquired its metaphorical meaning of head and commander thanks to his respected exhortations.

Although American for the name and the endeavour to be systematized, the cybernetic thinking can be traced back to the natively multi-disciplinary thinking of the German and Austro-Hungarian intellectuals, who were forced to emigrate to the United States for the Nazism [31]. The basic idea is feedback, i.e., the fact that "some of the output energy of an apparatus or machine is returned as input" and also the intuition that "a uniform behavoristic analysis is applicable to both machines and living organisms, regardless of the complexity of the behavior" (ibid.) These two ideas were applied to the idea of the *Cybersin*, the "cybernetic synthesis" of the actions of the individual workers and the productive capacity of factories and plants to be applied on the nationalized sector of Chile's economy during the Unidad Popular Government (1971–1973) in order to integrate data into a global network, economic data and decisions [28]. This projects envisions, for the first time, the idea of a nation as a living organism, where animals (including humans) and machines coexist, as components of the same system and as systems themselves, so tightly interconnected (structurally coupled) to be recognized as elements of the same network.

Systems Thinking emerged in the 1940s in reaction to scientific reductionism and to solve problems effectively through the ad-hoc combination of heuristics and multiple approaches. Probably just for this *pluralistic* attitude, in "systems thinking the use of words is not a straightforward exercise even though it influences our engagement with context" [6]. Among the most important expressions in system thinking one could rightly consider *socio-techical system* [14].

This expression was coined at the Tavistock Institute in London in the 1950s to denote a new way to look at organizational change, an approach that can be traced back to the Kleinian interpretation of the Freud's psychoanalysis and that considers both humans and machines essential for the emergence of specific forms of work, indeed socio-technical systems. These systems do not preexist their animate and inanimate components (cf. Aristotle) mentioned above, but rather emerge and unfold in the continuous inter-relation between those components and mutual fit, and in their turn affect their components, their mutual arrangement and behaviors. The first socio-technical researchers (including Eric Trist, Ken Bamforth, Joan Woodward and Fred Emery) observed this phenomenon in all those forms of work where the division of labor, for the sake of efficiency, creates distinctions and hierarchies, and in those where the same quest for efficiency imposes the clear distinction between theory (and hence planning) and practice (that is execution of plans)—a distinction affirmed by Taylor through his Scientific Management but already *in nuce* in the *theorein* of Aristotle and *idea* of Plato—and hence the quantification and measurement of performance and the consequent alienation of the workers involved. "Different technologies impose different kinds of demands on individuals and organizations, and those demands had to be met through an appropriate structure" [38].

Thus, from these seminal studies on, in systems thinking and in many similar and related approaches, socio-technical system has become one of the most common expressions to account for when humans and technologies "go together". Notwithstanding its popularity, or maybe right because of it, this expression also presents some shortcomings. Although systems thinking advocates a holistic approach to the study of systems by focusing on the features of the whole that emerge from the interaction of its parts, speaking of socio-technical system still emphasizes the existence and ontological (not necessarily functional) independence of the parts of a system, at least of the social and technical parts. Moreover, although systems thinking acknowledges the complex ways in which the parts of a system can interact with each other, and can exhibit unexpected behaviors as a whole that no part alone could produce by itself, it also assumes that systems are *structured, ordered functional* units.

In light of this, the expression socio-technical system, which looks reasonable for many practical and theoretical aims, also facilitates the neglect of two related, perhaps counter-intuitive, ideas. Shortly put these are: first, the social and the technical, in their dynamic and situated partaking in a single unitary system, actually cannot never be taken as distinct parts of this system and extracted as individual objects of study (or design). Second, looking at real socio-technical settings in terms of systems is conceptually tempting but paradoxically way too abstract and reductionist to allow for the faithful and effective account of their behavior and continuous change, especially when such an account is aimed at building programs to positively affect their construction and evolution over time.

To overcome these two shortcomings, in this position paper we will argue for a different phrase (and related analytical attitude), which could better denote autopoietic socio-technical settings and inspire different ways to design *for* them: the *cybork*. We introduce this new concept in the socio-technical theory discourse to emphasize the need to move from a model-driven, component-oriented and intrinsically static view of this kind of systems to a more organic one, where the complex entanglement between the social and the technical, as well as between the human and the artificial, is not only claimed but also acknowledged in the very representations by which we try to capture it. This leads to considering *community morphogenesis* as a new topic in the socio-technical discourse and taking the challenge to develop concepts and tools to both study and foster it.[1] To argue in favor of this stance, we will first address the shortcomings that a structural and ontological view of socio-technical settings can hide, and then argue more positively towards alternative metaphors and new proposal.

2   What Socio-technicality Can Hide

Multiplicitism. William of Ockham once said that "entia non sunt multiplicanda praeter necessitatem". Distinguishing between humans and technologies seem totally reasonable for many practical or theoretical aims, but it is actually harmful to

---

[1]Morphogenesis seems to be the "pillars of Hercules" of computational thinking, as also prominent figures like Alan Turing have considered it as a matter of study, with limited success [3].

design technologies for the humans. Philippa Goodall in 1983 rightly stated that "design *for* use is design *of* use" [15]. Rightly so, any design is the *design of work*, and *for its change*. The point is that technologies are one with the techniques by which they are put to use; and humans are at one with their extended body of tools and devices [35, Chap. 1]. This is so much the case that even the human body itself could be considered the first technology (ibidem): it is essentially human the cultural use of the body as expression of the self and as first communication medium. Human sociality then, which is a cultural phenomenon, is enabled by technology and cannot be given without it. This is because technology should not be narrowly intended: rather, also language should be considered a human technology [7] and indeed one of the most important and characteristic of our species ("language is the first technology", ibid.)., which involves the use of the body with techniques that are compatible with our physiology (of course) but also socially acquired and refined over years of social interaction requiring agreed conventions and mutual expectations.

Thus, distinguishing users from their tools is as much serious as common mistake of perspectives: a hammer lying on a table, which is not even considered by a potential user as a potential object by which to hammer something, is not a hammer. Here we are not proposing a variation of the argument of George Berkeley (1710), as we are not daring to say that the hammer does not exist as a material thing unless one perceives it. Rather, we say that that thing is not a hammer until it is used as a hammer by a "hammerer", that is until it is not involved in an intentional hammering.[2]

Staticism. We likely partake in (multiple) socio-technical systems any given moment. As curious observers of these human phenomena, looking at a socio-technical system is as easy as it is to belong to one, since what we would experience—the movements, the conversations, the material production of artifacts and their inscriptions, any continuous transformation of the state of affairs—would be *the* socio-technical system before, or better yet, around us. However, when we want to see any such system with the eyes of the mind, that is with that *theoretical* attitude that from Plato on distinguishes (and separates) the direct experience of the things from their detached contemplation and study, we need linguistic metaphors [20] that are isomorphic to the phenomena experienced.

3   A New Metaphor to Account for Change

Intelligence closely regards the capability to bring things together (cf. inter-lĕgo) and to stand in the midst of them (which is the literal meaning of the term *to understand*): an intelligent gaze on things and events sees and conceives relations between them (e.g., the basic relation of cause and effect), both relations holding *in presence* (cf. the paradigmatic relation that Saussure calls metonymy) and also *in*

---

[2]Not necessarily enacted, but also only imagined by an agent.

absentia (what Saussure calls metaphors). In this regard, Nietzsche was one the first Western thinkers to denote the tendency to see things where actually just actions are[3], or better yet a doing[4], that is to acknowledge the potentially harmful tendency to *reify* dynamic processes into metaphoric, yet static, entities.[5]

Thus, the very word *system* (from the Greek "ensemble of things put together") suggests to look for (and hence at) ordered arrangements of entities, where mutual relations can be variously relevant to constitute the above order, or even the nature of the related things themselves [2].

Other (intended isomorphic) metaphors have spread and gained general appeal in scholarly communities, including the communities engaged in the organizational studies and the design sciences: their members like to speak of *models* (small-scale representations of a system, pruned off of unnecessary details), *frames* [30], *structures* [17], and even *infrastructures* [9].

We here make the point, partly inspired by the theses of linguistic relativism [37][6], that these metaphors, besides affecting our comprehension of socio-technical systems (like any metaphor actually does), do also affect our comprehension and design of these systems through an overemphasis of the static, ontological and objectivistic phenomena that they exhibit.

Gestell and Gebild. This influence regards what the German philosopher Heidegger [19] denoted as Gestell, literally a frame, a structure of shelves, or the enframing structure that can be imposed on people, processes, and things and any sort of system by any sort of technology, among which also language [7]. However, as also noticed by Ciborra and Hanseth [12], the words Ge-stell and sys-tem indicate just the same concept (literally), in two different (but yet often converging) linguistic traditions.

In [8, 36], an alternative metaphor is discussed in regard to how we can know and understand the systems in which we also reside and work: instead of Gestell (or Gestalt), Gebild. This latter word derives from and is closely related to Bildung (growth, formation). This distinction was first put forth by Goethe in his "The metamorphosis of plants" from 1790 [16]. In hiw own words:

> The Germans have a word for the complex of existence presented by a physical organism: Gestalt. With this expression they exclude what is changeable and assume that an inter-related whole is identified, defined and fixed in its character. If we look at all these Gestalten, especially the organic ones, we will discover that nothing in them is permanent,

---

[3]If Nietzsche was among the first ones, Becker is probably among the latest ones, when he writes that "things are just people acting together" (p. 46) [5].

[4]In his words: "[...] there is no *being* behind the doing, acting, becoming. *The doer* is merely made up and added into the action—the act is everything" (On the Genealogy of Morals, treatise I, 13, tr. W. Kaufmann).

[5]The etymology of *thing*, i.e., a public assembly of people discussing "things of concerns" (from which it comes the metonymy by which the latter ones got the name of the former one) is a common place that we just hint at here.

[6]Simply put, linguistic relativism states that the language by which we describe the world affects our interpretation of it.

nothing is at rest or defined—everything is in a flux of continual motion. This is why German frequently and fittingly makes use of the word Bildung (formation, development) to describe the end product and what is in the process of production as well. Thus [...] we should not speak of Gestalt, or if we use the term, we should at least do so only in reference to an idea, a concept, or to an empirical element that s held fast for a mere moment of time. When something has acquired a form it metamorphoses immediately to a new one[7]

Gebild is then the "shaping form" [36] considered in a continuous evolution. The same object can be considered both as Gestalt, i.e., something standing firm and constant over time, and as Gebild, a sort of elusive image (or a picture of a fact, a là Wittgenstein). However, Goethe points out that looking at the continuous change of Nature, the reassuring and comforting certainty of the Gestalt is but an illusion (and perhaps even a delusion). Likewise, it is an illusion the idea that one form (one structure) can be given once and for all, and as such this is stable over time [36]. Thus, while Gestalt expresses the idea of something that has got a definitive and static shape (form), Gebild and Bildung express dynamic concepts, related to an ever-changing and ever-growing process, that is Bildung, as well as the thing resulting from this process, that is Gebild. This latter entity is the *organism*, which is another apt term in our argument.

Organism. This term is intertwined with the ideas of action and deed: "what by means of which work is done", "that which is wrought or made", but also "what makes and does". This word comes from one the deepest linguistic roots our language shares with the others, *werg- that stands for "to do".[8]

Organisms can be natural, of course, but also artificial, when machines are complex enough to exhibit autonomous actions and behaviors. Moreover, claiming the continuity between life and technique, and between human beings and the machine is no longer eccentric, especially after the "blasphemy" purported by Haraway in the late 20th century, which she called the *cyborg*: "a cybernetic organism, a hybrid of machine and organism [made of human beings in their] unchosen 'high-technological' guise as information systems, texts, and ergonomicallly controlled labouring, desiring, and reproducing systems [intertwined with] machines [...] as communication systems, texts, and self-acting, ergonomically designed apparatuses" [18]. After all, "nothing is more human than a machine" [11](p. 8).[9]

---

[7]cf. Goethe's Botanical Writings, pp. 215–19, cited in [33].

[8]"Cognates: Greek ergon "work," orgia "religious performances;" Armenian gorc "work;" Avestan vareza "work, activity;" Gothic waurkjan, Old English wyrcan "to work," Old English weorc "deed, action, something done;" Old Norse yrka "work, take effect". Online Etymology Dictionary, © 2001–2016 Douglas Harper.

[9]The Greek word for machine, mechané, means "any artificial means or contrivance (i.e., device/arrangement/expedient) for doing a thing": the machine cannot be decoupled from either its skillful use or the goal it is aimed at. Likewise, and differently from many mainstream translations of the treatise by Aristotle about machines, we translate its beginning as follows: *"Remarkable things occur [not in accordance with nature but rather] along and beyond it [parà phýsin], which are produced through techne for the advantage of humanity [...] whenever it is necessary to produce an effect [prâxai] beyond nature [parà phýsin]. [...] Therefore we call that part of techne [méros tes téchnes] solving such difficulties, a machine."*

Similarly, Longo in [23] proposed the concept of *symbiont*, in the metaphorical mould that had been clearly drawn first by Licklider [22], who used the expression *man-computer symbiosis* in the 1960s. However, this phrase is as much evocative as misleading, for its indulgence in making machines anthropomorphic (as they would give to have something back in return); and, even worse yet, substantially *different from* the human, rather than recognizing them part and parcel of the culture and hence of the human.

More correctly one could speak of *structural coupling* [26] between the technical element and the human element. Structural coupling between two systems, taken as "plastic composite unities", takes place whenever they "undergo recurrent interactions with structural change but without loss of organization" [26](p. xxi). Moreover, every time there is behavioral coordination in the realm of structural coupling, also communication takes place. For Maturana and Varela [27], who were strong opponents of the Shannon model of communication in terms of message exchange through a tube [4], "there is no transmitted information in communication" (p. 195), but rather this latter one is the result of the coordination of communicative behaviors which occur in *social coupling*.

From the cyborg to the cybork. Thus, also the idea of cyborg must be overtaken: the idea that a single organism can be augmented by some artificial prosthesis is simplistic for at least two reasons: first, because it does not consider the bigger context that makes the prosthesis either possible (who built it?) or effective (i.e., what configuration of forces and competences makes it useful, e.g., the power grid supplying energy to any computational device); second (and worse yet) because it does not consider the aims by which the augmentation has been pursued, that is the intentional activities that the newly designed hybrid organism can perform better, or now accomplish. Thus, it is important to focus on what, although grounded on the human and even on single individuals, goes beyond the individual and makes a collective effort concrete: *work*.

This concept in the main Latin languages is associated with ideas of fatigue and pain (e.g., the Italian *lavoro* comes from the Latin labor, i.e., toil, effort; the Spanish *trabajo*, as well as the French *travail*, come both from *tripalium*, a particular yoke for slaves and pack animals). In fact, as said above *work* (what in German is Werk, i.e., neither Arbeit, nor Mühe) comes from the same root behind the Greek *érgon* (literally, work) and from there, after a long but yet direct semantic trajectory, our *organization*. Work then is not related to exertion, pain, atonement; but rather to energy, expression of force, accomplishment, and (what produces) wealth. In one word, to effective action.

The *cybork* is then a portmanteau that blends together two semantic worlds and related traditions: the *cyborg*, i.e., an organism where natural and artificial elements are inexstricably intertwined and mutually fit to each other; and the *work*, that is a set of intentional activities that are *mutually dependent* and accordingly coordinated in reaching an objective [32]. The *cybork* is then a *collective organism*; a *hybrid agency*; a *network of actants* [21]; a "humanchine networks constituted out of the activities of humans and nonhumans acting collectively (although not necessarily universally in concert)" [1]; a whole configuration of active forces "that is greater than the sum of its parts", or better yet (citing Koffka) "that is *other* than the sum of the parts": a sort of *collective* (of humans and non-humans).

We make the point that these collectives need a different ontology and episte-mology to be detected, observed and studied, like those under development in the recent wave of sociology that has been recently dubbed the "sociology of associ-ations" ("associology") [21] to highlight its discontinuity from the so called "so-ciology of the social", i.e., the traditional sociology in the mould of Durkheim [25]; and a different design to be supported (and evolved), like the contrarian de-design approaches that we have just begun to outline in a previous contribution [10].

Therefore, The idea that is denoted by such a hybrid word itself, cybork, is that it is an idle question to understand[10] what element, between the human-social one and the artificial-technical one, is more necessary; as well as how to design the latter one to support, or substitute!, the former one. The idea of the cybork is that where humans and their tools go together there is only action to be observed; ways in which action is "fed back" by other action; there is only work and reflection, and how the coupling between these two unfolds over time and transforms the world.

4 Conclusions

The will to a system is a lack of integrity.

Friedrich Nietzsche[11]

A quick skim on this contribution could make it appear a paper stuck in the nominalistic side of socio-technical theory, the one struggling to find the better ways to denote complex phenomena. Or worse yet, an over-ambitious proposal to discard important terms in traditional socio-technical theory, like system and structure.

As a matter of fact, we propose this contribution as a short advocacy towards considering again the actual semantic roots of these seminal terms, which some IT discourse and the general grand narrative of business management and business modelling have slowly but clearly drifted towards the idea of an artificially detached and accurate *staticness*.

As a matter of fact yet, structure comes from *structus*, originally a heap or pile, something that is piled up one layer at a time, and *structūra* is indeed a building, built on layers of bricks, one brick at a time. Both the words come from *strŭo*, that is "to make by joining together, to build, erect, form, construct": *structure* was then the result of a process of undetermined piling up of materials, we would say, not predefined by any project or previous design, which only in later times indicated an

---

[10]Here again we recall that to understand means "to stand in between" as if it were always possible, by discerning the relata from the relation itself.

[11]Orig.: Der Wille zum System ist ein Mangel an Rechtschaffenheit. Götzen-Dämmerung, § 26,

ordered arrangement (especially in Cicero, but yet regarding language and rhetorical art, not physical systems).

On the other hand, also system, as hinted above, is a term with a long story behind: it derives from the ancient Greek *sýstema*, that stands for 'complex' and is (obviously) connected to *sýnthesis*, i.e., the action noun of the verb syntíthenai 'to put together, combine'. Clearly, *sýnthesis* is the opposite of *análysis*, that namely stands for 'breakdown', 'resolution of anything complex into simple elements'.

Since hoping in a revival of these linguistic roots for these common terms would be utterly overambitious, we rather aim to repropose the metaphors of *Gebild*— ever-growing structure, *Organism*—organic and self-organizing structure, from which we extrapolate a new term that subsumes those latter and all the similar ones —the *cybork*. This is done just to prepare the ground for new and more convinced studies in system thinking towards the ever changing bond between the social and the technical, without getting stuck in *understanding* (or worse yet, modeling) what the components and the single elements are, but rather focusing on the processes, of transformation and *translation*, which occur "where the action is" [13].

Thus, we have proposed the vision of a multitude of local and small cyborks, i.e. *ever-evolving socio-technical systems that do some action, and do some work*. By looking from some distance, these cyborks can be recognized as just connected regions of a greater, global Cybork, which both enables and justifies them all. A global Cybork so much alike the visions of Mumford—the *megamachine* [29]— or by Lotman[12]—the *semiosphere*. In particular, this latter was defined as "the place of the continuous making of sense (semiosis)" [24] and nowadays would certainly encompass the Web, as well as any of the human utterances and expressions that are entrapped in the social media and personal apps that people use while being immersed in their activities, their social interactions and texture of practices. However, notwithstanding this multiplicity and manifest dispersion, "all semiotic space can be considered a single mechanism (*if not organism*). [In so doing] not this or that brick will appear as the foundation, but the 'great system' called semiosphere" [24] (our emphasis). The same holds for the cybork: even just two people writing a conference paper by exchanging emails and feverishly consulting the Web as well as their small personal libraries at home, to have *this* very work done. By tracking down all the other cyborks that made the Web pages possible and still available and those books concrete and still understandable, one does not see just the individual cyborks doing something, but rather the one Cybork of human beings and human objects, all mobilized by some inner and ineffable force.[13]

Humankind itself can be seen as a giant Cybork, constituted by smaller cyborks, an overall living system where the boundary between the artificial and the natural, the living and the machine tends to blur and fade away. That notwithstanding, while

---

[12]In semiotics, the stance by the Russian semiologist Jurij Michajlovič Lotman can be seen as an alternative perspective to the more traditional ones, both the Peircean and the Saussarian ones, and one strongly opposing any stance that sees the whole ontologically as sum of its parts.

[13]"To do things, like certain inanimate objects,[not necessarily] knowing what they are doing, as, for instance, fire burns" Aristotle, Metaphysics, 981a–b.

the human beings consider themselves parts contained within complex socio-technical systems, they are also called to contain their technologies, to keep them together and prevent any of them from dismembering the human with centrifugal forces that distance it from its responsibility.

Senge [34] defined systems thinking as a framework "for seeing interrelationships rather than things, for seeing patterns of change rather than static snapshots." The Goethe's metaphor of the Gebild, to account for the astonishing complexity of Nature, as well as the new metaphor of the cybork to account for the inextricability of hands and tools—nature and culture, in any kind of work capable of changing the world, shed light on the dynamic nature of any socio-technical system; and the evolutionary nature of any thinking.

References

1. Atkinson, C., & Brooks, L. (2005). In the Age of the Humanchine. *ICIS 2005 Proceedings*, 11, 123–135.
2. Barad, K. (2003). Posthumanist performativity: Toward an understanding of how matter comes to matter. *Signs, 28*(3), 801–831.
3. Bard, J., & Lauder, I. (1974). How well does Turing's theory of morphogenesis work? *Journal of Theoretical Biology, 45*(2), 501–531.
4. Barnett, G. A., & Thayer, L. (1997). *Organizationâ€ communication, emerging perspectives V: The renaissance in systems thinking*. Westport: Greenwood Publishing Group.
5. Becker, H. S. (2008). *Tricks of the trade: How to think about your research while you're doing it*. Chicago: University of Chicago Press.
6. Bednar, P. (2016). *Complex methods of inquiry: structuring uncertainty* (Doctoral dissertation, Lund University).
7. Bernstein, C. (1986). Living tissue/dead ideas. *Social Text, 16*, 124–135.
8. Bocchi, G., & Le, Varanini F. (2013). *vie della formazione*. Italy: Guerini e Associati. Milano.
9. Bowker, G. C., Baker, K., Millerand, F., & Ribes, D. (2009). *Toward information infrastructure studies: Ways of knowing in a networked environment. In International handbook of internet research* (pp. 97–117). Netherlands: Springer.
10. Cabitza, F. (2014). De-designing the IT artifact. Drafting small narratives for the coming of the socio-technical artifact. In *ItAIS 2014, Proceedings of the 11th Conference of the Italian Chapter of AIS*, Genova, Italy.
11. Canguilhem, G., Marrati, P., & Meyers, T. (2008). *Knowledge of life*. New York: Fordham University Press.
12. Ciborra, C. U., & Hanseth, O. (1998). From tool to Gestell: Agendas for managing the information infrastructure. *Information Technology & People, 11*(4), 305–327.
13. Dourish, P. (2004). *Where the action is: The foundations of embodied interaction*. Cambridge: MIT press.
14. Emery, F. E., & Trist, E. L. (1960). *Socio-technical systems, management sciences models and techniques* (Vol. 2). London: UK.
15. Fallan, K. (2008). De-scribing design: Appropriating script analysis to design history. *Design Issues, 24*(4), 61–75.
16. Goethe, J. W., & Miller, G. L. (2009). *The metamorphosis of plants*. Boston, MA: MIT Press.
17. Greenhalgh, T., & Stones, R. (2010). Theorising big IT programmes in healthcare: Strong structuration theory meets actor-network theory. *Social Science & Medicine, 70*(9), 1285–1294.

18. Haraway, D. (1991). *Simians, cyborgs, and women: The reinvention of nature Routledge*. NY, USA: NYC.
19. Heidegger, M. (1954). The question concerning technology. *Technology and Values: Essential Readings*, 99–113.
20. Krarup, T. M., & Blok, A. (2011). Unfolding the social: quasiâ€ actants, virtual theory, and the new empiricism of Bruno Latour. *The Sociological Review, 59*(1), 42–63.
21. Lakoff, G., & Johnson, M. (2008). *Metaphors we live by*. Chicago: University of Chicago press.
22. Latour, B. (2005). *Reassembling the social*. Hampshire: Oxford University Press.
23. Licklider, J. C. (1960). Man-computer symbiosis. *IRE Transactions on Human Factors in Electronics, 1*, 4–11.
24. Longo, G. O. (2005). Uomo e tecnologia: una simbiosi problematica. *Mondo Digitale, 2*, 5–18.
25. Lotman, J., & Clark, W. (2005). On the semiosphere. *Sign Systems Studies, 33*(1), 205–226.
26. Maturana, H. (2002). Autopoiesis, structural coupling and cognition: A history of these and other notions in the biology of cognition. *Cybernetics & Human Knowing, 9*(3–4), 5–34.
27. Maturana, H. R., & Varela, F. J. (1987). *The tree of knowledge: The biological roots of human understanding*. Boston: New Science Library/Shambhala Publications.
28. Medina, E. (2006). Designing freedom, regulating a nation: Socialist cybernetics in Allende's Chile. *Journal of Latin American Studies, 38*(03), 571–606.
29. Mumford, L. (1971). *Technics and Human Development: The myth of the machine* (Vol. I). Harvest Boo.
30. Orlikowski, W. J., & Gash, D. C. (1994). Technological frames: Making sense of information technology in organizations. *ACM Transactions on Information Systems (TOIS), 12*(2), 174–207.
31. Rosenblueth, A., Wiener, N., & Bigelow, J. (1943). Behavior, purpose and teleology. *Philosophy of Science, 10*(1), 18–24.
32. Schmidt, K., & Bannon, L. (1992). Taking CSCW seriously. *Computer Supported Cooperative Work (CSCW), 1*(1–2), 7–40.
33. Seamon, D. (1998). *Goethe's way of science: A phenomenology of nature*. New York: SUNY Press.
34. Senge P. M. (1999). The fifth discipline, the art & practice of the learning organization. Reprint 1999. London: Random House (1990).
35. Tenner, E. (2009). *Our own devices: How technology remakes humanity*. Vintage.
36. Varanini, F. (2009). Goethe: la conoscenza come morfogenesi. https://goo.gl/VXvWZe.
37. Whorf, B. L. (1956). *Language, thought, and reality. Selected Writings of Benjamin Lee Whorf*. Cambridge: MIT Press.
38. Woodward, J. (1965). *Industrial organization: Theory and practice*. London, VI: Oxford University Press.

Is Participatory Game Design Effective Over Time? Let's Assess Its Products

Alessandra Melonio

Abstract Participatory game design has been conducted with children for eliciting their expectations for games for them. However, game design is a complex inter-action design process: it takes various design tasks and demands different cognitive skills. This paper reflects on it considering the products of two participatory game design studies with children, conducted in two different years in diverse primary schools.

Keywords Game design · Participatory design · Gamification · Cooperative learning · Engagement · Quality of children's products

1 Introduction

In principle, *participatory design* (PD) methods or similar interaction design methods take children's ideas directly into design so as to meet children's expectations for games [1]. Children should be critically contributing to the design with their ideas as experts of their experience. Designers should turn into reflective practitioners so that design becomes an act of "knowledge co-construction" in the sense of [2], for creating a shared experience. According to the adopted method and its philosophy, designers become full partners, peers, guides or facilitators of children's expression, and bring in their professional expertise for the product under design.

However PD methods are also demanding on all participants; co-designing interactive products can require PD participants several resources [3, 4]. Games are the prototypical examples of interactive products that appeal to children and yet are demanding to design, in terms of time and commitment to learn: even the early design of a game can be complex to master and can require prolonged times in

A. Melonio (✉)
Free University of Bozen-Bolzano, Piazza Domenicani 3, 39100 Bolzano, Italy
e-mail: alessandra.melonio@unibz.it

© Springer International Publishing AG 2018
C. Rossignoli et al. (eds.), *Digital Technology and Organizational Change*,
Lecture Notes in Information Systems and Organisation 23,
https://doi.org/10.1007/978-3-319-62051-0_8

81

order to elaborate various elements of the game, ranging from its narrative to its organisation into levels.

Recently, the complexity of conducting an effective *participatory game design* (PGD) experience has led researchers to reflect on it. Assessing it becomes even more crucial when design moves into schools, which bring further requirements on design activities, e.g., [5]. This paper reports on two different PGD studies, one in 2014 and the other in 2015, in different primary schools, and assesses them critically. It does so by considering children's *game design* (GD) products over time.

Most commonly in PD the outcome is the actual artefact or design delivered at the end of the experience; then an outcome embodies decisions and considerations and, as such, it brings researchers epistemology insights as design knowledge [6]. This paper partly embraces such a view: outcomes are children's GD products, and epistemology is knowledge concerning such products. However, the paper also moves away from that view. Firstly, it considers products as the outcomes of collaboration and not of individual work, in line with what suggested in [5]. Secondly, the knowledge considered is not what specific game elements children could design at the end of their experience, as in [7]. Rather, this paper focuses on a complementary knowledge: what design issues recur over time in the GD process, by inspecting GD products by children. Therefore the paper is a reflection on PGD processes with children, and their unfolding over time, across two years of work.

Firstly the paper overviews related work for setting the context of the two PGD studies. Secondly, for space constraints, it only sketches their common PGD approach; for details, see [8]. Then the paper explains how two PGD processes for primary schools were organised, in 2014 and 2015. As GD products by children were evaluated in the same manner in both years, their evaluation approach and results are presented in a single section. Finally the paper discusses how children's GD products evolved over time, and what categories of issues recurred in their products. By considering both studies in primary schools instead of one, across two years of work, we can compare differences and see what's common across them in order to reason, on more general grounds, about outcomes of PGD with children, and about knowledge acquired through it concerning the PGD process in the conclusive part of this paper.

2   Related Work

A GD process is a complex interaction design process. At a fine-grained view, an early GD process is made of complex intertwined tasks, and specifically of: goal *analysis*; *conceptualisation*; *prototyping*. Game designers analyse the goal of the game, and create the game idea high-level conceptualisation, with the main rules for reaching the game goal. Designers conceptualise and prototype the core mechanics by refining the main rules and considering the progression across game levels. In case the game requires a storyline for stirring the game forward, within or across levels, designers conceptualise the storyline so as to make it consistent with the overall GD choices. If the game idea envisages an avatar, designers define that early, in conceptualisation documents and prototypes; in avatar-based gameplay modes, the player generally acts on the avatar, and mechanics rules are related to the avatar's actions in the game; interface and interaction choices for the avatar have to be in line with the other GD choices. See [9].

GD for children has been differently approached [10]. Some designers prefer an individualistic approach to GD. Others, such as [11, 12], prefer a player/user centered design approach, involving players in the GD process and placing them at its centre. In recent years, PD has been receiving an increasing attention for involving children in the PGD process itself, as early designers.

PD forces designers to look at things from another point of view, which proves useful when participants are children. According to PD researchers, engaging children in the design process can lead to ideas that adults alone cannot envisage of [13]. Different PD methods have been devised for designing interactive products with children, and lately for designing games with children. A comprehensive overview can be found in [8].

Several PD methods assume that intergenerational small teams of children and adults work together for prolonged times, outside schools, e.g., [4, 14]. However the PD literature also counts PD studies with few design experts conducted within school hours and classrooms, e.g., [15, 16], in line with the manifesto in [17], which in 2014 foresaw that "elementary school children [will] learn about designing and co-designing through practical and fun hands-on experiences". The studies reported in this paper, one in 2014 and one in 2015, follow the latter line of work. They required two researchers in the PGD processes within primary-schools: roles were well-specified in advance so as to make clear how and when adults would mediate children's contribution, as recently recommended in [15].

Surprisingly, the assessment of children's products in a PGD process, in relation to their evolution over time, is relatively under investigated in the PGD literature: despite the proliferation of PGD studies with children, at present, the "number of studies that provide a deeper understanding of the complex process of the design of games [with children] is limited" [18]. For instance, the research work of Moser counts different case studies of PGD with children, e.g., [19]. She conceived a GD framework with techniques for creating parts of games together with children, used in her case studies with children. However the PGD outcomes were not assessed in the case studies, as the focus was how to elicit children's expectations for games and not the quality of the outcomes in GD tasks (person. comm.). More recently, Bonsignore, who coauthored several papers on co-design with children, reported co-design work concerning alternate reality games in [20]. The work of Bonsignore and colleauges inspect when the design process seems difficult for children, according to observational field-note data. This paper shares similar concerns but inspects GD products by children for drawing its conclusions, across two years of experience.

3 The Participatory Approach to the Design of Games with Children

Gamified Co-design with Cooperative Learning (GaCoCo) is the PGD approach that was used in the 2014 and 2015 studies reported in this paper. Conceived in [21], it was incrementally refined across studies for allowing primary-school children to design games with researchers and their teachers in GD sessions of c. 2 h, spread over different weeks, e.g., [7].

In GaCoCo, children work in groups of 3–5 members to conceptualise and prototype their game ideas. In line with [22], a teacher acts as intermediary between researchers and her or his class. At the start of a design session, teachers illustrate the work organisation and material to be used, according to the session protocol. Moreover, they are in classroom together with GaCoCo researchers during the entire design activity: teachers assist in the communication with children for the scaffolding of groups' work, following a specific GaCoCo protocol for them. GaCoCo researchers have different types of expertise and roles. One is the *GD expert*, who delivers each group formative feedback through dialogue during a design session, and through written comments in between design sessions. The other, experienced of child development, is the *education expert*. This acts as observer during design sessions and maintains a constant dialogue with the other adults concerning children's well being.

Last but not least, GaCoCo uses cooperative learning, an educational methodology based on constructivism, and gamification for engaging all children in the design work, as explained in [23].

4 Design of the 2014 and 2015 Studies

4.1 Study Design in 2014: From a Given Story to Group Games

4.1.1 Participants and Aim

The GD study of 2014 involved two classes from two different primary schools in North-Eastern Italy. Children were, in total, 35 (59% females), coming from a variety of socio-economic backgrounds. Classes were of different ages and sizes: at the start of the study, the younger class was of $n = 15$ children, in grade 3, with mean age $M = 8.85$ years, $SD = 0.44$; the older class was of $n = 20$ children, in grade 4, with mean age $M = 9.72$ years, $SD = 0.47$. All children participated on a voluntary basis, and their parents authorised their participation through a written consent form. The study involved 2 researchers and 2 teachers. Roles were in line with GaCoCo and, in line with it, teachers and researchers divided children in small groups of 3–5 members, heterogeneous in terms of learning and social skills, before the GD process started.

4.1.2 The GD Process

Each group of children of a class was asked to work on a game, composed of two levels. Technology-related choices were fixed: children were asked to design games for tablets. Games had to be designed as avatar-based, starting from a storyline. This was chosen by school teachers and designers together, and read at school as part of a traditional instructional activity.

The GD process was organised in line with GaCoCo. In particular, cooperative learning strategies for small heterogeneous groups were set in the GaCoCo protocol for children. Different cooperative learning roles, such as those of ambassador and secretary, were assigned by teachers to learners; roles rotated among group members so as to ensure that all children had a chance to train different skills. Rules for managing group work were explained to the class by their teacher.

The GD process in each school took a total of four design sessions, whereas the first session mainly served to create the identity of groups. A session lasted circa two hours and a half, and sessions were spread across different weeks. Each session was presented as a *mission* to children, with its own products as goal, generative toolkits and gamified probes, such as a progression map, for conveying a sense of progression, control and cooperation; these are explained in [24]. Missions followed a recurring pattern. At the start of a mission, the teacher recapped what children had produced at the end of the previous mission (if any) and outlined the goal products of the daily mission. Then each mission continued with its specific tasks. In particular, from the second mission onward, each group performed design tasks and released incremental GD products, that is, a GD document and prototype. Each mission and its products are detailed in the remainder.

First Mission: Group Identity. All children were trained by their teacher to cooperative learning rules and roles. The GD expert explained them how GD would work using metaphors. Finally, each group was assembled and worked on creating their identity, e.g., each group created their own badge, which served to track their progression on a progression map.

Second Mission: Group Game Idea and Avatar. Each group released the so-called high-level concept document of their game, containing their game idea. The document was structured as a form with scaffolding questions. Starting from the story read in class acting as storyline, each group was asked to create their game idea for continuing the story by filling in the document. Afterwards groups worked on prototyping the game avatars and their objects, using a specific template.

Third and Fourth Missions: Group Levels. Starting from the high-level concept document and avatar prototypes, each group conceptualised two game levels, working first in pairs and then sharing results in group, releasing the chore mechanics document for the levels. The document was again structured as a form with scaffolding questions. The document was used for prototyping levels, again first in pairs and then sharing results in group, using the avatars and objects prototyped in the second mission.

Fifth Mission: Group Passage Conditions. Groups of children firstly conceptualised the passage conditions between levels, filling in the so-called progression

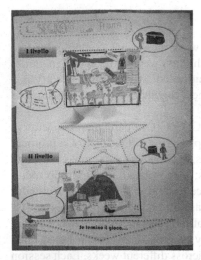
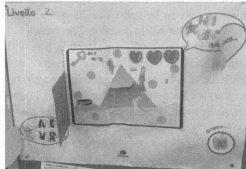

Fig. 1 Game prototypes of 2014 (*left*) and 2015 (*right*)

document. The document was again structured as a form with scaffolding questions. Secondly groups assembled their levels into a single game, using an ad hoc frame. See Fig. 1. They also presented their game to peers.

4.2 Study Design in 2015: From a Class Story to a Class Game

4.2.1 Participants and Aim

The GD study of 2015 involved two classes from another primary school in North-Eastern Italy. Children were, in total, 42 (45% females), coming from a variety of socio-economic backgrounds. Classes were in grade 4: one class was of $n = 19$ children, and the other with $n = 23$ children, with mean age $M = 10.02$ years at the start of the activity, $SD = 0.35$. All children participated on a voluntary basis, and their parents authorised their participation through a written consent form. The activity involved the same two researchers of 2014, and two new teachers. Before starting the GD process, classes were again divided into small heterogeneous groups of 3–5 members.

4.2.2 The GD Process

As in 2014, children were asked to design avatar-based games, starting from a storyline. However, the overall aim of GD in 2015 was a single game per class:

differently than in 2014, in 2015 each group worked on a single level of the single game of their class. The storyline of the game was created by the class as specified below, and not assigned by adults as in 2014.

The GD process was again organised in line with GaCoCo. As in 2014, cooperative learning strategies for small heterogeneous groups were set in the GaCoCo protocol for children. Cooperative learning roles for children were explained and used like in 2014.

As in 2014, the GD process in each school took a total of five design sessions, presented as missions to children, and the first session mainly served to create the identity of groups. Also in 2015, each mission had its own products as goal, generative toolkits and gamified probes, e.g., a progression map, see [24]. Missions followed a recurring pattern also in 2015.

However, given its slightly diverse design aim, the 2015 GD process differently scheduled GD tasks and products in missions. Specifically, training to GD was spread across missions, and not limited to the first mission as in 2014. The first two missions required class work more than group work for designing. Missions in 2015 were concluded with a sixth mission involving other children in assembling the levels of each class in a single game (see [8]). The main differences in missions of 2015 with respect to 2014 were as follows.

First Mission: Group Identity and Class Stimulus Cards. As in 2014, children were trained by their teacher to cooperative learning rules and roles; then each group was assembled and worked on creating their identity, e.g., their badge for the progression map. Differently than in 2014, the entire class was then engaged in a brainstorming, run like in cooperative learning. The brainstorming aimed at eliciting alternative ideas, written on so-called stimulus cards, at the class level, for creating alternative storylines for the class game, concerning a history topic previously discussed at school—eating habits in ancient cultures. The two class teachers, the GD expert and children worked together. Teachers were responsible for guiding and moderating the class in the brainstorming process; the GD expert organised children's ideas on the brainstorming panel, whereas the observer recorded them to produce so-called stimulus cards. *Second Mission: Class Storyline.* The cards of the first mission were used at the start of the conceptualisation stage of the second mission: each group selected cards for creating a group storyline. Each group released the group storyline document. The document was structured as a form with scaffolding questions. This was composed of four cards, corresponding to the main structures of narratives [25]. Afterwards, starting from the cards of the group storylines, the class worked under the direction of the GD expert, as in a focus group in order to create a single storyline document for the class game.

Third, Fourth and Fifth Missions: Group Level. Starting from the class storyline, each group ideated, conceptualised and prototyped a single game level, working like in the second, third and fourth missions of 2014. See Fig. 1.

5 Results of the 2014 of 2015 Studies

Data concerning the quality of GD products by groups of children were gathered at specific moments and analysed per group, as explained in details below.

5.1 Data Gathering

An expert review of an interactive product is an inspection method conducted by experts instead of users, usually in the early design. Expert reviews allow researchers to inspect issues for improving on design, e.g., see [26] for a general overview, and [27] for a working example. In 2014 and 2015, two GD experts evaluated the groups' GD products released at the end of each mission at school; one was the GD expert present at school. They used heuristics of [28] for informing and uniformly structuring their evaluation, as well as their GD expertise.

The GD experts tracked all the encountered negative issues, in brief, *issues*, reporting them in a structured format, mission per mission. The evaluation results were provided as formative feedback to the groups of participating children in the follow-up mission, in written format.

After both studies at school, issues in GD products were categorised inductively with a thematic analysis. As suggested in Chap. 5 of [26], gathering issues in categories is useful when certain areas of products are "causing the most issues"; categories should be few, "typically three to eight". The thematic analysis for discovering categories was run inductively and incrementally as follows, with peer reviews. Firstly, preliminary themes were created by the two GD experts. Then the emerged themes were independently assessed by two game developers. Finally, themes were jointly revised and refined into categories by maximising agreement so as to ensure that they could be applied consistently across GD products by groups of children [29]. Disagreements were resolved through discussions. The resulting *categories of issues* are as follows.

1. **Elements.** Elements are conceptualised in GD documents, such as secondary characters and objects, but not used in prototypes. Elements without specific functionalities, or inconsistent with other game elements, are also present.
2. **Goals.** The goals set in the high-level concept documents or in game levels are unclear, or inconsistently aligned in the final GD product.
3. **Storyline.** The interplay between the gameplay and the storyline is not maintained, e.g., no storyline elements are used in the gameplay.
4. **Player.** It is unclear what the player's role is and how the player interacts with the game, e.g., if the player is the avatar or another character.
5. **Incompleteness.** Gameplay or mechanics information is missing, which was requested explicitly, e.g., in GD documents. Specifically, children do not specify how to tackle challenges for winning or losing, or how to pass between levels.

In 2014, all the above categories of issues were applicable to the products of all missions from the second onward, except for *incompleteness*, which was only applicable from the third mission onward.

In 2015, categories of issues were applicable to products in missions as follows: *elements* and *storyline*, from the third mission onward; *goal*, only in the third mission; *incompleteness* from the fourth mission onward.

5.2 Data Analyses

The two GD experts assessed the products by groups of children in 2014 and 2015 against the above categories of issues, whenever applicable in a mission.

Specifically, using categories, "quality of product" of a group in a mission was defined and operationalised as follows. If a category of issues was applicable to all the products of a mission, then: if a product presented an issue in that category then the product received a negative *score* of 0; else the product received a positive score of 1. Next, the *quality of a (GD) product* in a mission was computed as a proportion: it is the sum of scores across categories, divided by the total number of categories applicable in the mission.

The division by the number of categories of issues, applicable in a mission, is a normalisation that enables to compare the quality of products across missions in a uniform manner, on a scale from 0 (worst) to 1 (best).

Using STATA 12.1 for Windows, descriptive statistics and intercorrelations for the quality of products were calculated as follows, per study.

The 2014 study. Table 1 reports the quality of product per group and per mission, mean (*M*) and standard deviation (*SD*) across groups in 2014, which indicate an evolution in quality of products over time. A non-parametric Friedman's test of differences among repeated measures was then conducted on the quality of products, and differences were found significant over time: $\chi^2(3) = 15.038$, $p = 0.002$.

The 2015 study. Table 2 reports the quality of products per group and per mission, mean (*M*) and standard deviation (*SD*) across groups in 2015, which indicate an evolution in quality of products over time. A non-parametric Friedman test of differences among repeated measures was also conducted on the quality of products, and again differences were found significant over time: $\chi^2(2) = 12.929$, $p = 0.002$.

Therefore, according to the conducted analyses, the effect of time on the considered quality of products was significant in both the 2014 and 2015 studies.

Table 1 Quality of product in 2014 for each group product and mission, from the second onward; means (*M*) and standard deviations (*SD*) across group products

Groups	Mission 2	Mission 3	Mission 4	Mission 5
Group 1	0.5	0.8	0.4	1
Group 2	0.5	1	1	1
Group 3	0.25	0.4	0.8	0.4
Group 4	1	0.6	1	1
Group 5	0	0.4	0.2	0.8
Group 6	0	0.2	0.2	0.6
Group 7	0	0.6	1	0.8
Group 8	0	0.6	0.6	0.8
Group 9	0	0.2	0.2	0.8
M	0.25	0.53	0.6	0.8
SD	0.35	0.26	0.36	0.2

Table 2 Quality of product in 2015 for each group and mission, from the third onward; mean (*M*) and standard deviation (*SD*) across groups

Groups	Mission 3	Mission 4	Mission 5
Group 1	0.5	0.25	1
Group 2	1	1	1
Group 3	0	0	0.75
Group 4	1	1	1
Group 5	0	0	0.5
Group 6	0.75	0.75	1
Group 7	0.75	1	1
Group 8	0.25	0.75	1
Group 9	0	0.75	1
Group 10	0	0.75	1
M	0.42	0.62	0.92
SD	0.43	0.39	0.17

6 Interpretation of Results and Conclusions

This paper reported two PGD studies with primary school children, one in 2014 and one in 2015, both fragmented over different weeks of work and conducted with the GaCoCo approach. The paper operationalised and assessed the quality of products by groups of children released at the end of missions (design sessions), and their evolution over time, in both the 2014 study and the 2015 study.

According to the conducted data analyses, in both years, the considered quality of products tended to significantly increase over time. The decrease may be due to the continuous GD expert's and peers' feedback given to children. Therefore the formative evaluation of children's products, mission per mission, seems promising for improving their quality, and should be maintained in future PGD experiences at school.

However, in the last mission, GD products still presented issues, e.g., they were still incomplete or had unclear functionalities of GD elements, as it is the case of powers attributed to game characters upon overcoming obstacles. Therefore children's products were in general clear but still in need of design revisions before being used as specifications for their development.

A subset of categories of issues were recurring across years 2014 and 2015. Such a situation may be due to the cognitive skills of 8–10 year olds. On the other hand, the remaining issues in children's products may well be due to the choice of generative design toolkits in both years. For instance, in both years, groups released GD paper-based documents and prototypes, which, alone, were not sufficient in for conveying interaction information. In future GD processes with children, their GD documents may be completed by GD experts, so as to fix remaining categories of issues concerning unclear functionalities and incompleteness of gameplay and mechanics elements. The GD expert, in classroom with children, seems a promising candidate for completing GD documents before passing them on to developers, in an act of collaboration across generations of participants.

Finally, we acknowledge that the work reported in this paper has its own limitations. Firstly, only two GD experts were involved in the assessment of the quality of products by groups of children, which may have created biases in their assessment. Secondly, this work was limited by the lack of adequate evaluation heuristics or guidelines for assessing early GD products, which may have affected the generality of our results. For instance, having heuristics would have allowed us to count issues for a category and a product, instead of indicating the presence of an issue for a category and a product as done in this paper.

However, this paper indicates the creation of guidelines or heuristics for assessing early GD products as a promising research direction [30]. Moreover it also purports the need of evaluation heuristics or guidelines specific for children's GD products. The categories of issues presented in this paper may be used as starting point for their creation.

References

1. Nesset, V., & Large, A. (2004). Children in the information technology design process: A review of theories and their applications. *Library & Information Science Research*, 26(2), 140–161. doi:10.1016/j.lisr.2003.12.002
2. Löwgren, J., & Stolterman, E. (2005). *Thoughtful interaction design*. Cambridge: The MIT Press.
3. Brederode, B., Markopoulos, P., Gielen, M., Vermeeren, A., & De Ridder, H. (2005). Powerball: The design of a novel mixed-reality game for children with mixed abilities. In: *Proceedings of IDC 2005*.
4. Mazzone, E. (2012). Designing with children: Reflections on effective involvement of children in the interaction design process. Ph.D thesis, University of Central Lancashire, Preston.
5. Sanders, E., & Westerlund, B. (2011). Experiencing, exploring and experimenting in and with co-design spaces. In: *Proceedings of the Nordic Design Research Conference*.

6. Frauenberger, C., Good, J., Fitzpatrick, G., & Iversen, O. S. (2015). In pursuit of rigour and accountability in participatory design. *International Journal of Human-Computer Studies 74* (0), 93–106. http://www.sciencedirect.com/science/article/pii/S1071581914001232.

7. Dodero, G., Gennari, R., Melonio, A., & Torello, S. (2014). Towards tangible gamified co-design at school: Two studies in primary schools. In: *Proceedings of the First ACM SIGCHI Annual Symposium on Computer-human Interaction in Play* (pp. 77–86). New York: CHI PLAY '14, ACM. http://doi.acm.org/10.1145/2658537.2658688.

8. Melonio, A. (2016). Participatory game design and children. Ph.D. thesis, Free University of Bozen-Bolzano, Bolzano.

9. Adams, E. (2013). *Fundamentals of game design* (3rd ed.). Pearson: Allyn and Bacon.

10. Vanden Abeele, V.A., & Van Rompaey, V. (2006). Introducing human-centered research to game design: Designing game concepts for and with senior citizens. In: *Extended Abstracts on Human Factors in Computing Systems* (pp. 1469–1474). New York: CHI EA '06, ACM. http://doi.acm.org/10.1145/1125451.1125721.

11. Alrifai, M., Gennari, R., & Vittorini, P. (2012). *Adapting with evidence: The adaptive model and the stimulation plan of TERENCE* (pp. 75–82). Berlin: Springer. http://dx.doi.org/10.1007/978-3-642-28801-2_9.

12. Di Mascio, T., Gennari, R., Melonio, A., & Tarantino, L. (2014). Engaging "New Users" into design activities: The TERENCE experience with children (pp. 241–250). Cham: Springer International Publishing. http://dx.doi.org/10.1007/978-3-319-07040-7_23.

13. Druin, A. (1999). Cooperative inquiry: Developing new technologies for children with children. In: *Proceedings of the SIGCHI Conference on Human Factors in Computing Systems* (pp. 592–599). New York: CHI '99, ACM. http://doi.acm.org/10.1145/302979.303166.

14. Fails, J. A., Guha, M. L., & Druin, A. (2013). *Methods and Techniques for involving children in the design of new technology for children*. Hanover, MA, USA: Now Publishers Inc.

15. Molin-Juustila, T., Kinnula, M., Iivari, N., Kuure, L., & Halkola, E. (2015). Multiple voices in ICT design with children—a nexus analytical enquiry. *Behaviour & Information Technology, 34*(11), 1079–1091. doi:10.1080/0144929X.2014.1003327.

16. Vaajakallio, K., Lee, J., & Mattelmäki, T. (2009). It has to be a group work!: Co-design with children. In: *Proceedings of Interaction Design and Children* (pp. 246–249). IDC'09, ACM.

17. Sanders, L., & Stappers, P. (2014). Designing to co-designing to collective dreaming: Three slices in time. *Interactions, 21*(6), 24–33.

18. Moser, C., Tscheligi, M., Zaman, B., Abeele, V.V., Geurts, L., Vandewaetere, M., et al. (2014). Editorial: Learning from failures in game design for children. *International Journal of Child-Computer Interaction 2*(2), 73–75. http://www.sciencedirect.com/science/article/pii/S2212868914000312, special Issue: Learning from Failures in Game Design for Children.

19. Moser, C. (2013). Child-centered Game Development (CCGD): Developing games with children at school. *Personal and Ubiquitous Computing, 17*, 1647–1661.

20. Bonsignore, E., Hansen, D., Pellicone, A., Ahn, J., Kraus, K., & Shumway, S., et al. (2016). Traversing transmedia together: Co-designing an educational alternate reality game for teens, with teens. In: *The 15th International Conference on Interaction Design and Children*.

21. Dodero, G., Gennari, R., Melonio, A., & Torello, S. (2014). Gamified co-design with cooperative learning. In: *CHI '14 extended abstracts on human factors in computing systems* (pp. 707–718). New York: CHI EA '14, ACM. http://doi.acm.org/10.1145/2559206.2578870.

22. Iivari, N., & Kinnula, M. (2016). 'It Has to Be Useful for the Pupils, of Course'—Teachers as Intermediaries in design sessions with children. In: *Proceedings of the Scandinavian Conference in Information Systems (SCIS)*.

23. Dodero, G., Gennari, R., Melonio, A., & Torello, S. (2015). "There is No Rose Without A Thorn": An assessment of a game design expereience for children. In: *11th Edition of CHItaly, the biannual Conference of the Italian SIGCHI Chapter*.

24. Gennari, R., Melonio, A., & Torello, S. (2016). Gamified probes for cooperative learning: A case study. multimedia tools and applications (pp. 1–25). http://dx.doi.org/10.1007/s11042-016-3543-7.

25. Stein, N. L., & Glenn, C. G. (1979). An analysis of story comprehension in elementary school children. In R. Freedle (Ed.), *Discourse processing: Multidisciplinary perspectives*. Norwood, NJ: Ablex.
26. Albert, W., & Tullis, T. (2013). *Measuring the user experience*. Burlington: Morgan Kaufmann.
27. De la Prieta, F., Di Mascio, T., Gennari, R., Marenzi, I., & Vittorini, P. (2014). User centred and evidence based design: An experience report. *International Journal of Technology Enhanced Learning, 6*(3), 212–236.
28. Desurvire, H., Caplan, M., & Toth, J. (2004). Using heuristics to evaluate the playability of games. In: *CHI '04 extended abstracts on human factors in computing systems* (pp. 1509–1512). New York: ACM.
29. Creswell, J. W. (2013). *Research design: Qualitative, quantitative and mixed methods approaches*. Thousand Oaks: SAGE Publications.
30. Dodero, G., & Melonio, A. (2016). *Guidelines for participatory design of digital games in primary school* (pp. 41–49). Cham: Springer International Publishing. http://dx.doi.org/10.1007/978-3-319-40165-2_5.

Part II
Organizational Innovation and Challenges

IT Managers' Relations and Value Creation: Complementary Insights from Four Theoretical Standpoints

Francesca Ricciardi, Alessandro Zardini and Sabrina Bonomi

Abstract Scholars investigating the importance of effective IT managers' relations tend to rely on two mainstream theoretical approaches: the resource-based view (RBV) and sister theories, on the one hand; and the business-IT alignment view, on the other hand. This study proposes that these two theories, although very effective in explaining several aspects of the importance of IT managers' relationships, are not sufficient, and could be usefully complemented by at least two further important theories: Lawrence and Lorsch's view of organisational differentiation and integration, and the cyclical model of organisational learning proposed by Zollo and Winter. Therefore, this study presents the contribution of these four theoretical approaches (RBV, business-IT alignment, organisational integration, and cyclical organisational learning) to explaining the importance of IT managers' relationships. For each theory, two propositions are deduced. The eight resulting propositions are briefly compared, in order to highlight the importance of theoretical cross-fertilisation and integration for a better scientific understanding of IT management value.

Keywords CIO · Relational capital · Organisational role of IT managers · Strategic value of IT · Innovation

F. Ricciardi (✉) · A. Zardini
University of Verona, Verona VR, Italy
e-mail: francesca.ricciardi@univr.t

A. Zardini
e-mail: alessandro.zardini@univr.t

S. Bonomi
eCampus University, Novedrate, Italy
e-mail: sabrina.bonomi@uniecampus.it

© Springer International Publishing AG 2018   97
C. Rossignoli et al. (eds.), *Digital Technology and Organizational Change*,
Lecture Notes in Information Systems and Organisation 23,
https://doi.org/10.1007/978-3-319-62051-0_9

1 Introduction

In the emerging e-business era, the processes enabled by Information Technologies (IT) tend to span a firm's whole value chain, from suppliers to client companies, dealers and final consumers. Selecting, designing, fine-tuning and managing these processes is often possible only through long-term intra- and inter-organisational cooperative interactions, where the active involvement of the IT managers is likely to be essential for success [1].

On the other hand, the growing phenomena of IT outsourcing and cloud computing also challenges the traditional role of IT management. IT managers must prove themselves capable of managing both formal (e.g., service level agreements) and informal (e.g., trust, interdependency and cooperation) mechanisms for interaction management, both within and across the firm's boundaries [2].

In this highly dynamic scenario, the very concept of IT governance and management is changing [3, 4]. These changes are occurring both within organisations and throughout their business networks. Consequently, several studies focus on the evolving role of IT management in enhancing the firm's capabilities to create strategic value even in turbulent business scenarios [5]. These studies often concentrate on the highest-ranking IT manager, the Chief Information Officer (CIO) [6, 7].

To date, researchers have often focused on the CIO's personal skills, including communication skills and business-oriented leadership [8, 9]. Researchers have also dedicated a great deal of attention to key organisational factors as possible antecedents of the CIO's leadership and influence, such as the CIO's role in the firm's hierarchical structure [10]. In fact, there is growing consensus that the CIO's capabilities and the organisation's attitudes towards IT do not develop in isolation. These two factors co-evolve and influence each other. It can be argued that the IT managers' strategic contribution consistently stems from their interactions with the organisational ecosystem [4]. If these interactions result in effective relationships over time, then the CIO/IT manager is more likely to boost the firm's capability and performance through the contribution of IT [11]. This view is agreed upon by several authoritative scholars. For example, Feeny and Willcocks [12] claim that the relationship-building ability of IT professionals has become a core capability of organisations. Chatterjee et al. [13] assert that IT management capabilities rely largely upon complex social relationships between IT functioning and the firm's internal and external stakeholders. According to Bassellier and Benbasat [14], the profile of the IT professional is changing from one in which technical skills are paramount to one in which the ability to form business relationships is at least equally important. There is strong consensus that the relational network of IT managers deserves greater attention: the "next generation of IT value studies should focus on the co-creation of value through IT rather than on IT value alone. [...] IT value is increasingly being created and realised through actions of multiple parties" [14, p. 28].

However, even if scholars tend to agree on the importance of IT managers' relational networks, many aspects of these relations are surprisingly under-investigated. Some potentially crucial IT managers' relationships, although mentioned as relevant in some conceptual studies, need further empirical investigations. On the other hand, the possible theoretical explanations of the impact of IT managers' relations have been only partially explored so far [15].

Scholars focusing on the importance of effective IT managers' relations tend to rely on two mainstream theoretical approaches: the resource-based view (RBV) and sister theories, on the one hand [16]; and the business-IT alignment view, on the other hand [17]. This study proposes that these two theories, although very effective in explaining several aspects of the importance of IT managers' relationships, are not enough, and could be usefully complemented by at least two further important theories: Lawrence and Lorsch's view of organisational differentiation and integration [18], and the cyclical model of organisational learning proposed by Zollo and Winter [11, 19].

Therefore, this study will present the possible contribution of these four theoretical approaches (RBV, business-IT alignment, organisational integration, and cyclical organisational learning) to explaining the importance of IT managers' relationships. For each theory, two propositions will be deduced. In the Conclusions section, the eight propositions deduced from the four theories will be briefly discussed and compared, in order to highlight the importance of theoretical cross-fertilisation for a better scientific understanding of IT management value.

2 IT Managers' Relations in the RBV and Sister Theories

Mata et al. [16] make the following point regarding the RBV: "It is the ability of IT managers to work with each other, with managers in other functional areas in a firm, and with managers in other firms that is most likely to separate those firms that are able to gain sustained competitive advantages from their IT and those that are only able to gain competitive parity from their IT. These skills, and the relationships upon which they are built, have been called managerial IT skills in this paper. Future research will need to explore, in much more detail, the exact nature of these managerial IT skills, how they develop and evolve in a firm, and how they can be used to leverage a firm's technical IT skills to create sustained competitive advantage" (p. 500).

After the seminal paper by Mata et al. [16], the RBV is by far the most frequently adopted theory to explain the strategic importance of IT managers' relationships for IT value [20]. According to the RBV, the key strategic goal of firms is sustained competitive advantage, which can be achieved only by leveraging valuable, rare, imperfectly imitable and non-substitutable (VRIN) resources [21]. Firms, then, must own or control VRIN resources to outperform competitors. The RBV has been utilised extensively to study both the direct and the indirect influence of IT resources on firm performance [22].

There is growing consensus that the indirect influence of IT on performance is more interesting than the direct one, because it is more soundly supported by empirical data, and because IT resources, per se, are often non-VRIN resources [11]. In most cases, scholars concentrate on organisational capabilities as the variable mediating the relationship between resources and firm performance [23, 24]. A capability is the capacity to integrate tangible and intangible resources in order to perform a task or activity [25]. Because the total effect of the resources is more difficult for competitors to copy, a capability can also be seen as a higher-level resource; therefore, the joint value of the complementary resources enabling a capability is higher than the total value of the same resources taken individually.

Nonetheless, the process through which IT resources generate key organisational capabilities is rather indecipherable if investigated only through classical RBV concepts [26]. For this reason, scholars often complement the RBV with sister, compatible theories, such as the relational view of the firm [27, 28], the knowledge-based view of the firm and theory of knowledge networks [29].

Studies on the importance of relational networks have primarily been developed at the inter-organisational level due to the relational view of the firm [28]. Scholars soon realised that a network of high-quality, effective relationships is difficult to imitate; such networks generate knowledge and capabilities that are impossible to achieve—even by those who imitate the most successful IT solutions. The relational view of the firm focuses on idiosyncratic linkages as sources of relational rents. Relational rents are superior returns co-generated in a specific, idiosyncratic exchange relationship, returns that could not be generated by an isolated partner. This approach highlights the possible importance of the CIO/IT manager as an actor in inter-organisational relationships, particularly with key suppliers, customers and/or IT outsourcers [15]. Consistent with these contributions, the CIO's inter- and intra-organisational network of collaborative relations creates IT-enabled resources and capabilities that are heterogeneous and imperfectly mobile; these resources and capabilities potentially contribute to competitive advantage [30].

According to the knowledge-based view of the firm and the theory of knowledge networks, (expert) actors' innovation capabilities are dramatically boosted if their collaborative interactions allow access to heterogeneous knowledge stocks [29, 31]. Grigoriou and Rothaermel [32] consistently found that the extent to which a manager's relationships connect different and distant parts of the organisation's network predicts the organisation's innovation performance. This predictor is even stronger than the manager's productivity. Similarly, if the IT managers effectively collaborate with subjects that otherwise would not be linked (such as the organisation's customers and IT people), they can bridge knowledge silos and act as 'information brokers'. Field studies confirm that information brokers who recombine knowledge coming from distant clusters are more likely to be capable of creative problem-solving [33], leading to better ideas [34] and better adaptation to changes [35]. More importantly, such 'relational stars' [32] cause the people around them to be more effective at knowledge recombination, thus spreading the positive effects of their networking activities [29, 36]. In a similar vein, through extensive coordination and communication, IT managers share a vision for the role of IT within the business; meanwhile, business executives share the risk and accept responsibility for IT projects. As a consequence, it is more likely that the CIOs will be able to anticipate business needs and devise appropriate IT-enabled solutions [12, 30].

Based on this theoretical framework, we can deduce the following Propositions:

Proposition 1 *Idiosyncratic, purposeful business relations of IT managers will positively influence the firm's competitive advantage.*

Proposition 2 *IT managers with a wide range of effective social relationships, bridging diverse and separated knowledge silos, will positively influence innovation capabilities and competitive advantage.*

3   IT Managers' Relations and the Business-IT Alignment Literature

Since the 1990s, there has been wide consensus among both Information Systems (IS) scholars and practitioners that the most important strategic challenge for IT managers is the alignment between business and IT [27, 37, 38]. Alignment is commonly defined as 'the extent to which the IS strategy supports, and is supported by, the business strategy' [39, p. 204].

Despite its broad use, this definition has been criticised as being difficult to apply. If taken literally, it implies that one should be capable of thoroughly assessing both business strategy and IS strategy [40] in a certain organisation at a certain time while simultaneously being able to measure their reciprocal support. However, the real key strategies can be idiosyncratic, emergent, blurred, tacit, provisional or even totally latent at the moment the researcher seeks to measure them [39]. Indeed, business and IT continuously co-evolve [41]; therefore, their alignment is difficult to understand if captured as a static 'balance' between two different phenomena. Moreover, supposing that the researcher succeeds in finding and measuring the 'perfect alignment' within an organisation, the situation assessed at a certain time may hide contradictions and fragilities bound to emerge later. Consequently, scholars are becoming more interested in studying the alignment between business and IT as an ongoing process. In other words, management studies now identify the factors that enhance the organisation's capability to align over time, which is perceived as more interesting and feasible than seeking to depict the actual exact alignment status of a certain organisation at a certain time [41].

Thus, similar to what has been observed in studies on the CIO role, a more dynamic approach is also emerging in business-IT alignment studies. For example, Luftman [37] proposes a business-IT alignment maturity model, which is based on the idea that alignment results from a set of activities that "management performs to achieve cohesive goals across the IT (Information Technology) and other functional organisations (e.g., finance, marketing, H/R, manufacturing)... Alignment *evolves into a relationship* where the function of IT and other business functions adapt their strategies together" (p. 2; italics ours). Even more explicitly, Huang and Hu [42] mention integrated planning, effective communication, active relationship management and an institutionalised culture of alignment as the four key elements of IT-business alignment. According to Tallon [43, 44], it is very important that the CIO builds a shared perception among top executives regarding the extent and locus of IT impacts. Thus, studies on business-IT alignment display a growing interest in the relational dimension of IT management.

On the other hand, studies on business-IT alignment rarely link IT to firm performance. In this stream of research, scholars usually focus on the factors that can be viewed as antecedents of alignment (e.g. cognitive consonance) and on the direct consequences (e.g. process efficiency) of the top-down processes of educated strategic planning enabled by alignment [45]. Therefore, based on the business-IT alignment literature, the following two Propositions can be deduced:

Proposition 3 *Organisational practices and designs enabling and facilitating the alignment between IT managers and the TMT will positively influence the contribution of the firm's IT to business effectiveness.*

Proposition 4 *Organisational practices and designs enabling and facilitating the alignment between IT managers and the operations departments will positively influence the contribution of the firm's IT to process efficiency.*

4 IT Managers' Relations and the Theory of Organisational Integration

Lawrence and Lorsch's seminal study [18] on organisational differentiation and integration states that, in dynamic competitive environments, different parts of the organisation become increasingly specialised, and each part tends to diverge from the others as for its people's shared goals, beliefs and attitudes. Therefore, organisations rapidly evolve into systems where people in different units think and act differently. However, excessive differentiation, if not balanced by effective integration, can cause inefficiencies and conflict. Differentiation and specialisation are successful strategies in dynamic environments only if the differing specialised parts of the organisation remain capable of understanding each other in order to collaborate for common goals.

Coordination and collaboration issues emerge wherever operational interdependencies are present, including both intra- and inter-organisational relationships between key sub-systems [46]. Active, creative cooperation becomes even more important when innovation needs emerge [47–49]. For these reasons, the organisation should develop formal and informal organisational mechanisms that enable and encourage integration [50], and managers should strive continuously and creatively for integration [51]. Managers that drive projects and activities involving the whole organisation are the best candidates for strong integration roles [18]. IT managers, including the CIO, are certainly among them, since IT itself plays a pivotal role in business process integration [50, 52–55]. The IT managers' contribution to firm performance and competitive advantage largely depends on these managers' ability to understand and support the evolving business needs and processes [56, 57]. This ability may be developed only if the IT management is at the centre of an effective and well-structured network of intra- and inter-organisational relationships [58]. In fact, in today's networked economy, increasingly based on extensive IT outsourcing and e-business, the possible strategic role of IT goes far beyond the boundaries of a single firm [59]. Thus, along with traditional interactions with the so-called internal customer, IT management is also more and more involved in inter-organisational interactions, especially with the firm's customers, IT providers and outsourcers and non-IT suppliers [60]. Therefore, IT managers should be able to, and put in the condition to, actively and collaboratively interact with different parts of the organisation's ecosystem, not only to avoid, minimise or solve conflicts, misunderstandings and inefficiencies, but also to contribute to strategic growth through product, process and market innovation [4].

Consistently with this literature stream, these Propositions can be developed:

Proposition 5 *Active involvement of IT managers in cross-functional teams and task forces will positively influence the development of effective IT-supported coordination and problem solving.*

Proposition 6 *A large range of effective intra-and inter-organisational relationships of IT managers will positively influence the development of IT as an effective mechanism of organisational integration.*

5 IT Managers' Relations and the Theory of Cyclical, Adaptive Organisational Learning

In the evolutionary view, existing routines, which embed previously successful knowledge, both constrain and enable further learning. The pre-existing knowledge base includes a complex body of routines. This complex body of routines is hard-wired in the organisation through culture, reward/sanction systems, social bonds, and/or technological artefacts. These routines shape interactions and result in consequences, which, in turn, facilitate or hinder further learning [61]. Therefore, organisations need to cyclically re-activate the capability to question existing routines and to generate new ones. Agile organisations are capable of re-activating a learning process at a time and in a way that generates the best options to address emerging threats and opportunities. These organisations are the most likely to survive and thrive [62].

The current management literature is growingly highlighting the importance of finding an equilibrium between exploration and exploitation, learning and unlearning processes in organisations. Many scholars agree that cyclical, spiraling, or zigzagging dynamism rather than static balance is the best way to address such paradoxical tensions [63, 64]. Zollo and Winter [19] propose a cyclical model of learning that seems ideal to illustrate this topic. Their model identifies three types of learning mechanisms that explain the generation and evolution of routines: experience accumulation, knowledge articulation, and knowledge codification [11].

At the level of *experience accumulation*, procedural memory stores organisational routines and allows automatic or quasi-automatic responses building on the knowledge resources that the organisational eco-system selected in the past. The knowledge is mostly either tacit or stored as highly inertial routines (e.g., as software code). Low levels of conscious volition are enough to activate these knowledge resources. The second learning level, *knowledge articulation*, occurs at a different level than experience accumulation. Although the accumulation of routines from experience tends to result in organisational inertia, Zollo and Winter [19] emphasise that, paradoxically, existing routines also play an essential role in activating and enabling the creative processes through which the organisational eco-system becomes capable to change the routines themselves. For these processes to be significant, social interaction, discussion, and negotiation must take place together, so that people combine efforts to make tacit knowledge explicit and questionable. The third learning level is *knowledge codification*. During codification, people clarify their understanding of causal linkages by translating their understanding in novel explicit and formalised routines. They then test the effectiveness of the new routines against real-world situations.. The cycle closes with either the selection or the rejection of each routine. Successful routines will soon become habits and submerge in the deeper layers of experience accumulation, from which they will possibly influence further knowledge cycles [11].

From the IT management standpoint, Zollo and Winter's model [19] views the existing IT infrastructure as a key component of knowledge accumulation. In fact, the IT infrastructure provides a firm with a system of automatic routines, resulting from previous experiences and choices, and shapes most organisational processes. On the other hand, the success of the articulation phase requires intense and diverse social interaction and collaboration for capability building [5]. Therefore, wide-ranging, trustful, and purposeful relationships between the IT department and the business environment are important during the articulation phase, to allow a seamless transition to the next level, the codification phase. Based on this view of organisational learning, the following Propositions can be developed:

Proposition 7 *Effective IT managers' relations will enable smoother and more effective cyclical transitions from a phase of organisational learning (accumulation, articulation, codification) to the following.*

Proposition 8 *IT managers' active involvement during the cyclical knowledge articulation phases will positively influence adaptive organisational learning and agility.*

6 Conclusions

Our literature survey shows that the two mainstream theoretical views considered in this study (RBV and business-IT alignment) may be usefully complemented by two further theoretical approaches (organisational integration and cyclical organisational learning) that have been quite overlooked by IT management scholars so far (Table 1).

The joint explanatory power of these four theories is quite interesting and we hope that further studies will leverage this possible theoretical cross-fertilisation to shed light on the relevance of effective IT managers' relationships. These results suggest that IT managers' relations influence organisational life and performance in several intertwining ways. Therefore, depending on the specific business contexts, phase, and expected outcomes, different organisational solutions and IT managers' capabilities should be developed and leveraged. We hope that this study encourages theoretical cross-fertilisation and integration, in order to achieve a wider understanding of the role of IT management in organisations.

Table 1 Synthesis of the Propositions deduced from the literature survey

Code (theory)	Proposition
1 (RBV)	Idiosyncratic, purposeful business relations of IT managers will positively influence the firm's competitive advantage
2 (RBV)	IT managers with a wide range of effective social relationships, bridging diverse and separated knowledge silos, will positively influence innovation capabilities and competitive advantage
3 (align.)	Organisational practices and designs enabling and facilitating the alignment between IT managers and the TMT will positively influence the contribution of the firm's IT to business effectiveness
4 (align.)	Organisational practices and designs enabling and facilitating the alignment between IT managers and the operations departments will positively influence the contribution of the firm's IT to process efficiency
5 (integr.)	Active involvement of IT managers in cross-functional teams and task forces will positively influence the development of effective IT-supported coordination and problem solving
6 (integr.)	A large range of effective intra-and inter-organisational relationships of IT managers will positively influence the development of IT as an effective mechanisms of organisational integration
7 (learn.)	Effective IT managers' relations will enable smoother and more effective cyclical transitions from a phase of organis. learning (accumulation, articulation, codification) to the following
8 (learn.)	IT managers' active involvement during the cyclical knowledge articulation phases will positively influence adaptive organisational learning and agility

References

1. Liang, H., Saraf, N., Hu, Q., & Xue, Y. (2007). Assimilation of enterprise systems: The effect of institutional pressures and the mediating role of top management. *MIS Quarterly Management Information Systems, 31,* 59–87.
2. Lacity, M. C., Khan, S. A., & Willcocks, L. P. (2009). A review of the IT outsourcing literature: Insights for practice. *The Journal of Strategic Information Systems, 18*(3), 130–146.
3. Piccoli, G., & Ives, B. (2005). IT-dependent strategic initiatives and sustained competitive advantage: A review and synthesis of the literature. *MIS Quarterly, 29,* 747–776.
4. Chen, D. Q., Preston, D. S., & Xia, W. (2010). Antecedents and effects of CIO supply-side and demand-side leadership: A staged maturity model. *Journal of Management Information Systems, 27,* 231–272.
5. Sambamurthy, V., Bharadwaj, A., & Grover, V. (2003). Shaping agility through digital options: reconceptualizing the role of information technology in contemporary firms. *MIS Quarterly, 27,* 237–263.
6. Gupta, Y. P. (1991). The chief executive officer and the chief information officer: the strategic partnership. *Journal of Information Technology, 6,* 128–139.
7. Hunter, G. (2010). The Chief Information Officer: A Review of the Role. *Journal of Information Technology, and Organizations, 5,* 125–143.
8. Willcocks, L., Feeny, D., & Olson, N. (2006). Implementing core IS capabilities: Feeny-Willcocks IT governance and management framework revisited. *European Management Journal, 24,* 28–37.
9. Applegate, L. M., & Elam, J. J. (1992). New information system leaders: A changing role in a changing world. *MIS Quarterly, 16,* 469–490.
10. Banker, R. D., Hu, N., Pavlou, P. A., & Luftman, J. (2011). CIO reporting structure, strategic positioning, and firm performance. *MIS Quarterly, 35*(2), 487–504.
11. Zardini, A., Rossignoli, C., & Ricciardi, F. (2016). A bottom-up path for IT management success: From infrastructure quality to competitive excellence. *Journal of Business Research, 69,* 1747–1752.
12. Feeny, D. F., & Willcocks, L. P. (1998). Core IS capabilities for exploiting information technology. *Sloan Management Review, 39,* 9–21.
13. Chatterjee, D., Richardson, V. J., & Zmud, R. W. (2001). Examining the shareholder wealth effects of announcement of newly created CIO positions. *MIS Quarterly, 25,* 43–70.
14. Bassellier, G., & Benbasat, I. (2004). Business competence of information technology professionals: Conceptual development and influence on IT-business partnerships. *MIS Quarterly, 28,* 673–694.
15. Zardini, A., Ricciardi, F., & Rossignoli, C. (2015). The relational capital of the IT department: Measuring a key resource for strategic value creation. *Journal of Intellectual Capital, 16,* 835–859.
16. Mata, F. J., Fuerst, W. L., & Barney, J. B. (1995). Information technology and sustained competitive advantage: A resource-based analysis. *MIS Quarterly, 19,* 487–505.
17. Ullah, A., & Lai, R. (2013). A systematic review of business and information technology alignment. *ACM Transactions on Management Information Systems (TMIS), 4*(1), 4.
18. Lawrence, P. R., & Lorsch, J. W. (1967). Differentiation and Integration in Complex Organizations. *Administrative Science Quarterly, 12,* 1–47.
19. Zollo, M., & Winter, S. G. (2002). Deliberate learning and the evolution of dynamic capabilities. *Organization Science, 13,* 339–351.
20. Wade, M., & Hulland, J. (2004). Review: The resource-based view and information systems research: review, extension, and suggestions for future research 1. *MIS Quarterly, 28,* 107–142.
21. Barney, J. (1991). Firm resources and sustained competitive advantage. *Journal of Management, 17*(1), 99–120.

22. Santhanam, R., & Artono, E. (2003). Issues in linking information technology capability to firm performance. *MIS Quarterly, 27*, 125–153.
23. Bharadwaj, A. (2000). A resource-based perspective on information technology capability and firm performance: An empirical investigation. *MIS Quarterly, 24*, 169–196.
24. Bhatt, G. D., & Grover, V. (2005). Types of information technology and their role in competitive advantage: An empirical study. *Journal of Management Information Systems, 22*, 253–277.
25. Makadok, R. (2001). Toward a synthesis of the resource-based and dynamic-capability views of rent creation. *Strategic Management Journal, 22*, 387–401.
26. Liang, T.-P., You, J.-J., & Liu, C.-C. (2010). A resource-based perspective on information technology and firm performance: A meta analysis. *Industrial Management & Data Systems, 110*, 1138–1158.
27. Wagner, H. T., Beimborn, D., & Weitzel, T. (2014). How social capital among information technology and business units drives operational alignment and IT business value. *Journal of Management Information Systems, 31*, 241–272.
28. Dyer, J. H., & Singh, H. (1998). The relational view: Cooperative strategy and sources of interorganizational competitive advantage. *Academy of Management Review, 23*, 660–679.
29. Reagans, R., & McEvily, B. (2003). Network structure and knowledge transfer: the effects of cohesion and range. *Administrative Science Quarterly, 48*, 240–267.
30. Ross, J. W., Beath, C. M., & Goodhue, D. L. (1996). Develop long-term competitiveness through IT assets. *Sloan Management Review, 38*, 31–42.
31. Reagans, R., & Zuckerman, E. W. (2001). Networks, diversity, and productivity: The social capital of corporate R&D teams. *Organization Science, 12*, 502–517.
32. Grigoriou, K., & Rothaermel, F. T. (2014). Structural microfoundations of innovation: The role of relational stars. *Journal of Management, 40*(2), 586–615.
33. Fleming, L., Mingo, S., & Chen, D. (2007). Collaborative brokerage, generative creativity, and creative success. *Administrative Science Quarterly, 52*, 443–475.
34. Burt, R. S. (2004). Structural holes and good ideas. *American Journal of Sociology, 110*, 349–399.
35. Gargiulo, M., & Benassi, M. (2000). Trapped in your own net? Network cohesion, structural holes, and the adaptation of social capital. *Organization Science, 11*, 183–196.
36. Galunic, C., & Rodan, S. (1998). Resource recombinations in the firm: knowledge structures and the potential for Schumpeterian innovation. *Strategic Management Journal, 19*, 1193–1201.
37. Luftman, J. (2000). Assessing business-IT alignment maturity. *Communications of the Association for Information Systems, 4*, 1–51.
38. Roepke, R., Agarwal, R., & Ferratt, T. W. (2000). Aligning the IT human resource with business vision: the leadership initiative at 3M. *MIS Quarterly, 24*, 327–353.
39. Ciborra, C. (2002). *The Labyrinths of Information*. Challenging the Wisdom of Systems: Oxford University Press.
40. Chen, D. Q., Mocker, M., Preston, D., & Teubner, A. (2010). Information systems strategy: Reconceptualization, measurement, and implications. *MIS Quarterly, 34*, 233–259.
41. Benbya, H., & Mckelvey, B. (2006). Using coevolutionary and complexity theories to improve IS alignment: A multi-level approach. *Journal of Information Technology, 21*, 284–298.
42. Huang, C. D., & Hu, Q. (2007). Achieving IT-business strategic alignment via enterprise-wide implementation of balanced scorecards. *Information Systems Management, 24*, 173–184.
43. Tallon, P. P. (2007). A process-oriented perspective on the alignment of information technology and business strategy. *Journal of Management Information Systems, 24*, 227–268.
44. Tallon, P. P. (2011). Value chain linkages and the spillover effects of strategic information technology alignment: A process-level view. *Journal of Management Information Systems, 28*, 9–44.
45. Reich, B. H., & Benbasat, I. (2000). Factors that influence the social dimension of alignment between business and information technology objectives. *MIS Quarterly, 24*, 1–59.

46. Whang, S. (1995). Coordination in operations: a taxonomy. *Journal of Operations Management, 12,* 413–422.
47. Ettlie, J. E. (1992). Organizational integration and process innovation. *Academy of Management Journal, 35,* 795–827.
48. Jansen, J. J. P., Tempelaar, M. P., van den Bosch, F. A. J., & Volberda, H. W. (2009). Structural differentiation and ambidexterity: The mediating role of integration mechanisms. *Organization Science, 20,* 797–811.
49. Millson, M. R. (2013). Exploring the moderating influence of product innovativeness on the organizational integration-new product market success relationship. *European Journal of Innovation Management, 16,* 317–334.
50. Volkoff, O., Strong, D. M., & Elmes, M. B. (2005). Understanding enterprise systems-enabled integration. *European Journal of Information Systems, 14,* 110–120.
51. Barki, H., & Pinsonneault, A. (2005). A model of organizational integration, implementation effort, and performance. *Organization Science, 16,* 165–179.
52. Ranganathan, C., & Brown, C. V. (2006). ERP investments and the market value of firms: Toward an understanding of influential ERP project variables. *Information Systems Research, 17,* 145–161.
53. Berente, N., Vandenbosch, B., & Aubert, B. (2009). Information flows and business process integration. *Business Process Management Journal, 15,* 119–141.
54. Mangan, A., & Kelly, S. (2009). Information systems and the allure of organisational integration: A cautionary tale from the Irish financial services sector. *European Journal of Information Systems, 18,* 66–78.
55. Cheung, C. M., Mocker, M., Schlagwein, D., Sunyaev, A., & Turowski, K. (2015). IOS 2.0: New aspects on inter-organizational integration through enterprise 2.0 technologies. *Electronic Markets, 25*(4), 263–265.
56. Peppard, J. (2007). The conundrum of IT management. *European Journal of Information Systems, 16,* 336–345.
57. Ding, F., Li, D., & George, J. F. (2014). Investigating the effects of IS strategic leadership on organizational benefits from the perspective of CIO strategic roles. *Information & Management, 51,* 865–879.
58. Cravens, D. W., Piercy, N. F., & Shipp, S. H. (1996). New organizational forms for competing in highly dynamic environments: The network paradigm. *British Journal of Management, 7,* 203–218.
59. Chun, M., & Mooney, J. (2009). CIO roles and responsibilities: Twenty-five years of evolution and change. *Information & Management, 46,* 323–334.
60. Kohli, R., & Grover, V. (2008). Business value of IT: An essay on expanding research directions to keep up with the times. *Journal of the Association for Information Systems, 9,* 23–39.
61. Ricciardi, F. (2011). Beyond Darwin: The potential of recent eco-evolutionary research for organizational and information systems studies. In: Carugati, A. and Rossignoli, C. (Eds.), *Emerging Themes in Information Systems and Organization Studies.* pp. 63–77. Springer. ISBN:978-3-7908-2738-5.
62. Li, D. Y., & Liu, J. (2014). Dynamic capabilities, environmental dynamism, and competitive advantage: Evidence from China. *Journal of Business Research, 67,* 2793–2799.
63. Boumgarden, P., Nickerson, J., & Zenger, T. R. (2012). Sailing into the wind: exploring the relationships among ambidexterity, vacillation, and organizational performance. *Strategic Management Journal, 33,* 587–610.
64. Ricciardi, F. (2013). *Innovation processes in business networks. managing inter-organizational relationships for innovational excellence.* Springer. ISBN: 978-3-658-03438-2.

Creative Sparks for Collaborative Innovation

Antonio De Nicola and Maria Luisa Villani

Abstract We present a methodology to support innovation processes in business contexts. The methodology consists of three phases. First, an innovation team composed of stakeholders, domain experts and knowledge engineers collects domain knowledge. This knowledge is used as source for creative sparks, which are representations of preliminary ideas for innovation. In the second phase of the methodology, creative sparks are identified to ignite a collaborative activity by the innovation team, which may lead to identification of new innovative ideas. Thus we provide hints on how to search and select the creative sparks and how to organize brainstorming activities. In the third phase, selected ideas are elaborated and validated in the specific business context. In this paper we focus on the first two phases and present an innovation management system to support them. In particular, we describe the CREAM software system that allows generation of creative sparks from a knowledge base comprising predefined idea patterns, a domain ontology and a set of business rules. Although the proposed methodology is general purpose here we show an application in the business intelligence sector.

Keywords Computational creativity · Collaborative innovation · Knowledge-based system · Business model

1 Introduction

This work proposes a methodology to support generation of innovative ideas by means of a new innovation management system. Such methodology originates from two insights. One is that an idea can be represented by a conceptual model; the second is that sometimes disruptive innovative ideas might have been discarded in

A. De Nicola (✉) · M.L. Villani
ENEA—CR "Casaccia", Via Anguillarese, 301, 00123 Rome, Italy
e-mail: antonio.denicola@enea.it

M.L. Villani
e-mail: marialuisa.villani@enea.it

© Springer International Publishing AG 2018   109
C. Rossignoli et al. (eds.), *Digital Technology and Organizational Change*,
Lecture Notes in Information Systems and Organisation 23,
https://doi.org/10.1007/978-3-319-62051-0_10

the first place as deemed not feasible or even absurd. A paradigmatic example is the case of Muhammad Yunus, the founder of the Grameen Bank, who introduced the microcredit [1], an innovative business model created by offering a traditional value proposition (i.e. money loan) to an unusual customer segment (i.e. poor people from Bangladesh). Here we aim at reproducing such reshuffling of business concepts to propose creative insights, i.e. creative sparks. Then we aim at supporting brainstorming on such insights among smart and open-minded people interested in disruptive innovation.

The methodology is organized in three phases. The first phase involves an innovation team composed of stakeholders, domain experts and knowledge engineers and begins with a set of activities aimed at collecting different types of knowledge to be gathered in a ontology and in a rules repository. Then one or more design patterns are defined to represent idea models and to generate creative sparks. The second phase concerns a collaboration process by the innovation team on a set of activities aimed at selecting creative sparks, discussing on them and, possibly, modifying them to achieve the final innovative ideas to be tested in the third phase in the real world context.

Here we focus on the first two phases of the methodology and we present the architecture of an innovation management system conceived to support them. In particular we present CREAM (CREAtivity Machine), a software component to generate creativity sparks that ignite the above-mentioned collaboration process.

The methodology is general purpose. In this paper we show how it can be applied to support definition of business models in firms operating in the business intelligence sector.

The rest of the paper is organized as follows. Section 2 presents related work concerning the innovation process and the ICT systems used to support it. Section 3 provides an overview of the methodology we propose. Section 4 focuses on innovation knowledge building and enhancement and describes automatic generation of the creative sparks. Section 5 illustrates the collaborative activities to be performed by the participants of the team to define innovative ideas. Section 6 presents the application concerning the business models generation for business intelligence firms. Finally Sect. 7 presents conclusions.

2 Related Work

This paper deals with the innovation process. One of the seminal works concerning this research topic is TRIZ (the Russian acronym for Theory for Inventive Problem Solving) [2]. This book faces the problem of "*inventing methods of inventing*" and defines some rules for brainstorming concerning how to build the "*idea-generating team*", the time limit for expressing ideas, the behavior to be held by participants (e.g., no criticism is allowed), and which ideas should be considered (e.g., also the frivolous ones). Another theoretical method is lateral thinking [3], a method to solve problems with creativity based on not obvious reasoning. According to [3], the vertical thinking approach tries to find the best solution to a problem whereas lateral thinking generates as many alternative solutions as possible. With respect to them we propose to use artificial intelligence techniques (i.e. based on an ontology) to support the innovation process.

Existing works on supporting the innovation processes leveraging on ontologies are [4, 5]. With respect to these, our solution is more flexible as it is not tied to a specific ontology or upper model.

On the other hand, we share the computational creativity approach with [6, 7]. This consists in using technologies to assist humans in thinking novel, disruptive, and unlikely ideas. However with respect to them we propose to use artificial intelligence techniques based on an ontology.

Existing collaboration systems, as BSCW, Slack and Trello, are general purpose and not explicitly conceived to support new ideas and innovations. *Innocentive* [8] is a platform that aims at stimulating new solutions and ideas leveraging on crowdsourcing technologies and a rewarding system. As Innocentive, *ideascale* is an innovation management platform based on crowdsourcing technologies. Finally our work is complementary to these systems as we propose to automatize the preliminary activities of idea generation and, hence, to stimulate the collaboration process with preliminary models of ideas generated by a software system.

3 A Knowledge-Based Methodology to Foster Innovation

According to the Merriam-Webster dictionary, one of the definitions of idea is *a visible representation of a conception or a replica of a pattern*. As such, this work proposes to represent an idea by a conceptual model derived from a previously defined *idea pattern* (i.e. a design pattern). Then it proposes an incremental methodology to generate a successful idea, which involves ICT systems, humans and a real-world experimentation. We distinguish three phases of the innovation process devoted to generation of a successful idea.

First a software application generates a preliminary model of an idea that has not been evaluated yet by humans. We name such model as a *creative spark*.

Then a group of humans taking part in an innovation team evaluates the generated creative sparks within a collaboration process supported by a software application. Hence, the creative sparks not considered as promising are discharged and named *bad ideas*. Please note that, since the evaluation process is subjective, those ideas can also be considered as *missed opportunities*. Furthermore, a bad idea could be considered as innovative in subsequent iterations of the innovation process. Instead, in case the innovation team deems that a creative spark is promising, it will focus on it and, possibly, will elaborate some variations to finally produce an *innovative idea*.

The third phase deals with the effective elaboration of the innovative idea in the real world, to end up either with a *successful idea*, in case the innovative idea is really used, or with a *failure* and, possibly, a *lesson learnt*. Failures and lessons

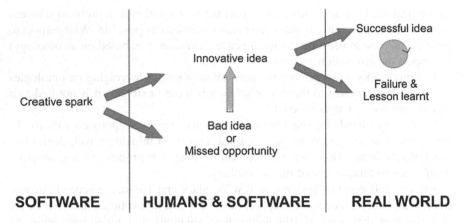

Fig. 1 Lifecycle of an idea: from the creative spark(s) to a successful idea for innovation

learnt could be used to refine the knowledge base but also to improve the definition of innovative ideas in subsequent iterations of the innovation process.

The lifecycle of an idea, from a creative spark to a successful idea as result of the iterative innovation process, and the knowledge-based methodology for innovation are depicted, respectively, in Figs. 1 and 2.

The aim of this work is to illustrate how the first two phases are supported by means of a new software environment we defined, namely the CREAM-based system depicted in Fig. 3. The third phase deals with the collaborative work to be performed by the innovation team based on the ideas produced in the second phase and will be treated in more details in future work.

As already mentioned the innovation team includes both stakeholders and domain experts to provide business knowledge concerning the specific application and knowledge engineers to support elicitation, collection and formalization of that knowledge. Even if we do not prescribe any particular organizational model for the team, we would suggest a "democratic approach", distinguishing two roles: innovation participant and innovation leader. The former contributes to the activities (e.g., knowledge collection, debate, …) whereas the latter has the responsibility of methodology advancement and group coordination.

4   The Approach for Creative Sparks Generation

This Section refers to the first phase of the innovation process, and describes in more details set up and usage of the CREAM-based system for automatic generation of the creative sparks. The environment consists of a suite of semantics-based tools that are used in human-based creative activities for knowledge construction in a specific domain. Such knowledge, in turn, is used to search for new ideas. Indeed, in our approach, human creativity for business innovation is stimulated by means of

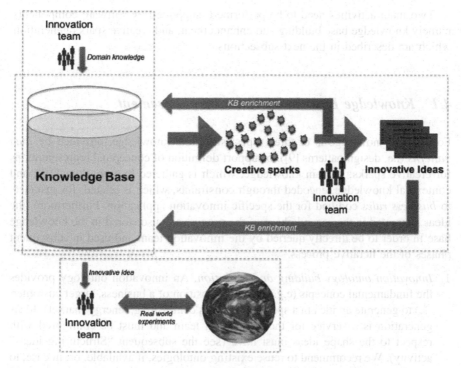

Fig. 2 Knowledge-based methodology for innovation as an iterative process

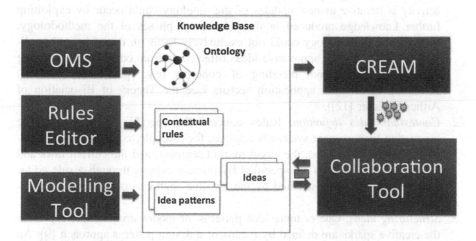

Fig. 3 CREAM-based system

automatically generated ontology-grounded conceptual models (the creative sparks), which, if relevant, contribute to further enhance the knowledge of that domain.

Two main activities need to be performed, supported by software components, namely knowledge base building and enhancement, and creative sparks generation, which are described in the next subsections.

4.1   Knowledge Base Building and Enhancement

Formalized knowledge is of three types: structural knowledge, provided by *idea patterns* (i.e. design patterns [9]) to support definition of conceptual representations for creative sparks; domain knowledge, which is gathered in a *ontology* [10]; and contextual knowledge, encoded through constraints, which is related, for instance, to *business rules* codified for the specific innovation application. Furthermore, the ideas generated in the second phase of the process are also stored in the knowledge base in order to be directly queried by the innovation team and used in subsequent phases of the iterative process.

1. *Innovation ontology building and evolution.* An innovation ontology provides the fundamental concepts (e.g., value proposition of a business, target customer, ...) to generate an idea in a specific business context (e.g., energy market). Ideas generation is a service for the innovation team and must be configured with respect to the shape ideas must have (see the subsequent "Structuring ideas" activity). We recommend to reuse existing ontologies, if available, or, in case, to build a new one following lightweight methodologies considering social involvement of a group of experts and stakeholders such as [11]. Note that this activity is iterative as new updates of the ontology could occur by exploiting further knowledge produced in the subsequent phases of the methodology. Furthermore the ontology could not exclusively focus on the addressed application domain. In fact, innovative ideas often come from contamination among different domains, from blending of concepts (e.g., problems, solutions) belonging to different application sectors (see the Theory of Bisociation of Arthur Koestler [12]).

2. *Contextual rules definition.* Rules concern the specific context where the innovation management system is applied, for example, considering the location, the temporal period, the target market segment, and the current laws and regulations. These rules are specified by domain experts through a rule editor and are required to be satisfied by the creative sparks as outcome of the generation process.

3. *Structuring ideas.* One or more idea patterns, or model structures, to represent the creative sparks are defined by means of a design patterns approach [9]. An example of model structure is the business model defined in [13], or else a part of it, like the one used for our case study in Sect. 6. Such a model consists of abstract concepts and relationships, usually belonging to upper level models for the domain ontology. Indeed, creative sparks will be identified by CREAM within the set of concepts and relationships, at the lowest possible level of

specialization in the ontology. Domain and application experts define these patterns through a modeling tool.

4. *Ideas classification.* The ideas elaborated by the innovation team, based on the creative sparks, are classified in the knowledge base according to three dimensions: bad ideas, missed opportunities and innovative ideas.

4.2   The CREAtivity Machine

This is a novel software component driving our innovation management system, as it plays the active role of generation of the creative sparks to be supplied to the innovation team. Technically, creative sparks for a given model structure are conceived as semantic bindings between abstract entities of that structure and domain-specific entities of the ontology, in order to represent possible concrete innovative ideas for the business domain at hand. Given an ontology represented in OWL/RDF, the semantic binding activity of a model structure with specific concepts of the ontology is implemented through a SPARQL [14] query. This is configured at run time by using three types of knowledge: from the design pattern that represents the model structure, from the domain and from the context.

Specifically, a pattern-based query is first constructed by accounting for the concepts and relationships that are used in the given design pattern, to retrieve all of their specializations from the domain ontology. Let us give a model structure represented by a pattern consisting of the entities: Entity_1,..., Entity_n, and object properties: objProp_ij, for i, j = 1,...,n, where objProp_ij is a relationship from Entity_i to Entity_j. Entities represent component abstractions of a domain model, and object properties semantic links between them. In the business domain, *Business Activity* and *Resource* are examples of entities and *requires* and *produces* are two possible object properties linking them.

Figure 4 shows an excerpt of the SPARQL query related to the given pattern, where we highlighted the main steps. Namely, the first step is finalized to selection of all the subclasses of the pattern entities. In the business domain example, *Production*, *Administration*, and *Software Development* are subclasses of *Business Activity*, and *Software*, *App*, and *Invoice* are subclasses of *Resource*. Then, the abstract ontological pattern referring to the model structure is specified. In the code, step 2 includes retrieving all of the specializations of the object properties objProp_ij, connecting Entity_i subclasses with the Entity_j subclasses retrieved in step 1, and belonging to the pattern. Examples of specialization of the object property *produces* could be *producesSW*, linking *Software Development* with *Software*, and *producesDoc* linking *Administration* and *Invoice*.

The subsequent code is finalized to retrieving, from each set, just those subclasses that are leaf concepts. Thus, *Invoice* and *App* could be leaf concepts in the example used. The effect of the above piece of query is a set of creative sparks resulting by linking each ontology relationship of the pattern to one of the object

```
PREFIX : <http://www.../BInnovationOntoName#>
.................
SELECT DISTINCT ?e_1 ?e_2 .... ?e_n
WHERE {

# selection of all entity subclasses
?e_11 rdfs:subClassOf Entity_1 .
....................
?e_n1 rdfs:subClassOf Entity_n .

# pattern definition
......................
?ipros_ij a owl:ObjectProperty;
  rdfs:domain ?ei1 ;
  rdfs:range ?ej1 ;
  rdfs:subPropertyOf objProp_ij .
  FILTER (! (?ei1 = Entity_i))
......................

# selection of leaf concepts only, among the selected \\
# specialization entities in block 1
?e1 rdfs:subClassOf Entity_1 .
  FILTER NOT EXISTS {
  ?sub_e1 rdfs:subClassOf ?e1 .
  ?sub_e2 rdfs:subClassOf ?e1 .
  FILTER (! (?sub_e1 = ?sub_e2)) }
  FILTER EXISTS {
  ?e1 rdfs:subClassOf ?e11 .}
......................
?en rdfs:subClassOf Entity_n .
  FILTER NOT EXISTS {
  ?sub_e1 rdfs:subClassOf ?en .
  ?sub_e2 rdfs:subClassOf ?en .
  FILTER (! (?sub_e1 = ?sub_e2)) }
  FILTER EXISTS {
  ?en rdfs:subClassOf ?en1 .}

# contextual rules
# example
FILTER (
!(?e1 in (C1Entity_1,  ...., CkEntity_1)) )
......................
}
```

Fig. 4 Pattern-based query excerpt

properties specializing it, and each entity involved in that relationship to a leaf subclass of the corresponding concept. The output on the given example would contain "*Sales producesDoc Invoice*" and "*Mobile Software Development producesSW App*" pattern instances.

This pattern-base query can be refined with contextual rules, each providing a filter SPARQL statement. The last fragment of the query in Fig. 4 shows one example of contextual rules, to eliminate from the specializations set of Entity_1 the concepts of the ontology belonging to the set {C1Entity_1,..., CkEntity_1}. In our example, if the concept *Administration* were eliminated through a contextual rule, then the final result would just contain the app development pattern instance.

CREAM was implemented in Java, based on the Apache Jena framework including the ARQ library [15], which implements a SPARQL 1.1 engine. The application is configurable with respect to the ontology, contextual rules and query patterns (idea patterns), by means of a XML file.

5 Collaborative Definition of Innovative Ideas

This step takes as input the creative sparks generated by CREAM and aims at selecting a (sub)set of them as components of the envisaged innovative idea. This phase includes an analysis of the candidate creative sparks.

Our main assumption is that a creative spark can be promoted from its candidate status to a "full-fledged" innovative idea if it is creative and, hence, novel and valuable [16]. Techniques from computational creativity could be used to speed up the advancement of creative sparks towards innovative ideas. Computational creativity is a branch of research devoted to defining methods and tools, mainly from artificial intelligence, to support creative processes, such as those for creative design. Here creative design aims at generating models for innovative ideas, that is, conceptual descriptions for new instances of business models. This process relies on the collaborative work of various stakeholders involved in the innovation management process, leveraging on their experience and different expertise, creativity and problem solving capabilities, and supported by the CREAM-based application.

According to the definitions given in [17], creative design processes can be achieved through (some of) the following actions.

- *Combination*, i.e. the process that combines features from existing designs into a new combination or configuration. Applied to our problem, this action consists in the generation of a new creative spark by combining parts of two or more (already known) creative sparks or innovative ideas.
- *Transformation*, i.e. the process that modifies the form of some particular features of an existing design. In our case, this action consists in the generation of a new creative spark by modifying parts of a (already known) creative spark or innovative idea.

- *Analogy*, i.e. the process in which specific coherent aspects of the conceptual structure of one problem or domain are matched with and transferred to another problem or domain. This process can be applied, for example, to generate a new creative spark by taking into account successful ideas for similar (or different) business objectives.

These actions can be implemented by the use of our CREAM-based system, by exploiting intelligent search features, such as reasoning and similarity based techniques. Examples of usage of such types of actions to the business intelligence case study are given in Sect. 6.

Having a method to evaluate ideas is a precondition to predict their success [18]. In this context, we envisage three approaches of incremental complexity to assess the creativity level of the generated creative sparks and, hence, to define innovative ideas, namely: human selection, intelligent search, and creative brainstorming.

- *Human selection of creative sparks*. This approach requires feedback on the value of creative sparks from the users through, for instance, interviews and questionnaires. To this purpose we propose a simple questionnaire to be sent to experts and stakeholders of the business sector to be innovated. The questionnaire template is filled with a creative spark candidate to be an innovative idea and two questions: *"have you ever considered this idea?"* and *"do you think a firm should take care of this idea?"*. The former aims at assessing its novelty whereas the latter its value. Both of them are measured by means of a multi-items ordinal scale, as the Likert's one [19].
- *Intelligent search of creative sparks*. This approach aims at improving the search for creative sparks by leveraging on creativity measures. However whereas assessing relevance of a creative spark can be done (at least in principle) by assigning a relevance weight to its elements and assessing its novelty can be done by measuring how much it is different from ideas already considered [16], the main difficulties concern its plausibility. The issue here is to determine how much the creative spark is reasonable and/or likely. For this reason full automation of this approach requires availability of a formal specification of common-sense knowledge that is currently an open issue in the artificial intelligent research field [20]. Then human intervention is required to make the final decision as described in the former approach.
- *Creative brainstorming*. This approach is the most complex as it encompasses two different types of activities. The former aims at idea assessment by promoting creative sparks from their candidate status to innovative ideas by means of the previously presented approaches. The latter aims at elaborating and refining ideas in a collaborative manner and with a brainstorming approach devoted to foster discussions and opinions exchange in a community of users. We envisage to use creative sparks that were discarded in the previously mentioned approaches as hints for identifying new ideas. Different methods can be adopted to this purpose. A promising one is the appreciative inquiry (AI) methodology [21]. This seems to be particularly suitable in our case as the

first step of the AI methodology is to recognize the best in the item to be discussed (and, hence, even the best in the unlikely creative sparks) as baseline to imagine something completely new (as new ideas) to be determined in subsequent steps of the brainstorming activity. Finally this approach can be used to elicit new knowledge from the users and, consequently, enrich the knowledge base. In fact new ideas arising from brainstorming activities could be an input for ontology enrichment whereas discarded creative sparks could originate new contextual rules or ontology updates.

6 Business Intelligence Application

In this section we illustrate one type of application of our CREAM-based innovation methodology, aiming at creation of business models in the field of business intelligence. We focus on the generation of creative sparks and we show a couple of interesting examples to be considered for discussion, brainstorming and real world experimentation. We present further examples to show how creative sparks can be further improved to achieve the final innovative ideas.

According to [13, 22], a *business model* describes the rationale of how an organization creates, delivers, and captures value. A widely accepted tool to design a business model is the "business model canvas" which resembles a painter canvas and allows depicting business models. It consists of nine essential building blocks working supportively together. For the sake of simplicity here we consider an idea pattern consisting of only five building blocks. The *customer segment* building block defines the different groups of people or organizations an enterprise aims to reach and serve. The *value proposition* building block describes the bundle of products and services that create value for a specific customer segment. The *channel* building block describes how a company communicates with and reaches its customer segments to deliver a value proposition. The *key activity* building block describes the most important things a company must do to make its business model work. The *key partnership* building block describes the network of suppliers and partners that make the business model work. The other building blocks not considered in this example are *customer relationship*, *revenue stream*, *key resource* and *cost structure*.

We formalized a part of business ontology for the business intelligence sector by specializing the concepts corresponding to the above-mentioned building blocks [23]. We also defined some business (contextual) rules to constraint the search for the creative sparks. Figure 5 shows an example of rule we applied, according to which data providers are not allowed to collaborate with intelligence agencies. Then we ran the pattern-based query over the ontology and we selected the following two creative sparks from the set generated by CREAM.

```
FILTER NOT EXISTS {
?cs rdfs:subClassOf BusinessIntelligenceOnt:IntelligenceAgency .
?kp rdfs:subClassOf BusinessIntelligenceOnt:DataProvider .
}
```

Fig. 5 SPARQL statement implementing a contextual rule

Creative Spark 1

Value Proposition (VP): Targeted Political Campaign
Channel (Ch): Sales Force
Customer Segment (CS): Political Party
Key Partner (KP): Data Provider
Key Activity (KA): Identification Of Social Networks Influencers

Description of Creative Spark 1

A company offers *targeted political campaign* as value proposition to political parties. The channel to sell it consists in the *sales force* composed of a group of people with marketing experiences. The key activity of the business consists in *identifying influencers in social networks* by analyzing information obtained from *data providers* (e.g., social network platforms as LinkedIn and Facebook).

Creative Spark 2

Value Proposition: Real-time Analyzer of Wellness and Poverty
Channel: Secured Web Service
Customer Segment: Charity Organization
Key Partner: Data Provider
Key Activity: Data Processing

Description of Creative Spark 2

A company offers a service aimed at *analyzing real-time wellness and poverty* in a specific geographical region as value proposition to *charity organizations*. The channel to sell it consists in *secured web services*. The key activity of the business consists in *data processing* (including data harvesting and algorithm execution) performed against data from a *data provider*.

As discussed in Sect. 5, *combination* is a type of action for creative design. Figure 6 shows how two creative sparks can be further refined and elaborated, for instance, during creative brainstorming. Accordingly, *innovative idea 1* originates from the *channel*, the *customer segment*, and the *key partnership* of *creative spark 1*, and from the *value proposition*, *key partnership* and *key activity* of *creative spark 2*.

As a result, *innovative idea 1* describes the business model of a company that offers a service aimed at *real-time analysis of wellness and poverty* in a specific geographical region as value proposition to *charity organizations*. The channel to sell it consists in the *sales force* composed of a group of people with marketing experiences. The key activity of the business consists in *data processing* (including

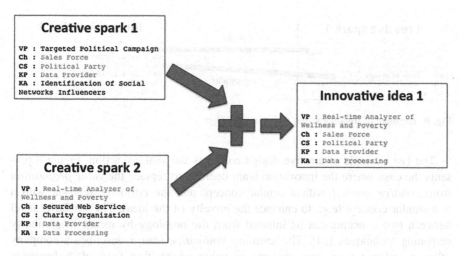

Fig. 6 Example of *combination* of two creative sparks

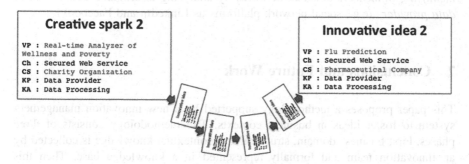

Fig. 7 Example of *transformation* action for creative design

data harvesting and algorithm execution) performed against data from a *data provider*.

Transformation is another action for creative design that can be performed during creative brainstorming. Figure 7 presents an example where *creative spark 2* is transformed to *innovative idea 2* by changing *value proposition* and *customer segment*. The new elements can be defined collaboratively once retrieved by means of intelligent queries (e.g., by using SPARQL) on a ontology. The resulting innovative idea describes a company offering a service aimed at *predicting flu* as value proposition to *pharmaceutical companies*. The channel to sell it consists in *secured web services*. The key activity of the business consists in *data processing* (including data harvesting and algorithm execution) performed against data from a *data provider*.

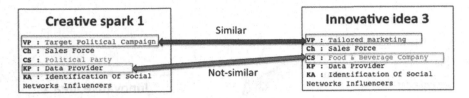

Fig. 8 Example of *analogy* action for creative design

The last example of creative design concerns the analogy action. Figure 8 presents the case where the innovation team decided to replace the *value proposition* from *creative spark 1* with a similar concept and the *customer segment* with a non-similar concept (e.g., to enhance the novelty of the idea). The similarity level between two concepts can be inferred from the ontology by means of similarity reasoning techniques [24]. The resulting *innovative idea 3* describes a company offering *tailored marketing* services as value proposition to *food & beverage companies*. The channel to sell it consists in the *sales force* composed of a group of people with marketing experiences. The key activity of the business consists in *identifying influencers in social networks* by analyzing information obtained from *data providers* (e.g., social network platforms as LinkedIn and Facebook).

7 Conclusions and Future Work

This paper proposes a methodology supported by a new innovation management system to foster ideas in business contexts. The methodology consists of three phases. First business domain, structural and contextual knowledge is collected by an innovation team and formally represented in a knowledge base. Then this knowledge is used to generate creative sparks and, hence, to stimulate the innovation team in discussing new ideas. Finally selected ideas are tested in real world environments. Here we focus on the core of the innovation management system, the CREAM component, which is used in the first phase.

We presented an exemplary application related to definition of a business model for business intelligence firms. Some other examples of application of the methodology were presented in previous works [25, 26] and focus on supporting creativity in emergency scenarios definition, concerning, respectively, supply-chains and complex socio-technological systems as smart cities. Finally, as a work in progress, we are applying our methodology to risks assessment in the water systems industry, as a follow up to the work presented in [27].

Acknowledgements We wish to thank Michele Melchiori (Università di Brescia) and Alex Coletti (Syneren) working together with us in this topic and the anonymous reviewers for their suggestions and comments.

References

1. Yunus, M. (2007). *Creating a world without poverty: Social business and the future of capitalism*. PublicAffairs.
2. Altshuller, G. S., Shulyak, L., & Rodman. S. (1999). *The innovation algorithm: TRIZ, systematic innovation and technical creativity*. Technical Innovation Center, Inc..
3. De Bono, E. (1970). *Lateral thinking*. Harper and Row.
4. Yan, W., Zanni-Merk, C., Cavallucci, D., & Collet, P. (2014). An ontology-based approach for inventive problem solving. *Engineering Applications of Artificial Intelligence, 27*, 175–190.
5. C. Zanni-Merk, D. Cavallucci, & F. Rousselot. (2009). An ontological basis for computer aided innovation. *Computers in Industry*, 60(8):563–574. Computer Aided Innovation.
6. Apostolou, D., Zachos, K., Maiden, N., Agell, N., Sanchez-Hernandez, G., Taramigkou, M., et al. (2016). Facilitating creativity in collaborative work with computational intelligence software. *IEEE Computational Intelligence Magazine, 11*(2), 29–40.
7. Zachos, K., Maiden, N., & Levis, S. (2015). Creativity support to improve health-and-safety in manufacturing plants: Demonstrating everyday creativity. In *Proceedings of the 2015 ACM SIGCHI Conference on Creativity and Cognition, C&C'15*, pp. 225–234, New York, NY, USA, ACM.
8. Allio, R. J. (2004). CEO interview: the innocentive model of open innovation. *Strategy & Leadership, 32*(4), 4–9.
9. Gangemi, A., & Presutti, V. (2009). Ontology design patterns. In Steffen Staab & Rudi Studer (Eds.), *Handbook on Ontologies* (pp. 221–243)., International Handbooks on Information Systems Berlin Heidelberg: Springer.
10. Gruber, T. R. (1993). A translation approach to portable ontology specifications. *Knowledge acquisition, 5*(2), 199–220.
11. De Nicola, A., & Missikoff, M. (2016). A lightweight methodology for rapid ontology engineering. *Communications of the ACM, 59*(3), 79–86.
12. Koestler, A. (1964). *The act of creation*. London Hutchinson.
13. A. Osterwalder and Y. Pigneur. *Business model generation: a handbook for visionaries, game changers, and challengers*. John Wiley & Sons, 2010.
14. Pérez, J., Arenas, M., & Gutierrez, C. (2006). Semantics and complexity of SPARQL. In Proceedings of *ISWC'06*, pp. 30–43. Springer.
15. Apache Jena, version 2.11.1, 2013. Available at: http://jena.apache.org.
16. Pease, A., Winterstein, D., & Colton, S. (2001). Evaluating machine creativity. In *Workshop on Creative Systems, 4th International Conference on Case Based Reasoning*, pp. 129–137.
17. Gero, J. S. (2000). Computational models of innovative and creative design processes. *Technological Forecasting and Social Change, 64*(2–3), 183–196.
18. Forde, A. N., & Fox, M. S. (2016). A proposed approach for idea selection in front end of innovation activities. *Technology Innovation Management Review, 6*(8), 48–55.
19. Likert, R. (1932). A technique for the measurement of attitudes. *Archives of psychology*.
20. Speer, R., Havasi, C., & Lieberman, H. (2008). Analogyspace: Reducing the dimensionality of common sense knowledge. In *Proceedings of the 23rd National Conference on Artificial Intelligence* (Vol. 1, pp. 548–553). AAAI Press.
21. Cooperrider D. L., & Whitney, D. (2011). What is appreciative inquiry.
22. Osterwalder, A. (2004). The business model ontology: A proposition in a design science approach. Dissertation, University of Lausanne, Switzerland: 173.
23. De Nicola, A. (2016). *Diffusion of Interests in Social Networks*. PhD thesis, University of Rome Tor Vergata.
24. Formica, A. (2008). Concept similarity in formal concept analysis: an information content approach. *Knowledge-Based Systems, 21*(1), 80–87.
25. De Nicola, A,. Melchiori, M., & Villani, M. L. (2014). *A lateral thinking framework for semantic modelling of emergencies in smart cities*. In *Database and Expert Systems*

Applications, volume 8645 of *Lecture Notes in Computer Science*, pp. 334–348. Springer International Publishing.

26. A. De Nicola, M. Melchiori, and M. L. Villani. A semantics-based approach to generation of emergency management scenario models. In *Proc. of I-ESA'14*, volume 7, pages 163–173. Springer, 2014.

27. Coletti, A., De Nicola, A., & Villani, M. L. (2016). Building climate change into risk assessments. *Natural Hazards, 84*(2), 1307–1325.

E-HRM Adoption and Usage: A Cross-National Analysis of Enabling Factors

Alessandra Lazazzara and Eleanna Galanaki

Abstract The present study builds on diffusion of innovation (DOI) and institutional theories to address the current lack of cross-national studies on e-HRM adoption and usage. The core research question asks about the factors influencing e-HRM adoption and usage for HRM. We analysed direct effects related to country, organizational and HRM factors among 3815 organizations in 21 countries in a multilevel approach. The results largely supported the hypotheses. Specifically, national systems supporting innovative behaviours determine the extent of e-HRM adoption. The economic sector of activity, size, global competition and educational level were associated with e-HRM adoption and usage at the organizational level. Moreover, a strategic orientation of the HR function seems to be a prerequisite for e-HRM adoption and usage. The theoretical and practical implications are discussed.

Keywords E-HRM adoption · E-HRM usage · Diffusion of innovation theory · Institutional theory · Global innovation index · Cranet

1 Introduction

E-HRM is an "umbrella term covering all possible integration mechanisms and contents between human resource management (HRM) and IT aimed at creating value for targeted employees and managers" [1]. It t is considered such an interesting topic in the HR field because the adoption of e-HRM is expected to confer many advantages on organizations, such as a more efficient and strategically oriented HR function and an increased competitive advantage [2–7].

A. Lazazzara (✉)
Department of Educational Human Sciences, University of Milano-Bicocca, Milan, Italy
e-mail: alessandra.lazazzara@unimib.it

E. Galanaki
Department of Marketing and Communication, Athens University of Economics
and Business, Athens, Greece
e-mail: eleanag@aueb.gr

© Springer International Publishing AG 2018
C. Rossignoli et al. (eds.), *Digital Technology and Organizational Change*,
Lecture Notes in Information Systems and Organisation 23,
https://doi.org/10.1007/978-3-319-62051-0_11

Factors behind e-HRM adoption decisions have usually been addressed by exploring both the organizational and HRM contexts [4, 8–10]. However, there is still no general agreement on the factors influencing e-HRM adoption. Additionally, a third element related to the influence of country-level factors such as culture, governmental policies and market forces on the adoption of e-HRM innovation has rarely been tested [11–13]. Indeed, reviews of the extant e-HRM literature [1, 9] revealed a dearth of research in analysing institutional factors affecting e-HRM adoption, which is even more apparent when considering that cross-national e-HRM studies are mainly restricted to English-speaking [14, 15] or European countries [11–13].

Concerning the functional focus, most studies address the overall adoption of e-HRM, while others focus on specific functional subsets of e-HRM, such as e-recruiting, e-selection, or e-learning [11, 12]. Although dichotomous measures are commonly used in innovation diffusion research (e.g., questions asking whether or not organizations have any e-HRM tools), e-HRM adoption alone does not imply e-HRM sophistication and embeddedness within HR practices. Conversely, only a few papers analyse both e-HRM adoption and the degree or intensity of e-HRM innovation [10].

Building on diffusion of innovation theory (DOI) [16] and the institutional literature [17], this paper aims to contribute to the HRM literature by addressing the current lack of cross-national empirical data regarding factors associated with the deployment of e-HRM within organizations. The core research question posed by this paper is the following: What factors influence e-HRM technology adoption and usage for HRM? In exploring this question, we apply a holistic approach that encompasses national, organizational and HRM strategic aspects and that distinguishes between technological and HRM aspects of e-HRM adoption. Moreover, we distinguished between two aspects of e-HRM, namely, the extent of e-HRM adoption and e-HRM usage.

To explore these issues, we first develop the theoretical framework and identify possible factors contributing to adoption at the national, organizational and HRM level. We then employ a cross-national large-scale survey to test our hypotheses on a sample of 3815 organizations in 21 countries by applying a multilevel analysis strategy. Finally, we discuss the results and derive conclusions for future research.

2   Theoretical Framework

E-HRM generally refers to the implementation and application of information and communication technology for HR purposes [12]. E-HRM can be considered an innovation in terms of HRM [5]. This results not only because information technology enables the design of HRM tools and instruments that would not be possible otherwise but also because it creates opportunities to reshape employee-management relationships, enables HRM departments to improve their strategic orientation, reduces costs/gain efficiency and improves client services [5]. However, technology has both a physical and a procedural dimension [18]. Therefore, to better define e-HRM, both dimensions should be taken into account. In particular, Thite, Kavanagh, and Johnson [19] distinguish between human resources information systems (HRIS) and e-HRM on the basis of the degree of information technology versus the human resource management focus. In this vein, HRIS is more focused on systems and technology (e.g., hardware, software, IT infrastructure) supporting the move to e-HRM, whereas e-HRM tends to be more HR-function oriented. Therefore, the technological focus is more related to the degree of the physical presence of information technologies that allow HR activities, while the HRM focus is the degree to which e-HRM is used to enable HR activities [20].

Analysing the adoption of IS innovations in the HR field poses several challenges due to the physical and procedural dimensions it encompasses. Indeed, this process involves multiple actors with information technology specialists designing and acquiring the information systems to first support the move to e-HRM, which is followed by the adoption of e-HRM technology by the HR function and employees.

The e-HRM adoption process consists of several stages that can be seen as the "Planning, implementation and application of information technology for both networking and supporting at least two individual or collective actors in their shared performing of HR activities" [9] from a process perspective. More specifically, Martin [21] was one of the first scholars arguing that the diffusion of innovation (DOI) theory [16] is a promising yet neglected perspective in the study of the process by which e-HRM innovations spread across and within organizations. Following the same line of reasoning, this theoretical framework has been applied to the adoption of e-HRM and HRIS in several studies [2, 14, 22].

The DOI perspective [16] represents an interesting theoretical foundation on which to explore the process of e-HRM technology spreading within organizations. However, the starting point of this theory is the adoption of innovations by individuals or entities over five stages, namely, knowledge, persuasion, decision, implementation and conformation. During these five stages, five innovation-specific attributes influence the likelihood of an innovation's adoption: relative advantage, complexity, compatibility, trialability and observability. Following Rogers' [16] proposal, the organizational adoption of e-HRM refers to the decision-making process that initiates and implements IT to network and support employees and managers in performing HR tasks. The diffusion of e-HRM is then based on the accumulated adoption of these kinds of innovations within organizations. Therefore, the DOI theory [16] provides valuable insight for the analysis of both e-HRM adoption and usage.

2.1 Country Level Factors Enabling E-HRM Adoption and Usage

Diverse internal and external factors—parameters that directly or indirectly further or hinder the adoption of e-HRM [12]—trigger the adoption and usage of IT for HR purposes. With regard to the socioeconomic and political contexts of these factors, few studies have used institutional theory to understand the adoption and usage of IS/IT [23] or, more specifically, of e-HRM [24], particularly in a cross-national context.

The literature on institutional theory is complex and varied and has been used for several decades by various researchers to study the impact of external forces on organizational behaviour, structures and ideals [17, 25]. At the heart of institutional theory are both the notion of institutions as "socially constructed, routine-reproduced programmes or rule systems" [26] and the fact that organizations operate in institutional environments governed by elaborate rules and requirements to which they must conform in order to gain acceptance and legitimacy and to endure [17, 25]. This forces organizations to meet the expectations embedded in the institutional context in order to survive and thus become isomorphic [25].

According to Weerakkody et al. [23], organizations in different socioeconomic and political contexts often react differently to similar internal and external challenges, particularly those that involve IT-induced change resulting from constraints imposed by the environment in which they operate. Furthermore, a well-developed argument in the HRM field assumes that contextual national characteristics lead to different models of HRM [27]. Accordingly, e-HRM adoption and usage will vary on a cross-national basis due to country-specific factors.

By applying an institutional perspective to the diffusion of innovation, we can argue that institutional settings (more specifically, national policies supporting innovative behaviours) are nation-based and that organizations necessarily act within the frame of such "national systems of innovation" to gain legitimacy and recognition [27]. This argument is rooted in the view that every country is characterized by these national systems, which consist of elements such as R&D outputs, business and public research organizations, funding and taxation arrangements, and support systems [28, 29]. If such systems foster the emergence and success of innovation practices and enable conditions in which innovation flourishes, they will trigger innovation adoption. Organizations located in countries scoring high on innovation will more likely have a higher e-HRM adoption and usage rate. *(H1) The national innovation system will positively influence the extent of e-HRM adoption and usage.*

2.2   *Organizational Factors Enabling E-HRM Adoption and Usage*

Previous research has revealed that companies operating in technology-intensive sectors seek to adopt IT tools early to enhance their external image [11]. Other studies reference the task characteristics of an industry and more specifically the incidence of clerical and stationary tasks (e.g., banking) that would predict e-HRM adoption [12]. Moreover, according to the institutional perspective, the adoption of organizational innovation is triggered by bandwagon pressures that lead organizations to adopt conformist behaviours driven by social pressures towards isomorphism [17].

To sum up, due to mimetic isomorphic pressures, the greater the number of adopters there are in an industry, the greater the pressure is towards innovation adoption to gain organizational legitimacy [17] and ensure survival [25]. Organizations located in industries in which the adoption rate is higher will be more likely to have a higher e-HRM adoption and usage rate. *(H2) The economic sector of operation will influence the extent of e-HRM adoption and usage.*

At the organizational level, company size is one of the main factors predicting the adoption and diffusion of e-HRM systems [2, 10–12]. Size plays a key role in driving the adoption of innovative systems because the larger a company is, the more likely it is to reach a "critical mass" demanding enhanced delivery of HRM services and greater effectiveness on the part of the HR function [5]. Moreover, as larger organizations are more likely spread over different buildings and locations, they benefit more from the automation and standardization of HR practices [12]. Furthermore, larger companies can more easily invest resources and absorb the risks associated with adopting and implementing innovations because they are more likely to obtain a return on their investment in e-HRM and thereby recoup the original cost due to economy of scale effects [10–12]. Therefore, larger organizations will more likely have a higher e-HRM adoption and usage rate. *(H3) The size of an organization will positively influence the extent of e-HRM adoption and usage.*

Similarly, especially for organizations operating in global markets, e-HRM facilitates collaboration and information sharing, thereby playing a key role in supporting virtual teams and network organizations [30]. Those organizations are continuously faced with what has been defined as "institutional duality", which refers to the different layers of institutional contexts (global-local) that simultaneously influence HRM configuration [31] and affect the success of combining telecommunications and information technologies to accomplish organizational tasks [32]. However, for these companies the drive to be competitive in all business aspects and the pressure on HR to reduce costs and fulfil the role of strategic partner leads them to adopt and use e-HRM tools [10]. Therefore, organizations competing in global markets will more likely have a higher e-HRM adoption and usage rate. *(H4) Global competition will positively influence the extent of e-HRM adoption and usage.*

Finally, when asking whether to adopt an e-HRM system, organizations may be influenced by another organizational characteristic: the educational level of the employees. Indeed, e-HRM requires a certain degree of technical competence, and employees' level of education has been found to be positively associated with innovation adoption in general [33] and with HRM innovation in particular [34]. Therefore, companies with a greater proportion of highly educated employees might be expected to be more inclined to adopt interactive e-HRM systems, since higher education that includes basic IT skills and familiarization with electronic tools facilitates e-HRM adoption [8]. *H5. The educational level of an organization should positively influence the extent of e-HRM adoption and usage.*

2.3 HRM Factors Enabling E-HRM Adoption and Usage

Several studies have recognized the essential role of top management in influencing e-HRM innovation adoption [10, 14, 35, 36]. The role of HR executives as business champions is essential for HRM innovation in terms of creating a supportive climate and providing adequate resources [37]. However, their ability to identify business opportunities and realize a strategic fit between IT, HR and corporate strategy also play a crucial role in the decision to introduce e-HRM systems [38]. Along with a strategic HRM orientation, the participation of the head of HR on the Board of Directors enhances business acumen and orientation by involving him/her in business strategy development [39] and is essential to bringing about the adoption of e-HRM and facilitating the link between organizational and HRM goals [12]. *H6. The HR director's involvement on the executive Board of Directors and in the development of business strategy will positively influence the extent of e-HRM adoption and usage.*

Finally, the long-term success of an HRM strategy based on IT applications should centre on the availability of skilled e-HRM professionals, as both IT and HR knowledge is required [10]. However, HR departments have traditionally been characterized by their lack of IT knowledge and skills. According to the strategic view that companies outsource activities for which they lack the necessary resources and capabilities and perform the activities for which they possess strategic resources and capabilities in-house [40], it is expected that at least in the first stages of e-HRM adoption, the HR function may decide to outsource IT services to limit financial investment. However, as long as e-HRM becomes more strategic and a source of competitive advantage, companies will be more likely to implement it in-house [41]. *H7. E-HRM outsourcing will positively influence the extent of e-HRM adoption.* The hypothesized model for this study is illustrated in Fig. 1.

3 Method

3.1 Sample and Procedures

The data employed in this study mainly stem from two sources. The first is the Cranet survey, one of the most representative large-scale international comparative surveys of HRM systems. The survey provides comprehensive information about the HRM practices of organizations and uses the participating companies' HR directors as the key informants (for a detailed description of the Cranet approach see [42]).

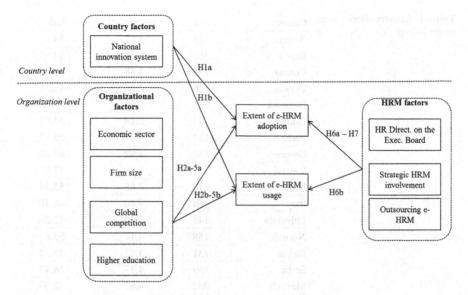

Fig. 1 The hypothesized theoretical model

The 2014–2015 dataset covers 3815 organizations across 21 countries, i.e., Austria, Brazil, Croatia, Cyprus, Denmark, Estonia, Finland, Greece, Iceland, Israel, Italy, Lithuania, Norway, Russia, Serbia, Slovakia, Slovenia, Spain, Sweden, Switzerland, and the USA. The second source of data is the 2015 Global Innovation Index (GII) [43], which is an international comparative measure addressing countries' institutional settings and more specifically the estimated innovation by firms and industries and the implementation of national policies supporting innovative behaviours.

Of the companies examined, 2251 (70.4% of sample) were in the trade and services sector, 842 (26.19% of sample) were in the manufacturing sector, and only 122 (3.49% of the sample) were in the primary sector of the economy. The majority of the organizations, 2486, were private, while 912 were public, 167 were not-for-profit, and 180 were mixed. Finally, 1141 organizations (29.91% of the sample) were multinationals. In 64.70% of the companies, the most senior person in HRM had a seat on the Board of Directors. The majority of the companies also involved HR people in HRM strategy (Table 1).

3.2 The Study Variables

Dependent variables. There are two dependent variables in this study. One measures whether e-HRM has been adopted and the other measures the degree or intensity with which this innovation has been adopted by the HR function. The first

Table 1 Country distribution of data sample (N = 21)

Country	Freq.	Percent (%)	GII
Austria	223	5.85	54
Brazil	352	9.23	34.95
Croatia	171	4.48	41.70
Cyprus	86	2.25	43.51
Denmark	175	4.59	57.70
Estonia	83	2.18	52.81
Finland	182	4.77	59.97
Greece	184	4.82	40.28
Iceland	110	2.88	57.02
Israel	110	2.88	53.54
Italy	168	4.40	46.40
Lithuania	145	3.80	42.26
Norway	158	4.14	53.8
Russia	131	3.43	39.32
Serbia	159	4.17	36.47
Slovakia	262	6.87	42.99
Slovenia	157	4.12	48.49
Spain	91	2.39	49.07
Sweden	285	7.47	62.40
Switzerland	211	5.53	68.30
USA	372	9.75	60.10
Total	3815	100	

dependent variable, *extent of e-HRM adoption*, was measured as a formative measure of the technological sophistication of e-HRM; it has a minimum of 0 and a maximum of 3. It was calculated by adding three categorical (yes/no) questions from the CRANET questionnaire: (a) Human resource information system or electronic HRM systems for HRM activities (HRIS); (b) manager self-service for HRM activities (manager self-service); and (c) employee self-service for HRM activities (employee self-service). The second dependent variable, *extent of e-HRM usage*, is a formative measure of the penetration of e-HRM in multiple HRM functions with a minimum of 0 and a maximum of 4. This variable was calculated by adding four categorical (yes/no) questions from the CRANET questionnaire: (a) the vacancy page on the company website as a recruitment method (e-recruitment); (b) online selection tests as the selection method (e-selection); (c) bottom-up or top-down electronic communication (e-communication); and (d) the use of computer-based packages/e-learning for career management (e-learning).

Country context. The 2015 Global Innovation Index (GII) [43] scores were used as a proxy for estimating the national innovation system [44]. The GII was developed by Cornell University, INSEAD and the World Intellectual Property Organisation (a UN organization), where the overall innovation performance ranking of a country is a composite score based on 79 indicators across a range of innovative policy and firm behaviour themes. Scores are normalized in the 0–100 range.

All the other independent variables identified in the research model are based on the Cranet questionnaire.

Organizational context. *Organizational size* was the natural logarithm of the total number of employees in the organization. *Global competition* was measured by asking the respondents to characterize the main market(s) for their organization's products or services based on a 5-point Likert scale (1 = "local", 2 = "regional", 3 = "national", 4 = "continent-wide", 5 = "worldwide"). A six-point scale was adopted to measure the *proportion of the workforce with a higher education/university qualification* (1 = "0%", 2 = "1–10%", 3 = "11–25%", 4 = "26–50%", 5 = "51–75%", 6 = "76–100%"). For the *economic sector*, a categorical variable portraying the sector of economic activity of the organization was used as follows: 1 = "primary sector", 2 = "manufacturing" and 3 = "trade & services".

HRM context. *HRM position on the Executive Board* was measured via a categorical (yes/no) variable ("Does the person responsible for HR have a place on the board or equivalent top executive team?"). Moreover, the *strategic involvement of HRM* was measured via a 4-item Likert scale answering the question: "If your organization has a business/service strategy, at what stage is the person responsible for HRM involved?" (0 = "not consulted", 1 = "on implementation", 2 = "through subsequent consultation", 3 = "from the outset"). Finally, *e-HRM outsourcing* was measured via a 5-item Likert scale (0 = "not outsourced", 4 = "completely outsourced").

Descriptive statistics and correlations are presented in Table 2.

3.3 Analysis

Structural equation modelling (SEM) analysis was deemed necessary to test the model. The STATA14, module SEM- GSEM and the STATA SEM path diagram modules were used.

The analysis involved two steps. In the first step, regular SEM analysis (method: maximum likelihood with missing values) was conducted to confirm the model for the firm-level relations. In this analysis, all variables were included except the Global Innovation Index (GII), which is a country-level variable. Then, in the second step, generalized SEM was applied, as it allows for the introduction of multilevel variables, so the higher (country) level variable GII was included, as in the model portrayed in Fig. 2.

In the first step, all indices for SEM were acceptable. The model achieved an $R^2 = 0.22$ (22% of the total variance), which is an acceptable level for research in management science.

In the second step, generalized SEM was employed to test whether the linear inclusion of GII improves the model. Indeed, the LR (maximum likelihood) test

Table 2 Means, standard deviations and correlations (N = 3815)

		Mean	SD	1	2	3	4'	5	6	7'	8	9
1	E-HRM adoption	1.44	1.13	1								
2	E-HRM usage	1.71	0.91	0.21*	1							
3	Organizational size	6.29	1.41	0.28*	0.21*	1						
4'	Economic sector	2.66	0.55	0.09*	0.07*	0.02	1					
5	Global competition	3.16	1.39	0.08*	0.07*	0.02	-0.40*	1				
6	Proportion higher education	3.85	1.35	0.14*	0.07*	-0.08*	0.27*	-0.01	1			
7'	HRM position on Board	0.64	0.48	0.14*	0.14*	0.12*	0.00	0.02	-0.00	1		
8	Strategic involvement of HRM	2.16	1.02	0.10*	0.15*	0.12*	0.06*	-0.03	-0.00	0.33*	1	
9	E-HRM outsourcing	1.07	1.38	0.17*	0.05*	0.02	0.06*	-0.05*	0.08*	0.07*	0.03	1

Note Correlations marked with * are statistically significant at the 0.05 level. For economic sector (4') and HRM position on the Executive Board (7'), Spearman's Rho correlations are reported (non parametric)

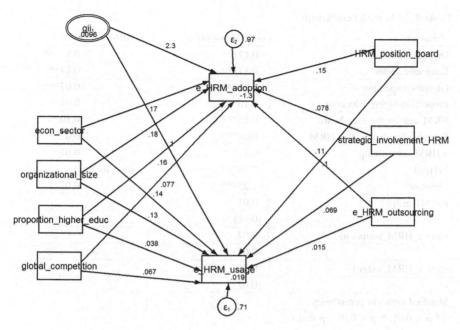

Fig. 2 GSEM diagram

revealed that the inclusion of a random intercept based on GII significantly improved the simpler model (LR chi2(2) = 108.15, p < 0.01). Therefore, including GII as an intercept significantly improved the predictive power of the model.

4 Results

Table 3 presents the coefficients' estimates for the SEM model. As expected, the national innovation system was positively related to both the degree of e-HRM presence and e-HRM usage for HRM.

The set of hypotheses related to the effect of organizational factors on e-HRM presence and usage (H2-5) were almost all significant and positive. Hypothesis 2 concerned the relationship between the economic sector of activity and e-HRM presence and usage. The statistical analyses confirmed that the former relationship was significant and positive. Overall, organizational size and operation in a global market increased the likelihood that companies would adopt e-HRM and would have a higher e-HRM usage rate. The educational level of employees was positively related to e-HRM presence and usage.

Turning now to the HRM context, the HR director's involvement on the main Board of Directors was positively related to e-HRM's physical presence and e-HRM usage. Among the HRM factors, the strategic involvement of the HR

Table 3 SEM model coefficients

Variables	e-HRM adoption	e-HRM usage
Organizational size	0.17***	0.13***
Economic sector	0.17***	0.14***
Global competition	0.08***	0.07***
Proportion higher education	0.16***	0.04***
HRM seat on the exec board	0.15***	0.10***
Strategic involvement of HRM	0.08***	0.07***
e-HRM outsourcing	0.11***	0.01
M1[gii]	2.35***	1 (constrained)
Constant	−1.25***	0.02
var(M1[gii])	0.01	
	(0.01)	
var(e.e_HRM_adoption)	0.97	
	(0.03)	
var(e.e_HRM_usage)	0.71	
	(0.02)	
Standard errors in parentheses		

*** $p < 0.01$, **$p < 0.05$, *$p < 0.1$

function also appeared to be the more salient since it is positively related to both e-HRM adoption and usage. As expected, HRIS outsourcing had a significant positive effect on the adoption of e-HRM but not on e-HRM usage.

5 Discussion and Conclusion

The aim of this chapter was to address the current lack of cross-national analysis on factors associated with the deployment of e-HRM within organizations. We built on diffusion of innovation theory [16] and the institutional literature [17] to disentangle the factors enabling HRM innovation. We created three groups of factors: institutional, organizational, and HRM. Furthermore, we not only investigated whether organizations adopted e-HRM but also ascertained the intensity of the adoption and diffusion among HRM practices.

Empirically, our results partially confirmed previous studies. However, they also offer new insights into unexplored factors and patterns influencing e-HRM adoption and usage. Confirming previous results, organizational size significantly influenced not only e-HRM adoption but also its usage for HRM. In addition, organizations facing global competition—those operating in a global market—are more likely to have higher e-HRM adoption and usage rates because of the need to facilitate collaboration across organizational and geographical borders. This suggests that larger organizations and those operating in a global market are increasingly leveraging e-HRM to become more competitive and reduce costs [10]. Our results revealed that employees' educational level positively influences e-HRM adoption and usage. This is possibly because of lower probability of failure in its adoption when employees are more educated, but also because of the nature of the tasks typically carried out by employees with high educational levels. In our study, we confirm the role of industry membership in e-HRM adoption and usage and support the role of mimetic isomorphic pressures at the industry level whereby companies operating in industries characterized by a high level of e-HRM adoption and usage will be more prone towards innovation adoption and diffusion to achieve organizational legitimacy [17].

An unexplored factor in our study was the role of national systems in supporting innovative behaviours. Confirming our hypothesis, the results revealed that the extent of e-HRM adoption and usage in HRM is influenced by external national forces as well as organizational and HRM ones. By revealing the way in which the institutional settings and interactions between different social entities influence HRM innovation, this study demonstrates how the contextual environment affects the organizational structure as well as the role that e-HRM plays in organizations. Therefore, we advocate for a stronger emphasis in the e-HRM literature on the analysis of interactions with other enterprises and the social cultural environment as important determinants of e-HRM adoption and usage. To reach the expected advantages that organizations aim to obtain through e-HRM [2–7] and to accelerate innovation, a stronger interaction between different actors such as organizations, policy makers, education, research organizations, and trade associations would be crucial.

Finally, the strong role of the strategic orientation to successfully implement e-HRM emerged from the analysis of the HRM context. In particular, the involvement of the HR director on the Board of Directors, particularly his/her involvement in business strategy formulation, was a positive factor influencing e-HRM adoption and usage by overcoming possible resistance, creating a supportive climate and providing adequate resources [37]. Clearly, championing not only the HR executive but also (and especially) the strategic involvement of the HR function is essential to bringing about the adoption and usage of e-HRM [14]. Therefore, a systematic link between business and HR strategies is essential to developing and sustaining HRM innovativeness. Moreover, although HRIS outsourcing may help with undertaking e-HRM adoption (at least during the initial stages), then the development of IT knowledge and skills among HR professionals is required to transform e-HRM into a strategic asset if the HR function wants to pursue an IT-based HRM strategy [45].

Despite several limitations due to the cross-sectional nature of the data and the possible lack of other important factors, we expect this study to contribute to the existing literature through two primary channels. First, this study integrates two theoretical frameworks that stem from two different domains. Indeed, institutional theory has been extensively adopted in organization studies while not sufficiently applied in information system (IS) research [23]. With this study, we start answering the call for a wider adoption of institutional theory in IS research [46].

Second, the study analysed the effect of the implementation of national policies supporting innovative behaviours on the adoption and diffusion of e-HRM. In so doing, we applied a cross-national perspective that included large varieties of countries characterized by institutional diversity. Although cross-national papers on e-HRM have mainly adopted a clustering strategy and assumed that e-HRM adoption does not vary within clusters [11, 12], given the high heterogeneity characterizing our sample, we tested country-level effects in a multilevel approach that allows accurate model contexts and lower-level effects. Therefore, we have not only answered the recent call for empirical cross-national studies exploring those factors that might foster e-HRM adoption [12], but we have also started unravelling e-HRM adoption and diffusion as a multilevel phenomenon that goes beyond the single HR function or organization. At the practical level, the study can suggest to HR practitioners aiming to adopt e-HRM within their organizations how this process would be easier and more successful if linked with a broader HR and business strategy based on innovativeness. In addition, for those actors involved in policy making at the national and organizational levels, the current findings offer compelling insights into the role of institutional factors in influencing innovative activities.

References

1. Bondarouk, T., & Ruel, H. (2009). Electronic human resource management: Challenges in the digital era. *International Journal of Human Resource Management, 20,* 505–514.
2. Florkowski, G., & Olivas-Lujan, M. (2006). The diffusion of human resource information technology innovations in US and non-US firms. *Personnel Review, 35,* 684–710.
3. Bondarouk, T., Ruël, H., & Van der Heijden, B. (2009). E-HRM effectiveness in a public sector organization: A multi-stakeholder perspective. *The International Journal of Human Resource Management, 20,* 578–590.
4. Marler, J. H., & Fisher, S. L. (2013). An evidence-based review of E-HRM and strategic human resource management. *Human Resource Management Review, 23,* 18–36.
5. Ruel, H., Bondarouk, T., & Looise, J. (2004). E-HRM: Innovation or irritation. An explorative empirical study in five large companies on web-based HRM. *Management Revue, 15,* 364–381.
6. Ruël, H., & van der Kaap, H. (2012). E-HRM usage and value creation. Does a facilitating context matter? *Zeitschrift für Pers./German Journal of Human Resource Management, 26,* 260–281.
7. Marler, J. (2009). Making human resources strategic by going to the net: Reality or myth? *The International Journal of Human Resource, 20,* 515–527.
8. Panayotopoulou, L., Vakola, M., & Galanaki, E. (2007). E-HR adoption and the role of HRM: Evidence from Greece. *Personnel Review, 36,* 277–294.
9. Strohmeier, S. (2007). Research in e-HRM: Review and implications. *Human Resource Management Review, 17,* 19–37.
10. Teo, T. S. H., Lim, G. S., & Fedric, S. A. (2007). The adoption and diffusion of human resources information systems in Singapore. *Asia Pacific Journal of Human Resources, 45,* 44–62.

11. Panayotopoulou, L., Galanaki, E., & Papalexandris, N. (2010). Adoption of electronic systems in HRM: Is national background of the firm relevant? *New Technology, Work and Employment, 25,* 253–269.
12. Strohmeier, S., & Kabst, R. (2009). Organizational adoption of e-HRM in Europe: An empirical exploration of major adoption factors. *Journal of Managerial Psychology, 24,* 482–501.
13. Galanaki, E., & Panayotopoulou, L. (2009). Adoption and success of E-HRM in European Firms. In T. Torres-Coronas & M. Arias-Oliva (Eds.), *Encyclopedia of human resources information systems: Challenges in e-HRM* (pp. 24–30). Hershey, PA: Information Science Reference.
14. Olivas-Luján, M. R., & Florkowski, G. W. (2008). Diffusion of HR-ICTs, an innovations perspective. In G. Martin, M. Reddington, & H. Alexander (Eds.), *Technology, outsourcing & transforming HR* (pp. 231–256). Oxford, UK: Butterworth-Heinemann.
15. Olivas-Luján, M. R., & Florkowski, G. W. (2009). The diffusion of HRITs across English-Speaking Countries. In T. Torres-Coronas & M. Arias-Oliva (Eds.), *Encyclopedia of human resources information systems: Challenges in e-HRM* (pp. 242–247). Hershey, PA: Information Science Reference.
16. Rogers, E. M. (2003). *Diffusion of innovations.* New York: Free Press.
17. DiMaggio, P., & Powell, W. (1983). The iron cage revisited: Industrial isomorphism and collective rationality in organizational field. *American Sociological Review, 48,* 147–160.
18. Orlikowski, W. J., & Scott, S. V. (2008). Sociomateriality: Challenging the separation of technology, work and organization. In J. P. Walsh & A. P. Brief (Eds.), *The academy of management annals* (pp. 433–474). Philadelphia: Taylor & Francis.
19. Thite, M., Kavanagh, M. J., & Johnson, R. A. (2012). *Human resource information systems: Basics, applications, and future directions.* Thousand Oaks, CA: Sage.
20. Marler, J. H., & Parry, E. (2015). Human resource management, strategic involvement and e-HRM technology. *The International Journal of Human Resource Management, 5192,* 1–21.
21. Martin, D. P. (2006). Relation d'emploi et mutualisation des ressources humaines entre entreprises d'un même territoire: le cas des pratiques de rémunération des groupements d'employeurs. In: *Acts. of the 17th Congress of AGRH.*
22. Lau, G., & Hooper, V. (2008). Adoption of e-HRM in large New Zealand organizations. In T. Torres-Corronas & M. Arias-Oliva (Eds.), *Encyclopedia of human resource information systems* (pp. 31–41). Hershey, PA: IGI Global.
23. Weerakkody, V., Dwivedi, Y. K., & Irani, Z. (2009). The diffusion and use of institutional theory: A cross-disciplinary longitudinal literature survey. *Journal of Information Technology, 24,* 354–368.
24. Comacchio, A., & Scapolan, A. C. (2004). The adoption process of corporate e-learning it Italy. *Education+ Training, 46,* 315–325.
25. Meyer, J., & Rowan, B. (1977). Institutional organizations: Formal structure as myth and ceremony. *American Journal of Sociology, 83,* 340–363.
26. Jepperson, R. (1991). Institutions, institutional effects, and institutionalism. In W. Powell & P. DiMaggio (Eds.), *The new institutionalism in organisational analysis* (pp. 143–163). Chicago: University of Chicago Press.
27. Brewster, C. (2006). Comparing HR policies and practices across geographical borders. In G. Stahl & I. Bjorkman (Eds.), *Handbook of research in International human resource management* (pp. 68–90). Cheltenham: Edward Elgar.
28. Freeman, C. (1995). The "National System of Innovation" in historical perspective. *Cambridge Journal of Economics, 19,* 5–24.
29. Lundvall, B. A. (2007). National innovation systems—Analytical concept and development tool. *Industry and Innovation, 14,* 95–119.
30. Parry, E., & Tyson, S. (2011). Desired goals and actual outcomes of e-HRM. *Human Resource Management Journal, 21,* 335–354.

31. Tempel, A., Edwards, T., Ferner, A., Muller-Camen, M., & Wächter, H. (2006). Subsidiary responses to institutional duality: Collective representation practices of US multinationals in Britain and Germany. *Human Relations, 59,* 1543–1570.
32. Ghiringhelli, C., & Lazazzara, A. (2016). Perceived training needs for effective virtual teams: An exploratory study. In: F. D'Ascenzo, M. Magni, A. Lazazzara & S. Za (Eds.), *Blurring the boundaries through digital innovation. Individual, organizational, and societal challenges* (pp. 20–34). Berlin: Springer International Publisher.
33. Zhang, Y. (2005). Age, gender, and internet attitudes among employees in the business world. *Computers in Human Behavior, 21,* 1–10.
34. Kossek, E. E. (1987). Human resources management innovation. *Human Resource Management, 26,* 71–92.
35. Lin, C. Y.-Y. (1999). Human resource information systems: Implementation in Taiwan. *Research and Practice in Human Resource Management, 5,* 57–72.
36. Thatcher, S. M. B., Foster, W., & Zhu, L. (2006). B2B e-commerce adoption decisions in Taiwan: The interaction of cultural and other institutional factors. *Electronic Commerce Research and Applications, 5,* 92–104.
37. Wolfe, R. (1995). Human resources management innovations: Determinants of their adoption and implementation. *Human Resource Management, 34,* 313–327.
38. Tansley, C., & Watson, T. (2000). Strategic exchange in the development of HRIS. *New Technology, Work and Employment, 15,* 108–122.
39. Kelly, J., & Gennard, J. (1996). The role of personnel directors on the board of directors. *Personnel Review, 25,* 7–24.
40. Quinn, J. B., & Hilmer, F. G. (1994). Strategic outsourcing. *Sloan Management Review, 35,* 43–55.
41. Lacity, M. C., Willcocks, L. P., & Feeny, D. F. (1996). The value of selective IT outsourcing. *Sloan Management Review, 37,* 13–25.
42. Brewster, C., Hegewisch, A., Mayne, L., & Tregaskis, O. (1994). Methodology of the Price Waterhouse Cranfield Project. In C. Brewster & A. Hegewisch (Eds.), *Policy and practice in European human resource management* (pp. 230–245). London: Routledge.
43. Cornell University, INSEAD, WIPO. (2015). *The global innovation index 2015: Effective innovation policies for development.* Fontainebleau, Ithaca, and Geneva.
44. Jackson, P., Runde, J., Dobson, P., & Richter, N. (2015). Identifying mechanisms influencing the emergence and success of innovation within national economies: A realist approach. *Policy Sciences,* 1–24.
45. Lazazzara, A., & Ghiringhelli, C. Strategic HRM and e-HRM adoption: An empirical study. In: A. Harfouche & M. Cavallari (Eds.), *The social relevance of the organisation of information systems and ICT.* Berlin: Springer International Publisher.
46. Currie, W. L. (2009). Contextualising the IT artefact: Towards a wider research agenda for IS using institutional theory. *Information Technology & People, 22,* 63–77.

Consumer Satisfaction and Loyalty in Digital Markets: Exploring the Impact of Their Antecedents

Ivan Russo, Ilenia Confente and Antonio Borghesi

Abstract Customer loyalty is even more important in the e-commerce since the costs of serving customers decrease as long as the customers' number increases. Convenience, variety seeking, trust, security, social interaction, returns policy are helpful elements to predict e-satisfaction, and this latter, constitutes the primary cause of e-loyalty. The aim of the paper is to better explore the impact of different drivers in enhancing the satisfaction and loyalty perceived by customer when purchasing online in a B2C context. Results show that not all the antecedents represent drivers enhancing customer satisfaction and loyalty. In particular, the constructs related to ease of use and trust on the e-retailer/s are found to be always positively linked to all the three dependent variables (satisfaction, repurchase intention and WOM), while monetary savings and security do not impact on these three outcomes. Considering the effect of return policy, it impacts both on satisfaction and overall loyalty.

Keywords Customer loyalty · Customer satisfaction · Ease of use · Trust · Monetary savings · Security · Return policy · Word of mouth

1 Introduction

The turnover from e-commerce in Italy is estimated to have been worth 28.8 billion euros in 2015 with a growing by 19% compared to 2014 [1].

Moreover consumers are not only becoming more confident with the e-commerce but seem to be willing to share their purchasing experiences and their

I. Russo (✉) · I. Confente · A. Borghesi
Università degli Studi di Verona, Dipartimento di Economia Aziendale,
University of Verona, Verona, Italy
e-mail: ivan.russo@univr.it

I. Confente
e-mail: ilenia.confente@univr.it

A. Borghesi
e-mail: antonio.borghesi@univr.it

© Springer International Publishing AG 2018
C. Rossignoli et al. (eds.), *Digital Technology and Organizational Change*,
Lecture Notes in Information Systems and Organisation 23,
https://doi.org/10.1007/978-3-319-62051-0_12

feelings, giving a judgment that can become useful for other consumers as well. Four out of ten online retailers think giving the customers a sense of convenience and offering them support during the purchase process are other important factors that could boost the conversion rate. At the same time in today's environment the conversion rate doesn't mean to have the consumer's loyalty thus research is struggling to find a precise way of measuring online loyalty, although in our knowledge it does not exist just one way [2]. Then, high levels of e-service quality can increase the intentions of the consumers to revisit the web site and the chance of a positive word of mouth. Nevertheless satisfaction and loyalty depend both on context-general and context-specific determinants. Moreover consumers now have multiple touch points with brands (online, mobile, and in-store) and use all of them to inform their purchases. The benefits of online shopping go beyond the monetary saving, it is also a time saving purchasing process as it can be carried out with little efforts and at the most convenient time for the consumers. Maybe one of the greatest revolution that e-commerce brought has been the opportunity of a clear and constant comparison of price for the same good and across various brands. Despite this, according with DHL 2015 the 27% of all online-ordered clothes are returned by customers. It is increasingly important for e-tailers to offer the appropriate returns policy as this will attract online customers [3].

This activity represents one of the less explored driver and it consists of the ability by the e-retailer to manage returns product. The process of having to return the good, if it doesn't fit properly, might be seen as an excessive bother for the consumer therefore discouraging the transactions.

The aim of the paper is to better explore the impact of different drivers in enhancing the satisfaction and loyalty perceived by customer when purchasing online in a B2C context. In particular, a specific attention will be given to the capabilities of e-retailer to manage product returns and how this activity can contribute in building customer loyalty and in the intention to repurchase from the same e-retailer.

2 Literature Background

Loyalty is well known as an important element to investigate in order to enhance the relationship between the company and its customers. Particularly, e-loyalty is "the customer's favorable attitude towards an electronic business, resulting in repeat purchasing behaviour" [4, p. 42]. Consumer loyalty is even more important in the e-commerce since the costs of serving customers decrease as long as the customers' number increases. Convenience, variety seeking, trust, security and social interaction are helpful elements to predict e-satisfaction, and this latter, constitutes the primary cause of e-loyalty. As a consequence, e-retailers should invest in e-satisfaction to enhance e-loyalty [5, 6].

A precise way of measuring online loyalty does not exist, so Toufaily et al. [7] conducted a literature review to sum up what researchers have discovered about loyalty to a e-commerce platform. They noticed that the theoretical foundations of e-loyalty can be considered as the same of the classic one. Loyalty can be cognitive (brand performance aspects), affective (emotions), conative (intention to repeatedly purchase), action (conversion of intentions to action). Determinants of online customer loyalty are related to customer characteristics (trust, psychological elements), product attributes (quality, price perception), sellers characteristics (reliability and strategy) and website features (customization, content, design).

However, loyalty can be damaged by frustration incidents. Problems with loyalty programs awaken negative feelings that are expressed through a negative eWOM: low rating reviews, non-recommendations, switching initiatives, revenge [8]. Satisfaction and loyalty depend both on context-general and context-specific determinants. Ease of use and customer service, included in the context-general determinants, show a positive relation with satisfaction. Security also can affect loyalty, while reliability and information quality are good predictors of satisfaction and loyalty [9].

Moreover, trust is the key to maintain continuity in online retailing [10].

One important driver that this study has included as an antecedent of online outcomes, such as e-loyalty and e-satisfaction, is product returns management. Managing returns is one of the main drivers in the decision of buying online. The paper of Griffis et al. [11] deals with an e-commerce website that sells books, DVDs and CDs and focuses on the relationship between an experience of product returns and subsequent shopping behaviour in the book context. Returns experienced consumers purchase more frequently, more items per order and items with a higher value than consumers who have never experienced a return. Even if restocking and managing returns practices, that facilitate product returns by immediately (or at an agreed date and time) taking back, are costly, the increased customers' loyalty covers them.

While many studies look at product returns as an extra cost, recent research has started to perceive them as a way to lower the perceived risk of current and future purchases [12]. Petersen et al. [13] found that a company can increase its short and long-term profits if it is able to account for the perceived risk related to product returns and if it manages the related costs.

Thus, the return policy is a mixed signal, since some e-tailers use it to communicate quality and, at the same time, some consumers perceive it as a quality signal [12, 14, 15].

The goal of the paper is to better explore the impact of the above characteristics in consumer satisfaction, loyalty and WOM. Table 1 lists the hypothesis of our study.

3 Methodology

We conducted a nationwide (in Italy) online survey among 283 respondents. We invited them through an online link to the survey and we asked them to respond to a set of questions that described themselves and their behavior as online shoppers.

Table 1 Hypotheses

Hypotheses	
Monetary saving deriving from online purchasing enhances customer satisfaction (H1a) customer loyalty (H1b) and WOM widespread intention (H1c)	H1
The easy of use of adopting the online retailer's platform enhances customer satisfaction (H2a) customer loyalty (H2b) and WOM widespread intention (H2c)	H2
The perceived security of the online retailers' platform enhances customer satisfaction (H3a) customer loyalty (H3b) and WOM widespread intention (H3c)	H3
The perceived trust to the online retailers' platform enhances customer satisfaction (H4a) customer loyalty (H4b) and WOM widespread intention (H4c)	H4
The product returns management of the online retailer enhances customer satisfaction (H5a) customer loyalty (H5b) and WOM widespread intention (H5c)	H5
Customer satisfaction leads to improve customer loyalty (H6a) and willingness to widespread WOM (H6b)	H6

Table 2 Descriptive statistics

Variables	Min	Max	Average mean	St. Dev.	Items (n.)	Cronbach (α)
Monetary savings	1	7	5.24	1.36	3	0.87
Easy of use	1	7	5.68	1.12	4	0.80
Security	1	7	5.62	1.08	4	0.88
Trust	1	7	5.58	1.11	4	0.89
Product returns management	1	7	4.80	1.38	4	0.85
Customer satisfaction	1	7	5.99	1.02	4	0.92
Customer loyalty	1	7	3.94	1.14	9	0.90
Word of mouth	1	7	5.62	1.24	3	0.87

The survey is constituted by three parts: the first one related to the demographic characteristics of participants (age, gender, education, etc.), their previous purchases online (category of good/service; number of purchases, average spending, etc.) and information about e-retailers chosen by participants.

Second one, we asked respondents to provide their evaluation about a list of antecedents that can contribute in building e-loyalty (particularly monetary saving, easy of use, security, trust). Participants were asked to provide an evaluation of the importance of these elements when purchasing through an online retailer (using a 7 points-Likert scale from 1 = highly disagree to 7 = highly agree). We also added questions related to our dependent variables, that are the overall satisfaction related to the online retailer plus the willingness to widespread positive Word of Mouth (WOM) and to repurchase the product/service (customer loyalty) from the same e-retailer (evaluated in a range from 1 = very unlikely to 7 = very likely). All the constructs were adopted from previous research [2, 10, 12, 16–18]. Table 2 provides a detailed list of these variables. As indicated, the variables that are perceived as more important/relevant are easy of use (mean = 5.68) and security (mean = 5.62). About the outcome variables, respondents seem to be highly satisfied with the online retailer (average mean = 5.99) and very inclined to widespread positive WOM about it (mean = 5.62) but less loyal to it (mean = 3.94).

The third one of the survey regarded the evaluation of product return management, particularly the evaluation of recovery responsiveness and policy as one of the potential drivers for satisfaction and loyalty in the online context. So this section contained questions regarding the importance of this driver and the evaluation of the last (if any) product return experience by participants.

Data analysis was conducted through three regressions using SPSS software. The three dependent variables were e-loyalty, e-satisfaction and WOM.

4 Findings

Results show that not all the antecedents represent drivers enhancing customer satisfaction (SAT), loyalty (LOY) and the willingness to widespread positive word of mouth (WOM). In particular, the constructs related to ease of use and trust on the e-retailer/s are found to be always significant (p-value < 0.000) and positively linked to all the three dependent variables (satisfaction, loyalty and WOM). As a consequence, H2 and H4 are fully supported. With regards to the benefit related to monetary savings and security, these constructs do not impact on the three outcomes variables and so H1 and H3 are not supported.

Considering the effect of product return management and policy, it impacts on all the three variables supporting H5.

In addition our model tested the effect of satisfaction as a driver for building customer loyalty and also to enhance WOM wide spreading. Our findings support these two relationships, confirming our hypothesis 6 (a and b).

Among the demographic characteristics of the sample, we did not found any gender or age effects on all the outcomes, while one variable related to the frequency of purchasing online regardless the amount spent, affects all the three dimensions (p-value < 0.05). This means that participants who are heavy users of e-commerce for high volume of products and services are likely to perceive a higher satisfaction and are more willing to repurchase online again and say positive comment about the e-retailer.

5 Implications, Limitations and Future Research

The role of consumer loyalty as a key contributor to firm competitive advantage has been consistently highlighted by marketing scholars.

Consumers buying online are increasing on a daily basis and data prove that they are more interested in purchasing online.

A recent report by DHL [3, p. 30] concluded its recommendations with a specific direction for a company "*Omni-channel is here to stay. Companies that enable consumers to find, buy, receive, and return goods most conveniently and at the lowest cost are being rewarded with increased customer loyalty, revenue growth, differentiation, and profitability.*"

On the one hand our paper contributes to confirm the validity of previous models about the direct correlation between some specific antecedents of customer satisfaction and loyalty. This is the case of trust and ease of use variables that are important when deciding to purchase using a specific e-commerce platform. On the other hand some other drivers are not supported in our research. For instance monetary saving does not contribute to a positive experience: it is not particularly surprising in the era of the need to have online and offline channels integrated.

That is a new challenge for companies, starting with an analysis of the main issues on the online channel; one of the main concerns of companies is to align the consumers experience with their expectation, where returns policy is becoming a relevant part of that.

Then the major contribution of the study is related to the analysis of managing returns products with an important role of the purchase experience. Return experiences that require high levels of customer effort can have a negative impact on customer's satisfaction/loyalty with the return operations. This suggests that managers must critically evaluate their procedures for product returns. The present study represents an initial step into the analysis of the different drivers to deliver satisfaction, loyalty and WOM in the e-commerce.

This research enters several uncharted territories regarding the loyalty in the e-commerce context. The findings are restricted to the limitations of the study design and strictly linked with future research.

As such, one limitation of our study is that we considered an Italian sample of consumers of a specific age range.

Since returns policy assumes its relevance in the e-commerce context, future research should investigate this particular field, taking into account different websites and product categories, with the aim of assisting managers to develop good return policies and to find a precise guideline to encourage users to share their personal experiences in order to improve the reputation in managing returns.

Future research should explore how the impact of these antecedents on customer loyalty changes when other variables are considered or changed.

Nowadays cyber-security plays a central role in the global debate, however our data showed security is not significant for our sample. This probably happens for the millennials, who constitute our sample as they are digital native with high-confidence in internet usage. This controversial aspect needs further studies in the future.

Moreover, because of the complex reality in which the phenomena of customer loyalty manifests itself, some scholars sought to determine all the possible "recipes" that build strong customer loyalty, arguing that the application of the complexity theory tenets can provide a more accurate understanding of what generates customer loyalty [19]. Future studies and limitations on that stream could be conceptualized in a more complex way, particularly understanding other drivers in the era of servitization [20] that can be included in the model and compare among different regions and retailer's characteristics how to create loyalty in e-commerce context [21, 22]. Finally, another future research to develop would be to verify the moderation effect of product returns between customer satisfaction and customer loyalty.

References

1. https://www.casaleggio.it/focus/rapporto-e-commerce-in-italia-2015/.
2. Fang, Y., Qureshi, I., Sun, H., McCole, P., Ramsey, E., & Lim, K. H. (2014). Trust, satisfaction, and online repurchase intention: The moderating role of perceived effectiveness of E-Commerce institutional mechanisms. *MIS Quarterly, 38*(2), 407–427.
3. http://www.dhl.com/content/dam/downloads/g0/about_us/logistics_insights/dhl_trendreport_omnichannel.pdf (2015).
4. Anderson, R. E., & Srinivasan, S. S. (2003). E-satisfaction and e-loyalty: A contingency framework. *Psychology & Marketing, 20*(2), 123–138.
5. Valvi, A. C., & Fragkos, K. C. (2012). Critical review of the e-loyalty literature: A purchase-centred framework. *Electronic Commerce Research, 12*(3), 331–378.
6. Tontini, G. (2016). Identifying opportunities for improvement in online shopping sites. *Journal of Retailing and Consumer Services, 31*, 228–238.
7. Toufaily, E., Ricard, L., & Perrien, J. (2013). Customer loyalty to a commercial website: Descriptive meta-analysis of the empirical literature and proposal of an integrative model. *Journal of Business Research, 66*(9), 1436–1447.
8. Tuzovic, S. (2010). Frequent (flier) frustration and the dark side of word-of-web: Exploring online dysfunctional behavior in online feedback forums. *Journal of Services Marketing, 24*(6), 446–457.
9. Carlson, J., O'Cass, A., & Ahrholdt, D. (2015). Assessing customers' perceived value of the online channel of multichannel retailers: A two country examination. *Journal of Retailing and Consumer Services, 27*, 90–102.
10. Chen, S. C. (2012). The customer satisfaction–loyalty relation in an interactive e-service setting: The mediators. *Journal of Retailing and Consumer Services, 19*(2), 202–210.
11. Griffis, S. E., Rao, S., Goldsby, T. J., & Niranjan, T. T. (2010). The customer consequences of returns in online retailing: An empirical analysis. *Journal of Operations Management, 30*(4), 282–294.
12. Hsieh, P. L. (2013). Perceived opportunism (PO) in e-return service encounters. *Managing Service Quality: An International Journal, 23*(2), 96–110.
13. Petersen, J. A., & Kumar, V. (2015). Perceived risk, product returns, and optimal resource allocation: Evidence from a field experiment. *Journal of Marketing Research, 52*(2), 268–285.
14. Pei, Z., Paswan, A., & Yan, R. (2014). E-tailer's return policy, consumer's perception of return policy fairness and purchase intention. *Journal of Retailing and Consumer Services, 21*(3), 249–257.
15. Bonifield, C., Cole, C., & Schultz, R. L. (2010). Product returns on the Internet: A case of mixed signals? *Journal of Business Research, 63*(9), 1058–1065.
16. Mollenkopf, D. A., Rabinovich, E., Laseter, T. M., & Boyer, K. K. (2007). Managing internet product returns: A focus on effective service operations. *Decision Sciences, 38*(2), 215–250.

17. Kim, C., Galliers, R. D., Shin, N., Ryoo, J. H., & Kim, J. (2012). Factors influencing Internet shopping value and customer repurchase intention. *Electronic Commerce Research and Applications, 11*(4), 374–387.
18. Chiu, C. M., Wang, E. T., Fang, Y. H., & Huang, H. Y. (2014). Understanding customers' repeat purchase intentions in B2C e-commerce: The roles of utilitarian value, hedonic value and perceived risk. *Information Systems Journal, 24*(1), 85–114.
19. Russo, I., Confente, I., Gligor, D. M., & Autry, C. W. (2016). To be or not to be (loyal): Is there a recipe for customer loyalty in the B2B context? *Journal of Business Research, 69*(2), 888–896.
20. Confente, I., Buratti, A., & Russo, I. (2015). The role of servitization for small firms: Drivers versus barriers. *International Journal of Entrepreneurship and Small Business, 26*(3), 12–331.
21. Mola, L., Russo, I. (2016). From e-Marketplace to e-Supply chain: Re-conceptualizing the relationship between virtual and physical processes. In *Empowering Organizations* (pp. 133–145). Berlin: Springer International Publishing.
22. Russo, I., Confente, I. (2017). *Customer loyalty and supply chain management: Business-to-business customer loyalty analysis, routledge studies in business organizations and networks*. New York.

Unveiling the Big Data Adoption in Banks: Strategizing the Implementation of a New Technology

Eduardo H. Diniz, Simone S. Luvizan, Márcia Cassitas Hino
and Priscila Cardoso Ferreira

Abstract This study describes the process of big data adoption in three major Brazilian banks and unveils the process of implementing a new technology platform in a "pluralistic context". Besides requiring huge investments, big data implementation also demands an articulation between the many centers of power within the bank and a redefinition of concepts once dominant in the organization. The four moments of the translation model proposed by the Actor-Network Theory—problematization, interessment, enrolment and mobilization—are used as elements for describing and understanding the big data adoption journey. A cross-case analysis unveils a similar model for incorporating big data in the three studied banks. Initially brought into the bank by a small group of pioneers, the new concept of big data is explored by study groups created to amplify knowledge about the concept and related technologies. These pioneer groups then start working on connecting with other business areas, on the path to consolidate the need of big data in the bank. Thus the purpose of this study is to understand the process managers inside the organization from the point they became aware of the relevance of big data for their businesses and how they create conditions for it to be incorporated to the bank's corporative strategy.

Keywords Banking · Big data adoption · Strategizing process

E.H. Diniz (✉) · S.S. Luvizan · M.C. Hino · P.C. Ferreira
Escola de Administração de Empresas de São Paulo at Fundação
Getulio Vargas, São Paulo, São Paulo, Brazil
e-mail: eduardo.diniz@fgv.br

S.S. Luvizan
e-mail: sluvizan@hotmail.com

M.C. Hino
e-mail: marciahino@uol.com.br

P.C. Ferreira
e-mail: priscilacf@gmail.com

M.C. Hino
Instituto Superior de Administração e Economida do Mercosul,
Curitiba, Paraná, Brazil

© Springer International Publishing AG 2018   149
C. Rossignoli et al. (eds.), *Digital Technology and Organizational Change*,
Lecture Notes in Information Systems and Organisation 23,
https://doi.org/10.1007/978-3-319-62051-0_13

1 Introduction

This paper aims to contribute to the strategy-as-practice perspective by describing the adoption of strategic information systems, big data applications, in three major banks in the Brazilian market. As pointed out by some authors [1], strategy-as-practice needs to be understood in its materiality and can benefit from investigations in the field of information systems implementation. Big data implementation is seen as one opportunity for understanding Information System strategizing.

This strategizing process is continuously dealing with tensions between planned strategy and emergence, efficiency and flexibility, environment opportunities and uncertainties [2]. It is also influenced by knowledge and power [2], what reinforce the need of approaches that investigate the entire complexity of the ecosystem where it takes place.

By unveiling the process of implementing a new technology that promises to lead firms to a "long term strategic differentiator" [3] this paper intends to bring more light on the phenomenon of strategic IS implementation by allowing a further understanding on a truly critical challenge which is how to implement strategic change associated with this system and avoiding the inability "to realize the strategic intent of implemented, available system capabilities" [4].

Given its novelty and strategic role inside organizations, big data implementation process raises questions on emerging versus planned strategies inside banks, what provides opportunities to link this process with the strategizing literature. Previous IS strategizing studies describe tensions between formal and informal approaches, human and IT aspects, standardized and flexible procedures, highlighting the dynamics between IT and business personnel, however usually lacking the understanding of power considerations [2].

Banks can be considered as pluralistic organizations for being characterized by diffuse power and knowledge-based work processes [5]. In such pluralistic contexts, Actor Network-Theory (ANT) [6, 7] offers an opportunity to describe and explain how support networks are built inside banks during the process of adopting new technologies. This theoretical approach is particularly useful for describing the emergence of new strategic technology in organizations with significant fragmentation of power and objectives and is considered a sound alternative for investigating the adoption of new technologies particularly in such pluralistic contexts [5]. Since big data demands substantial investments and many internal changes in processes and policies, its adoption affects a broad number of people and areas in the bank.

Following the Actor-Network Theory precepts, this study was developed to provide a script to understand big data implementation in banks. A cross-case analysis within the studied banks unveils a similar model for big data incorporation, from the pioneers of the concept inside banks to the creation of study groups to expand knowledge about the concept and the technologies related to it. Articulation of this initial group with other areas in the bank and definition of the potential applications that will eventually justify the required investment come next on the path to big data adoption. This study also reveals how this articulation process takes place using specific communication elements, such as proof of concept, to exemplify the applications of such technology within the bank.

2 Emergence of Big Data in Banks

As pointed out by some researchers [3, 8], big data has captured the attention of senior managers like few other technologies did before. Thus, for the purpose of this study, more important than adopting a precise definition of big data, we seek to understand how and why those managers became aware of the relevance of this new technology for their businesses and started to create conditions for it to be incorporated to the banks corporative strategy. Previous studies recognize the importance of different actors, like vendors and adopters, building the discourses that support new technologies adoption, but highlight the lack of knowledge we have about it [9].

Banks are among organizations that have already envisioned the potential benefits of using big data [10, 11]. This is coherent with the banks' history of intensive use of ICT and with the challenges of data management and competition in this area [12]. As banks search for innovative approaches for dealing with the new data management challenges, big data emerges with solutions and tools for managing the incoming data and the traditional established database with great ability [10, 11].

On the other hand, the current challenges faced by banks are not limited to data volume or management, but have to do with other transformations in this market [11]. There are changes in the expectations of clients, who are more and more used to technological applications and virtual services [10]. Whether in emerging economies or in stabilized markets looking for new niches to compensate the saturation of traditional customers and banking products, there is a growing number of clients and services.

For major banks, particularly in the retail market, big data is being used to understand aspects of the customer relationship that they were previously unable to get at. For big banks, which are already struggling to deal with the huge amount of transactional data, the priority focus of big data implementation relies on structured data, rather than focusing on broader analysis based on customer services usage and consumption patterns [3]. However, others expect major impacts from big data coming from analysis on unstructured data, like sentiment analysis based on data gathered from bank clients on social media platforms [13].

The realization of big data potential benefits in banking goes beyond the technical aspects, implicating on the banking organizational structure and mobilizing a plurality of actors inside and outside the bank. The lack of historical information make the room to big data implementation strategy be defined as a dynamic, iterative and learning process, like observed in other researches analyzing the strategizing process in IS field as a whole [2].

3 Actor-Network Theory (ANT)

This study uses the ANT concepts to tell a story about big data adoption in three banks in Brazil, a conceptual approach that allows a holistic view of this phenomenon. ANT elements can appropriately frame the process by which this adoption took place, by identifying the actors, their relationships and how they evolved over time towards the objective of positioning big data solutions as the irreversible path for banks data management evolution.

ANT offers a vocabulary for interpreting and describing the adoption of a technology based on the connection (network) between human and non-human entities (actors), providing a social and technical description of the process of ordinance and associations of heterogeneous elements. This vocabulary allows the elaboration of a narrative that follows the entities involved in the incorporation process of a new strategic technology, like big data, without imposing a predefined analytical framework (structure, values, etc.).

ANT allows an understanding of big data adoption that goes beyond the technological issue, unveiling also the social connections developed to make it the emerging solution for the new data management problems in banks. The adoption of big data involves a relationship between an ample and diversified set of actors, since it impacts the organizational structure, and demands large investments and great changes in the internal and external policies of the banking environment. ANT allows the identification of how these actors link together within the networks to consolidate a translation strategy, focusing on the dynamics of this phenomenon's trajectory, instead of centering on the duality of cause/impact [14].

ANT is an alternative way of studying pluralistic contexts because it helps to describe and explain how it is possible to build networks that define technologies from a strategic standpoint [5]. ANT provides tools to describe and explain how, despite the fragmentation of power and goals, it is possible to create support around definitions of a particular technology up to the point it is taken for granted. For ANT, the adoption of a strategic technological artifact (e.g., big data) can be considered an organizational strategy, since its realization becomes true by the creation of an organizational actors (human and non-human) network that support it.

Among ANT's key elements [15], this study will especially employ the concept of "translation" that represents the interactive process occurring between the diverse "actants" in a social network through the consolidation process of one solution recognized as the only way of solving a given problem. In this study, the translation approach is used to describe the interactions between diverse groups inside the bank during the adoption of big data as a new technology platform for data management.

For ANT, there are four moments in translation: problematization, interessment, enrolment and mobilization [5]. Problematization identifies the moment when a problem is defined and a particular solution is presented by an initial set of actors as an "obligatory passage point". Interessment marks the movements of this initial group to line up the solution defined with the main actor's interests. Enrolment is characterized by the stages of consensus built up among the diverse actors around the negotiated solution. Mobilization comprehends the articulation needed to define an implementation model, considering the means to make it happen. In this way, the definition of a strategic decision for adopting a new technology that will impact many organizational processes is related to the creation of a network for supporting such a decision and that dynamically emerges through this translation process. Strategizing, in this sense, is a 'translation' process [5].

ANT has shown to be an appropriate alternative "for the generation of detailed and contextualized empirical knowledge" in the Information Systems field [16], particularly when there is a wish to unveil "implicit parts of techno-scientific devices" [17]. For similar reasons, other authors also encourage the use of ANT in IS research [15].

ANT also considers the ways in which certain objects can act as agents (named 'actants' by ANT researchers). For example, strategic plans, once constituted, can create affordances or constraints as far as concerns human actors. Thus, the use of ANT for investigating strategizing in pluralistic contexts is appealing [5]. The appropriateness of the ANT approach to this study is even more explicit if the many examples of its use in cases dealing with the implementation of technological artifacts are considered.

4 Methodological Procedures

Three major banks operating in Brazil were selected to participate in this study, representing each of the three macro-segments of this business sector (one public bank, one private Brazilian bank and one foreign institution). The participants agreed to supply information since the interviewees and institutions could not be identified.

Some dialogical principles are recommended to produce significance from empirical material in critical and interpretative research [18], such is the case of this study. They are: authenticity, plausibility, criticism, and reflexivity. The following description connects the methodological procedures employed in this research study to each one of these principles.

To guarantee authenticity, this study contains interviews carried out between May/2014 and May/2015 with 13 executives, 6 from business areas and 7 from IT areas, with an average of more than 20 years' service in their companies. The number of interviewees per bank was: 4 from the public bank, 3 from the multi-national bank, and 6 from the Brazilian private bank. Two interviews were conducted remotely, while the others were conducted personally, with an average duration of 1.3 h. The interviewees have an average time in the company of over 20 years and six of them (two in each bank) hold high-level executive positions. Authenticity is also guaranteed by the fact that two of the authors of this study have had significant professional experience with the studied banks. Internal documents from these banks and from *Febraban* (Brazilian Federation of Banks) publications about big data were also used as information sources.

To make sense of the story to be told and, therefore, guarantee the plausibility principle, interviews were recorded, ensuring the veracity of the gathered information and providing the possibility of detailed reviews of the collected data. All documents provided were the subject of careful analysis and checked for possible different interpretations among the authors.

The critical perspective of the study is supported by the theoretical approach used, which intends to make readers reexamine the assumptions made in the process of introducing new technology. ANT provides a theoretical alternative that goes beyond the description of diffusing new technology, showing that the stability envisioned in the diffusion models is provisional and represents "only the 'tip of the iceberg', hiding a multifaceted and complex set of social-technical practices" [5].

After listening to all interviews, we organized a storyline that made possible to identify a pathway where the translation moments could be described for each bank. Based on these storylines, we then created a reflexive cross case analysis to describe the translation moments related to the introduction of big data in each bank, providing a very personal interpretation of big data in the studied banks.

5   Cases Description

There follows a brief description of each case to provide the reader an overview of the context of the three banks investigated in this study.

5.1   Bank B1

At Bank B1, a public bank, the interest in big data technologies first appeared in 2010, when a new technological platform was prospected in order to deal with the challenge of the high volume of data being produced during implementation of the unified customer database. To the data coming from clients that were generated in the traditional channels was added a large volume of external information, in particular, non-structured data from mobile devices, like georeferenced data, and from social media, like Facebook and Twitter.

By 2011, Bank B1 was unable to find any technology in the market that could meet its requirements for integrating the massive amount of new data into the existing and fully functioning Customer Relationship Management (CRM) model that had been implemented in the bank almost one past decade. It was realized that adopting emerging technologies, which at the time were associated with big data, this evolution could be provided. In the words of one of the Bank B1 interviewees:

> Within the CRM functional model created in 2011, there was a component to which no technological solution could solve. Currently it's possible to realize that this demand can be easily attended by big data, with all processing power to deal with big volumes of data.

In 2012, big data was included in the strategic IT planning of Bank B1 and in 2013 a multidisciplinary team, including personnel from all IT subareas, was created. This group aimed at studying big data technologies to create a conceptual and structural model for coping with the new necessities of the bank's business areas. According to one of the Bank B1 interviews:

> The multidisciplinary team started to study and deepen in the technology. It was an initiative started by IT Board of Directors, involving people from IT Architecture, Development and infrastructure teams. All IT areas were represented

As this task could not be carried out only by IT personnel, people from business areas joined the team to facilitate the discussion of non-technical, although critical questions that emerged from the big data study. Since knowledge of this field was still very technical, a proof of concept, shaped in a small and limited application, was developed to facilitate the knowledge sharing process. After this proof of concept, one of the regional customer relationship areas requested the first application of big data in Bank B1. In the opinion of one IT manager at Bank B1:

> The big challenge [at that time] was to have everyone in the same page. That way should be possible to show the whole organization the advantages of this new technology, how far we can go with it.

The dissemination of the concept of big data to other business areas was made possible by spreading knowledge about the possibilities of this new data management platform. That was the role of the multidisciplinary team that then organized meetings with some business areas in order to design specific solutions to be tested in controlled environments.

By 2014, Bank B1 had already prepared an operational structure to support big data solutions, while it continued prospecting new technologies in the market.

5.2   Bank B2

At Bank B2, a multinational private bank, executives in the business areas first learned about big data in 2010 in a presentation made by technology suppliers during an international conference. In this initial contact, big data was introduced as a solution for the management of big repositories and the real value of investing in such a solution was still not very clear. One of the interviewees at Bank B2 reminded:

> The Big Data expression was first heard in some international conferences [...] this terminology, already used in the market [...] was presented as one of the solutions for huge volume of data repository [...] It was not clear what that meant.

In 2012/13, due to a drastic growth in data volume in Bank B2, the subject was once again brought to the table. Executives recognized that the existing data warehouse solution, which was only few years old, was insufficient for meeting the current capacity and response time needs. The bank intensified its search for a new approach to organizing its data environment and big data started being seen as an appropriate alternative to this end. However, the institution would need to understand that the current technology was exhausted and adopting a new one was a point of no return. Although they knew that important changes should be done to implement this new solution, there was some inertia in the process. As one executive of Bank B2 said:

> We realize that it was a no return point when we tried to improve the technological solution used that time, and there was nothing else to do. We contacted the supplier, and they asked us to change things, to implement others, but, in fact, nothing changed.

In 2013, with the support of their international headquarters, a multidisciplinary forum was created to make strategic decisions regarding data management. From this forum emerged the necessity of establishing a CDO (Chief Data Officer) position within the bank and the need to create a pattern and indicators for monitoring data quality and control. One interviewee from Bank B2 said:

> many decisions related to data management were distributed in the company [...] some committees to discuss data strategy were created and I started to attended them. It was when the need of a CDO (Chief Data Officer) started to be discussed, as well as implementation of data quality standards and control over sensitive data.

This forum initially comprised people from business areas, but without the participation of the IT area. As these discussions would demand a more technological point of view and few people in that group had any technical knowledge, when sub-groups were created to deal with specific questions, and technology was one of them, the IT people were invited to join.

During 2014, this multidisciplinary group initiated discussions on which technology would better fit the institution's needs, and they already included big data. The strategy was to create a data management environment to serve the demands of the business areas. This strategy was supported by the international headquarters, which already had a platform for housing big data projects. The headquarters team also disseminated ideas about big data and its benefits to the bank and provided guidance about how to get the maximum value from existing data. Big data cases were shared to guide and stimulate new project initiatives.

In 2015, for the first time, Bank B2 considered replacing the current technology by a big data solution. As noted by one the Bank B2 executives:

> In 2015, we opened a discussion about how the change from the Data Warehouse to a Big Data structure. The current solution was no longer attending us for years.

Questions were no longer being asked as to whether the bank would invest in big data, but rather how its cost would be apportioned within the company. One challenge identified at Bank B2 was building an unified data environment.

5.3 Bank B3

At Bank B3, a Brazilian private bank, the term big data came up to cope with the need of processing the large volumes of data coming from electronic channels. According to one of the interviewees in Bank B3, even though only dealing with structured internal databases, the challenge of processing this huge volume was an obstacle for some requested analysis:

> That time, the Director of Electronic Channels wanted to have the electronic channels log analyzed, what was being hard to deliver.

In 2011/12, a group of IT specialists and a few people from business areas started researching big data technologies, initially on visiting to companies in Silicon Valley.

At the time, a working group was created inside the bank since the technology suppliers and consultants working with Bank B3 could not provide the needed support because they were also at the big data learning stage. One of the interviewees at Bank B3 was in this group and reminded:

> Technical discussions occurred with the objective of understanding the Big Data concept. I also went to USA with the mission of deepen the understanding of Big Data.

Bank B3's IT executives were introduced to big data in 2012, during presentations by the pioneer working group. In a meeting with seven IT directors, a consensus was created about big data being part of the new data architecture to be developed.

However, it was not yet clear on which applications big data should focus. As few innovative cases in banks were known, the working group asked for support from external consultants to identify proper solutions for fulfilling Bank B3's needs. Then this group proposed a proof of concept to exemplify the value of this new technology to the bank. In the words of one Bank B3 interviewee:

> We discussed the feasibility of an internal case within the modeling team, and we decided to run a proof of concept of big data involving people from the company.

The processing of statistical credit risk models, based on a large volume of data, became the opportunity needed for proposing the first big data application. This proof of concept was then presented to the executive committee, which endorsed it. In the first four months of 2013, with other demands for big data applications coming in, the big data group inside the bank realized that when data quality is low, not even big data technologies can come up with good results. The importance of reinforcing data quality was recognized as being an important part of the big data process in the organization. One Bank B1 interviewee reminded:

> We learnt that enrich the data, data quality, is part of Big Data process.

Paradigm changes were needed to allow the design of big data architecture within Bank B3. There was a lot of confusion between traditional statistical modeling and big data. Even the technology procurement process had to be changed to acquire big data infrastructure solutions. One of the statements reinforced this idea:

> Some companies had already commented about the difficulties, but one thing is to hear about, other thing is to live the experience [...] It was not clear that existed a data quality issue [...] It was a paradigm shift, a learning process.

Suppliers and consultants' recommendations were important, but the internal studies developed were determining factors to consolidate big data in Bank B3, as expressed in one of the interviews:

> It was only possible because were assigned internal people to study about [...] just like a center of excellence.

6 Adoption of Big Data by Banks

The big data discourse was raised by a pioneer group within the banks—people from the IT area in banks B1 and B3; people from business areas in B2 Bank—after recognizing the limitations imposed by current data management platforms, especially regarding volume and data formats. This is the moment of problematization, when big data appears as a potential solution for these banks.

Realizing that the use of this new technology will demand many changes in a bank's data management concepts, study groups were created to generate and share knowledge about big data. This is when interessment is installed. Forums, which are still limited to the groups that first brought the concept to the bank, are then organized. The study groups in banks B1 and B3 were basically formed by IT staff, while in B2 Bank the team was multidisciplinary and dominated by business areas.

In the groups from Business or IT areas searching for technological alternatives for solving specific bank needs, big data emerged as the only solution available or the "obligatory passage point". Multidisciplinary study groups and debate forums about concepts and applications spread the idea of big data as the solution for meeting the challenges of multiple areas inside the banks. Proof of concept and idealization of sound projects helped to establish the alliances and working groups necessary for boosting the adoption of big data in banks. Leaders in the initiatives for big data make the necessary resources available for developing big data projects in banks. Table 1 presents a comparative summary of the cases according to the ANT translation model rational.

The applicable big data solution only materializes if and when IT and the different business areas in the bank work together to define what the main projects should be. To make this enrollment moment happen, it was necessary to develop specific communication instruments. In the case of banks B1 and B3, proof of concept was the key element for convincing the decision makers and creating consensus about the need for big data and the potential benefits of adopting it.

Table 1 Comparative summary of cases in the translation model

	Bank B1	Bank B2	Bank B3
Problematization	IT area; Need to manage data volumes for channel integration; BD emerges as a solution to new volume and the inclusion of mobile and external data from social networks	Teams outside of IT; Contact BD in international conferences; Potential to overcome established limits of Data-Warehouse	Analysis of electronic channels logs; Expertise disseminated to IT and business areas; Simulations for representing potential benefits
Interessment	Multidisciplinary IT team to study of BD solutions available in market	International corporate team requests suggestions for new projects; Forums to disseminate knowledge	Statistical risk model impossible to process with existing tools; risk areas and other viewing BD as a solution for large volumes of data
Enrollment	Proof of Concept sensitizes business areas about BD potential benefits	Multidisciplinary groups; Discussion of concepts to carry out projects	Spread the concept to key leaders of the organization; Responsibility for projects: IT and business; international consultancies help define conceptual model
Mobilization	Demand to develop new applications	Project implementation not started yet	Resource approval by the executive committee to develop database applications; Break paradigm: configuration servers and purchase of IT solutions

Materializing projects means defining who pays the bills. Once the priorities for big data implementation have been defined, it is necessary to decide how to share the costs, thus providing the resources for transforming big data ideas into concrete technological artifacts. On the one hand, modifications in IT structures required by the new demands of big data should not be accounted for in the business areas; on the other, applications' development costs are usually paid by the requesting areas. At Bank B2, the discussion about sharing costs is still on going and, so, no application has been implemented. At banks B1 and B3, proofs of concept helped secure the necessary political support for releasing the resources needed for developing the projects.

The influence of external actors in the big data adoption process in all translation moments was also captured from the interviews, reinforcing the movements that generate the support network that will make such technology available in the organization [1]. Although we could not make any interview with people from outside the banks, in the interviewees' discourse we identified a recurring reference to vendors and the intense external search for better knowledge about big data in conferences and banking sector meetings.

7 Concluding Remarks

Based on the ANT analysis of the three cases, it was possible to describe the strategizing process of implementing big data in banks by showing patterns of strategic decision being established through the creation of networks that lead, in practice, to a translation process in the data management structure of each studied bank. Following the ANT precepts, this study unveiled the stages to be overcome in the process of implementing strategic projects, such as big data, and how this process can be translated into strategizing by building networks inside organizations on the path to create a common view of the technology solution.

Since in pluralistic organizations there are many instances of power and multiple objectives to be accomplished, this strategizing process can only be constructed in synchrony with the network that defines it [5]. By understanding this process of strategic systems implementation as translation, executives and managers, either from business and technology areas, can develop active engagement around objectives that will determine a sequence of routine events leading to strategic orientations inside banks.

This study intends to make an interesting case by using ANT for understanding big data implementation in banks, what brings some level of novelty. Instead of a prescriptive discussion on big data implementation [19], ANT provides a more critical perspective. ANT as a research strategy, in particular on this topic of big data, puts a strong emphasis on empirical enquiry, in part composed of the careful tracing and recording of relational networks, showing "how ordinary and mundane they often are" [16].

Although the study focuses on the Brazilian banking scenario, the degree of technological sophistication of the sector in the country [20] arouses an interest in the results of this study in other contexts.

As limitations of this study, it should be emphasized that it is still at an initial phase and the 13 interviews carried out provided only partial information about this process. It does not include of all the organizations' representatives actors, from inside and outside the banks. Learn about the vendors perspective would be particularly important because of their role in building the dissemination of the big data inside the banks [9].

By focusing on the initial phases of the big data implementation process, this study could also not check if the intended strategic change was successfully achieved by this implementation. Nevertheless, it can show how firms pursuing strategic change go through a process of incorporating a set of highly specialized features introduced by a new strategic technology, such as big data.

References

1. Whittington, R. (2014). Information systems strategy and strategy-as-practice: A joint agenda. *The Journal of Strategic Information Systems, 23*(1), 87–91.
2. Marabelli, M., & Galliers, R. D. (2016). A reflection on information systems strategizing: the role of power and everyday practices. *Information Systems Journal.*
3. Davenport, T. H., & Dyché, J. (2013, May). Big data in big companies. International Institute for Analytics.
4. Arvidsson, V., Holmström, J., & Lyytinen, K. (2014). Information systems use as strategy practice: A multi-dimensional view of strategic information system implementation and use. *The Journal of Strategic Information Systems, 23*(1), 45–61.
5. Denis, J. L., Langley, A., & Rouleau, L. (2007). Strategizing in pluralistic contexts: Rethinking theoretical frames. *Human Relations, 60*(1), 9–215.
6. Callon, M. (1986). The Sociology of an Actor-Network: The case of the electric vehicle. In M. Callon, J. Law, & A. Rip (Eds.), *Mapping the Dynamics of Science and Technology* (pp. 19–34). London: Macmillan Press.
7. Latour, B. (2005). *Reassembling the social: An introduction to actor-network-theory.* Oxford: Oxford University Press.
8. Ekbia, H., Mattioli, M., Kouper, I., Arave, G., Ghazinejad, A., Bowman, T., et al. (2015). Big data, bigger dilemmas: A critical review. *Journal of the Association for Information Science and Technology, 66,* 1523–1545.
9. Miranda, S., Kim, I., & Wang, D. D. (2015). Whose talk is walked? IT decentralizability, vendor versus adopter discourse, and the diffusion of social media versus big data. In *Thirty Sixth International Conference on Information Systems.* Fort Worth.
10. Bedeley, R., & Iyer, L. S. (2014). Big Data Opportunities and Challenges in Banking Industry. In *Proceedings of the Southern Association for Information Systems Conference,* March 21st–22nd, 2014. Macon, GA, USA.
11. Diniz, Eduardo H. (2014). Tecnologias de Back-Office: desafios no mundo interconectado. Administração Bancária: uma visão aplicada. Org.: Clovis De Faro. 1ed.Rio de Janeiro: Editora FGV, 2014, v. 1, pp. 177–200.
12. Constantiou, I. D., & Kallinikos, J. (2015). New games, new rules: big data and the changing context of strategy. *Journal of Information Technology, 30*(1), 44–57.
13. Srivastava, U., & Gopalkrishnan, S. (2015). Impact of big data analytics on banking sector: Learning for Indian banks. *Procedia Computer Science, 50,* 643–652.
14. Heeks, R., & Seo-Zindy, R. (2013). ICTs and Social Movements under Authoritarian Regimes: An Actor-Network Perspective. In *UK Academy for Information Systems Conference Proceedings.*
15. Walsham, G. (2013). Actor-network theory and IS. In *Information Systems and Qualitative Research: Proceedings of the IFIP TC8 WG 8.2 International Conference on Information Systems and Qualitative Research Philadelphia,* (p. 466). Pennsylvania, USA: Springer.
16. Doolin, B., & Lowe, A. (2002). To reveal is to critique: actor-network theory and critical information systems research. *Journal of information technology, 17*(2), 69–78.
17. Heeks, R. (2013) *Development studies research and actor-network theory.* Actor-Network Theory for Development. Working Paper Series. Paper No. 1. Centre for Development Informatics. University of Manchester. Available at http://www.cdi.manchester.ac.uk/resources/ant4d.
18. Pozzebon, M., Rodriguez, C., & Petrini, M. (2014). Dialogical principles for qualitative inquiry: A nonfoundational path. *International Journal of Qualitative Methods, 13,* 293–317.

19. Sanyal, M. K., Bhadra, S. K., & Das, S. (2016). A Conceptual framework for big data implementation to handle large volume of complex data. In *Information Systems Design and Intelligent Applications*, (pp. 455–465). India: Springer.
20. Urdapilleta, E., & Stephanou, C. (2009). Banking in Brazil: Structure, performance, drivers, and policy implications. Policy Research Working Paper 4809. 39p.
21. Lee, N., & Brown, S. (1994). Otherness and the actor network: the undiscovered continent. *The American Behavioral Scientist, 37*(6), 772.

E-learning Effectiveness from a Students' Perspective: An Empirical Study

Leonardo Caporarello, Beatrice Manzoni and Martina Bigi

Abstract E-learning is pervading higher education, being a convenient training opportunity in a busy and demanding society. Despite being a popular phenomenon both in research and in practice, e-learning is however far from being successfully implemented in any context. This is a matter of both inadequate exploration of the learners' perspective and insufficient reflection about the implications for the instructors. This paper focuses on the first aspect, surveying 277 university students about their opinion and experience of e-learning. The results are partially unexpected and expected: first, despite recognizing a positive future trend for e-learning, students are still confused with regard to its meaning and have a only limited awareness of its potentialities. Secondly, despite the general familiarity with its use, there is still a high percentage of students who haven't used e-learning yet and who are uninterested in using it. Thirdly, e-learning seems to present more advantages than disadvantages, yet there are still many areas to work on to make e-learning really works. Based on these findings, we develop some managerial implications for instructors and educational organizations.

Keywords E-learning · Students' satisfaction · Technology-based education · Implications for instructors

1 Introduction

Technology is becoming progressively widespread in education. In particular e-learning is pervading higher education [1, 2], representing a tool for accelerating the formal and informal learning effectiveness [3–6] and being a convenient opportunity in a busy and demanding society.

L. Caporarello (✉) · B. Manzoni
Bocconi University, Milan, Italy
e-mail: leonardo.caporarello@unibocconi.it

M. Bigi
KPMG, Milan, Italy

© Springer International Publishing AG 2018
C. Rossignoli et al. (eds.), *Digital Technology and Organizational Change*,
Lecture Notes in Information Systems and Organisation 23,
https://doi.org/10.1007/978-3-319-62051-0_14

Numerous are the definitions of e-learning in the literature [e.g. 1, 7, 8]; here we refer to this phenomenon as it has been recently defined as "the use of Internet and new multimedia technologies to advance the quality of lear-ning by providing access to resources and services as well as enabling remote exchange and collaboration" [9].

Yet despite being popular, e-learning is far from being successfully implemented in any context.

Although the debate in both academic and practitioner literatures is wide and extensive, the effective contribution of e-learning systems is still an open issue also because most discussions have focused more on technical, financial and adminis-trative aspects than didactic issues [10]. Even those studies focusing on didactic issues have predominantly studied ways for the instructors to use technology. With few exceptions [e.g. 10–12], the students' perspective, in terms of readiness, sat-isfaction, performance with regard to e-learning, is rarely addressed. Instead, especially now that e-learning is widespread, investigating learners is key for making significant improvements in the way we use e-learning systems.

Given this, the aim of this paper is to understand whether e-learning can be considered as a valid and powerful learning system for students' learning and to provide some managerial implications and recommendations for instructors based on the learners' viewpoint.

The paper is structured as follows. First we review the debate on e-learning advantages and disadvantages and critical success factors taking into account the instructors' perspective mainly. Secondly we explore the students' general opinions towards e-learning, and the main advantages and disadvantages they experience in the e-learning context, based on the data we collected. Finally we offer instructors food for thoughts with regard to effective design and use of e-learning systems, by listing some managerial implications.

2 Effective or Ineffective E-learning Systems: This Is the Quest

Information and communications technology are quickly evolving and are now pretty much pervasive in our professional and personal life. Consequently, the use of technology for educational purposed is evolving as well, and e-learning repre-sents one of its most relevant applications [4].

Despite their use, e-learning however remains underutilized [13] particularly if we take into account its potentialities. The real effectiveness of e-learning systems and how to make them really widespread are therefore still under debate.

The adoption of e-learning in education, especially for higher educational institutions has several benefits. E-learning is considered among the best methods of education and has motivated universities to invest their resources on implementing Web-based or online courses. Many studies and authors have provided benefits derived from the adoption of e-learning technologies into schools [14]. These benefits are in particular flexibility, interactivity and efficiency: e-learning can be done at any time, at any place and from anyone; it frees instructors and learners from physical interaction constraints; it is more affordable and it can save time and money [15, 16]. Ensuring the realisation of these benefits is a way to ensure e-learning's effectiveness as well [17].

Instead, the high cost of technology and the lack of a strategy [18, 19] together with a lack of ability to stimulate active interaction within the e-learning course [20] are the main ones driving ineffectiveness.

In general research has proved that understanding these factors is essential to improve e-learning utilization, satisfaction and performance [21].

Starting from them, research has theorized factors affecting the successful implementation of e-learning. For example, Wu et al. [22] identified the learners' cognitive beliefs (self-efficacy and performance expectations), the technological environment (system functionality and content feature), and the social environment (interaction and learning climate); while Basak et al. [16] suggested an even more omni-comprehensive model, including technological, institutional, pedagogical, management, ethical, evaluation, resources, social interaction factors.

However, these models have been predominantly developed and tested from the instructors' point of view, despite the relevance of understanding how all these variables come into play in the learner's experience from his/her own perspective.

In the literature, there is only a limited number of very recent studies investigating how students perceive e-learning, comparing students' preference and self-assessment of learning for onsite, online and hybrid delivery methods [23]; revealing students' readiness [24] and implementation issues with regard to e-learning [12]; exploring the factors that affect online performance in collaborative distance learning environments [10]; understanding the critical success factors for their success [2].

Despite these attempts educational organizations require more research to achieve successful strategies, including the delivery, effectiveness, and acceptance of the courses [15]. In fact, the solution does not lie into offering any conceivable course and attempting to replicate classroom, it surely cannot meet the students' expectations and may lead to failure.

Given this, this study aims at investigating the following three issues, in order to equip instructors and education organizations with insights on the use they can make of e-learning:

- The general opinion university students have towards e-learning, both with regard to what they mean by e-learning, and to its future trends.
- The experience students make of e-learning, taking into account their frequency of use, the reasons why they use it and their satisfaction.
- The advantages and disadvantages students recognize in the e-learning systems.

3   Methodology

The empirical research was conducted in 2015 among university students, collecting a sample of 277 students who answered an online questionnaire. The questionnaire included both multiple choices, and Likert scales questions about the personal experience of e-learning, its future developments, advantages and disadvantages.

The sample can be described as follows. 56.4% are female and 43.6% male respondents, aged between 19 and 30 years old. Within the women sub-sample, the distribution compared with age follows general data in a more constant way, whereas the male sample presents a high concentration of students aged between 28 and 30, and a higher presence of students older than 34, compared with the age range immediately preceding (between 31 and 33 years old).

With regards to nationality, the sample is mainly composed of Italian students (88.99%), with the remaining part being Spanish (3.52%), French (2.20%), and Russian (2.20%). Other nationalities accounted for 3.08%.

39.65% of the sample attends a Graduate course, followed by 21.15% of students who attends a Master's Degree program. The remaining sample is thus distributed: 18.94% of students attend Undergraduate studies courses, 15.42% attends other courses, and 4.85% attends a Ph.D. program.

Business and Economics is the main discipline studied (42.73%), followed by Engineering (14.54%), Humanities (13.66%), Social Sciences (11.89%), Science (9.69%) and others (7.49%).

The psychometric properties of the scales were assessed in terms of internal consistency. In fact, Cronbach's alpha for each construct exceeds 0.65, confirming the internal consistency.

4   Results

4.1   Students' Opinions Towards E-learning, Today and in the Future

A first area of questions aimed at investigating the students' self-awareness with regards to e-learning's meaning and trends.

45.81% of students think that e-learning consists in using electronic devices to learn (including the delivery of content via electronic media, such as internet, audio, video, satellite broadcast, interactive TV, CD-ROM...). 30.84% retains that it's a mixture of processes aimed at knowledge acquisition and use, where this knowledge is mainly distributed through electronic devices depending on networks and computers. Finally 23.35% defines e-learning as the technology shifting the Web to turn it into a participatory platform, in which people not only consume content (via downloading) but also contribute and proceed new content (via uploading).

This highlights that there is still confusion with regard to a common e-learning definition, which means that, despite being a widespread concept, e-learning requires greater clarity.

With regard to the prospective use of e-learning, the data shows us a positive trend: 64.76% of students believe that e-learning will strongly grow in the future, with positive outcomes on its development. 17.62% of students retain, on the contrary, that e-learning will not experience an expansion, and will even decline in the coming years, while a similar percentage thinks that it will not experience any significant modification, both positive and negative.

This general positive trend is linked to the widespread opinion (according to 67.40% of the sample) that e-learning systems can facilitate learning and motivate students.

4.2 Students' Experience of E-learning

A second area of questions aimed at understanding the students' familiarity with e-learning. 48.02% of the interviewees attended an e-learning course, while 21.59% stated to never having attended an e-learning course, but could take the idea into consideration in the following 24 months. 20.26% of the sample was not interested in any e-learning course and this data can be interpreted in light of the disadvantages e-learning presents and which will be described in the following part of the paper (Table 1).

In the survey, students were also asked to reflect upon their satisfaction with regards to e-learning. Overall, e-learning is perceived as a suitable, effective option for delivering training. Half participants were satisfied with their courses. All things considered, 86% of the sample would like to take another e-learning class in the future and suggest the same experience to others (Table 2).

Moreover, the survey also shows that most of the respondents (84.40%) believe they have learnt what they needed. However only 47% of those who learnt something shared the acquired knowledge with other students. This possibly suggests that e-learning mainly promote individual type of learning rather than social type learning.

With regard to how they use e-learning systems, students report that they see these systems as mainly an online platform, a place where you can download and

Table 1 Have you ever attended an e-learning course?

Yes, in the last 12 months	35.68%
Yes, in the last 24 months	6.17%
Yes, not in the recent past	6.17%
No, but I'm willing to attend one in the next 12 months	6.17%
No, but I'm willing to attend one in the next 24 months	3.96%
No, but I would like to do it in the future	21.59%
No, and I'm not interested in	20.26%

Table 2 Rate you satisfaction of your e-learning courses	Strongly satisfied	10.09%
	Satisfied	40.37%
	Neutral	35.78%
	Dissatisfied	11.93%
	Strongly dissatisfied	1.83%

Table 3 Perceived advantages of e-learning (more than one answer is possible)

Increasing flexibility (time and place)	129
Sharing of teaching materials	107
Downloading teaching materials (e.g. slides)	100
Updating teaching materials	82
Improving interaction processes with teachers	68
Getting a quick feedback	68
Improving collaboration and coordination among students	46
Improving the development of student's knowledge and skills	43
Fostering interaction processes among students	41
Total	684

share materials. More than 55% of students admit to use e-learning as a sharing tool and as a way to download materials. This presumably suggests that the knowledge and the awareness about e-learning systems are pretty limited. Students underestimate the possibility to use the e-learning systems to review concepts, take self-assessments, and interact with other participants and with the instructors, outside the class's physical boundaries.

4.3 The Perceived Advantages and Disadvantages of E-learning

In the survey, students were also asked to reflect on the positive and negative aspects of the e-learning system they experienced.

The major advantages are flexibility in terms of time and space, easiness and speed in sharing material and the possibility of receiving material from the teacher via a download (Table 3).

With regards to disadvantages, a first observation relates to the fact that they are fewer than the advantages: 463 against 684. The highest rated disadvantage of e-learning system is the "reduced social interaction" compared to a traditional learning context (Table 4).

Results partially differ among different sub-groups, depending on gender and age, while in previous sections no significant difference among sub-groups was registered.

Table 4 Perceived disadvantages of e-learning (more than one answer is possible)

Reducing social interactions	122
Increasing extra costs in terms of technological equipment	62
Reducing the opportunity to understand the students' learning style	60
Facing some technological-related issues	59
Working better for students with technological and computer skills	59
Lacking of readiness of faculty members	58
Being difficult to self-organizing the learning schedule	43
Total	463

With regard to gender, female respondents have reported a higher score than male respondents on the following three variables: getting a quick feedback, improving collaboration and coordination among students, and updating teaching materials.

With regard to age, it is worthy of note that younger students are more critical than older ones towards e-learning: in fact they underline many more disadvantages than advantages.

5 Managerial Implications and Conclusions

This study provides insights for educational organizations to understand what changes are needed in e-learning processes and systems, providing an updated overview of the students' perspective on e-learning and linking this perspective with the existing models of e-learning effectiveness (e.g. [16]) (see Table 5).

First we suggest that there is still confusion with regard to what e-learning is, even if it is thought that it improves learning and motivation and it is going to grow as a phenomenon. This confusion was also reported by Akaslan et al. [12], due to the fact that individuals and organizations use e-learning for many different activities and e-learning is implemented using different technologies.

In order to increase clarity, instructors and organizations should invest on both technological factors to make the use of technology even easier and institutional ones to make a cultural change happen in terms of learning culture [25].

Secondly, according to our data, for many students e-learning is mainly a technological platform enabling the download of materials. This suggests that students have had only limited chances to experiment the other potentialities of e-learning in terms of interaction and assessment for example. They have therefore only a limited understanding of what they can do with e-learning systems and how these systems can improve their satisfaction as well as their learning performance.

This should make instructors pay attention to institutional factors, in order to make people understand how to learn, and be familiar with e-learning systems even before using it. This might also imply initiating and managing a change in the learning culture. Moreover it also implies working on pedagogical factors, to ensure

Table 5 Students' perceptions and implications for instructors

Areas of investigation	Main findings	Managerial implications for instructors and educational organizations
Students' opinion towards e-learning	• There is confusion about a common and agreed definition of e-learning • There is a diffused belief that e-learning is going to grow in the future • E-learning can facilitate learning and increase motivation	• Foster a change in study habits and in the learning culture and ensure institutional support as well as financial one to make this change happen • Improve the technological factors, in terms of ease of use, reliability, efficiency, but also technical support for instructors and students to facilitate a broader adoption of e-learning systems
Students' use experience of e-learning	• E-learning is perceived as an effective option for delivering training • E-learning seems to mainly promote individual type of learning rather than social type learning • E-learning is mainly an online platform for sharing materials. Its potentialities are underestimated	• Change the mind-set of the learners to broaden their understanding of e-learning • Design e-learning systems taking into account pedagogical factors, that include content analysis, audience analysis, learning strategies • Improve the technological factors to be able to exploit all the potentialities of e-learning in terms of functionalities
Students' perception of advantages and disadvantages of e-learning	• Reported advantages are more than disadvantages • The major advantages are flexibility in terms of time and space, easiness and speed in sharing material and the possibility of receiving material from the teacher via a download • The major disadvantage is the "reduced social interaction" compared to a traditional learning context	• Invest in social interaction factors, creating occasions for social interaction among participants and with the instructor • Provide tools and occasions for evaluation, developing learning assessments and allowing for easy and continuous feedback • Ensure the right support from a management team in charge of developing contents and managing the delivery. This team should support both instructors and learners

the proper design and implementation of e-learning courses. Technological factors are also critical to support the pedagogical ones, because instructors should also think about strengthening those functionalities that are in particular underused (e.g. the ones related to social interaction) and creating learning opportunities that comprises a wider use of the e-learning possibilities.

According to our data there is still a significant percentage of students who had no experience in e-learning and no interest in experiencing it. This asks educational organizations and instructors to investigate the reason why: is it a matter of non curiosity, or of perception of too many disadvantages in this type of learning experience or of too limited occasions to use them? Depending on the answer, instructors should focus on changing the learning attitudes, making the use of technology easier, improving the learning experience or providing more diverse occasions for use.

Thirdly, we confirm that there are several recognized benefits in the e-learning systems, but still many disadvantages as well, mainly related to the limited inter-action among participants and with the instructors. This presents significant prac-tical implications: when instructors design their e-learning offer, they have to consider not only the technical aspects, but also social interaction factors, as well as management, evaluation and resources factors. Creating occasions for social interactions, having the right competences and sufficient resources to manage the online content development process, developing a system to offer feedback and evaluation are all critical factors.

References

1. Welsh, E. T., Wanberg, C. R., Brown, K. G., & Simmering, M. J. (2003). E-learning: emerging uses, empirical results and future directions. *International Journal of Training and Development, 7*, 245–258.
2. Caporarello, L., & Sarchioni, G. (2014). E-learning: the recipe for success. *Journal of e-learning and Knowledge Society, 10*(1), 107–118.
3. Wong, W. T., & Huang, N. T. N. (2011). The effects of e-learning system service quality and users' accpetance on organizational learning. *International Journal of Business and Information, 6*(2), 205–225.
4. Murillo, L. F. L., & Velázquez, F. J. L. (2008). E-learning as a key aspect for the future of higher education. In *DEXA Workshops IEEE Computer Society, 431*–435.
5. Za, S., Spagnoletti, P., & North-Samardzic, A. (2014). Organisational learning as an emerging process: The generative role of digital tools in informal learning practices. *British Journal of Educational Technology, 45*(6), 1023–1035.
6. North-Samardzic, A., Braccini, A. M., Spagnoletti, P., & Za, S. (2014). Applying media synchronicity theory to distance learning in virtual worlds: A design science approach. *International Journal of Innovation and Learning, 15*(3), 328–346.
7. Rosenberg, M. J. (2001). *E-learning: Strategies for delivering knowledge in the digital age.* New York: McGraw-Hill.
8. Terry, L. (2000). Get smart online. *Upside, 12*(5), 162–164.
9. Alptekin, S. E., & Karsak, E. E. (2011). An integrated decision framework for evaluating and selecting e-learning products. *Applied Soft Computing, 11*, 2990–2998.
10. Biasutti, M. (2011). The student experience of a collaborative e-learning university module. *Computers & Education, 57*, 1865–1875.
11. Keller, C., & Cernerud, L. (2002). Students' perceptions of e-learning in university education. *Journal of Educational Media, 27*(1–2), 55–67.
12. Akaslan, D., Law, E.L-C., & Taskin, S. (2012). Analysis of issues for implementing e-learning: The student perspective. New York: IEEE.

13. Lee, Y. H., Hsieh, Y. C., & Hsu, C. N. (2011). Adding innovation diffusion theory to the technology acceptance model: Supporting employees' intentions to use e-learning systems. *Educational Technology & Society, 14*(4), 124–137.
14. McLoughlin, C. E., & Lubna Alam, S. (2014). A case study of instructor scaffolding using Web 2.0 tools to teach social informatics. *Journal of Information Systems Education, 25*(2), 125.
15. Dutta, A. K., Mosley, A., & Akhtar, M. M. (2011). E-learning in higher education: Design and implementation. *International Journal of Computer Science Issues, 8*(4), 509–516.
16. Basak, S. K., Wotto, M., & Bélanger, P. (2016). A framework on the critical success factors of learning implementation in higher education: A review of the literature. *International Journal of Social, Behavioural, Economic, Business and Industrial Engineering, 10*(7), 2259–2264.
17. Baldwin-Evans, K. (2004). Employees and eLearning: What do the end-users think? *Industrial and Commercial Training, 36*(7), 269–274.
18. Elloumi, F. (2004). Value chain analysis: A strategic approach to online learning. In A. Anderson & F. Elloumi (Eds.), *Theory and practice of online learning* (pp. 61–92). Athabasca, Canada: Athabasca University.
19. Saadé, R. G. (2003). Web-based education information system for enhanced learning, EISL: Student assessment. *Journal of Information Technology Education, 2*, 267–277.
20. Rodrigues, J. J. P. C., Sabino, F. M. R., & Zhou, L. (2011). Enhancing e-learning experience with online social networks. *IET Communications, 5*(8), 1147–1154.
21. Al-hawari, M. A., & Mouakket, S. (2010). The influence of technology acceptance model (TAM) factors on students' e-satisfaction and e-retention within the context of UAE e-learning. *Education, Business and Society: Contemporary Middle Eastern Issues, 3*(4), 299–314.
22. Wu, J.-H., Tennyson, R. D., & Hsia, T.-L. (2010). A study of student satisfaction in a blended e-learning system environment. *Computers & Education, 55*, 155–164.
23. Castle, S. R., & McGuire, C. J. (2010). An analysis of student self-assessment of online, blended, and face-to-face learning environments: Implications for sustainable education delivery. *International Education Studies, 3*(3), 36.
24. Akaslan, D., & Law, E.L-C. (2011). Measuring student e-learning readiness: A case about the subject of electricity in higher education institutions in Turkey. In *Proceedings of the 10th International Conference on Web-Based learning*. Hong Kong.
25. Caporarello, L., & Inesta, A. (2016). Blended learning approach: How is the learning educational paradigm changing? Reflections and a proposed framework. In F. D'Ascenzo, M. Magni, A. Lazazzara, & S. Za (Eds.), *Blurring the boundaries through digital innovation*. Germany: Springer.

The JamToday Network: The European Learning Hub for Applied-Games for Learning Environments

David Crombie, Pierre Mersch, Iana Dulskaia and Francesco Bellini

Abstract The paper presents early results of the first European applied game-jam network called JamToday. The JamToday Network was set-up in 2014 with the support from the European Commission Programme CIP-ICT-PSP being the first pan-European Network dedicated to applied game design. It brings together different types of partners (such as creative clusters, game companies, education and research institutes, public sector institutions, municipalities etc.) from various sectors, fields and expertise for running game jams across Europe to make a real change in making games on themes like eSkills, Health & Wellbeing and Learning Maths and applying them in learning environments. The paper presents the work achieved by the JamToday Network in the first two years and very concrete and practical tools and methodologies developed by the JamToday Network to support game-design approaches for learning environments from design to transfer and evaluation.

Keywords Game-based learning · Applied-game design · Game jam · Co-design

D. Crombie (✉) · P. Mersch
HKU University of the Arts Utrecht, Utrecht, The Netherlands
e-mail: david.crombie@hku.nl

P. Mersch
e-mail: pierre.mersch@hku.nl

I. Dulskaia · F. Bellini
Eurokleis srl, Rome, Italy
e-mail: iana.dulskaia@eurokleis.com

F. Bellini
e-mail: francesco.bellini@eurokleis.com

© Springer International Publishing AG 2018
C. Rossignoli et al. (eds.), *Digital Technology and Organizational Change*,
Lecture Notes in Information Systems and Organisation 23,
https://doi.org/10.1007/978-3-319-62051-0_15

1 Introduction

In recent years, the Game Jam approach has been increasingly effective in bringing together the appropriate stakeholders around broad themes and challenges. There is now a need to focus on establishing a sustainable learning hub for raising awareness of educational games and their use within learning environments. The European Game Jam Learning Hub, JamToday,[1] aims to establish a central networking hub for the sustainable implementation and uptake of the next generation of educational games across Europe. Game Jams have been instrumental in stimulating innovation in the creation, implementation and deployment of educational games. JamToday is supporting this by creating toolkits and providing support for events across Europe, at local, regional and national levels. And given the emerging focus on new learning environments, JamToday is also supporting the move towards games as contextual interventions and foster awareness-raising and innovation between the games and learning sectors with the intention of demonstrating real-life impact. The JamToday hub thus provides stewardship for this emerging area and ensures that stakeholders maintain a balanced understanding of the main issues and the implementation hurdles that need to be overcome. JamToday seeks to provide a replicable model of good practice in the design of transformative environments and to provide methods and tools that have been validated from several perspectives. Each year, JamToday is setting up game jams in at several locations across Europe. Every JamToday Competition focuses on a particular theme. Combining observatory and knowledge-base functions, JamToday provides methods for measuring and assessing the impact of different approaches.

2 Theoretical Background

2.1 What Is Applied-Game Design?

Nowadays, game-based learning has gradually gained recognition at policy and academic level and many universities offer training and research in 'serious games'. However, in many instances the serious games—being developed with sacrifice of fun and entertainment in order to achieve a desired effect—resulted in a poorly designed solution that is rarely accepted by the intended users.

As game-based learning is focused on achieving the particular objectives of given educational content through game play, players' attempts to solve problems are maintained throughout the learning session. Learning strategies and gaming strategies adopted to implement problem solving strategies in game-based learning may be the primary factor behind the high achievements in both learning and gaming [1].

---

[1]http://www.jamtoday.eu/.

Game jam could be defined as: an accelerated opportunistic game creation event where a game is created in a relatively short timeframe exploring given design constraint(s) and end results are shared publically [2].

The European Game Jam Learning Hub, JamToday is a pan-European network that seeks to support the development of game-based prototypes through so-called game-jams. JamToday approach to game design is based around the idea of 'applied games' that are defined as *'games that are deployed for purposes like training, education, persuasion, physical exercise; i.e. all games that bring about effects that are useful outside the context of the game itself'* [3]. In this approach, it is the way that a game is *applied* that defines its usefulness outside the *context* of the game itself. At the core of this approach lies the idea that applied game-design tries to retain core game design concepts in the wider areas of application and the broader context of use. Indeed the approach has been deployed across many diverse fields, from education and healthcare to defence and museums.

However, this is a complex process, as finding a good balance between the *fun* and the *applied* part of the game is often a challenge. Moreover, people who work in game companies are mostly not experts in the field for which the game is being created. For these reasons, the JamToday network aims at building bridges between game designers and other stakeholders in order to maximise the impact of applied games. Game jam is one of the instruments used by the JamToday Network to create these bridges and develop game concepts for a specific thematic area.

The JamToday Network aims to develop game-based prototypes for training environments. Through game jams, the network aims to reinforce the links between game professionals and professionals from the context of use in order to maximise impact and take-up of games in learning and training environments.

JamToday provides a replicable framework for the co-design and co-development of game-based prototypes for learning environments. It also provides tools to facilitate the implementation and validation of game prototypes in learning and training contexts.

2.2 Games for Learning and Training Environments: The Policy Context and Main Barriers

Over the last decade, the European Learning and Training sector went through significant changes supported by central authorities at National and European levels. For example, with the European Framework for Key Competences for Lifelong Learning, we observe that the focus is shifting from the provision of *knowledge* towards the provision of *competences*. The Europe2020 Strategy [4] also calls for further innovation in the education sector as one of the key elements in smart growth for Europe.

Over recent years, the value of game-based learning has slowly been recognised and initiatives are emerging to support game-based learning in formal education programmes. In order to support further use of games in education, the European Schoolnet and the Interactive Software Federation of Europe have for example recently organised a set of online workshops on the use of Games in Schools.

As the use of games by children is rivalling that of television [5] and studies reveal that young people all over Europe are playing computer games on a regular basis the recognition of the value of games in learning to support the development of key competences is slowly emerging [6]. However, educators have been ambivalent about this, as technology is still only marginally applied in educational contexts [7].

A report called "Report on the educational use of games" [8] explains the value of games in learning contexts by pointing out that *"there is a widely held view that games software is capable of developing a degree of user engagement which could be usefully harnessed in an educational context"*. The area of game-based learning and Digital Game-Based Learning and teaching examines all types of digital games use from the perspective of learners and teachers [9]. It is a relatively new field, which has only recently been reviewed, and has largely focused on school-based education and some aspects of life-long learning (see for example [10–12]). However, the value of using game design principles to address the needs of the learner has proven to be an innovative addition to the traditional teaching methods.

Learning is perceived by most researchers as a multidimensional construct of learning skills, cognitive learning outcomes, (e.g. procedural, declarative and strategic knowledge), and attitudes. The state of the art pedagogy indicates that *"designing effective learning environments where knowledge is generated from integrated experience with complex tasks may be more appropriate for many domains of learning compared to isolated, instructivist activities that separate knowledge from action and theory from practice, like learning and practicing separately"* [13]. Computer games have a great potential to provide such learning environments [14]. As such, games have a power of engagement that can be explained via intrinsic motivation, reflection and transfer [15].

"Like any innovation, games must be deployed in a measured and systematic way that maximizes their benefits while minimizing the negative consequences" [16]. The discussion over the inclusion of games in learning environments has been running for some time and can be characterized in the following way. For some, there is little place for games and gamification in education. This argument rests primarily on the absence of empirical evidence showing that real learning takes place and secondly arguing that skills acquired through gaming are not transferable to the real world. Other negative issues include: the cost of introducing games, distraction from learning other skills, social isolation and shortened attention span.

Furthermore, a Report published by the European Schoolnet 'How are digital games used in schools?' [17], found that the main obstacles mentioned for not using games in school were (in ranking order): (1) cost and licensing, (2) timetable of the school, (3) finding suitable games, (4) attitudes of other teachers, (5) training and support, (6) inappropriate content, (7) worries about negative aspects, (8) insufficient evidence of value, and (9) examinations.

Moreover, despite a rise in the recognition of the value of game-based learning, some authors point out that often little attention is given to how to implement them in learning environments and how to ensure there are significant learning outcomes [18].

3 Case Study: The JamToday Network: Game-Jams for Applied-Games for Learning Environments

Based on a thorough literature review and consultation with experts, the European Game Jam Learning Hub, JamToday has developed a framework with validated methodologies and tools to harness the potential of game-based learning from design to deployment and evaluation. The JamToday Network seeks to provide a replicable model to provide concrete answers for the introduction of applied-games into learning environments.

Through the active involvement of different stakeholders in so-called game jams for the development of game-based learning prototypes and by providing guidelines on how to implement these educational games in thematic areas the JamToday Network seeks to provide a replicable model to bridge the gap between game professionals and professionals from the context of use.

This way, the JamToday network aims at engaging teachers in the design and deployment of game-based learning prototypes thus raising awareness about the potential of games for learning and training environments and supporting the deployment of games into learning environments.

Game Jams have been successfully organised for several years around the world and are a powerful instrument to stimulate innovation in the creation, development and deployment of educational games. They offer the possibility to develop an idea into a potentially innovative solution around specific themes while at the same time offering the opportunity to explore the process of development (e.g. programming, game and interaction design, narrative exploration or artistic expression).

Typically, game jams last 48-h. Over a weekend people from different sectors are brought together to brainstorm and develop game-based solutions for tricky problems. JamToday is the first network specifically organising game jams for applied games.

Each year, JamToday sets up game jams in several locations across Europe focusing on a particular theme.

In order to assist game-jam organisers, the JamToday networks has developed an online Toolkit that provides a detailed overview in 5 modules of the different steps to organise a successful game-jam.

The JamToday Toolkit is conceived as a step-by-step guide explaining how to run a game jam following the JamToday formula and how to implement the outcomes with help of the JamToday network into learning environments. It deals with aspects such as:

- Stakeholders and target participants
- Legal aspects
- Funding and finance
- Communication and Promotion
- Practicalities
- Transfer and assessment

The JamToday model is open, transparent, versatile and replicable. While game jams are at the core of its methodology, the JamToday network is more than a platform seeking to bring people together for just a weekend.

Prior to each game jam, JamToday fosters the identification of the most relevant regional stakeholders to invite to take part in the game jam for maximising the impact. JamToday provides guidance on how to carry out a stakeholder mapping analysis and how to mobilise the right stakeholders before, during and after the game jam. These are for example game and sound designers but also thematic experts, teachers, parents, problem owners, investors, representatives from local and regional authorities etc. In this way, JamToday aims to make the processes at stake in the creation of applied games more transparent to all stakeholders by providing the necessary know-how and expertise and by bringing together the different people who are involved in the process of designing and deploying game-based approaches to learning.

In order to be the most effective, JamToday does not only provide the tools to bring relevant stakeholders together in the most meaningful way. It also provides tools to assess the potential of applied games and a framework to evaluate the best outcomes from each game jam. At the end of each game jam, a jury assesses each game prototype. Following that, a group of experts evaluates further the best outcomes of each game jam on different criteria:

- Game transferability in the learning sector
- Coherence with the proposed assignment
- Pedagogical potential of the game
- Innovativeness of the games
- Motivation

Ultimately, after the evaluation of the potential of a game concept, prototypes should be introduced into the thematic area. It has to be noticed that the outcomes of game jams are merely game prototypes that cannot be treated as fully functional and completed games in transfer activities.

The JamToday Network has therefore developed a set of versatile tools to facilitate the implementation of these educational game prototypes into learning and training contexts:

- Games-Scope is a tool developed to validate/evaluate the potential of a game-prototypes and to learn to critically analyse a game prototype and discuss elements that make a good concept

- GameSpark is another tool that is developed to evaluate a playable prototype of an applied game. Since the tested game prototypes are in a very early stage of development, Game Spark intends to gather data on the potential for further development rather than actually testing its effect. Game Spark consists of a Teacher Expert Observer Form (TEOF), and a Student Expert Player Form (SEPF). The SEPF is developed in two versions: a version for the very young (SEPF Junior), using very basic questions and smileys as answer scale, and a version for older children. We recommend the Teacher Expert to choose the most suitable version.

To support the transfer in learning and Training environments, JamToday also hosts workshops with professionals from the learning sector aimed at introducing the best games from the JamToday game jams into the education environments and to enable educators to use educational games in their classrooms.

4 Lessons Learned from the First Game Jams on "Improving ICT Skills" and "Adopting Healthier Lifestyles"

Each year, JamToday tackles a specific thematic area and enters in dialogue with experts and professionals from the field of application in order to best address the theme and formulate an assignment for the game jams. In 2014, the theme addressed was "Improving ICT skills" and in 2015, the theme addressed was "adopting healthier lifestyles". This section presents the annual themes addressed by the JamToday Network, the common assignment to the different game-jams and the main outcomes and lessons learned from the first editions of the JamToday game-jams.

4.1 Improving ICT Skills and Adopting Healthier Lifestyles: Policy Context and Exiting Initiatives Relevant for the JamToday Game Jam Assignments

In 2014, the thematic area addressed by JamToday was "Improving ICT skills" and in 2015, the theme addressed was "Adopting healthier lifestyles". This section provides some contextual information on the policy context and existing initiatives in Europe related to these themes.

Both at European and national levels, there is broad consensus among policy makers about the crucial importance of e-skills for Europe in the knowledge-based economy: e-skills shortages, gaps and mismatches and a digital divide will affect negatively growth, competitiveness, innovation, employment and social cohesion in

Europe. As new technologies are developing rapidly, e-skills are increasingly sophisticated and need to be constantly updated. There is a critical need for individuals with creativity, innovation and higher-level conceptual skills. A recent study for the European Commission interested in the "international Dimension and the Impact of Globalisation" [19] on eSkills recently highlighted the crucial need for integrated policies as the world is confronted with a growing e-skills gap that can in turn curb economic competitiveness and recovery. The report highlights that "As part of the new global sourcing models, different skill sets are required in different regions, and new technologies keep demanding changes in the type of skills required. These new technological trends are likely to act as further drivers of increased demand for ICT practitioners over the coming years."

For many years, the development of digital skills has therefore been identified by European policy makers as one of the most pressing issues to address. The Europe2020 Strategy [4] identifies digital literacy as a key competence for the younger generation. Before that, digital skills were already supported by the eLearning initiative at the dawn of the millennium and further elaborated in the Communication on e-Skills [19]. Recently, the lack of ICT skills has been identified by the European Digital Agenda [20] as one of the seven most important obstacles to harnessing the potential of ICT. This has for example lead Policy makers to call for further innovation in the education system for smart growth in Europe (Europe 2020)

At national level, there also are very high levels of activity in the Digital Literacy domain and in the e-Skills area where the focus is on ICT practitioners and professionals rather than the population at large [21]. A mapping of policies dealing with e-skills in the EU-28 recently found that there are some 100+ policies dealing broadly with e-skills (including in particular policies such as digital literacy/user skills and e-inclusion).

Generally speaking, the report on the "international Dimension and the Impact of Globalisation" [19] identifies twelve key policies from the analysis of the existing policies dealing with eSkills across Europe:

- Including ICT in education reform is considered to be a key factor
- Teacher training curricula needs to include ICT
- Immigration policy reform should be implemented to attract talent
- ICT career opportunities and career paths should be strongly promoted
- Labour market monitoring is needed at national and EU level
- The uptake of the e-Competence framework should be promoted
- Member States should consider multi-stakeholder partnerships
- ICT training and educational curricula should meet labour market demand
- Up-skilling and re-skilling measures help ICT professionals to take new jobs
- Matching of jobs and ICT professional competences needs to increase
- ICT education for girls should be promoted
- Member States should create a dedicated entity to design and implement a coherent and consistent long term e-skills strategy (e.g. ICT skills sector council, national coalition etc.)

Based on an extensive literature review and consultation with experts from the ICT and Learning sector through an Expert Advisory Group meeting held in Brussels on 28 February 2014, JamToday has defined a common assignment for all the game jams that were held in the context of JamToday.

Following that workshop, a general assignment was defined with a short introductory text. This assignment has been used in all game-jams.

While being specific and open at the same time the assignment aims at tackling issues that emerged from the literature review carried out by the JamToday Consortium and the consultation of thematic experts that participated in the Expert Advisory group. Moreover, the JamToday evaluation Framework and selection criteria have been defined as a replicable model tailored to the annual theme. In 2014, the assignment was

We don't want to address learners in a vacuum. We want to address both teachers and learners.

We don't want to address coding in a vacuum. We want to address not just the coding but also the experience and impact and in this way address meaningful coding as a way of reinforcing critical thinking.

For some, just solving the puzzles is enough. But the fun of coding lies in solving the puzzle and by doing so, building something that works and something that gives pleasure to others.

So, the assignment is:

"Develop a game that stimulates teachers and learners to work together with coding logic in order to promote critical thinking, creativity and design".

In 2015, the annual theme addressed by JamToday was "adopting healthier lifestyles". With the input of the expert advisory group, the game jam in the second year of JamToday focused on adopting healthier lifestyles with the following guidelines in mind.

The objective was to use a new concept of health and well-being that is currently being appropriated in the preventative health care sector. The definition is changing to one of 'positive health' with a correspondingly stronger focus on self-empowerment and resilience, rather than curing and medication.

Games can approach health and well-being from a human perspective instead of a medical perspective. For the game jam assignment, JamToday proposed to focus on the broader personal context and motivational habits in a playful way instead of a proscriptively medical way.

JamToday invited participants to develop games that should encourage collaborative play and interchangeable role-play to support not only behavioural change, but behavioural maintenance. Play together and change roles to understand one another's perspective.

As game designers, participants were also invited to keep a strong focus on the end-users and pay special attention to the learning environment.

For the second year, the assignment was less specific than in the first year and a JamToday decided to use a catch phrase or an image to spark creativity, debate and surprising concepts rather than a too specific assignment.

4.2 Towards Applied-Games for Learning Environments

Based on the JamToday Toolkit and the JamToday model, in 2014, game jams were successfully organized in 8 European locations from June till October 2014. In 2015, game jams have been organised on the theme of health in 13 European locations. In all locations, jammers worked on the common assignments presented above. The assignment were introduced to the jammers on the first day of the game jam.

In total more 498 *participants* participated in one of the JamToday game jams and more than *100 game-based learning prototypes* were successfully developed. JamToday constantly monitors its activities and the following chart summarises the main figures (Fig. 1).

A wide range of participants participated in the game jams with very different profiles. The youngest participant was 5 year-old and the oldest was over 50 year-old.

All game-prototypes are available from the JamToday online Learning Hub.

Each organizing country selected a winning game, and external experts then evaluated these games.

The evaluation framework combined quantitative and qualitative data and evaluated the game prototypes on several criteria:

- Technical evaluation of the games
- Focus of the games on the assignment
- Learning sectors and transferability

The evaluation of the game highlighted that the technical quality of the games developed is in general more than satisfying, especially considered the particular environment (the Game Jams) in which they were developed, and the largely non-professional composition of the various development teams. The games developed did tackle the assignment proposed, and they proved to be able to foster

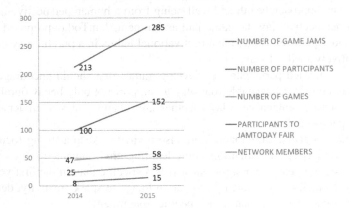

Fig. 1 JamToday main key performance indicators

the key skills required by the assignment. The games were tackling in general mostly the K-12 and High School sectors of learning; however, some of the games proved to be applicable also in other learning sectors.

As pointed out earlier, the ultimate aim of applied-game is the meaningful application of game-based principles in the fields of application. To reach this objective, the JamToday Network has entered in consultation with experts from various fields in order to define the game-jam assignment and professionals from the field of application have also taken part in the game-jams. Furthermore, the best games have also been presented to professionals from learning and training environments in regional training workshops. These workshops were organised in 7 regions to introduce the best games from the JamToday game jams into educational environments and to enable educators to use educational games in their lessons to improve students' coding skills. Workshops were organised in Stuttgart, Germany, Sofia, Bulgaria, Barcelona, Spain, Turin, Italy and Milan, Italy, Leuven, Belgium and Graz, Austria.

The success of the first editions with game jams organised in a total of 16 EU locations shows that the JamToday Toolkit is a useful tool that has enabled partners without experience in running game-jams to successfully run and attract participants.

The experience from the game jams held in the context of the JamToday Network highlighted a great variety of approach from the game jam organisers. Some partners had no previous experience in running game-jams while others had been organising game jams for many years in other contexts such as the Global Game-jam. Similarly, there was a great difference in the experience partners had in working with game companies. This open approach has enabled the Network to reach a large number of participants with very different profiles. At the end, while some game-jams gathered professional and semi-professional participants (such as students in game design) others have gathered a mix of children and adults without necessarily previous experience in coding or developing games. As a consequence the games developed also have very diverse identities: some are rather simple video games others are more advanced while other teams have opted for analogue board games.

The analysis of these JamToday game jams shows that there is a consensus amongst game-jam organisers on the relevance of the game-jam instrument as an efficient way to quickly develop and explore new solutions to a problem, raise awareness about the potential of applied-game design and bring together stakeholders from different horizons with a potential to have concrete socio-economic impact. From the games developed during the game-jams, some are now being taken further to market, jammers decided to work together beyond the jam, some are now pre-incubated in local incubators etc.)

Organisers of jams where jammers with no previous experience in programming were positively impressed by the efficiency of the JamToday model, which allowed people with no programming background to develop video games.

As anticipated, involving experts and industry professionals was mentioned as one of the key factors to success. Experts and industry professionals are particularly useful to provide context information related to the theme or help teams to adjust their expectations and support them in keeping align with the assignment.

The flexible approach followed by JamToday has enabled organisations with different profiles and agendas to successfully run a game-jam. Impact of the approach can be identified not only for the learning environments for which the games are developed. In fact, the positive impact of the JamToday approach can be measured on other variables such as:

- Capability to broaden the network for game jam organisers
- Peer-learning for game-jam participants
- Capacity to attract people that would normally not work with games and impact on the awareness about the potential of applied games for people outside the gaming sector
- Capacity to trigger interest in working on new themes for game-developers or with other fields of application
- Impact on game companies that can experiment with new contexts and new themes
- Capability of the game-jam to bring participants in contact with new economic actors at regional levels
- Talent discovery
- Improving collaborative creation of applied games
- Opportunities for new collaboration for participants
- Entrepreneurial discoveries

5 Conclusions and Future Research

JamToday is a pan-European network that was established in 2014. It is the first network dedicated to the organisation of game jams for applied games. Each year, JamToday tackles a thematic area. JamToday seeks to provide a replicable model that helps maximising the impact of game-design for learning environments. At the core of the JamToday methodology is the organisation of game-jams. The JamToday framework offers support from planning to evaluating and transfer of game-based learning prototypes.

Between 2014 and 2016, close to 500 participants took part in one of the JamToday game jams to develop close to 100 game-based prototypes on a common assignment. JamToday provides the tools to identify and attract the right stake-holders and be a platform to meaningfully bring stakeholders with different back-grounds and expertise together in co-design exercise thus fostering dialogue, mutual learning, co-creation and quick prototyping sessions.

The experience from JamToday highlighted that game jams are an effective tool to foster such cooperation, which in turn can yield changes in attitudes towards game-based learning and foster dialogue between stakeholders for the promotion and development of game-based solutions for learning environments and a way to raise awareness about the potential of applied-game design.

Game Jams are also a good way for people external to the game world to get an insight into game-design processes.

JamToday also provides tools to facilitate the implementation and validation of game prototypes in learning and training contexts.

The lessons learned from the successful editions of the JamToday game-jams will help the JamToday network to enhance the tools developed to support the organisation of game jams, which in turn can be used by new members willing to join the JamToday network to become a sustainable learning hub for raising awareness of educational games and their use within learning environments. In 2016 the theme addressed will be "Improving the learning of mathematics" and game jams will take place in Europe, North Africa and North America.

References

1. Kim, B., Park, H., & Baek, Y. (2009). Not just fun, but serious strategies: Using meta-cognitive strategies in game-based learning. *Computers & Education, 52*(4), 800–810.
2. Kultima, A. (2015). Defining game jam. In *Proceedings of foundations of digital games conference* (vol. 15).
3. Van Roessel, L., & Van Mastrigt-Ide, J. (2011). Collaboration and team composition in applied game creation processes. DIGRA Conference http://www.digra.org/wp-content/uploads/digital-library/11301.53001.pdf.
4. European Commission. (2010). *Europe 2020 A strategy for smart, sustainable and inclusive growth*, Com(2010) 2020 final see http://eur-lex.europa.eu/LexUriServ/LexUriServ.do?uri=COM:2010:2020:FIN:EN:PDF.
5. Greenberg, B. S., Sherry, J., Lachlan, K., Lucas, K., & Holmstrom, A. (2010). Orientations to video games among gender and age groups. *Simulation & Gaming, 41*(2), 238–259.
6. Blamire, R. (2010). *Digital games for learning: Conclusions and recommendations from the IMAGINE project*, European Schoolnet.
7. European Commission: COM 669. (2012). *Rethinking education: Investing in skills for better socio-economic outcomes*. Communication for the Commission to the European Parliament, the Council, the European Economic and Social Committee.
8. McFarlane, A., Sparrowhawk, A., & Heald, Y. (2002). *Report on the educational use of games: TEEM*.
9. Stewart, J., & Misuraca, G. (2013). *The industry and policy context for digital games for empowerment and inclusion: Market analysis, future prospects and key challenges in videogames, serious games and gamification*, Retrieved from http://ipts.jrc.ec.europa.eu/publications/pub.cfm?id=6099.
10. Egenfeldt-Nielsen, S. (2005). *Beyond edutainment: Exploring the educational potential of computer games*. Copenhagen: IT University of Copenhagen.
11. Ellis, H., Heppell, S., Kirriemuir, J., Krotoski, A., & McFarlane, A. (2006). *Unlimited learning: Computer and video games in the learning landscape*. London: Entertainment and Leisure Software Publishers Association.
12. FAS. (2006). *Harnessing the power of video games for learning*. Washington, DC: Federation of American Scientists.

13. Vygotsky, L. S. (2007). *Mind in society*. In M. P. J. Habgood (ed.), *The effective integration of digital games and learning content*. Cambridge, MA: Harvard University Press. 1978 Retrieved from http://steelminions.com/zd/Habgood%202007%20Final.pdf.
14. Cagiltay, K., Reinhardt, R. (2010). *Green paper European network for growing activity in game-based learning in education—ENGAGE*.
15. Habgood, M. P. J. (2007). *The effective integration of digital games and learning content*, Retrieved from http://steelminions.com/zd/Habgood%202007%20Final.pdf.
16. Marquis, L. (2013). *Debatest about gamification and game-based learning in education*, Retrieved from http://classroom-aid.com/2013/04/07/debates-about-gamification-and-game-based-learninggbl-in-education/.
17. Wastiau, P., Kearney, C., & Van den Bergh, W. (2009). *How are digital games used in schools? Complete results: Final report*. European schoolnet EUN Partnership AISBL, Brussels, Belgium.
18. Shaffer, D. W. (2009). 'Wag the Kennel: Games, frames, and the problem of assessment. In R. Fertig (Ed.), *Handbook of research on effective electronic gaming in education* (vol. II, pp. 577–592). Hershey, PA: IGI Global.
19. IVI. (2014). *e-Skills: The international dimension and the impact of globalisation*. http://ec.europa.eu/DocsRoom/documents/7040.
20. European Commission. (2010). *A digital agenda for Europe*, COM(2010) pp. 245 final/2 see http://eur-lex.europa.eu/LexUriServ/LexUriServ.do?uri=COM:2010:0245:FIN:EN:PDF.
21. Empirica. (2014). *e-Skills in Europe: Final report measuring progress and moving ahead*. http://ec.europa.eu/DocsRoom/documents/4574.

Let's Learn Together: Team Integration Climate, Individual States and Learning Using Computer-Based Simulations

Leonardo Caporarello, Massimo Magni and Ferdinando Pennarola

Abstract The present study analyses individual learning in a computer-based simulation setting (business game). In particular, the study points out the importance of the team environment in stimulating individual states that may foster individual learning. By taking into account 402 individuals who participated in a computer-based simulation, we underscore that individual perception of integration climate fosters individual curiosity and decreases individual aggressiveness. Moreover, we outline that individual curiosity does have an impact on individual learning.

Keywords Business game · Team learning · Curiosity · Technology-based education

1 Introduction

As employee learning plays a pivotal role for organizational innovation and competitive advantage [1], business schools are increasingly seeking approaches that allow enhancing individual learning. Indeed, learning has been outlined as a fundamental element for reaching sustained performance and to prepare individuals and organizations to continuously react and adapt to shifting goals, priorities, and environmental challenges. Due to the increased importance of learning, business schools are enhancing their efforts in order to design training interventions, which may foster individual learning [2].

In pursuing this goal, educational institutions are leveraging on the opportunities offered by the pace of technological innovation through incorporating technology-based tools for stimulating individual learning. The increased importance

---

Authors are listed alphabetically.

L. Caporarello · M. Magni (✉) · F. Pennarola
Bocconi University, Milan, Italy
e-mail: massimo.magni@unibocconi.it

© Springer International Publishing AG 2018
C. Rossignoli et al. (eds.), *Digital Technology and Organizational Change*,
Lecture Notes in Information Systems and Organisation 23,
https://doi.org/10.1007/978-3-319-62051-0_16

of technology based tools in managerial training can be traced back to the fact that technology is considered as a key resource for providing participants' enhanced learning experiences [3]. Such a perspective is also confirmed by previous research, which underscored that participants' interest in and demand for technology-based learning are increasing over time [4].

From a research standpoint, technology-mediated tools received attention with a primarily descriptive approach, or by comparing it to traditional management education (e.g. [5]).

One of the most popular and recognized methods for creating an enhanced experience in the classroom relies on computer-based simulations or business games [6], defined as interactive computer-simulated work environments in which trainees assume different roles to enact real-life scenarios [7]. Such a perspective is also corroborated by an interview to Roberto and Edmondson from the Harvard Business School: "Simulations provide one way to provide some variety in pedagogy. They also provide that rapid feedback on student decision-making which is so critical for their learning" and "A sim requires action and decisions. Students are right in the mix having an experience as opposed to reading about an experience. Team-based sims have the added value of getting students to deal with team dynamics-just like in real life."

Computer simulations in management universities or business schools are often defined as business games. Notwithstanding the wide interest generated by business games, many calls have still to be addressed with regards to design and utilization. Managerial business games are fertile ground for experimentation. If compared with paper-based case histories, they seem to be less consolidated in terms of design methodologies, usage suggestions and results measurement. The aim of this article is to collect empirical evidence on the design and the utilization aspects of a computer-based business game in teams. The use of business games in a learning context is based on several assumptions that can be traced back to learning theories that look at interactive approaches for fostering individual learning and on the complementary assumptions of collaborative learning [8].

Many studies have shown that a positive climate among subjects is fundamental to improve the productivity of their learning process [5]. Thus, group dynamics have a strong impact on learning results within a team-based context, such as the collaborative learning environment. Moreover, group relational dynamics are even more relevant when the team is engaged in solving challenges that require an exchange of information and social interaction [9], and the impact of such relationships is more effective when the challenge to be faced is complex and characterized by interdependencies among individuals [10]. We argue that team dynamics and processes may activate individual states that favour individual learning in a computer-based simulation context.

Drawing on the theories of individual learning and team processes, we develop a model which considers team behavioral integration as positive contextual element that may activate individual curiosity and decrease individual level of aggressiveness, thus allowing individuals to reach higher levels of learning in a simulation-based setting. Figure 1 depicts the research model.

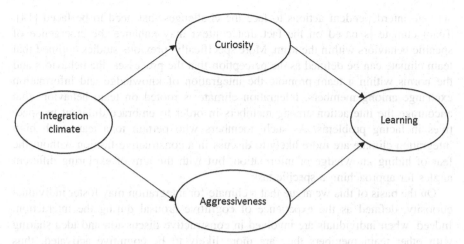

Fig. 1 Research model

2 Theory and Hypotheses

2.1 Social Learning in Simulation-Based Context

The effectiveness of a business game can be related to the mechanism that it can activate both at the individual and group level in order to connect information and develop knowledge. In particular, cognitive theories refer to learning as an active and constructive process carried out by the individual [11], and this it is better achieved when individuals are actively involved in the process itself with the acquisition, generation, analysis and elaboration of information. In a complementary fashion, Vygotsky argues that learning is a social process, initially shared by individuals, and then internalized and personalized by each subject [12]. Thus, the individual learning is better activated not only by involving the subject, but also by developing a social setting of collaborative learning. Through discussion, conversation and comparison, participants develop interpretations of and solutions to the proposed problem-solving situation. Such approaches are even more effective when knowledge of the general problem-solving strategies is acquired through practical resolution of complex problems [13].

2.2 Team Integration Climate and Individual States

Psychological climate plays a pivotal role in influencing individual behavior and it represents an appropriate perspective for developing a better understanding on how context may affect individuals' states. Such an effect is particularly relevant in localized settings, where individuals are immersed in situations where they need to activate interdependent actions to face the challenges that need to be faced [14]. Team climate is based on the fact that context may enhance the emergence of specific behaviors within the team. More specifically, previous studies outlined that team climate can be defined as the perception that the processes, the behaviors and the norms within a team promote the integration of knowledge and information exchange among members. Integration climate is rooted on team behaviors that encourage the interaction among members in order to embrace different perspectives in facing problems. As such, members who pertain to a team with high integration climate are more likely to discuss in a constructive fashion without the fear of hiding knowledge or information, but with the aim of exploring different angles for approaching a specific task

On the basis of this we argue that a climate for integration may foster individual curiosity, defined as the experience of cognitive arousal during the interaction. Indeed, when individuals are involved in constructive discussion and idea sharing with other team members they are more likely to be cognitive activated, thus increasing their desire to find new ways to solve a problem and to proactively contribute to the group activity. Thus, as the individual perceive to be immersed in a context that stimulates sharing of ideas and knowledge, they would develop a cognitive state that favors exploration and it is inquiring. In other words, individuals who are immersed in such kind of situation are likely to be more curios and better explore the simulation and its dynamics.

Besides activating a positive state, we argue that individual's perception of integration climate may smoothen the occurrence of negative states that may hamper the individual learning process in a group setting. Indeed, when individuals feel that they are immersed in a context where the norm is sharing information and knowledge, they would be less likely to develop defensive attitudes that may be in contrast with the environment, which they are embedded in. Indeed, if the climate fosters norm of collaboration and sharing, individual behaviors is likely to be influenced by such norms, thus making less likely that individuals embrace individualistic oriented states, such as aggressiveness. Aggressiveness state is indeed characterized by an attitude toward competitiveness and taking advantage of individual opportunities even if not beneficial for the group [15]. An aggressive state is likely to foster individuals' focus on themselves and on outperforming others. Therefore, a climate that stimulates interaction and sharing among team members is likely to diminish the occurrence of such negative state. Thus, individuals immersed in a computer based simulation, but who share an integration climate, would be more likely to play having in mind the goals of the group. Therefore they would approach the simulation with the intent of favoring the team outcomes rather than their personal outcomes. On the light of these arguments, we state the following:

H1: Integration climate will be positively associated with individual curiosity
H2: Integration climate will be negatively associated with individual aggressiveness

2.3 Individual States and Learning

Individuals who are experiencing a curiosity state present higher levels of attention to the external stimuli in order to satisfy their need for cognitive challenge [16]. Such higher degree of attention brings individuals to be more prone to acquire all the information [17] that are provided by the simulation and all the knowledge coming from other members. In such a way, being more inquisitive in approaching the simulation may lead them to be more likely to understand the dynamics of the simulation and the related contents. For such a reason, individuals who present high degree of curiosity are more likely to present higher levels of learning when immersed in a computer based simulation.

Conversely individuals, who perceive a high degree of aggressiveness when interacting with the group in a simulation setting, are more focused on protecting their information and to understand how to maximize their outcome from the situation [18]. For this reason their attention is focused on issues that are not related to knowledge acquisition and to the inquire state that is associated with learning. In so doing their attention toward the simulation content is not enough for activating an effective learning process.

According to the above-mentioned reasoning we underscore the following:

H3: Curiosity will be positively associated with learning
H4: Aggressiveness will be negatively associated with learning

3 Method

3.1 Sample and Measures

Participants are 402 individuals who participated in a training seminar on team management and leadership adopting a team-based computer simulation. Team members are seated around a table, in front of a computer station, and able to freely talk with each other throughout the game. The simulation is developed in five rounds and the team members play the role of a cross functional team which has to launch a new product on the market. On the basis of their decisions, the simulation reacts and provides a different scenario. To be successful as individuals and as a team, members must unify their efforts (such as interpreting the different set of information provided by the simulation). Indeed, when team members pool their knowledge and data, better decisions can be taken, which in turns positively affect both individual and team simulation scores. The simulation is developed in a way that complexity and knowledge integration necessity are higher at each step. Thus, on the basis of the simulation reactions, members may learn that in such kind of team-based situation information sharing and joint decision-making lead to advantages both for the individual and for the whole team. After the five rounds, a questionnaire has been distributed to each team member in order to assess the interactions with the teammates as well as the interaction with the simulation. Then simulation results were shown and subjects were debriefed.

Data have been gathered through a fully standardized questionnaire (five-point likert scale) developed upon scales already validated in prior research studies.

Individual learning. We adopted a six-item scale relying on the work of Hoegl and Gemuenden [19]. The scale was adapted to the simulation context. The cronbach alpha of the scale was 0.85.

Behavioral integration climate. We measured the individual perception of integration climate by adopting 4 items derived from Li and Hambrick [20]. The coefficient alpha was 0.80, which is consistent with previous studies.

Curiosity was assessed with two items from Agarwal and Karahanna [16] and tapped into the extent the experience arouses an individual's sensory and cognitive curiosity. The cronbach alpha of the scale was 0.64.

Aggressiveness was measured with two items assessing the degree of competitiveness and lack of supportiveness from Erdogan et al. [18]. The cronbach alpha of the scale was 0.56. Whereas the cronbach alpha is lower than the usual average values, we maintained the scale because both items were strongly loading on the aggressiveness factor.

3.2 Analyses and Results

We used partial least square (PLS) to analyze our data. PLS is a structural equation modelling technique which adopts a component-based technique to calculate the relationship between constructs, and variance explained by the theoretical model.

According to Agarwal and Karahanna [16] data analysis process was split in two phases. In the first step we established the psychometric validity of the measures, while in the second we tested our hypotheses. The psychometric properties of the scales were assessed in terms of items loading, internal consistency, and discriminant validity. All items loaded respectfully on their corresponding factor. In order to assess the discriminant validity the square root of the average variance extracted (AVE) should be higher than the interconstruct correlations. All the constructs share more variance on their indicator than other constructs. Overall, we conclude that the measures testing the model all display good psychometric properties.

Figure 2 reports the significant paths coefficients and the explained variance for the model. Following Agarwal and Karahanna [16] we avoided the confounding of results based on specific individual characteristics including in the analysis two control variables: age and gender. As none of the controls were significant, they were dropped from the final model. These results support hypotheses 1 and 2 thus

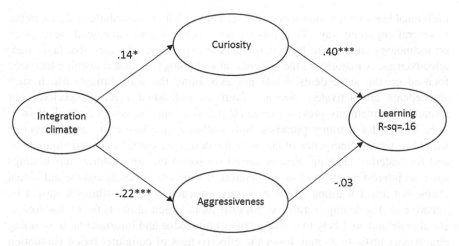

Fig. 2 Results. $^*p < 0.05$, $^{***}p < 0.001$

underscoring a positive effect of integration climate on curiosity and a negative effect on aggressiveness. Moreover, results corroborate hypothesis 3 underscoring a positive influence of curiosity on learning, while they do not support H4. The overall variance explained in individual learning is acceptable (R-sq = 0.16).

4 Discussion

The objective of this research was to understand the mechanisms that activate learning in a team based simulation setting. Our study thus makes a number of contributions to the learning literature and broader education and information systems field. It puts factors associated with cognitive states and team processes in the study of simulation-based training. In particular, the paper shows that team context shapes the emergence of individual states that favor learning. Research on computer mediated simulations remains lacking form this perspective and there are several calls for shedding light on the relationship between learning environment and individual states. Moreover, our study also extends learning research by identifying contextual influences on the expression of individual emergent state in a learning setting, integrating individual learning and team learning domains.

First, our results show that individual states improve individual learning and they represents important mechanisms through which the group environment influences the individual learning process in a computer based simulation setting. As such, curiosity emerges as important enabler in this context. Second, we see that the role of aggressiveness does not affect learning. This suggests that curiosity and aggressiveness affect learning independently of one another. Moreover, it appears that team integration climate represents an important trigger for supporting individual learning in a simulation setting. These findings contribute to the literature in several important ways. First, this research contributes to and extend the research on technology simulations by better understanding the mechanisms that favor their effectiveness. A majority of the research on technology-mediated learning has been focused on the antecedents, while not explaining the way through which such antecedents are activated. Second, from an individual level perspective, our research complements previous research pointing out the positive effect of individual states for learning purposes, thus outlining that university and instructors should foster the emergence of curiosity for designing computer based simulations and for fostering learning. Finally, based on social learning theories our findings show an interesting effect of the perception of team environment and the individual states that affect learning. In other words, instructors and institutions should be attentive in developing learning environments in which individuals are fostered to collaborate and are likely to exchange their knowledge and information. In so doing educational institutions may foster the effectiveness of computer based simulation for learning purposes.

References

1. Edmondson, A. (1999). Psychological safety and learning behavior in work teams. *Administrative Science Quarterly, 44*, 350–383.
2. Meyer, J. P. (2003). Four territories of experience: A developmental action inquiry approach to outdoor-adventure experiential learning. *Academy of Management Learning and Education, 2*(4), 352–363.
3. Alavi, M., & Leidner, D. (2001). Research commentary: Computer mediated learning—A call for greater depth and breadth for research. *Information System Research, 12*, 1–10.
4. Lundgren, T. D., & Nantz, K. S. (2003). Student attitudes toward internet courses: A longitudinal study. *Journal of Computer Information Systems, 43*(3), 61–66.
5. Alavi, M. (1994). Computer-mediated collaborative learning: An empirical evaluation. *MIS Quarterly, 18*(3), 159–174.
6. Michaelson, R., Helliar, C., Power, D., & Sinclair, D. (2001). Evaluating FINESSE: A case-study in group-based CAL. *Computers & Education, 37*(1), 67–80.
7. Proserpio L., & Magni, M. (2005). Learning through business games. In *Encyclopaedia of multimedia technology and networking,* Hershey: Idea Group Publishing.
8. Johnson, D. W., & Johnson, R. (1999). *Learning together and alone: Cooperative, competitive, and individualistic learning* (5th ed.). Boston: Allyn & Bacon.
9. Gladstein, D. L. (1984). Groups in context: A model of task group effectiveness. *Administrative Science Quarterly, 29*, 499–517.
10. Thompson, J. D. (1967). *Organizations in action.* New York: McGraw-Hill.
11. Shuell, T. J. (1986). Cognitive Conceptions of Learning. *Review of Educational Research, 56*(4), 411–436.
12. Vygotsky, L. S. (1978). *Mind in society: The development of higher psychological processes.* Cambridge, MA: Harvard University Press.
13. Pellegrino, J. W., & Glaser, R. (1982). Analyzing aptitudes for learning: inductive reasoning. In R. Glasser (Ed.), *Advances in instructional psychology* (pp. 269–345). Hillsdale, NJ: Erlbaum Associates.

14. Weiss, M., Hoegl, M., & Gibbert, M. (2011). Making virtue of necessity: The role of team climate for innovation in resource constrained innovation projects. *Journal of Product Innovation Management, 28*(s1), 196–207.
15. O'Reilly, C. A., & Caldwell, D. F. (1985). The impact of normative social influence and cohesiveness on task perceptions and attitudes: A social information processing approach. *Journal of Occupational Psychology, 58,* 193–206.
16. Agarwal, R., & Karahanna, E. (2000). Time flies when you're having fun: cognitive absorption and beliefs about information technology usage. *MIS Quarterly, 24*(4), 665–694.
17. Berlyne, D. E. (1960). *Conflict, arousal, and curiosity.* New York City: McGraw-Hill Companies.
18. Erdogan, B., Liden, R. C., & Kraimer, M. L. (2006). Justice and leader-member exchange: The moderating role of organizational culture. *Academy of Management Journal, 49*(2), 395–406.
19. Hoegl, M., & Gemuenden, H. G. (2001). Teamwork quality and the success of innovative projects: A theoretical concept and empirical evidence. *Organization Science, 12*(4), 435–449.
20. Li, J. T., & Hambrick, D. C. (2005). Factional groups: A new vantage on demographic faultlines, conflict, and disintegration in work teams. *Academy of Management Journal, 48*(5), 794–813.

Part III
Societal Innovation and Challenges

The Perception of the Benefits and Drawbacks of Internet Usage by the Elderly People

Dilwar Hussain, Penny Ross and Peter Bednar

Abstract This project looks into the perception of the benefits and drawbacks of Internet usage by elderly people, born from the mid 1920s to the early 1940s, also known as the 'silent generation' (Lustria et al. in Health Informatics Journal 17 (3):224–243, [1]). As governmental services are gradually becoming online, elderly people are required to use the Internet in order to complete the compulsory task(s). The Internet can be a challenging technology for the silent generation due to their experience and knowledge in using the computer and Internet. At the same time elderly people are anxious about Internet security, as they believe they can be victimised, hence the reason why the generation avoids the technology as much as possible. Participants also believed there was no need to use the Internet, as they have managed without the technology throughout their career. The paper also discusses the key elements by outlining the benefits and drawbacks relating to age-related disabilities, affordability, and privacy/security issues. In addition accessibility, usability and design issues are discussed and how that benefits and affects interaction with the Internet from a socio-technical perspective. During the observations participants were observed on how they interact with the Internet. The research suggests participants' experienced accessibility, usability and design issues (i.e. using the mouse, keyboard, font-size, and logging-in).

Keywords Internet · Computer · Technology · Elderly · Silent generation · Senior · Internet banking · Online shopping · Accessibility · Usability · Web design · Training · Privacy · Security · Risk · Keyboard · Mouse · Socio-technical systems

D. Hussain (✉) · P. Ross · P. Bednar
School of Computing, University of Portsmouth, Portsmouth, UK
e-mail: dilwarhussain655@gmail.com

P. Ross
e-mail: penny.ross@port.ac.uk

P. Bednar
e-mail: peter.bednar@port.ac.uk

P. Bednar
Department of Informatics, Lund University, Lund, Sweden

© Springer International Publishing AG 2018   199
C. Rossignoli et al. (eds.), *Digital Technology and Organizational Change*,
Lecture Notes in Information Systems and Organisation 23,
https://doi.org/10.1007/978-3-319-62051-0_17

1   Introduction

The inspiration behind this project originates from the researcher's family background experience on the adoption of Internet technology by the seniors. The researcher initially observed how family members struggled when using the technology, which inspired the author to conduct further research in regards to the topic.

The Internet can be seen as the core communication medium in the Network Society [2]. The Network Society is associated to the social, political, economic and cultural changes, which is caused by the spread of networks, communication technologies and digital information [2]. The Internet plays an important part in our everyday life and is the biggest computer network in the world, connecting millions of computers. This paper discusses research conducted with the elderly people (silent generation - born in the mid 1920s to the early 1940s) [3]. The research was designed to analyse and observe participant's perception and interaction with the Internet (World Wide Web). The findings are examined based on a socio-technical perspective, as the analysis is supported by numerous academic literatures.

The majority of today's silent generation has limited knowledge and experience in using and interacting with the Internet and computers [4]. Our research findings suggest that those participants who have adopted the Internet mentioned (80%) they gain benefit by searching and browsing information on the Internet, such as health related information. However those who gave not adopted the Internet felt uncomfortable and insecure using the Internet, as they felt they have managed without the Internet all their life, therefore the participants did not feel the need to adopt to the Internet. A number of research questions have been identified in order to break down and accomplish the overall objectives of the study. Answering these research questions will provide a better understanding of the subject and the factors influencing it.

1.1   Research Questions

1. Do elderly people benefit from accessing the Internet?
2. What are the reasons for not using the Internet amongst the target group?
3. What types of problems do elderly people encounter accessing the Internet?
4. Do elderly people prefer to use the Internet or prefer manual transactions? i.e. physically going to the bank instead of online banking or pen and paper applications instead of online applications.
5. Does Internet technology make everyday life style tasks easier? i.e. online banking, electronic governmental services, online shopping etc.

When it comes to Internet use experienced as useful by individual human being the question becomes clearly a socio-technical issue [5]. One reason for why people do not use the Internet is because it is not experienced as useful from their own perspective. The 'beginner Internet learning classes' are described as a socio-technical system of elderly people, incorporating varied worldviews [6] that exists within the system and factors influencing perceived usefulness of solutions. The author then outlines two different types of users (Internet and non Internet-users), which determine purposes, and perception of the benefits and drawbacks of Internet usage.

2 Background

A selected number of topics have been chosen to investigate 'the perception of the benefits and drawbacks of Internet usage by elderly people'. Initially the term 'elderly' is defined in the context of the study. However different countries around the world had different perception in defining the term elderly. Therefore the study was aimed based on a generation, called the 'silent generation' (born in the mid 1920s to the early 1940s) as majority of the authors from the literature defined elderly within this category. Key elements of the Internet usage will be outlined to explain the benefits and barriers the elderly encounter. The literature review consisted of exploring barriers relating to Internet adoption such as age related disabilities, expenditure and affordability, privacy, security, trust relations and risks elderly people encounter whilst adopting the Internet. Research was also carried out on the accessibility, usability and design of the webpages and how that affects the elderly's interaction with the Internet. Other research was conducted on how the elderly retrieve valuable training and support in using the Internet, for example if the participants are achieving some level of experience by attending the Internet tutorial classes.

3 Research Method

Throughout the investigation of the topic, primary and secondary research has been conducted by adhering to the Triangulation research methodology. The primary research consisted of two research tools, including observations and structured/semi-structured interviews, which provided a mixture of quantitative and qualitative data. The scope of the project included investigating the perception of the benefits and drawbacks of Internet usage by the elderly people (silent generation). The selection of participants was restricted to Portsmouth (Hampshire) and Swindon (Wiltshire). Furthermore observations were conducted by attending local community centres and libraries, which provided training courses for the beginner elderly Internet/computer users. In total 8 different beginner training classes were attended in order to observe how elderly users interacted with the Internet. Moreover in depth interviews were conducted with 14 participants, 6 being Internet

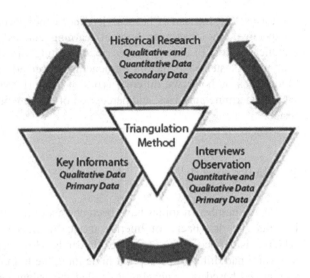

users and 8 being non-Internet users, as this provided the perception of both users.
Electronic survey was considered, however this method was not undertaken as it
could lead to the results being biased because not all users have access to or uses the
Internet [7]. For this study the research methodology was inspired by the
Triangulation Methodology illustrated in Fig. 1.

Triangulation is a method used to analyse the data collected in a study by using
multiple methods to collect data on the same topic [9]. The method assured validity
of the research by using variety of approaches to collect data on the same subject.
There are four types of triangulation methods [10], such as Data Triangulation. This
is when data is gathered through different sampling strategies where parts of the
data are collected during different time periods and social situations and on a variety
of people. Investigator Triangulation is when more than one researcher is involved
in the research to gather and analyse the data. Theoretical Triangulation is when
more than one theoretical position is used in interpreting data and Methodological
Triangulation is when more than one method is used to gather primary data by the
researcher. After considering all four methods the Data Triangulation and
Methodological Triangulation was adhered. This is because the data was gathered
from two different sources by multiple methods and increased the validity of the
data [10]. Additionally data triangulation provides an advantage in social research,
as it provides confidence in the collected data, with clear and deeper understanding
of the phenomena [11]. The Triangulation Methodology provided additional
sources of information and often gave more insight into the selected topic. The
methodology was also beneficial when inadequacies found in one-source data is
minimised when multiple sources confirmed the same or similar data. For example
multiple sources provided verification, assurance and validity while complementing
similar data [11]. Moreover the data and information is supported in multiple types
of research, which provided ease to analyse data to draw conclusions.

Total Participants: 75 (Total Number of Organisations: 8)					120 minutes
Number of times seeking assistant: 211			Trainee's experienced level of achievement: 70		
Keyboard *Typing*	Mouse *Usability*	Display	Step-by-step note taking	Accessibility Issues	Trouble Logging-in
44	40	25	31	34	24

Fig. 2 Observation results/template

Initially the focus was on planning and designing the research tools and strategy, for the interview questions and the structured template to record the results of the observation. The interview questions were identified based on the secondary literature research and was piloted and evaluated further. While testing the data collection form, feasible amendments and improvements were made. For example reflecting on the way the questions were asked during the interviews to reduce the bias by listening to or revising the previous interview scripts/recordings.

The review of the academic research materials has been used to develop foundations of knowledge of elderly people's perception on the Internet technology usage. For example how they believe the Internet will be useful and the benefits and barriers they encounter whilst interacting with the Internet. The observation study template (Fig. 2) monitors the difficulties the users encountered whilst using the Internet. The common barriers identified were accessibility, usability and design issues as well as experiencing difficulties logging-in i.e. emails. The research data was analysed using social-technical framework of reference to systemically comprehend the complexity of the topic [6, 12]. Figure 2 illustrates 75 participants have been observed in total of 8 different observations classes, as the participants required assistance/help 211 times. Out of the 75 participants 70 believed they achieved some level of experience by attending the tutorial class. Taking notes by pen and paper was common (31 users) as it helped the participants learn and remember the tasks and procedures.

4 Data Analysis

The interviews gathered a large amount of qualitative data, which enabled the researcher to gain a deeper insight and understanding of the topic. The results of the interviews were used to compare the findings with the observation results. Whilst conducting the interviews two different templates were used, one for Internet users and the other for non-Internet users. The templates consists of pre-defined questions, however as the interviews were structured and semi-structured the questions varied depending on how the interviewees answered the questions [13, 14].

Textual analysis coding method was used in order to analyse the interview results by highlighting the key themes and categorising the responses into appropriate groups [13, 14]. Below illustrates a number of examples of the interview responses being analysed by highlighting the most frequent and repetitive responses. For example Table 1 illustrates the analysis of Internet users, where 6 participants stated the Internet could be used to improve knowledge and skills.

Table 1 Types of benefits users think they can gain by using the internet

Data item—categories	Number of occurrences	Total
Research purposes	*XX*	2
Improve knowledge and skills	*XXXXXX*	6
Solving problems	*XXX*	3
Hobby	*XXXX*	4
Perform tasks in own comfort	*XXXX*	4
Socialise and network	*XX*	2
Save money	*X*	1

Analysis Internet Users (Table 2)

Table 2 Types of problems encountered accessing the internet

Data item—categories	Number of occurrences	Total
Connection failure	*XXX*	3
Slow connection	*XX*	2
Resolving technical issues	*XXX*	3
Pop-ups	*XXXX*	4
Usability issues	*XXX*	3

Analysis Non-Internet Users (Table 3)

Table 3 Reason for not using the internet

Data item—categories	Number of occurrences	Total
No knowledge	*XXXXXX*	6
Don't require it	*XXXXX*	5
No access	*XX*	2
Complicated and confusing	*XXXXXX*	6
Disability	*XX*	2
Expenditure	*XX*	2
Don't feel safe	*XXX*	3

5 Research Topic

5.1 Generation

Firstly the underlying worries were defining the term "who are the elderly?" This is because after carrying out the literature search (secondary research), it appeared that different countries around the world had different perceptions when defining the term "elderly". This has led the researcher to come to a conclusion and conduct the primary research based on a generation. The generation that was chosen was the "silent generation", where people were born in the mid 1920s to the early 1940s [7]. The generation "baby boomer" was considered (born between 1946 and 1964) [7]. However the "silent generation" was selected because the majority of authors in the literature defined elderly within this category.

5.2 Benefits of Internet

After interviewing two groups of participants; Internet users and non-Internet users, the researcher intended to discover what benefits elderly people think they can gain by using the Internet or if they were to use the Internet. The interview results suggest that all participants believed the Internet could be a useful tool for improving general knowledge and skills, whereas 50% of the non-Internet users had the same perception. In addition 65% of elderly participants who use the Internet mentioned, the Internet could be used for hobby purposes and 57% of participants stated it could also be useful for performing tasks in your own time and comfort. However there does not seem to be enough evidence from the literature review that suggests the perception of elderly people regarding why they believe the Internet can be a useful tool. On the other hand the findings have agreed with Eastman's [15] and Castells [16] study, where both Internet users and non-Internet users thought the Internet could be useful for communicating [2] and networking with families and friends around the world. In addition participants believed it can save money, i.e. you do not have to use your landline to communicate with people in different countries.

The interview results attempts (Internet users) to answer the first research question 'Do elderly people gain benefits accessing the Internet?' After interviewing users that practice using the Internet, 80% of the respondents mentioned they gain benefit by searching health related information. This shows positive correlation with the literature review where Robertson-Lang et al. [17] research also discovered the Internet was a significant resource for searching health related information. This topic is the most common searched field the elderly perform online [8]. It was also found in the secondary and primary research that elderly people generally used the Internet for searching holidays, travel information and checking the weather online [3, 18]. Fifty percent of the participants used the

Internet for communication purposes, such as emailing and social networking. Once again the primary research was consistent with the secondary research, as emailing was one of the most common activities on the Internet the elderly performed [15]. However participants that did not use the Internet for emailing was because they experienced problem-remembering their login details i.e. username and password.

The primary research discovered, a participant found the Internet beneficial by using the 'click and collect' facility. This has found to show some level of similarities with the secondary research, as the literature review suggests elderly people adopt the Internet for various reasons such as online shopping [19]. On the other hand the primary research indicates 65% of the participants used the Internet for watching and reading the news and 50% used the Internet to listen to music and watch videos. However the researcher did not come across any research where elderly people tend to use the Internet to listen to music and watch videos. This was an unexpected surprise, as the researcher was not expecting elderly people to watch videos and listen to music online. An assumption was made beforehand that elderly people would prefer to watch videos on TV or listen to music from a tape recorder or radio.

5.3   Reasons for not Using the Internet

'What are some of the reasons for not using the Internet?' was the second research question the researcher intended to retrieve answers from by interviewing non-Internet users. Seventy-five percent of the participants mentioned they do not use the Internet because they do not have enough knowledge about the technology and did not know how to use a computer. These findings were also supported by Jokisuu's [20] study. Further research by Ogozalek's [21] study discovered that elderly people who did not use the computer mentioned they do not require a computer at all, hence why they don't use the technology. This was found to be partially accurate in the primary research, as 63% of the non-Internet users commented they do not require using the technology. Where one participant stated "I *don't require using it for any sort of reason*". Six out of eight non-Internet users seemed to be finding the technology complicated and confusing, hence the reason for not adopting the Internet. Olphert et al. [22] describes the cost of accessing the Internet can also be an important factor. Where 15.4% of Lee's [23] participants stated, "It cost too much to purchase Internet access". These findings show to be similar with the primary research, where 25% of the interviewees found expenditure as a barrier for not using the Internet.

5.4 Internet Security

Another barrier for not using the Internet is because not all users felt it was safe [24]. A study by Lee [23] justifies the perception and the barriers of Internet security which elderly people encountered. The secondary findings suggest elderly people avoid tasks on the Internet, which involve providing financial information [25]. This was because of fearing their personal information may be at risk as elderly users were concerned about security issues [24]. These findings were found to be accurate by the primary research, where 82% of Internet users and 86% of non-Internet users felt anxious and worried about Internet security, especially regarding financial information. Despite the fact there are security features available to protect users from theft and fraud [24], the majority of the participants preferred not to carry out tasks involving personal data. This explains why one of the participants in the primary research claimed they had been victimised in the past.

A participant also mentioned when they are browsing on the web and carry on the search, the next day the same search is displayed on the screen. This made the user anxious thinking they are being followed or watched. However this was relating to "cookies" as the participant was not educated in this area. This finding was unexpected and turned out to be important, which was not identified in the secondary research. The study has taught the researcher it is important that users are educated about Internet security in order to make them feel a little more confident when using the technology.

5.5 Usability Issues

The researcher conducted interviews and observations to examine the types of problems elderly people encounter whilst accessing the Internet (research question 3). According to the interview (Internet users), 66% of participants explained they encountered usability issues, such as finding pop-ups as a big frustration and problematic. These findings were supported by Gatto and Tak's [26] study, which suggest positive correlation, where participants experienced spam and pop-ups to be the biggest cause of frustration, which potentially leads to viruses. In addition interview results suggests 50% of the participants found connection failure and resolving technical issues challenging, which led the participants to not use the system. These findings turned out to be critical, which was not discovered in the secondary research.

As participants experienced usability issues, they decided to keep a list of step-by-step instructions of how to use the website they frequently visit [27]. These findings are supported by the observation results, as 45% of the beginner Internet learners took step-by-step notes whilst attending the tutorial sessions. An Internet user also commented the step-by-step notes could become invalid as the design/layout of websites can occasionally change. This was also echoed by

Nielsen [27], as the author's study explains the notes can become irrelevant when the design of the website changes. This led to further challenges as users had to re-learn and understand the new design and take new notes. The observation result also suggests 58% faced problems using the keyboard. For example participants were confused when using specific symbols and functions. Another usability issue identified during the observation was the difficulty in using the mouse. Users were occasionally confused between the right and left mouse click. These findings are also supported by Gatto and Tak's [26] research, whose findings showed similarities with regards to usability issues.

5.6 Accessibility Issues

Good et al. [18] study discovers participants faced accessibility issues whilst using the Internet, which was generally caused by visual impairments [28]. Visual impairments led to participants having difficulties to read written instructions and manuals from the display screen [29]. This behaviour was also observed during the observation as 45% of participants encountered accessibility issues, such as eyesight problems. In addition the findings show correlation with the interview results, as 25% of the elderly Internet users and all the non-Internet users explained they experience eyesight problems. Therefore showing positive correlation between the primary and secondary findings as users with visual impairment experienced difficulties to see written content on the display screen. This implies that not all elderly users are aware of the 'font enlargement' feature or possibly the websites are not applying to the W3C standards and regulations [30].

The analysis of Internet users and non-Internet users discovered participants having 'shaky hands', which led to difficulties in using the mouse and keyboard. However during the observation it was identified those participants were using special keyboards and ergonomic mouse in order to assist them to use the Internet. This is described by Mitzner et al. [31] study, as the author states there are adaptive features and hardware available to support users with accessibiliy issues.

5.7 Internet or Manual Transactions

The fourth research question focussed on "if elderly people preferred to use the Internet or manual transactions to complete tasks". For example if the participants preferred to use the Internet or preferred face-to-face interaction, i.e. physically going out to shop instead of online shopping, going to the bank instead of online banking. The primary results indicate 67% of the silent generation preferred face-to-face interaction. This was found to be accurate with Beneke et al. [4] research. The author highlights, participants preferred face-to-face communication instead of using the Internet. However on the other hand 16% mentioned they do prefer to use the Internet or it may depend on the situation. Moreover 2 users stated they do prefer online shopping as it allows more comfort and avoids queuing up and carrying shopping bags. This research showed consistency with Sum et al. [19] study where using the Internet for online shopping provided an advantage, as shoppers do not have to carry shopping bags home. It can be agreed online shopping can be advantageous, however there are disadvantages as 66% of elderly people disliked online shopping because they did not feel secure and confident providing their financial information [25].

5.8 E-Government

Both Internet and non-Internet users were interviewed to get their perception on the governmental services going online (E-Government). The majority of the Internet users believed the service could be beneficial as the process could be quicker and efficient. This shows similarities with the secondary research as the elderly Internet participants used the Internet for governmental services, such as paying bills and taxing their vehicles [4, 32]. However the Internet users argued the service should be optional by having both facilities available, as not everyone knows how to use a computer and the Internet. Moreover 50% of the interviewees mentioned they do prefer pen and paper applications, where the other 50% did not mind using either facility. The non-Internet participants were not pleased about e-government service as they claimed they "don't like technology". All the non-Internet participants argued that there should be alternative methods available. Despite the fact governmental services are going online, it still does not encourage all elderly participants to adopt the Internet. Participants believed they can discover alternative methods i.e. getting their family members to complete tasks.

5.9 Computer Training

The primary research has discovered 37% of non-Internet users are aware of the free public computer training sessions for elderly people. This shows similarities with the secondary research, as there are public libraries that provide both Internet access and training for elderly beginner users [33]. Therefore this leads 63% of non-Internet users not being aware of the free computer training sessions. This suggests that perhaps the classes are not being advertised appropriately as the majority of the elderly people were not aware of the facility. Fifty percent of the participants mentioned they would consider attending the free classes. The other 50% stated they would not attend the class because they did not feel the need to use the Internet as they have managed without it throughout their career. Eighty-seven percent of the participants that do not use the Internet tend to seek assistance from other members if a task requires using the Internet. This information was interesting, as the researcher did not manage to find any similarities during the secondary research.

6 Conclusion

The project emphasised the perception of the benefits and drawbacks of Internet usage by the elderly people (silent generation). However after completing the study, it can be perceived that the drawbacks of Internet usage are being commonly discussed, while the benefits are being overlooked. Despite the challenges of using the Internet, It can be suggested those elderly people who have adopted the Internet do benefit from the technology. While the non-Internet participants who have no experience of using the technology had a negative perception and did not show much interest.

Although the use of the Internet can be beneficial for the silent generation and in some situations has a positive impact in their life style, it can also come across equally having several drawbacks. Overall, the research suggests those elderly people that have adopted the Internet and attended the socio-technical environment [11] to learn to use the Internet seemed to gain some level of benefit by using the technology. Elderly people with negative perceptions of the technology, result in lack of motivation [17, 34] and determination to learn to use the Internet. Non-Internet users believed they managed without the technology throughout their career; therefore they can carry on without it. One of the key underlying reasons for not using the Internet is because a number of participants were not willing to learn to use the technology. This can be due to the socio-technical environment as not all participants found the beginner learning classes convenient i.e. location [35]. However those who are practicing to use the Internet did seem to find the technology challenging and complicated. This suggests, perhaps web developers should consider making web pages more user friendly in order for it to be accessible, usable and less complex [6] for all types of users, enabling simpler interaction between people and technology.

Expenditure and affordability was identified as a barrier, as not everyone believed it was worth paying for the technology if they were not going to make good use of it. The cause of Internet security threats and online hacking has also made elderly people anxious in using the technology. A number of participants felt worried and insecure when it relates providing financial and personal information; therefore the generation prefers face-to-face interaction [36] like the "old fashioned" way.

Numerous participants did not provide the researcher consent to carry out the observation study, which was a limitation. This was because a number of users felt uncomfortable and anxious learning, whilst being observed by an external researcher [11]. The barriers and challenges stated as the limitations of the research could be seen as potential future recommendations. One of the recommendations for future research will be to conduct both electronic and paper based surveys. The electronic survey was not carried out on its own because it may provide biased results, as responses from non-Internet users will not be achieved.

References

1. Lustria, M. L. A., Smith, S. A., & Hinnant, C. C. (2011). Exploring digital divides: an examination of eHealth technology use in health information seeking, communication and personal health information management in the USA. *Health Informatics Journal, 17*(3), 224–243.
2. Bednar, P. M., & Welch, C. (2008). Bias, misinformation and the paradox of neutrality. *Informing Science, 11*, 85–106.
3. Karavidas, M., Lim, N. K., & Katsikas, S. L. (2005). The effects of computers on older adult users. *Computers in Human Behavior, 21*(5), 697–711.
4. Beneke, J., Frey, N., Chapman, R., Mashaba, N., & Howie, T. (2011). The grey awakening: A South African perspective. *Journal of Consumer Marketing, 28*(2), 114–124.
5. Bednar, P. M. (2009). Contextual analysis: A multiperspective inquiry into emergence of complex socio-cultural systems. In G. A. M. Minati & E. Pessa (Eds.), *Processes of emergence of systems and systemic properties: Towards a general theory of emergence* (pp. 299–312). Singapore: World Scientific.
6. Checkland, P., & Scholes, J. (1999). *Soft systems methodology in action: A 30 year retrospective.* Chichester: Wiley.
7. Horevoorts, N. J., Vissers, P. A., Mols, F., Thong, M. S., & van de Poll-Franse, L. V. (2015). Response rates for patient-reported outcomes using web-based versus paper questionnaires: Comparison of two invitational methods in older colorectal cancer patients. *Journal of medical Internet research, 17*(5), e111.
8. Miroshnikova, G. (2014). An evaluation of public participation theory and practice: The Waterloo Region case (Unpublished doctoral thesis). University of Waterloo, Canada. Retrieved from https://uwspace.uwaterloo.ca/bitstream/handle/10012/8863/Miroshnikova_Galina.pdf?sequence=3.
9. Jupp, V. (2006). *The Sage dictionary of social research methods.* London: SAGE.
10. Denzin, N. K. (1970). *The research act: A theoretical introduction to sociological methods.* New Brunswick: Transaction Publishers.
11. Mumford, E. (2013). Designing human systems—The ETHICS Method.
12. Von Bulow, I. (1989). The bounding of a problematic situation and the concept of system's boundary in soft systems methodology. *Journal of Applied Systems Analysis, 16*, 35–41.
13. Corbin, J., & Strauss, A. (2014). Basics of qualitative research: Techniques and procedures for developing grounded theory (4th ed.). Thousand Oaks: Sage.
14. Goulding, C. (1999). *Grounded Theory: some reflections on paradigm, procedures and misconceptions.* Retrieved from http://hdl.handle.net/2436/11403.
15. Eastman, J. K., & Iyer, R. (2004). The elderly's uses and attitudes towards the Internet. *Journal of Consumer Marketing, 21*(3), 208–220.
16. Castells, M. (2011). The rise of the network society: The information age: Economy, society, and culture (Vol. 1). New York: Wiley.
17. Robertson-Lang, L., Major, S., & Hemming, H. (2011). An exploration of search patterns and credibility issues among older adults seeking online health information. *Canadian Journal on Aging, 30*(4), 631–645.
18. Good, A., Stokes, S., & Jerrams-Smith, J. (2007). Elderly, novice users and health information web sites-issues of accessibility and usability. *Journal of Healthcare Information Management, 21*(3), 72–79.

19. Sum, S., Mathews, R. M., & Hughes, I. (2009). Participation of older adults in cyberspace: How Australian older adults use the internet. *Australasian Journal on Ageing, 28*(4), 189–193.
20. Jokisuu, E., Kankaanranta, M., & Neittaanmäki, P. (2007). Computer usage among senior citizens in Central Finland. *Agora Human Technology Centre: Univeristy of Jyvaskyla.*
21. Ogozalek, V. Z. (1994). A comparison of the use of text and multimedia interfaces to provide information to the elderly. *Proceedings of the SIGCHI conference on human factors in computing systems* (pp. 65–71). Boston: ACM.
22. Olphert, C. W., Damodaran, L., & May, A. J. (2005, August). Towards digital inclusion–engaging older people in the 'digital world'. In *Accessible design in the digital world conference* (pp. 23–25).
23. Lee, B., Chen, Y., & Hewitt, L. (2011). Age differences in constraints encountered by seniors in their use of computers and the internet. *Computers in Human Behavior, 27*(3), 1231–1237.
24. Akhter, S. H. (2015). Impact of internet usage comfort and internet technical comfort on online shopping and online banking. *Journal of International Consumer Marketing, 27*(3), 207–219.
25. Tatnall, A., & Lepa, J. (2003). The internet, e-commerce and older people: An actor-network approach to researching reasons for adoption and use. *Logistics Information Management, 16*(1), 56–63.
26. Gatto, S. L., & Tak, S. H. (2008). Computer, internet, and e-mail use among older adults: Benefits and barriers. *Educational Gerontology, 34*(9), 800–811.
27. Nielsen, J. (2013). Neilson Norman Group: Seniors as web users. Retrieved from http://www.nngroup.com/articles/usability-for-senior-citizens/.
28. NHS. (2014, February 02). *Age-related cataracts.* Retrieved October 19, 2015 from National Health Service: http://www.nhs.uk/conditions/Cataracts-age-related/Pages/Introduction.aspx.
29. Sinclair, A., Ryan, B., & Hill, D. (2014). Sight loss in older people the essential guide for general practice. Retrieved November 1, 2015, from Royal College of General Practitioners: http://www.rcgp.org.uk/ ~ /media/Files/CIRC/Eye%20Health/RCGP-Sight-Loss-in-Older-People-A-Guide-for-GPs.ashx.
30. W3C. (1999). *Web content accessibility guidelines 1.0.* Retrieved from https://www.w3.org/TR/WCAG10/wai-pageauth.pdf.
31. Mitzner, T. L., Boron, J. B., Fausset, C. B., Adams, A. E., Charness, N., Czaja, S. J., et al. (2010). Older adults talk technology: Technology usage and attitudes. *Computers in Human Behavior, 26*(6), 1710–1721.
32. Hill, R., Beynon-Davies, P., & Williams, M. D. (2008). Older people and internet engagement: Acknowledging social moderators of internet adoption, access and use. *Information Technology & People, 21*(3), 244–266.
33. Xie, B. (2012). Improving older adults'e-health literacy through computer training using NIH online resources. *Library & information science research, 34*(1), 63–71.
34. Douglas, D. (2006). Intransivities of managerial decisions: A grounded theory case. *Management Decision, 44*(2), 259–275.
35. Checkland, P., & Holwell, S. (1997). *Information, systems and information systems: Making sense of the field.* Chichester: John Wiley & Sons Ltd.
36. Stowell, F. (2012). The appreciative inquiry method—A suitable candidate for action research? *Systems Research and Behavioral Science, 30*(1), 15–30.

Collaboration Dynamics in Healthcare Knowledge Intensive Processes: A State of the Art on Sociometric Badges

Davide Aloini, Chiara Covucci and Alessandro Stefanini

Abstract Modern organizations, particularly in Healthcare, increasingly adopt knowledge Intensive Processes (KIPs) and use work teams to perform knowledge intensive tasks and coordination activities. Despite a growing interest on the topic of KIPs, studies analyzing the role of interactions among knowledge workers and their collaboration dynamics as drivers of process performance are still lack in the literature. This research aims to offer a methodological support towards a more quantitative and systematic analysis of such process dynamics. Thus, a state of the art is assessed by a structured and in-depth investigation of the academic literature. Results focus on Sociometric badges/sensors as an innovative way and potential valuable tool to quantitatively analyze social dynamics of collaboration in KIPs by measuring participant interactions and group behavior. Main benefits and possible alerts are identified and analyzed in order to provide valuable directions for applications and further research.

Keywords Knowledge intensive process · Sociometric badges · Healthcare · Literature review

1 Introduction

Unstructured processes, also known as Knowledge Intensive Processes (KIPs), are defined as processes where execution is mainly driven by contingent decisions taken by the actors so that the process is rarely characterized exactly by the same pattern. These kind of processes are quite common in a variety of business

D. Aloini (✉) · C. Covucci
University of Pisa, Pisa, Italy
e-mail: davide.aloini@dsea.unipi.it

A. Stefanini
University of Roma Tor Vergata, Rome, Italy
e-mail: alessandro.stefanini@uniroma2.it

© Springer International Publishing AG 2018   213
C. Rossignoli et al. (eds.), *Digital Technology and Organizational Change*,
Lecture Notes in Information Systems and Organisation 23,
https://doi.org/10.1007/978-3-319-62051-0_18

applications. Think, as just an example, at the many R&D activities aiming at New Product Development, or also to highly customized professional services. In Healthcare, for example, highly-structured work involves most of the organizational processes including some production and administrative activities (diagnostic exams, patient admission/discharge, appointment scheduling, etc.). However, other business services are hardly dependent on the patient case, medical knowledge and evidence. Hence, they involve collaborative features and unstructured processes that do not have the same level of predictability< (e.g. clinical procedures, medical treatment processes). See Kemsley [19] for a detailed classification of structured and unstructured processes.

Evidence shows that unstructured processes are at the core of many business activities and the understanding of surrounded dynamics is critical for managers. In this setting, in fact, traditional Process Management Systems aiming at improving operations in the work environment offer a limited support and are hard to adapt since they mostly apply to fully structured processes with controlled interactions between participants. A major assumption and limitation to PMS suitability is that such processes, after having been modelled, can be repeatedly instantiated and executed.

Numerous works in the Business Process Management (BPM) literature focused on the issues of how to model low or un-structured processed, trying to identify and formalize in a flexible way the activity sequencing and related decision logic [6, 7]. However, while offering a methodological support to deal with KIPs' coordination system, just few of them [15, 24, 26, 38] explicitly focus on the analysis of interactions among knowledge workers and their collaboration dynamics, which instead seem really to be the performance drivers of this kind of processes.

Modern organizations, in fact, increasingly adopt work teams to perform knowledge intensive tasks and coordination activities [10, 14, 45] so that the comprehension of the collaboration dynamics is becoming more and more important to improve their performance. Healthcare KIPs, for example, are very ad hoc processes [13, 30], highly subjected to human collaboration, and participants—including patients sometimes—have the expertise and autonomy to decide their own working procedures. Therefore, these processes have a high degree of freedom and variability, the order of execution is non-deterministic but strongly affected by social interactions among process participants (e.g. surgery activity as in [17, 12, 39]).

The debate on the topic is still developing and there is a need to shed further light on how collaboration dynamics and interactions among process participants could drive performance of KIPs. Particularly this paper would be a first step in order to identify valuable ways to study behavioural dynamics within such class of processes in order to enable a more robust and reliable technical/managerial analysis. A first step in this direction is here accomplished by a systematic and in-depth investigation of the literature.

2 Research Background

2.1 Knowledge Intensive Processes: Features and Challenges

Panian [36] defined KIPs as "knowledge-centric processes" performed by Knowledge workers "they create, acquire, distribute and finally apply knowledge through experiences and collaboration with others". As a consequence, the coordination structure of KIPs is goal-oriented and mostly driven by knowledge. In this setting, both formal/informal and tacit/explicit knowledge is fundamental for process decisions and progress. Also, the collaborative nature of the process work stresses the importance of interactions and behavioral collaboration dynamics for the outcome. In this section, we offer a preliminary overview of KIPs features and current research challenges.

KIPs are usually considered as a distinct class of processes because of their specific characteristics, which are reported here following (Fig. 1 presents a framework explaining KIPs' structure). See also Di Ciccio et al. [6].

1. **Knowledge Intensity**. Knowledge is the key element that drives the knowledge workers' behaviour and the evolution of the process path. The knowledge workers are the main constrains in the process development.
2. **High Variability**. KIPs do not share a general workflow structure. Every case might change in an unpredictable way because of the high number of different variables that affect the process. Also external events, or interrelated cases, may strongly affect the main business case, changing the previously used pattern and the knowledge workers' decision making.

Fig. 1 KIPs framework
(*Source* [6])

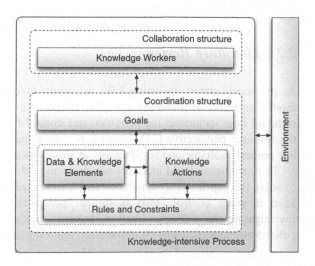

3. **Information Complexity**. Information required for process decisions is a critical issue in KIPs. Experience has a fundamental value in these processes and serves as a guide in processing future activities. In order to influence correctly the pursuance of the KIPs process, information must be available at the right time.

4. **Collaboration and coordination**. Collaboration and coordination along the process are usually guaranteed by different ways: interviews, informational exchanges, meetings, team work and similar ones. The presence of multiple participants and roles with a high degree of autonomy make the management of collaboration and coordination more complex.

5. **Time Variance**. The unpredictability and the external influence on the process make it difficult to evaluate in advance the time required for process execution. The standard processes' measures, as time and cost, are hardly applicable.

6. **Goal Oriented**. KIPs might require a long time to be carried out, so that a series of intermediate milestones and goals are usually defined to monitor the progress of the activities.

Due to this complexity, engineering of knowledge-intensive processes is far from being mastered [6]. Up to date, the BPM community has mostly focused on supporting the coordination structure (relying on the traditional notion of process models, valid for structured processes), and has often neglected collaboration aspects which instead are typical of KIPs. Nevertheless, nowadays KIPs are considerably important as they represent a consistent part of modern business processes both at a managerial and operational level. A first methodological issue to be solved is how to model and analyze this kind of processes in order to understand process determinants. Thus, enabling a more systematic KIPs' analysis is one of the main challenge in order to define the right design parameters and keep them under control, possibly finding a "balance between practices and procedure" [36].

2.2 Literature Review

As previously stated, analyzing KIPs is a tricky task since it firstly requires a hard modelling effort to transform complex process knowledge and interactions in a standard flow including: the activities and control-flow; the data perspective; and the resource perspective [25]. Up to date, traditional tools and methodologies are not properly suitable and/or adaptable to this purpose.

Thus, studies in BPM literature which try to address KIP perspective mostly aim to solve the gap between dynamism and standardization of the process in order to keep it under control. Two prominent perspective can be identified: studies investigating the KIP coordination structure and studies trying to support KIP collaboration mechanisms. Summarizing, main streams can be classified as follows:

- Knowledge Management and Information System studies which aim at coding and standardizing knowledge and experience of process participants (e.g. creating an integrated database of cases to collect relevant reference patterns). These knowledge and patterns can be transferred and applied—also through new information systems—in new cases to flexibly support process coordination and agile workflow management [6, 36].
- Modelling studies developing flexible declarative languages that can be effectively used to support modelling activities. Resulting models have no rigid control-flow structure. Nonetheless, they try to introduce formal objects to indicate the environmental elements that might affect the process [6].
- Collaboration and Behavioural studies. Research focuses on the development and refinement of collaboration tools in order to better support information and knowledge exchange within and throughout the KIPs. This is in the aim to manage the complexity and the dynamism of these processes [31, 36].Other studies analyse behavioural patterns in KIPs, i.e. the way in which people organized and accomplish their work in order to identify regularity in patterns and possible relations with process performances [7, 37]

This work belongs to this last stream and particularly contribute to investigate process interaction between team members in collaborative tasks.

3 Research Objectives

The ultimate aim of this research is to explore how the collaboration among knowledge workers can affect performance of Healthcare KIPs. In so doing, this paper would be a first step in order to understand how process interactions and collaboration dynamics between KIPs' participants could be effectively measured and analyzed in a direct and quantitative fashion.

Research on collaborative processes, inside real organizations, is usually done through interviews, direct observations, questionnaires and IS reports [5, 3]. These data collection methods are affected by subjectivity of observed and observers, and limit richness, quality and reliability of data [2, 23, 27, 33]. At our best knowledge, in this context, many methodological concerns are still open and studies analyzing this point are lack in the literature.

Thus, we assess a systematic and in-depth investigation of the literature in order to understand current approaches, focusing in particular on studies reporting quantitative analysis of social interactions using Sociometric badges. Sociometric badges, in fact, might offer a novel and more systematic way to quantitatively investigate KIPs collaboration dynamics. These tools (invented by the group of Pentland at the MIT Media) can automatically and directly measure individual and collective dynamics in a quantitative way [33]. Thanks to direct and quantitative measurement, the Sociometric badges seem to be able to overtake the most important limit in the studies of collaborative processes.

Here following the main research objectives:

- Investigate the applicability of Sociometric badges to the KIP analysis
- Identify potential strengths/benefits and possible risk/alerts for Sociometric badges adoption.

4 Research Methodology

Stage 1—Data collection. The examined papers consist of articles and conference papers indexed by *SCOPUS* database. Therefore, we checked the studies published by the most important worldwide specialists: Emerald, IEEE, Science Direct, Springer and the other most important journals and conferences. We used the keywords *SOCIOMETRIC BADGE* and *SOCIOMETRIC SENSOR* in *abstract, keyword* and *title*, for the initial phase of data collection. In this way, we were reasonably confident that the main works, in the analyzed field of study, were selected.

Initially we collected 31 papers: 8 journal articles and 23 conference papers. After a preliminary screening of the studies, 4 conference papers were considered out of the scope of analysis. After that, a second and more in-depth analysis of the documents was performed in order to select the works definitively consistent with the methodological purpose of this research. We discarded the studies not properly focusing on Sociometric measurement (3 documents) and those analyzing the same case study from a similar perspective (3 conference papers reports evidence by the same case study). We decided to keep only one of them. Figure 2 shows the main phases of the data collection and refinement. The final sample of interest was made of 22 papers, of which 8 articles and 14 conference papers. It is a small sample still but interesting considering the novelty of the field.

Two paper out of 22 treat *Sociometric sensor* rather than *Sociometric badges*. Even if we did not consider differentiation between these two tools in the analysis, it is valuable to notice that Sociometric badges catch measurement about physical activity, relative and absolute position, and speech activity whereas Sociometric sensor just collect data only on the relative and absolute position.

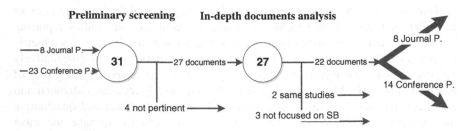

Fig. 2 Data collection

Stage 2—Data analysis. Once selected, papers were analyzed as follows:

- In a first step, we analyzed the time-trend of published documents, distinguished between conference papers and journal articles.
- A second step consisted of a very in-depth analysis of the selected papers, in order to provide a comprehensive picture of the current research in the field, especially from a methodological viewpoint: using Sociometric badges to analyze unstructured processes. At this stage, we have classified contributions according to the following four dimensions:

1. *Research type*, we distinguished among Technical research, Empirical research, Review, and Research proposal/Theoretical papers.
2. *Field of application*, we identified the field in which the study was carried on. We recognize some research as *Social Science*, because some studies do not focalize on a particular economic sector but only on the personal or social behaviours/attitudes.
3. *Research scope*, we distinguished between Individual Research and Social Research. The Individual Research focuses on the personal behaviour, trying to link the individual sociometric data with attitudes, personal nature and/or individual performance. Rather, the Social Research focalizes on the aggregated behaviour, trying to link the sociometric data with group (team) attitudes, group nature and/or group performance. Some studies might involve both the approaches.
4. *Process Performance*, we have discriminated between papers that tried to link sociometric data with process performance and those not. In fact, to understand how the KIPs' dynamics influence process performance is at the core of our proposal.

Stage 3—Discussion. Contributions were analysed in order to catch how Sociometric badge technologies can support or facilitate a quantitative analysis of unstructured processes. Preliminary findings allow to get some direction on Pros/Cons and about possible interesting directions for further research in healthcare.

5 Findings

5.1 Time-Trend of Published Documents

Our analyses show the novelty of the research in the field of Sociometric sensor, with the first studies dated back to 2008. In addition, the time-series show that this field of study is slowly maturing, with the growth of more robust research presented by scientific journal. Direct and quantitative approaches are highly desirable to investigate collaboration dynamics and behavioural issue in KIPs. Definitely, Sociometric badges still have a great potential in this direction. Methodological recommendations could be of huge value for researchers at this maturity stage.

5.2 State of the Art

Table 1 presents papers classified according to the **Research type**. As expected, empirical research is dominant in this field. This preliminary evidence seems to support the utility and suitability of Sociometric tools for improving and extending research on collaboration, both inside organizational contexts and in society.

Table 2 presents papers classification according to the **Field of application**. We distinguished among *Service, Social Science, Manufacturing*, and *Simulation*. As for *simulation*, we considered the application of Sociometric badges in simulated settings rather than in a real environment. Research using Sociometric badges mainly addresses the service sector. This fact suggests a full applicability of sociometric approach to the service setting, where there is a relevant incidence of KIP. Analysing studies on services, we can underline a major presence of software firms and research institutions/universities. Some works also concern to healthcare, we point out one research study in a ward, Post-anesthesia care unit (PACU), inside the Boston hospital [34]. In addition, Yu et al. [44] simulated the use of Sociometric badges inside an Emergency Room in order to demonstrate the applicability of such technique in that contest.

Table 1 Research type

	List of papers
Empirical research	*Stehlé et al.* [40]; *Chancellor et al.* [4]; *Orbach et al.* [35]; *Johannes et al.* [16]; *Alshamsi et al.* [1]; Kalimeri et al. [18]; Do et al. [8]; Watanabe et al. [42]; Lepri et al. [28]; Tripathi and Burleson [41]; Dong et al. [9]; Niinimäki [32]; Olguín et al. [34]; Kim et al. [21]; Kim et al. [20]; Wu et al. [43]
Technical research	*Olguín et al.* [33]; *Yu et al.* [44]
Review	Kim et al. [22]; Fischbach et al. [11]
Research proposal/Theoretical	*Kim et al.* [23]; Lyra et al. [29]

Journal articles in italics

Table 2 Field of application

	List of papers
Service	*Chancellor et al.* [4]; *Olguín et al.* [33]; *Kim et al.* [23]; Do et al. [8]; Watanabe et al. [42]; Lepri et al. [28]; Tripathi and Burleson [41]; Dong et al. [9]; Niinimäki [32]; Olguín et al. [34]; Kim et al. [21]; Fischbach et al. [11]; Lyra et al. [29]; Wu et al. [43]
Social science	*Stehlé et al.* [40]; *Alshamsi et al.* [1]; Kalimeri et al. [18]; Kim et al. [20]
Manufacturing	*Orbach et al.* [35]
Simulation	*Yu et al.* [44]; *Johannes et al.* [16]

Journal articles in italics

Table 3 shows papers according to the *Research scope*. It demonstrates that sociometric badges/sensors can be proficiently applied both to Individual and Social research. Therefore, the sociometric method can be used to link the individual sociometric data with attitudes and individual performance, and in parallel, to link the group sociometric data with group (team) attitudes and group performance. These elements shed further light on the great potential of this tools in exploring collaboration structure of KIPs.

In Table 4 papers investigating *Process Performance* are reported. Some papers were considered *Not Pertinent* to the classification (literature reviews). Results show that Sociometric badges could support researchers to link the individual behaviours and attitudes, and group (team) behaviours and attitudes to the individual and/or group (team) performance. In particular, almost all contributions [9, 20, 34, 39–43] are focused on the identification and measurement of team (or other work group) performance. To understand how the process dynamics influence performance is one of the most interesting and challenging question to grasp for KIP management and the sociometric approach is relevant and valuable in this purpose.

Table 3 Research scope

	List of papers
Individual studies	*Olguín et al.* [33]; *Chancellor et al.* [4]; *Alshamsi et al.* [1]; *Yu et al.* [44]; *Johannes et al.* [16]; *Stehlé et al.* [40]; Kalimeri et al. [18]; Kim et al. [21]; Lepri et al. [28]
Social studies	Orbach et al. [35]; Do et al. [8]; Watanabe et al. [42]; Kim et al. [20]; Wu et al. [43]; Tripathi and Burleson [41]; Niinimäki [32]; Lyra et al. [29]
Individual and social studies	*Kim et al.* [23]; Dong et al. [9]; Olguín et al. [34]

Journal articles in italics

Table 4 Process Performance

	List of papers
Process performance	Lepri et al. [28]; Watanabe et al. [42]; Dong et al. [9]; Tripathi and Burleson [41]; Olguín et al. [34]; Kim et al. [20]; Wu et al. [43]
Without process performance	*Orbach et al.* [33, 35]; *Chancellor et al.* [4]; *Alshamsi et al.* [1]; *Yu et al.* [44]; *Johannes et al.* [16]; *Stehlé et al.* [40]; Do et al. [8]; Niinimäki [32]; Lyra et al. [29]; Kalimeri et al. [18]; Kim et al. [21]; Kim et al. [23]
Not pertinent	Kim et al. [22]; Fischbach et al. [11]

Journal articles in italics

6 Discussion and Conclusions

Preliminary findings from the literature allow to understand some important aspects, strengths and limitations, about the applicability of sociometric methodology inside organizational settings, in particular to analyze the collaborative processes of Healthcare organizations.

One of the most important challenges in studying collaborative processes is due to data collection that is frequently assessed by interviews, direct observations, questionnaires and reports [3, 5]. Thus, data collection is not real time but mediated and performed in batch and discontinuous way which imply a lower data richness, quality and reliability. In addition, standard methods to measure and evaluate human behavior often suffer from subjectivity and memory effects [33], or face problems with the influence of the observer on the system [2, 23, 27].

Sociometric badges can automatically and directly measure individual and collective patterns of behavior, predict human behavior from unconscious social signals, identify social affinity among individuals working in the same team, and, eventually, enhance social interactions by providing feedback to the users of system [33]. Therefore, the Sociometric badges are able to measure individual and collective patterns of behavior directly and in a quantitative way, overtaking the most important limit in the studies of collaborative processes. Furthermore, Sociometric badges are able to guaranty the privacy; in fact, it is impossible to determine the content of the conversation or identify the speaker from the sociometric data. In this way, these badges are likely to be far less intrusive than a human observer, potentially limiting any social facilitation distortions to the data [33].

On the other hand, the Sociometric badges methodology presents even some weaknesses. Researchers find relationships between sensor data and individual/organizational attitudes or performance, but they generally do not identify causal relationships. The approach is more useful in discovering correlations between the data, rather in detecting possible explanations of phenomenon (e.g. [9, 34]). Another open issue, about sociometric approach, is the influence on the results by the specific contest under investigation. Indeed, the patterns of behavior, attitudes etc. may be affected by various external factors as the specific organizational environment, the national culture, the sector of activity, the educational level, etc. This fact may introduce the problem in the generalization of the results obtained with the Sociometric badges methodology. Therefore, in the research design phase, it is fundamental to pay attention to the various external factors that could affect the collected data.

Lastly, although the data capture and processing is relatively simple, the data management could be relative difficult due to the large volumes of data usually obtained in this type of research.

Concluding despite the existent weaknesses of this review mostly due to the very nascent stage of research, evidence is mostly positive and encourages researchers to adopt Sociometric badges or at least test them in a wider set of organization.

In further development, we aim to use Sociometric badges in healthcare organization for the study of collaborative processes. Currently we have identified a preliminar test case and we are refining the research design and data collection protocol.

References

1. Alshamsi, A., Pianesi, F., Lepri, B., Pentland, A., & Rahwan, I. (2016). Network diversity and affect dynamics: The role of personality traits. *PLoS ONE, 11*(4), e0152358.
2. Barley, S. R. (1990). Images of imaging: Notes on doing longitudinal field work. *Organization Science, 1*(3), 220–247.
3. Chambers, D., et al. (2012). Social network analysis in healthcare settings: a systematic scoping review. *PLoS ONE, 7*(8), e41911.
4. Chancellor, J., Layous, K., & Lyubomirsky, S. (2014). Recalling positive events at work makes employees feel happier, move more, but interact less: A 6-week randomized controlled intervention at a Japanese workplace. *Journal of Happiness Studies, 16*(4), 871–887.
5. Cunningham, F. C., et al. (2012). Health professional networks as a vector for improving healthcare quality and safety: A systematic review. *BMJ Quality & Safety, 21*(3), 239–249.
6. Di Ciccio, C., Marrella, A., & Russo, A. (2015). Knowledge-intensive processes: Characteristics, requirements and analysis of contemporary approaches. *Journal on Data Semantics, 4*(1), 29–57.
7. Diamantini, C., Genga, L., Potena, D., & Storti, E. (2014). Discovering behavioural patterns in knowledge-intensive collaborative processes. In *New frontiers in mining complex patterns* (pp. 149–163). Berlin: Springer.
8. Do, T. M. T., Kalimeri, K., Lepri, B., Pianesi, F., & Gatica-Perez, D. (2013). Inferring social activities with mobile sensor networks. In *Proceedings of the 15th ACM on international conference on multimodal interaction* (pp. 405–412). New York: ACM.
9. Dong, W., Olguin-Olguin, D., Waber, B., Kim, T., & Pentland, A. (2012). Mapping organizational dynamics with body sensor networks. In *Wearable and Implantable Body Sensor Networks (BSN), 2012 Ninth International Conference on* (pp. 130–135). IEEE.
10. Ferriani, S., Cattani, G., & Baden-Fuller, C. (2009). The relational antecedents of project-entrepreneurship: Network centrality, team compositionand project performance. *Research Policy, 38*(10), 1545–1558.
11. Fischbach, K., Gloor, P. A., Lassenius, C., Olguin, D. O., Pentland, A. S., Putzke, J., et al. (2010). Analyzing the flow of knowledge with sociometric badges. *Procedia-Social and Behavioral Sciences, 2*(4), 6389–6397.
12. Guerlain, S., Adams, R. B., Turrentine, F. B., Shin, T., Guo, H., Collins, S. R., et al. (2005). Assessing team performance in the operating room: development and use of a "black-box" recorder and other tools for the intraoperative environment. *Journal of the American College of Surgeons, 200*(1), 29–37.
13. Gupta, S. (2007). Workflow and process mining in healthcare. Master's Thesis, Technische Universiteit Eindhoven.
14. Hoegl, M., & Proserpio, L. (2004). Team member proximity and teamwork in innovative projects. *Research Policy, 33*(8), 1153–1165.
15. Ilgen, D. R., Hollenbeck, J. R., Johnson, M., & Jundt, D. (2005). Teams in organizations: From input-process-output models to IMOI models. *Annual Review of Psychology, 56*, 517–543.
16. Johannes, B., Sitev, A. S., Vinokhodova, A. G., Salnitski, V. P., Savchenko, E. G., Artyukhova, A. E., et al. (2015). Wireless monitoring of changes in crew relations during long-duration mission simulation. *PLoS ONE, 10*(8), e0134814.

17. Kaissi, A., Johnson, T., & Kirschbaum, M. S. (2003). Measuring teamwork and patient safety attitudes of high-risk areas. *Nursing Economics, 21*(5), 211.
18. Kalimeri, K., Lepri, B., & Pianesi, F. (2013). Going beyond traits: Multimodal classification of personality states in the wild. In *Proceedings of the 15th ACM on international conference on multimodal interaction* (pp. 27–34). New York: ACM.
19. Kemsley, S. (2011). The changing nature of work: From structured to unstructured, from controlled to social. In *Business process management* (p. 2). Berlin: Springer.
20. Kim, T., Chang, A., Holland, L., & Pentland, A. S. (2008). Meeting mediator: Enhancing group collaboration using sociometric feedback. In *Proceedings of the 2008 ACM conference on computer supported cooperative work* (pp. 457–466). New York: ACM.
21. Kim, T. J., Chu, M., Brdiczka, O., & Begole, J. (2009a). Predicting shoppers' interest from social interactions using sociometric sensors. In *CHI'09 extended abstracts on human factors in computing systems* (pp. 4513–4518). New York: ACM.
22. Kim, T., Olguín, D. O., Waber, B. N., & Pentland, A. (2009b). Sensor-based feedback systems in organizational computing. In *International conference on computational science and engineering, 2009. CSE'09* (Vol. 4, pp. 966–969). IEEE.
23. Kim, T., McFee, E., Olguin, D. O., Waber, B., & Pentland, A. (2012). Sociometric badges: Using sensor technology to capture new forms of collaboration. *Journal of Organizational Behavior, 33*(3), 412–427.
24. Kozlowski, S. W., & Ilgen, D. R. (2006). Enhancing the effectiveness of work groups and teams. *Psychological Science in the Public Interest, 7*(3), 77–124.
25. La Rosa, M., Dumas, M., Ter Hofstede, A. H., & Mendling, J. (2011). Configurable multi-perspective business process models. *Information Systems, 36*(2), 313–340.
26. Leonard, M., Graham, S., & Bonacum, D. (2004). The human factor: the critical importance of effective teamwork and communication in providing safe care. *Quality and Safety in Health Care, 13*(suppl 1), i85–i90.
27. Leonard-Barton, D. (1990). A dual methodology for case studies: Synergistic use of a longitudinal single site with replicated multiple sites. *Organization Science, 1*(3), 248–266.
28. Lepri, B., Staiano, J., Rigato, G., Kalimeri, K., Finnerty, A., Pianesi, F., et al. (2012). The sociometric badges corpus: A multilevel behavioral dataset for social behavior in complex organizations. In *2012 international conference on privacy, security, risk and trust (PASSAT), and 2012 international confernece on social computing (SocialCom)* (pp. 623–628). IEEE.
29. Lyra, O., Karapanos, E., & Kostakos, V. (2011). Intelligent playgrounds: Measuring and affecting social inclusion in schools. *Human-Computer Interaction–INTERACT 20*, 560–563.
30. Mans, R., Schonenberg, H., Leonardi, G., Panzarasa, S., Cavallini, A., Quaglini, S., et al. (2008). Process mining techniques: An application to stroke care. *Studies in Health Technology and Informatics, 136*, 573.
31. Marjanovic, O., & Freeze, R. (2011, January). Knowledge intensive business processes: Theoretical foundations and research challenges. In *2011 44th Hawaii international conference on system sciences (HICSS)* (pp. 1–10). IEEE.
32. Niinimäki, T. (2011). Face-to-face, email and instant messaging in distributed agile software development project. In *2011 sixth IEEE international conference on global software engineering workshop (ICGSEW)* (pp. 78–84). IEEE.
33. Olguín, D. O., Waber, B. N., Kim, T., Mohan, A., Ara, K., & Pentland, A. (2009a). Sensible organizations: Technology and methodology for automatically measuring organizational behavior. *IEEE Transactions on Systems, Man, and Cybernetics, Part B: Cybernetics, 39*(1).
34. Olguín, D. O., Gloor, P. A., & Pentland, A. S. (2009b). Wearable sensors for pervasive healthcare management. In *3rd international conference on pervasive computing technologies for healthcare, 2009. Pervasive health 2009* (pp. 1–4). IEEE.
35. Orbach, M., Demko, M., Doyle, J., Waber, B. N., & Pentland, A. S. (2015). Sensing informal networks in organizations. *American Behavioral Scientist, 59*(4), 508–524.
36. Panian, Z. (2011). A promising approach to supporting knowledge-intensive business processes: Business case management. *World Academy of Science, Engineering and Technology, 75*, 642–648.

37. Rebuge, Á., & Ferreira, D. R. (2012). Business process analysis in healthcare environments: A methodology based on process mining. *Information Systems, 37*(2), 99–116.
38. Rosen, M. A., Dietz, A. S., Yang, T., Priebe, C. E., & Pronovost, P. J. (2014). An integrative framework for sensor-based measurement of teamwork in healthcare. *Journal of the American Medical Informatics Association*, amiajnl-2013.
39. Sexton, J. B., Helmreich, R. L., Neilands, T. B., Rowan, K., Vella, K., Boyden, J., et al. (2006). The safety attitudes questionnaire: Psychometric properties, benchmarking data, and emerging research. *BMC Health Services Research, 6*(1), 1.
40. Stehlé, J., Charbonnier, F., Picard, T., Cattuto, C., & Barrat, A. (2013). Gender homophily from spatial behavior in a primary school: A sociometric study. *Social Networks, 35*(4), 604.
41. Tripathi, P., & Burleson, W. (2012). Predicting creativity in the wild: Experience sample and sociometric modeling of teams. In *Proceedings of the ACM 2012 conference on computer supported cooperative work* (pp. 1203–1212). New York: ACM.
42. Watanabe, J. I., Fujita, M., Yano, K. I., Kanesaka, H., & Hasegawa, T. (2013). Resting time activeness determines team performance in call centers. In *2012 international conference on social informatics* (pp. 26–31). IEEE.
43. Wu, L., Waber, B. N., Aral, S., Brynjolfsson, E., & Pentland, A. (2008). Mining face-to-face interaction networks using sociometric badges: Predicting productivity in an it configuration task. Available at SSRN 1130251.
44. Yu, D., Blocker, R. C., Sir, M. Y., Hallbeck, M. S., Hellmich, T. R., Cohen, T., et al. (2016). Intelligent emergency department: Validation of sociometers to study workload. *Journal of Medical Systems, 40*(3), 1–12.
45. Zaccaro, S. J., Marks, M. A., & DeChurch, L. A. (2012). Multiteam systems: An introduction. *Multiteam systems: An organization form for dynamic and complex environments.* pp. 3–32.

Generation X and Knowledge Work: The Impact of ICT. What Are the Implications for HRM?

Daria Sarti and Teresina Torre

Abstract This chapter aims to demonstrate the positive impact of the use of ICTs and knowledge work content on employees' wellbeing. Our focus is on generations at work, and specifically generation X, which is underexplored in the current research debate but relevant in terms of the organizations' human capital. The relationship between knowledge work content and wellbeing of Generation X has been explored along with the impact that the use of ICT may have in this relationship. The findings of the analysis, carried out on a sample of 5,557 employees in Europe (data source: WVS 2010–14), demonstrate that the use of ICT is important for the wellbeing of all generations. We also demonstrate that different levels of knowledge work content have an impact on employees' wellbeing, and this relationship is stronger for Generation X, while increase in ICT usage may have an adverse effect on it. Our results offer interesting stimuli for a debate between scholars and practitioners in the management of employees, calling for attention to the controversial effect of ICT usage and to this mid-generation, too.

Keywords Generation X · Generations · Knowledge work · ICT · HRM

1 Introduction

Many scholars, as well as practitioners in organizational contexts have emphasized for some decades the importance of managing diversity in organizations as a relevant challenge in the management of human resources [1–7]. Also, authors have suggested that each organization has to identify specific strategies and methods to

D. Sarti (✉)
Department of Economics and Management, University of Florence, Firenze, Italy
e-mail: daria.sarti@unifi.it

T. Torre
Department of Economics and Business Studies, University of Genova, Genova, Italy
e-mail: teresina.torre@economia.unige.it

© Springer International Publishing AG 2018   227
C. Rossignoli et al. (eds.), *Digital Technology and Organizational Change*,
Lecture Notes in Information Systems and Organisation 23,
https://doi.org/10.1007/978-3-319-62051-0_19

ensure that all employees have the opportunity to maximize their potentials and to enhance workers' self-development, to enlarge their contribution to the organizational goal [8, 9]. By the way, Williams and O'Reilly [10: 120] concluded that 'diversity is most likely to impede how organizations function. In order to reap the benefits of workforce diversity, organizations must actively manage it'. According to seminal studies [10–14], there are different sources of diversity in organizations. Some of them are considered in a narrow way focusing essentially on race and gender, while others are broad and include soft dimensions, such as values, personality, attitudes, religion, educational level, job tenure [15, 16]. For a long period, the second approach has been preferred. Indeed, current trends in demographics are hard-testing organizations in the management of 'so many diversities' connected to the age of workers [17–19].

A vast and deeply-rooted debate on generations at work [20] has been dominating the literature on diversity management over the past two decades [21–23]. Presently, this theme appears to be particularly topical than ever, due to the increasing interest in aging of workforce and to the emergence of inter-generational conflicts, which become more relevant in times of crisis.

Many scholars devote their attention to general aspects such as motivational factors for different generations of workers [24–26], variances in work values [27–29] and workplace attitudes as well as behaviours shown by various generations [27, 30]. As concerns the relationship between ICT and generations, most of the researchers' interest is dedicated to the so-called 'generation gap' [31].

In general, it seems that most care is dedicated to the relationship between aging and younger generations, while not much concern has been paid to middle generation employees, known as Generation X (i.e. people born between the Sixties and Seventies) [27, 32, 33].

The aim of this paper is to highlight this generation, suggesting its significance in terms of contribution to the overall human capital of organizations. Furthermore, in the theoretical perspective of Job Resource-Demand (JR-D) model, we are interested in proving that knowledge work content may represent an antecedent of employees' wellbeing, especially for the Generation X; while ICT usage may represent for people belonging to the so-called mid-generation a potential 'job resource' or a source of stress depending on the level of knowledge content of work. In other words, we think that for people belonging to Generation X, the introduction of ICT may play a crucial role and be a source of individual strain for those whose job profiles show high levels of creativity and intellect. For workers of Generation X in charge of manual and routine tasks, that is with low knowledge content, ICT may have a positive relationship with individual well-being.

The paper has been organized in the following manner: In the second part, the theoretical background is offered and our hypotheses are introduced; in the third paragraph, we present the analysis and the most relevant results. Finally, some preliminary suggestions in relation to our central question have been offered and considerations useful for future research activities proposed.

2 Theoretical Background

2.1 Generations and Knowledge Work

Two main perspectives emerge from studies about generations. The first is focused on the idea that a 'generation' is made by people born in the same time span [34] and that chronological age is associated with a set of attitudes and preferences [35]. The second, following Mannheim's approach [36: 302], suggestes that 'generations are connected through the transmission of persons passing through time, who come to share a common habitus and lifestyle'. According to this viewpoint, a generation is defined on the basis of the significant events which affect members of a group [30, 33]. This interesting viewpoint brings to a relevant problem in the operationalizing process of the concept. Otherwise, several researchers have identified generations' limits [33]. In our study, we refer to the more diffused classification, which considers three generations currently in the labour market. They are: Baby Boomers, Generation X and Generation Y [28, 37].

From our review of organizational and managerial studies, we find that there is a lack of research on the mid-generation. Indeed most of the researches are concerned on aging generations and on the youngest ones. Many studies focus on highlighting Baby boomers' difficulties in learning [38, 39] and their resistance to change as well as inflexibility [32]. Some authors point out the need to motivate aged workforce [40, 41] and suggest that to improve working conditions can increase their productivity [42], empowering key knowledge transfer and retention of core competencies in the organizations [43, 44]. Meanwhile, for the youngest generation at work—Generation Y—a lively and wide debate is on. It discusses their attitudes, motivators and socialization process [45] and it shows concern on effective ways to manage and lead such new generations of workers [46–48].

Despite few studies devoted on Generation X, we believe that more attention should be paid to it owing to its valuable participation in organization performance. Indeed, employees of this generation contribute significantly to the organizations' human capital on the basis of their knowledge and experience, which have to be transferred to younger co-workers. Indeed, members of Generation X are more educated than previous generations [49] and more easily trainable [50]. Further, they represent a vast proportion of overall workforce [51], while there is evidence of lower levels of satisfaction [52] and continuance commitment among them compared to other generations [53]. Studies demonstrate further that Generation X members may be more committed to their careers than their organisations [54, 55]. Also, authors [56] show a reduction in midlife concerns and strains when a successful adaptation to age-appropriate adult roles is achieved (e.g., high responsibility work roles). Therefore, considering the higher educational level of Generation X and the fact that its members work hard with regard both to the number of hours a week and to the engagement they show [49], we posit that:

- HP1. Members of Generation X demonstrate high levels of knowledge work content compared to the other generations.

2.2   ICT and Wellbeing

There are many publications on the beneficial and detrimental effects that the use of ICT may have on individuals. Some researches highlight the positive consequences, considering ICT as a source that can make individuals 'nearer' them, in terms of space and time, and feed their—already existing—social relations, thus impacting positively their working quality [57]. On the other hand, some studies suggest that ICT may cause isolation and antisocial behaviours [58]. However, this latter perspective does not appear to be coherent with the working environment where socializing is a crucial element of the definition of the organization itself. In this connection, we recall the classic notion of the organization proposed by Barnad [59]. He defines the enterprise as a cooperative system (exactly based on cooperation among individuals) in which the social nature of an organization is a constitutional element and communication represents an essential condition. In this perspective assuming the viewpoint of the work setting, we hypothesize a positive relationship between ICT use and individuals' wellbeing so that:

- HP2. The use of ICT has an overall positive impact on individuals' wellbeing.

2.3   Knowledge Work and Generations' Wellbeing

There is a wide debate on the importance of creativity and intellectual work, also known as knowledge work [60] for organizational success and individual wellbeing. Indeed, according to the authors enriched jobs are more challenging than simplified jobs, while relatively simple and routine jobs do not support high creativity. It is proved that job enrichment increases individual satisfaction [61]; further, empowerment and job enrichment are found as direct antecedents of job satisfaction [62]. Also, it is demonstrated that knowledge workers are more motivated compared to blue collars [63]. Thus, we posit that:

- HP3a. Knowledge work content has an overall positive impact on individuals' well-being.

  Studies on generations highlight that Generation X members and Baby Boomers value intrinsic rewards—that are directly connected with enriched work content— more than Generation Y. Thus, a work context that provides intrinsic rewards is more valued by generation X members compared to generation Y [64]. Also, it is proved that Generation X prefers organisations which offer skills development [33]. On the other hand, Baby Boomers, as the generation more proximal to retirement, tend to consider these dimensions less relevant, being more oriented towards a future without work. Thus, we posit:

- HP3b. Knowledge work content has a higher impact for Generation X's well-being compared to other generations.

2.4 ICT, Knowledge Work and Generations' Well-Being

Although the use of PC technology may be of great help in daily activities and for reducing the impact and strain arising from routine tasks, it may not aid success in creative and intellectual activities. This is especially true for mid-generation members, who have lived the change produced by the pervasive presence of technologies in the early stages of their lives.

If the diffusion of new social media increases the democratization of communication, those people holding a managerial role and occupying a nodal position in a communication network (that probably belongs to Generation X's members) have to devote more time and experience to a deep change of mind-set necessary in this different context. At the same time, the interactivity typical of social media induces the expectation of immediate feedback, producing situations of pressure towards the receivers of the communication itself. In this sense, we hypothesize that positions that are enriched in terms of work contents may as well see a reduction in the positive relationship existing between ICT and perceived sense of satisfaction (well-being). A previous study suggests that 'computer-mediated groups took longer to reach consensus than did face-to-face groups' [65: 1128], this might unfavourably impact such kinds of people, who most of the time have to take decisions or support the group in achieving solutions.

This reasoning finds theoretical support within the JD-R model perspective, a field of research studying job characteristics as determinants of organizational behavior [57, 66]. Following this stream, we posit that for Generation X knowledge works, the introduction of ICT may play a crucial role, coping with lower levels of well-being (and by consequence of life satisfaction) and be, more than for other generations, a source of individual strain. On the other hand, for people in charge of manual or routine tasks, that is low-level knowledge content of work, ICT may have a better relationship with individual well-being. Thus, we hypothesize that:

- HP4. High levels in use of ICT for Generation X reduce the positive relationship between work content and individuals' well-being and low levels of ICT use increase the relationship between work content and individuals' well-being.

3 Analysis and Results

Our research has been developed using a secondary source, which allows adequate observation of the phenomenon we are interested in. In this paragraph, we first present the methodological approach and then we describe the results obtained in order to verify the previously introduced hypotheses.

3.1 Method

The database of World Values Survey (WVS) is used in our analysis. Data are taken from the Wave 6 data covering the 2010–14. Only data available from EU countries are included in this work in order to consider a relatively homogeneous sample. Eight European Countries—see Table 1—are analysed since for these Countries data relevant to our analysis were available.

Only people who declared their status of employment are included in the final sample. It comprises 5,557 individuals belonging to different generations: Generation Y ($N = 1107$), Generation X ($N = 3148$) and Baby Boomers ($N = 1302$). The size of the three samples is large enough to allow comparisons. In Table 2, main characteristics about the samples are shown.

3.2 Variables in the Analysis

The dependent variable here considered is *individual well-being*. It is measured with the question: 'How much satisfied are you with your life?'. The range of response was based on a 10-point scale from 1 = completely dissatisfied to 10 = completely satisfied.

Table 1 Distribution of generations of our sample by Countries

	Generation Y		Generation X		Baby Boomers	
Cyprus	167	15%	310	10%	119	9%
Germany	250	23%	662	21%	242	19%
Netherlands	113	10%	511	16%	296	23%
Poland	126	11%	252	8%	112	9%
Romania	155	14%	384	12%	94	7%
Slovenia	54	5%	337	11%	121	9%
Spain	107	10%	305	10%	89	7%
Sweden	135	12%	387	12%	229	18%
	1107		3148		1302	

Table 2 Characteristics of our sample

		Generation Y (%)	Generation X (%)	Baby Boomers (%)
Gender	Male	54	52	53
	Female	46	48	47
Managerial role	Managerial role	23	34	37
	Non managerial role	77	66	63

The independent variables of this study are: ICT and knowledge work content.

ICT is measured with two different scales available in the WVS dataset. One is related to the frequency in use of PC technology; the other is connected with the use of new social media. The use of PC technology is assessed with the single-item question 'How often do you use a personal computer?'. The range of response was based on a three-point scale from 1 = never to 3 = always. The use of social media is measured with three items (frequency of use of mobile, email and internet) ranging from 1 = never to 5 = daily. Alpha was above the recommended value of 0.7.

Knowledge work is measured with two dimensions: intellectual-manual work content and creative-routine work content. Following previous studies [67, 68], creative work content is defined as the employees' generation of novel and useful ideas concerning products, procedures, and processes at work' [69: 964]. Intellectual work may be defined as 'the use of non–empirical form–abstractions which may be represented by nothing other than non–empirical, "pure" concepts' [70: 67]. Routine-creative is measured with a single question, which was: 'Nature of tasks: routine versus creative?'. The range of responses was based on a 10-point scale from 1 = mostly routine tasks to 10 = mostly non-routine tasks. The manual-intellectual content of work is measured with a single item question that was: 'Nature of tasks: manual versus intellectual?'. The range of response was based on a 10-point scale from 1 = mostly manual tasks to 10 = mostly non-manual tasks.

In order to identify different generations the following criteria are adopted [27, 71]: Baby Boomers are those subjects born between 1943 and 1960, Generation X are individuals born between 1961 and 1981. Finally, Generation Y's members are individuals born in 1982 and later. These are controlled in the analysis as dummy variables.

In the study, some control variables are used. These are: gender (1 = male; 2 = female), managerial position (1 = yes; 2 = no) and number of children.

3.3 Results

The Statistical Package of Social Sciences (SPSS Version 20) is used to analyse the data.

3.3.1 Levels of Work Content Among Generations: The Relevance for Generation X

Results of a descriptive analysis demonstrate that the major intellectual content of work is performed by Baby Boomers ($M = 6.1334$) and Generation X ($M = 5.9189$), while the level of intellectual content of work among employees of Generation Y is moderately lower ($M = 5.5807$). Also, creative work is on an average higher for Baby Boomers ($M = 5.4768$) and for Generation X

(M = 5.2518), while the level of creative work among employees of Generation Y is moderately lower (M = 4.9402).

In order to demonstrate the first Hypothesis, a one-way ANOVA is performed to compare the means of the two variables of intellectual and creative work content across the three generation groups mapped herein.

The results indicate that there is a significant effect of the generation on the level of intellectual work performed, $F(2, 5500) = 9.317$, $p < 0.001$ and on the level of creative work, $F(2, 5504) = 10.612$, $p < 0.001$.

The assumption of homogeneity of variance is violated; therefore, the Brown-Forsythe F-ratio and Welsh F-ratio are computed in both cases. Results $F(2, 3627) = 9.360$, $p < 0.001$ and $F(2, 2419) = 9.367$, $p < 0.001$—demonstrate a significant effect of the generation on the intellectual content of work. Also, data shows: $F(2, 3690) = 10.792$, $p < 0.001$ and $F(2, 2442) = 10.927$, $p < 0.001$ which is a significant effect of the generation on creative work. The Tukey post hoc test is used to demonstrate that Generation Y has significantly lower mean than other generations for both creative and intellectual work. In other words, Generation X and baby boomers do not differ significantly in intellectual and creative work content (HSD Tukey test).

Results prove that Generation X displays high levels of work content both intellectual and creative. In particular Generation X is paired with baby boomers in terms of high levels of intellectual and creative work content compared to lower levels for Generation Y. Thus, HP1 was supported.

3.3.2 ICT and Individuals' Well-Being: The Moderating Role of Work Content

In order to run a regression analysis an exploratory factor analysis (EFA) is applied to the independent variables. A principal component analysis with varimax rotation is used. Two factors based on eigenvalues-greater-than-one rule are identified: ICT (four items) and content of work (two items). The two factors explain 67.538% of the variance in the sample data. The Kaiser-Meyer-Olkin (KMO) measure of sampling adequacy is satisfactory at 0.685. The factors are used as independent variables for our regression analysis. A regression analysis is performed with life satisfaction as dependent variable in order to verify the other hypothesis. The analysis is performed in four different steps. At the first step the control variables are included: gender, managerial position and number of children. In the second step, a block entry of the dummy variables for generations (X, Y and Baby Boomers) is introduced. Later the main effect of the independent variables is added to the equation—i.e. the two factor identified through the EFA. In the fourth step two-way interaction terms are included—as it is recommended in the literature, this model includes all possible two-way interactions [72]—and also the three-way interaction term is entered in the same step in the full model (Table 3).

Results show a significant relationship between ICT and wellbeing, thus, supporting Hypothesis 2.

Table 3 Regression analysis for individual wellbeing

	Step 1	Step 2	Step 3	Step 4
Control variables				
Gender	0.017	0.018	0.004	0.004
Managerial position	−0.071***	−0.074***	−0.027[a]	−0.028[a]
Number of children	0.045**	0.062***	0.088***	0.089***
Generation				
Generation Y		0.041*	0.034[a]	0.034[a]
Generation X		0.001	−0.005	−0.005
Main effect				
Knowledge work content			0.149***	0.114***
ICT			0.113***	0.118***
Moderation effects				
Kn. work content*GenX				0.041[a]
Kn. work content*ICT				0.027
ICT*GenX				−0.011
Kn. work content*GenX*ICT				−0.055*
R^2 adj	0.014	0.015	0.040	0.042

Note Values are standardized beta values
[a]<0.10
***$p < 0.001$; **$p < 0.01$; *$p < 0.05$

Hypothesis 3a, according to which there is a positive relationship between knowledge work content and individuals' well-being is supported. Furthermore, it is found that this relationship is stronger for Generation X, thereby supporting Hypothesis 3b. Indeed, the interaction effect for Generation X is found in the relationship between knowledge work content and well-being ($\beta = 0.041, p < 0.1$) thereby demonstrating that for Generation X the relationship between knowledge work content and well-being is stronger than for other generations.

Figures in the regression table further show that the knowledge work content, ICT and Generation X in combination have a negative effect on wellbeing. Thus, it is proved that a moderation effect exists between knowledge work and ICT for Generation X compared to other generations.

In other words, the results demonstrate that an increase in ICT usage reduces the positive relationship between knowledge work and individuals' well-being in Generation X, and so, Hypothesis 4 is supported.

4 Conclusions, Limitations and Further Research

This paper wishes to investigate well-being, ICT and knowledge work content among generations at work. In particular, our focus is on Generation X, which is expected to be relevant in terms of organizations' human capital, despite it appears to be underexplored in current research. Indeed, in the first result of the present research, it is proved that individuals in Generation X perform intellectual and creative tasks at higher levels, like Baby-Boomers, compared to Generation Y.

More in detail, our aim is first to prove that a relationship exists between the use of ICT and individuals' well-being and to investigate the role played by the level of knowledge work content—which are differently influenced by ICT use itself—and well-being and then whether an interaction effect exists among these three variables. The question has a certain relevance, as it is ascertained that well-being represents an important condition for working well and, by consequence, it seems necessary that organizations make efforts to promote employees' well-being, particularly for those workers, who look weaker in this perspective. Also, the increase in the need for ICT tools as well as the enrichment of work are relevant phenomena that impact differently, according to specific features of each different generation. The evidence shown in this study demonstrates some important acquisitions, and the first of this is that ICT is important for all generations' well-being.

Furthermore, we demonstrate that different kinds of knowledge work contents impact the relationship between the use of ICT and well-being for Generation X. This conclusion confirms previous studies, which propose positive implications of structural flexibility in today's technologies and strengthens the classic idea that a qualitatively rich job may be more interesting for workers, especially for those engaged in creative and intellectual jobs, like the Generation X's members.

The current study demonstrates that when ICT is introduced for people belonging to the same mid-generation, whose tasks have low levels of intellectual and creative contents, the relationship between ICT interventions and individuals' well-being becomes stronger. It is possible to think that, for those positions, a positive impact in terms of perceived increase in job resources—that is, an increase in the ICT usage—may be experienced in terms of discretion and growth as well as learning opportunities.

The particular relevance of the topic and its preliminary stage of analysis suggest, of course, a particular attention in the conclusions. Hence, further and deeper research into different kinds of jobs and different kinds of technologies for any generation at work may be useful to look into the question we are interested in.

The importance of this is set to increase for the pervasive role that ICTs are continuing to play; a role which produces different effects, according to the experience of each generation. Also, it could be interesting to examine if culture, both organizational and national ones, influences well-being and its relationship with ICT.

This work aims to suggest insights that would enable HR departments to manage better, that is, more effectively, this mid-generation in coherence with one of the most acclaimed diversity management approach which is described as a 'diversified approach to management of human resources, whose aim is to create an inclusive working environment, to favour the expression of individual potential and to use it as strategy to reach the strategic objectives' [73: 14, our translation]. In other words, in this perspective, diversity is a reality to face and manage through effective and suitable strategies and actions rather than a value to pursue [74: 154], exactly like the presence of many generations in organizations [19, 75].

The present study has one major limitation: it is based on secondary data. This means that the population studied and the measures undertaken may not be exactly those which the researchers may have chosen to collect for the specific topic. Nevertheless, the use of a database such as WVS makes available the advantage of having a very large sample—which offers the statistical power required to obtain significant interactions; on the other hand, it raises questions about the reliability of the measures that—for this study—also lead to a low percentage of variance explained by the model.

Also, we are aware of the limitations associated with the use of a single-item measure for overall life satisfaction as a dependent variable, since it may be affected by a wide number of factors, apart from those investigated. However, previous studies have proved the high correlation of life satisfaction with job satisfaction and its usefulness in work-related studies [76, 77] and this is, according to our opinion, particularly true for individuals belonging to Generation X, which are at the 'peak' of their working life.

In conclusion, we think that our work contributes to get evidence of a this phenomenon on a wide sample of generations' members and provides interesting insights into a topic of increasing relevance in the current debate on generational relationships and on the role of ICTs in work organization and work conditions, since these fields are considered particularly tricky.

References

1. Egan, T. M. (2005). Creativity in the context of team diversity: Team leader perspective. *Advances in Developing Human Resources, 7*, 207–225.
2. Herring, C. (2009). Does diversity pay? Race, gender, and the business case for diversity. *American Sociological Review, 74*(2), 208–224.
3. Pelled, L. H., Eisenhardt, K. M., & Xin, K. R. (1999). Exploring the black box: An analysis of work group diversity, conflict, and performance. *Administrative Science Quarterly, 44*, 1–28.
4. Pfeffer, J. (1983). Organizational demography. *Research in Organizational Behavior, 5*, 299–357.
5. Dietz, J., & Petersen, L. E. (2006). Diversity management. In G. Stahl & I. Bjorkman (Eds.), *Handbook of research in international humane resource management* (pp. 223–244). Cheltenham, UK: Edward Elgar.
6. Schwabenland, C., & Tomlinson, F. (2015). Shadows and light: Diversity management as phantasmagoria. *Human Relations, 68*, 1912–1936.
7. Van Knippenberg, D., & Schippers, M. C. (2007). Work group diversity. *Annual Review of Psychology, 58*, 515–541.
8. Chartered Institute of Personnel and Development. (2005). *Managing diversity. Linking theory and practice to business performance*. London, CIPD: Change agenda.
9. European Commission. (2003). *The costs and benefits of diversity: A study on methods and indicators to measure the cost effectiveness of diversity policies in enterprises*. Brussels.
10. Williams, K. Y., & O'Reilly, C. A. (1998). Demography and diversity in organizations: A review of 40 years of research. In B. M. Staw & L. L. Cummings (Eds.), *Research in organizational behaviour. 20*: 77–140. Greenwich, CT: JAI Press.

11. Milliken, F. J., & Martins, L. L. (1996). Searching for common threads: Understanding the multiple effects of diversity in organizational groups. *Academy of Management Review, 21*(2), 402–433.
12. Cox, T., Jr., & Blake, S. (1991). Managing cultural diversity: Implication for organizational competitiveness. *Academy of Management Executive, 5*(3), 45–56.
13. Ellis, C., & Sonnenfeld, J. A. (1994). Diverse approaches to managing diversity. *Human Resource Management, 33*(1), 79–110.
14. Kerstern, A. (2000). Diversity management. Dialogue, dialectics and diversion. *Journal of Organizational Change Management, 13*(3), 235–248.
15. Ivancevich, J. M., & Gilbert, J. A. (2000). Diversity management. Time for a new approach. *Public Personnel Management, 29*(1), 75–92.
16. Rijamampianina, R., & Carmichael, T. (2005). A pragmatic and holistic approach to managing diversity. *Problems and Perspectives in Management, 1*, 109–117.
17. Leibold, M., & Voelpel, S. C. (2007). *Managing the aging workforce: Challenges and solutions*. Hoboken: Wiley.
18. Ng, E. S. W., & Burke, R. J. (2005). Person-organization fit and the war for talent: Does diversity management make a difference? *International Journal of Human Resource Management, 16*(7), 1195–1210.
19. Zemke, R., Raines, C., & Filipczak, B. (2000). *Generations at work: Managing the clash of Veterans, Boomers, Xers, and Nexters in your workplace*. New York: Amacom.
20. Benson, J., & Brown, M. (2011). Generations at work: Are there differences and do they matter? *The International Journal of Human Resource Management, 22*(9), 1843–1865.
21. Lieber, L. D. (2010). How HR can assist managing the four generations in today's workplace. *Employment Relations Today, 36*(4), 85–91.
22. Staudinger, U. S., & Bowen, C. E. (2011). A systemic approach to aging in the work context. *ZAF, 44*, 295–300.
23. Zacher, H. (2015). Successful aging at work. *Work, Aging and Retirement, 1*(1), 4–25.
24. Montana, P. J., & Petit, F. (2008). Motivating Generation X and Y on the job and preparing Z. *Global Journal of Business Research, 2*(2), 139–148.
25. Stanov-Rossnagel, C., & Hertel, G. (2010). Older workers' motivation: Against the myth of general decline. *Management Decision, 48*(6), 894–906.
26. Wong, M., Gardiner, E., Lang, W., & Coulin, L. (2008). Generational difference in personality and motivation. Do they exist and what are the implications for the workplace? *Journal of Managerial Psychology, 23*(8), 878–890.
27. Parry, E., & Urwin, P. (2011). Generational differences in work values: A review of theory and evidence. *International Journal of Management Reviews, 13*, 79–96.
28. Gursoy, D., Maier, T. A., & Chi, C. G. (2008). Generational differences: An examination of work values and generational gaps in the hospitality workforce. *International Journal of Hospitality Management, 27*, 448–458.
29. Hansen, J. C., & Leuty, M. E. (2012). Work values across generations. *Journal of Career Assessment, 20*(1), 34–52.
30. Kupperschmidt, B. R. (2000). Multigenerational employees: Strategies for effective management. *The Health Care Manager, 19*(1), 1–49.
31. Bailey, A., & Ngwenyama, O. (2010). Bridging the generation gap in ICT use: Interrogating identity, technology and interactions in community telecenters. *Information Technology for Development, 16*(1), 62–82.
32. Ng, T. W. H., & Feldman, D. C. (2012). Evaluating six common stereotypes about older workers with meta-analytical data. *Personnel Psychology, 65*, 821–858.
33. Smola, K. W., & Sutton, C. D. (2002). Generational differences: Revisiting generational work values for the new millennium. *Journal of Organizational Behaviour, 23*, 363–382.
34. Berkup, S. B. (2014). Working with generation X and Y in generation Z period: Management of different generations in business life. *Mediterranean Journal of Social Science, 5*(19), 218–229.

35. Zenger, T. R., & Lawrence, B. S. (1989). Organizational demography: The differential effects of age and tenure distribution on technical communications. *Academy of Management Journal, 32*, 353–376.
36. Mannheim, K. (1952). The problem of generation. In K. Mannheim (Ed.), *Essays on the sociology of knowledge* (pp. 276–322). London: Routledge.
37. Pritchard, K., & Whiting, R. (2014). Baby boomers and the lost generation: On the discursive construction of generations at work. *Organization Studies, 35*(11), 1605–1626.
38. Liaw, S., Chen, G., & Huang, H. (2008). Users' attitudes towards web-based collaborative learning systems for knowledge management. *Computers & Education, 50*, 950–961.
39. Lim, C. S. C. (2010). Designing inclusive ICT products for older users: Taking into account the technology generation effect. *Journal of Engineering Design, 21*(2–3), 189–206.
40. Lazazzara, A., Karpinska, K., & Henkens, K. (2013). What factors influence training opportunities for older workers? Three factorial surveys exploring the attitudes of HR professionals. *The International Journal of Human Resource Management, 24*(11), 2154–2172.
41. Lazazzara, A., & Bombelli, M. C. (2011). HRM practices for an ageing Italian workforce: The role of training. *Journal of European Industrial Training, 35*, 808–825.
42. Göbel, C., & Zwick, T. (2013). Are personnel measures effective in increasing productivity of old workers? *Labour Economics, 22*, 80–93.
43. Calo, T. J. (2008). Talent management in the era of the aging workforce: The critical role of knowledge transfer. *Public Personnel Management, 37*(4), 403–416.
44. Dunn-Cane, K., Gonzalez, J., & Stewart, H. (1999). Managing the new generation. *AORN Journal, 69*(5), 930–940.
45. Martin, C. A. (2005). From high maintenance to high productivity. What managers need to know about Generation Y. *Industrial and Commercial Training, 37*(1), 39–44.
46. Anderson, E., Buchko, A. A., & Buchko, K. J. (2016). Giving negative feedback to Millennials: How can managers criticize the "most praised" generation. *Management Research Review, 39*(6), 2–27.
47. Kultalahti, S., & Liisa Viitala, R. (2014). Sufficient challenges and a weekend ahead–Generation Y describing motivation at work. *Journal of Organizational Change Management, 27*(4), 569–582.
48. Kuron, L. K., Lyons, S. T., Schweitzer, L., & Ng, E. S. W. (2015). Millennials' work values: Differences across the school to work transition. *Personnel Review, 44*(6), 991–1009.
49. Miller, J. D. (2011). The generation X report. *A Quarterly Research Report from the Longitudinal Study of American Youth, 1*(1), 1–8.
50. Appelbaum, S. H., Serena, M., & Shapiro, B. T. (2004). Generation X and the Boomers: Organizational myths and literary realities. *Management Research News, 27*(11/12), 1–28.
51. Tulgan, B. (2000). *Managing Generation X: How to bring out the best in young talent*. New York: WW Norton & Company.
52. Lyons, S., & Kuron, L. (2014). Generational differences in the workplace: A review of the evidence and directions for future research. *Journal of Organizational Behavior, 35*(1), 139–157.
53. Costanza, D. P., Badger, J. M., Fraser, R. L., Severt, J. B., & Gade, P. A. (2012). Generational differences in work-related attitudes: A meta-analysis. *Journal of Business and Psychology, 27*(4), 375–394.
54. Cennamo, L., & Gardner, D. (2008). Generational differences in work values, outcomes and person-organisation values fit. *Journal of Managerial Psychology, 23*(8), 891–906.
55. Miller, P., & Yu, H. C. (2003). Organisational values and generational values: A cross cultural study. *Australasian Journal of Business & Social Enquiry, 1*(3), 138–153.
56. Van Aken, M. A., Denissen, J. J., Branje, S. J., Dubas, J. S., & Goossens, L. (2006). Midlife concerns and short-term personality change in middle adulthood. *European Journal of Personality, 20*(6), 497–513.

57. Demerouti, E., Bakker, A. B., Janssen, P. P. M., & Schaufeli, W. B. (2001). Burnout and engagement at work as a function of demands and control. *Scandinavian Journal of Work, Environment & Health, 27,* 279–286.
58. Kraut, R., Patterson, M., Lundmark, V., Kiesler, S., Mukophadhyay, T., & Scherlis, W. (1998). Internet paradox: A social technology that reduces social involvement and psychological well-being? *American Psychologist, 53*(9), 1017–1031.
59. Barnard, C. (1938). *The function of an Executive.* Mass: Harvard College.
60. Drucker, P. F. (1999). Knowledge-worker productivity: The biggest challenge. *California Management Review, 41*(2), 79–94.
61. Umstot, D. D., Bell, C. H., & Mitchell, T. R. (1976). Effects of job enrichment and task goals on satisfaction and productivity: Implications for job design. *Journal of Applied Psychology, 61*(4), 379–394.
62. Yang, S. B., & Lee, K. H. (2009). Linking empowerment and job enrichment to turnover intention: The influence of job satisfaction. *International Review of Public Administration, 14*(2), 13–24.
63. Huang, T. P. (2011). Comparing motivating work characteristics, job satisfaction, and turnover intention of knowledge workers and blue-collar workers, and testing a structural model of the variables' relationships in China and Japan. *The International Journal of Human Resource Management, 22*(04), 924–944.
64. Twenge, J. M., Campbell, S. M., Hoffman, B. J., & Lance, C. E. (2010). Generational differences in work values: Leisure and extrinsic values increasing, social and intrinsic values decreasing. *Journal of Management, 36*(5), 1117–1142.
65. Kiesler, S., Siegel, J., & McGuire, T. W. (1984). Social psychological aspects of computer-mediated communication. *American Psychologist, 39*(10), 1123–1142.
66. Bakker, A. B., & Demerouti, E. (2007). The job demands-resources model: State of the art. *Journal of Managerial Psychology, 22*(3), 309–328.
67. Amabile, T. M. (1988). A model of creativity and innovation in organizations. *Research in Organizational Behavior, 10*(1), 123–167.
68. Oldham, G. R., & Cummings, A. (1996). Employee creativity: Personal and contextual factors at work. *Academy of Management Journal, 39*(3), 607–634.
69. Hirst, G., Van Dick, R., & Van Knippenberg, D. (2009). A social identity perspective on leadership and employee creativity. *Journal of Organizational Behaviour, 30*(7), 963–982.
70. Sohn-Rethel, A., & Sohn-Rethel, M. (1978). *Intellectual and manual labour. A critique of epistemology.* London: Macmillan.
71. Howe, N., & Strauss, W. (2009). *Millennials rising: The next great generation.* New York: Vintage.
72. Allison, P. D. (1977). Testing for interaction in multiple regression. *American Journal of Sociology, 83*(1), 144–153.
73. Barabino, M. C., Jacobs, B., & Maggio, M. A. (2001). Il diversity management. *Sviluppo & Organizzazione, 184,* 19–31.
74. Flood, R. L., & Romm, N. (1996). Emancipatory practice: Some contributions from social theory and practice. *Systemic Practice and Action Research, 9*(2), 113–128.
75. Knight, R. (2014). Managing People from 5 Generations, HBR, September (2014).
76. Andrews, F. M., & Withey, S. B. (1976). *Social indicators of well-being.* New York: Plenum Press.
77. Judge, T. A., & Watanabe, S. (1993). Another look at the job satisfaction-life satisfaction relationship. *Journal of Applied Psychology, 78*(6), 939–948.

The Digital Employee Experience: Discovering Generation Z

Chiara Meret, Silvia Fioravanti, Michela Iannotta and Mauro Gatti

Abstract Nowadays, organizations face the co-presence of three generations of workers ("baby boomers", Xers and Yers). However, another generation will join the workforce in the next years: the generation Z. Accordingly, companies must be able to understand their characteristics and expectations, in order to manage their generation mix. This study aims to fulfill a consistent gap in the extant literature, also providing important managerial implications, when formulating three propositions: (a) there are specific aspects which Zers give more importance when choosing their job; (b) the use of technology and the typology of technological devices characterize the digital employee experience of the generation Z; and (c) the entry of the new generation of workers has an impact on diversity management practices within organizations. After a comprehensive review of the literature, we analyze and discuss the results of a survey among 298 young people, belonging to the generation Z. The findings reveal both a universal profile of the future generation of workers, together with their digital behaviors.

Keywords Generation Z · Digitalization · Diversity management · Aging · HRM

C. Meret (✉) · S. Fioravanti · M. Iannotta · M. Gatti
Department of Management, Sapienza University of Rome,
Via del Castro Laurenziano 9, 00161 Rome, Italy
e-mail: chiara.meret@uniroma1.it

S. Fioravanti
e-mail: silvia.fioravanti@uniroma1.it

M. Iannotta
e-mail: michela.iannotta@uniroma1.it

M. Gatti
e-mail: mauro.gatti@uniroma1.it

© Springer International Publishing AG 2018
C. Rossignoli et al. (eds.), *Digital Technology and Organizational Change*,
Lecture Notes in Information Systems and Organisation 23,
https://doi.org/10.1007/978-3-319-62051-0_20

241

1 Introduction

Companies around the globe are facing great changes driven by the current social and economic environment. These changes lead companies to consider different ways of managing diversity in the workforce. Human Resource Management (HRM) must take into account the identity of each individual and specific groups of people to proactively manage them, since the heterogeneity of the elements that make up the cultural and cognitive mix of human resources represents a positively related factor to the achievement of a durable, competitive advantage [1–7]. Among the others, the variety of age constitutes one of the fundamental issues of diversity management. People's behaviors, job needs and preferences and their attitudes towards digitalization change with age. This lead to a changed relationship between the company and workers [8]. The social sciences identify the time period ranging from approximately 16 to 25 years of every individual's life, the laps in which expectations and values are formed and developed, in relation to the social context of reference [9]. Organizations that take into account the importance of understanding this phenomenon reach distinctive advantages.

Nowadays, we see the co-presence of three generations within companies (the "baby boomers", the Xers and the Yers). In addition, another generation will join the workforce: the Zers. They represent the population of today's students and future workers and consumers and they are "digital natives". Their higher level of interconnectedness might shape the way this generation view and live relationships. Consequently, when taking into consideration the generational change phenomenon, organizations can intervene in two ways: (1) inducing a change through diversity and knowledge management, and the implementation of continuous training programs; or (2) through the turnover, entering new resources with different characteristics from those typical of previous generations. This second possibility is translatable in the insertion of young people in the company, but it must be preceded by a careful analysis of their own reality reference. Despite the urgency of considering this issue, only few studies have tried to sum up Zers' main traits. In detail, the extant literature reveals not consistently defined findings on their typical characteristics [10–13], leaving quite unexplored their potential attitudes towards organizations and their digital behaviors. In order to fill this gap, our study survey 298 young people belonging to the generation Z, revealing interesting results both for theoretical research and managerial practice.

The paper is structured as follows. The next section provides a review of the literature and the resulting research propositions. The third section presents the research methodology. In the fourth section we highlight main findings and provide a deepened discussion. Conclusions and further insights are presented in the final section.

2 Literature Review and Research Questions

2.1 Age in Diversity Management

In literature, diversity management is considered as an integrated approach to HRM, aimed at creating an inclusive work environment. This setting should be capable of promoting the expression of individual potentials, a strategic tool for achieving organizational goals [1].

While discussing the current literature, Di Mauro [14] highlights three main perspectives of intervention: (a) elimination of discrimination in favor of equality; (b) recognition and appreciation of differences; and (c) promoting the development of people and organizations. While the first one concerns the identification and the consequent elimination of inequalities and discriminations within the workplace, the second one refers to the creation and promotion of an organizational culture that can positively enhancing the aforementioned differences. Finally, the third perspective stresses on individual differences, which are considered in terms of capabilities and specific knowledge. In this context, HR practices should target the promotion of principles of inclusiveness, participation and collaboration. Contributions that individuals can make in terms of novelty and quality are reflected in the development of personal-based programs. The main objective shifts to the possibility of reaching a mutual growth, both individual and organizational. Consequently, as evidenced by Costa and Gianecchini [15], organizations have to abandon the stereotypes that have characterized them until a few years ago. Moreover, the variety of age constitutes one of the fundamental issues of diversity management. Specifically, there are several variables that affect aging impact on the organization; above all there is the generation gap between older workers and new entrants into the labor market [15]. These two groups of workers are profoundly different from each other and one of the most challenging goals for the company is to be able to combine their distinct characterizations, so as to enhance the mix. In fact, the combined effects of the demographic change in industrialized countries have led to a significant shift in the age structures of labor markets, resulting both in a decrease of necessary human resources and an increasing demand for highly skilled employees [16]. In line with these considerations, organizations aim to fully exploit the opportunities of diversity, avoiding all the related disadvantages [13, 17] by actively managing diversity [17–19].

According to sociological research, the term generation represents the set of individuals of around the same age. At the same time, however, it could refer to all the people who live in the same time frame, even having different ages [20].

This classification allows to study the phenomenon of social differentiation. According to this paradigm, different individuals within the same organization occupy different roles [21]. At the same time, they might occupy the same positions with different values, opinions, attitudes and behaviors [21].

The social sciences identify the time period ranging from around 16 to 25 years of every individual's life, the laps in which expectations and values are formed and developed, in relation to the social context of reference [9]. Organizations must consider the importance of understanding this phenomenon, in order to reach distinctive advantages. This will allow you to better manage the different generational groups consequent to prepare action plans [21].

2.2   The Generation Mix

Based on the literature and on events that have characterized the history of the labor market, it is possible to divide generations in five main categories: (a) traditionalists, also defined the silent generation; (b) baby boomers; (c) generation X; (d) generation Y; and (e) generation Z [21].

Following Howe and Strauss [22], it is possible to identify three major attributes to recognize the nature of a generation: (a) the perceived membership; (b) the common beliefs and behaviors; and (c) the common location in history. Moreover, expectations for the future has profoundly changed among different generations, shaped by main events characterizing each reference period, together with the weight attached to the significant features compared to the expected job, and the use of technology [23]. We will refer to these categorizations to analyze generational characteristics, and in the development of items in our empirical study. Accordingly, our first proposition is: *There are specific aspects which Zers give more importance, when choosing their job.*

Traditionalists represents extremely disciplined individuals, born between 1900 and 1945. They have mainly conservative and traditional ideologies. The costume and the consequences of international conflicts that have characterized this era have made these individuals very close to the formal logic of the organization, in which the leader is the center of an unquestioned subordination [24, 25]. The sense of ethics and the respect of the rules are the basic principles on which to base the employment relationship. A strong sense of loyalty is also deeply rooted in these people, characterizing their ability to work with connotations of dedication and sacrifice [25]. Much of their knowledge is experiential and this raises significant concerns for organizations, about the time when these individuals will not be able to pass it on to subsequent generations, leaving a gap extremely difficult to fill [22]. In line with this characteristics, the top five traits of this generation, provided by the Generational Differences Survey Report by the SHRM [25] are: (a) they plan to stay with the organization over the long term; (b) they are respectful of the organizational hierarchy; (c) they like structures; (d) they accept the authority of different figures in the workplace; and (e) they give their maximum effort.

The second generation of "baby boomers" represents people born in the decade after the end of World War II, currently facing retirement [9, 22, 24, 26]. Despite a diffusion of some stereotypes among the literature, baby boomers represent a generation with radically different desires and aspirations from those who preceded them [22, 27]. They are born in a rather prosperous period, beneficing of the explosion of the tertiary sector and a housing market on the cheap. In fact, this generation encompasses a substantial portion of the world's population, especially in developed countries [28]. One of their main characteristics is the risk-aversion. At the same time, they maintain a deep-rooted sense of loyalty to the organization (as happened for the previous generation). Technologically, however, they represent a critical issue in terms of skills and willingness to adapt [29]. According to the top five traits of this generation, provided by the Generational Differences Survey Report by the SHRM [25] are: (a) they give their maximum effort; (b) they accept the authority figures in the workplace; (c) they are results-driven; (d) they plan to stay within the organization over the long term; and (e) they tend to retain what they learn.

The third generation represents the so-called Xers, as a term popularized by Coupland [30]. The Cold War, the fall of the Berlin Wall and a significant reduction in the birth rate (a totally opposite phenomenon to the previous generation) are the most significant events that have influenced thoughts, values and beliefs of this generation. Xers are people born between 1965 and 1980 and some researchers call them "baby busters", highlighting "the drop-off or bust in births following the Baby Boomer generation after World War II" [30: 2]. Compared to previous generations, they appear to be more heterogeneous in terms of race, social class, religion, language and gender [22]. The typical personality of Xers is competitive, independent; they point to a career path that develops upwards, starting from the most operational levels [30–32]. Temperamentally, they seem to act more for their own advantage [30]. In addition, historical and economic events that have accompanied (and accompany) their working lives, making them skeptical not only of the previous generation, firmly tied to the position reached, but also considering the entrance of the youngest, because they have desirable characteristics for the labor market [30, 32]. The pervasive entry of new technologies in the economic environment makes them pioneers on the one hand, as well as incomplete on the other hand [25, 33–36]. The top five traits of this generation, provided by the Generational Differences Survey Report by the SHRM [25] are: (a) they became technologically savvy; (b) they are pioneers of informality; (c) they learn quickly; (d) they seek a work-life balance; and (e) they embrace diversity.

The fourth generation is represented by the Yers (also named Millennial Generation, Generation Next, Net Generation or Dot Generation) [37]. It generally refers to people born between 1981 and 1994 [30]. These individuals have made a difference in the definition of new ways of managing human resources, since they had access to technology from their youth (computers and mobile phones). This has meant new employers being updated with their strategies. The historical events that have marked this generation include the attack of September 11, 2001, the Enron's scandal, the development of Google and the financial crisis erupted in 2008 [9]. This generation lives in a flexible labor market characterized by and precarious jobs, where many possibilities for continuous updating and the "just-in-time" logic accompany the concept of prolonged "employability", as opposed to the typical reality of the previous generations [38]. The multimedia universe in which they are connected enables them to have experiences that go far beyond those that were considered normal experiences by Generation X [24, 39–41]. In practice, this generation challenges traditional organizational management models. To provide an example: the social dimension of interpersonal relations challenges traditional boss-subordinate relationships, as well as the interactive mode between collaborators. Communication becomes fundamental and it changes with the transition from "one-to-may" to "many-to-many" [42]. The use of new technologies makes this generation multi-tasking and more flexible, without sacrificing, but maintaining the right work-life balance [22]. They are less inclined to net hierarchical subdivisions and to formalism, while they appear to be more inclined to the development and maintenance of interpersonal relationships [40, 43]. Numerous studies supported by empirical evidence have focused on their ambitions, expectations and behaviors. Starting from them, HRM strategies and practices started to focus on the possibility of providing benefits for the promotion of the psychological well-being of young workers. Formalizing these characteristics, the Generational Differences Survey Report by the SHRM identified the following top-five traits [25]: (a) they are technologically savvy; (b) they like informality; (c) they embrace diversity; (d) they learn quickly; and (e) they need supervision. In fact, according to different studies [44–46] Yers did not result as independent requiring a certain degree of guidance from their supervisors (possibly behaving as mentors), notwithstanding flexibility.

The final generation on which literature is focusing and towards which all the most important business realities pose attention, is the generation Z. In the literature and among practitioners they are also called Generation M (for multitasking), Generation C for (Connected Generation), the Net Generation or the iGeneration [47]. The label used for this generation is not standardized, as well as the age range within which integrate individuals in question is not universally defined. In our research we consider the range of people born between 1990 and 2009 [10, 48]. They represent the first generation that has not experienced the pre-Internet world. Consequently, they can be considered as digital natives. Their historical background is the era of terrorism, the recession and the climate change, but they are considered to have the potential to reverse the course of this decline. They represent the population of today's students and future workers and consumers. For these reasons, it has still been difficult to highlight clearly all their typical characteristics, as currently in definition and evolution. Only few studies have tried to sum up some hypothetical traits, deriving them from findings of previous surveys among previous generations [49]. Regardless of any consideration on the fundamental impact of digitization on this generation, Neil Howe and William Strauss [12, 13] identify seven personality traits, basing on the analysis they conducted in the US: (a) they feel special, firmly believing in their ability to address the future trends and becoming builders of their own destinies; (b) they are protected, not only by their families, but also by their superiors; (c) they are confident and optimistic about the future; (d) they are quite conventional; (e) they are team-oriented, because of their increased possibility of connection with others, primarily related to the level of technological sophistication they bring. This might imply a greater propensity to cooperation; (f) they aim to feel blessed and aim to achieve greater personal fulfillment in the future, relying on a higher level of education; and (g) they feel under pressure and believe that success in the future is based on choices made today [50].

2.3   The Impact of Digitalization Among the Generation Mix

In recent years, ICTs has had a profound impact on human resources and continuous innovations in technology will fundamentally change the way HR work is accomplished (e.g. eHRM) [51–54]. Moreover, IT has the capacity of mediating the relationships between employees and supervisors, and between individuals in general and the whole organization, deeply modifying the ways by which communicate, and the way we connect to each other [51, 55, 56]. In accordance with different authors [29, 57], age is one of the factors that influence the intention to use an information system.

Kumar and Lim [59] analyze the use of IT systems among baby boomers, discovering they primarily use mobile phones for voice calls, and hardly ever use them for texting, or internet facilities (i.e. emails, downloads). Morris and Venkatesh [60] demonstrate that age differences in information processing have a strong impact on older workers' computer-based tasks and performance. Other researchers have also supported that older people have a more difficult time adapting to changes in their work environments, trying to refuge in more familiar methods [60, 61]. The authors also show that there are real differences in the relevance of different factors influencing technology adoption and usage in the workplace, linked to age [59, 60]. In particular, "younger workers appear to be more driven by underlying attitudinal factors whereas older workers are more motivated by process factors" [60: 392]. Accordingly, generational conflicts over technological issues are often representative of fundamentally different approaches to change [25]. Moreover, different generations prefer diverse methods of communication, having different levels of comfort with technology [25]. Differently from baby boomers, some of the Xers were raised on technology, with personal computers becoming common even early in their lifetime and workplaces, mainly using technology for convenience purposes [23, 25, 30, 45]. They also interact with technology, believing they need to have computer skills to be successful in their jobs [23]. On the other hand, according to Bannon et al. [49], Yers are more technology-savvy, since they grew up with wireless devices and they are connected with others through social networks. In addition, peers have grown up in online environments [62]. In line with these considerations, Junco and Mastrodicasa's [63] research outlined some typical behaviors related to Yers' digital behavior. Above all, they confirmed to be multitasking, and the 40% of them used the web to get the most of the news, while the only the 10% used television. We expect to get similar information from our investigation. According to Hershatter and Epstein [64], the most apparent difference between Yers and other generations is their distinctive relationship with technology, which has changed the way they see the world, their positive experience within organizations and institutions, and the way they interact with them. According to them, technology is considered their "sixth sense" and their use of ICTs clearly shows preferences for using technology to capture, systematize, broadcast their feelings, opinions, and experiences [64].

Gen Z is represented by "digital natives" but, according to Withe [10], despite their technology proficiency, Zers might prefer person-to person relationships to online interaction. Nevertheless, because of social media, they are comfortable with engaging with friends all over the world, so they seem to be well prepared for a global business environment [65]. Peer groups have increased their importance and they are always present. This higher level of interconnectedness might shape the way this generation view and live relationships. Similarly, to the previous generation, they expect everything to be immediately accessible through the Internet [66], but "Google" has become a verb for them. In line with the previous considerations, the last two generations, as early adapters to emerging technologies and "digital natives", should have an innate benefit in instinctively understanding potential applications and advantages, when rapid changes in technology occur. Consequently, our second proposition is: *The use of technology and the typology of technological devices characterize the digital employee experience of the generation Z*. As a consequence, the third proposition is: *The entry of the new generation of workers has an impact on diversity management practices within organizations*.

3 Research Methodology

In line with the exploratory purposes of this study, we performed a survey-based descriptive analysis, particularly useful for investigating the profile of Zers, as well as their interests and attitudes towards technologies. A sample of 323 participants was recruited using the snowball sampling procedure that "yields a study sample through referrals made among people who share or know of others who possess some characteristics that are of research interest" [67]. Initial participants were checked only for age. In line with the extant literature, which generally refers to Generation Z as people born between 1990 and 2009 [10, 48], we chose individuals aged between 16 and 26.

At first, the questionnaire was developed in the Italian language (source version); at a later stage, it was translated into English (target version) by a professional bilingual translator using the back-translation process [68, 69]. The comparison between the back-translated version and the source version has confirmed a good equivalence of meaning of the items. Finally, the questionnaire was distributed in both languages: Italian for residents in Italy, and English for participants of all other countries. In this way, the empirical investigation also takes account of cultural differences across countries. The questionnaire consisted of three main sections. The first section collected structural data of respondents, specifically their age, gender, nationality, country of origin, education, residential status and employment status.

The second section delved into the expectations of generation Z about their future ideal job (e.g., "What are your plans for the future?", "Where do you see yourself working in the future?"), using multiple choice questions. In addition, participants were inquired about the importance they attribute to several aspects of job, when considering a perfect job. They were status, autonomy, trust, career, salary, possibilities to learn and develop yourself, good relationships with colleagues, time flexibility, space flexibility (working from home), decision making, job security, knowledge sharing among colleagues, building relationships and networking. The degree of importance was detected through a 5-point Likert-type scale ranging from 1 to 5 where 1 is "Not significant" and 5 is "Very significant".

The third section collected responses about Zers' digital behaviour. More exhaustively, it intended to shed light on the present attitudes of Zers towards technologies in order to predict their future behaviours in organizational environments (i.e., "Which mean of communication do you use the most?", "How many different social media (Facebook, Twitter, Instagram) do you use?", "How many hours a day do you use the internet and your social media accounts?", "How often do you check your Facebook, Twitter, Instagram, etc.?"). When asked to answer on the usage of technology, the items were radio, TV, newspapers/magazines, online magazines and websites, and social media (Facebook, Twitter, Skype, LinkedIn, YouTube). A five point Likert-scale ranging from 1 ("Never") to 5 ("Always") assessed this question. Moreover, participants were asked to indicate the main motivation of using Internet (e.g., Social networks, Communication, Research, Emails), and the reasons why technology is important for them (i.e., "To get information anytime anywhere", "To connect with others", "To work and collaborate", "To be more productive", "Other").

Self-administered questionnaires were employed trough the online platform "Google Forms", and collected from April to May 2016. A total of 298 complete responses were coded for descriptive data analysis (25 were excluded due to partial responses).

4 Main Findings and Discussion

Since the survey had been closed, we collected 298 answers. Among the respondents, the 63% were female and the 37% male, with an average age of 22, 2 years old. The 70% of participants were Italian, while the 30% were from other countries, with a prevalence of people from the East of Europe. According to the target of our investigation, more than 70% of the respondents are attending high schools (33%) or a bachelor study program (41%), while the remaining part is attending a master program or has different occupations. Consequently, the 74% of the total amount of people declared to be a student, while the others are divided between employed and unemployed. Despite the expectations, only the 63% of respondents still live with their family; the others live alone or with flat mates.

According to the literature, our results confirm their tendency to build their future based on a higher level of education. In fact, the majority of respondents actually attending a high school and bachelor programs has expressed the intention to obtain a master degree. Moreover, regarding their plans for their future works, most of the respondents aim to join a multinational company. Surprisingly, the second choice in order of relevance is represented by the category of "other". This may represent both an incognizance of the significance of some terms (such as SME or NGO), or a contrast to the literature, which assumes that Zers are confident and optimistic about the future. In addition, the opportunity of becoming an entrepreneur only represents the 12% of respondents, which is in contrast to the prevalent literature that sees Zers as entrepreneurial people, becoming builders of their own destinies. In line with the explorative intent of our research, our results support the first proposition by highlighting Zers' responds, when asked to assess the most important aspects they consider, when choosing their first jobs. Despite the average results were quite homogeneous, we observed some important findings. Accordingly, people belonging to Z generation performed the following responses (Fig. 1).

Firstly, the majority of Zers believe the following aspects to be the most important ones: (a) building relationships and networking; (b) job security; (c) good relationships with colleagues; (d) possibilities to learn and develop yourself; (e) trust; and (f) autonomy. Specifically, the 75% of respondents judged the possibility to learn and develop themselves to be the main aspect in their future jobs. In the second and third positions are respectively trust and job security. This data reveals they actually look for a higher level of education and learning possibilities but, again in contrast with the literature, we interpret these three findings as indicators of a scarce confidence and optimism. In fact, the possibility to learn and

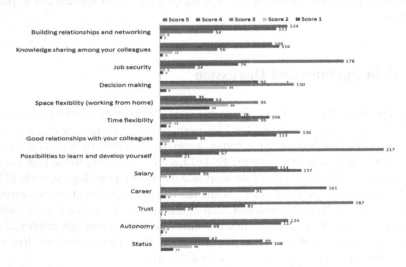

Fig. 1 Most important aspects of jobs among Zers. *Source* own elaboration

develop ourselves allows us to enlarge the amount of personal competences: this increases the chances of re-employment, in a progressively more flexible work environment. Furthermore, we noticed an absence of a quantitative effect by cultural diversity; despite the questionnaire was addressed to people from 25 different countries, we only observed small differences in percentage, related to the expressed preferences in: (a) space flexibility (Italian 5%, Other 6%); (b) status (Italian 6%, Other 7%); (c) trust (Italian 9%, Other 8%); and (d) autonomy (Italian 8%, other 7%).

Notably, the survey has provided impressive results compared to current managerial practices, which nowadays seem to increasingly converge towards the approach of smart working. In fact, the two aspects of Time and Space Flexibility turn out to be the ones where young people appear to give less importance ever. Consequently, we thought the result was linked to gender differences, as we collected a majority of female respondents. However, even confronting the average values in the male-female comparison, the results are consistent. In addition, we assumed that the results could be attributed to cultural differences. However, the comparison between Italian and foreign responses presented no conflicting values.

Going back to gender differences, we only detected a really low discrepancy when looking at a difference of 0.4 average point associated with the aspect of job security (females have expressed an average score of 4.6, while males of 4.2).

Therefore, we think that such results may be indicative of an increased convergence and homogenization of preferences among Zers, both in terms of gender and cultures, confirming the extant literature.

Finally, there is a strong commonality across respondents which upholds our second proposition by analyzing the digital behavior of Generation Z. The same variables (cultural differences and gender) are studied to investigate their effects on the use of social media among Zers. Firstly, it is notable that the mostly used ones are social networks (Facebook, Twitter, Skype, LinkedIn and YouTube), since the 83% of respondents declared to use them "always" (56%), and "very much" (27%). Secondly, on-line magazines and websites are used by the 64% of young people, with the 36% of them affirming to use them "always", while the 28% answered "very much". In line with our expectations, digital natives barely prefer to use magazines and newspapers. Furthermore, we investigated Zers' behaviors when interacting with social networks and social media. Our study confirms their most extensive use of social networks, revealing that the 35% of respondents use them for 1–2 h per day, the 36% have declared an equivalent use of 2–4 h per day, while the 27% make use of social networks for more than 4 h per day. In addition, Zers use social media mainly to entertain conversations with instant messaging tools (80%) and to make phone calls (14%). Sending an e-mail or a SMS are the most important functions only for the 2% of peoples. To execute the abovementioned activities, the 55% of respondents have from one to three social media accounts. Additionally, according to the literature [12, 13, 66] and in line with our expectations, the most important function of technology is represented by being connected with others and get information anytime and anywhere (81% of respondents). Again, we highlighted a neutral effect of nationality and gender.

5 Conclusions and Future Research

The current social and economic environment is challenging the way companies around the globe are facing profound changes in their business and in the workforce.

Furthermore, since the use of technology is becoming more and more pervasive, particularly among younger generations, it has changed the way individuals communicate, live and work. In line with these considerations, companies must consider different ways of managing diversity in the workforce. Thus, understanding the relevant characteristics of the new generation of workers will help HRM to induce a change through the combination and the adaptation of practices, involving different generations of workers. Strengthening our first proposition, we outlined that, the possibility to learn, job security and trust, are the top-three characteristics Zers consider in choosing the perfect job, without discrimination on gender and cultural differences between countries. This homologation drives to a major managerial implication, which supports our third proposition: with advancing years, diversity management should focus on Aging and not on cultural differences, when managing the generation mix. Moreover, the second major managerial implication concerns smart working. Changes in the economic environment require new approaches to organizing work: smart working is one of the most discussed among organizations. However, in contrast with the changes taking place, our survey reveals surprisingly relevant results. People belonging to Z generation do not seem to give importance to time and space flexibility, regardless of gender and country of origin. In line with this outcome, managers must find a way to combine different necessities and expectations among the generation mix, within their organization. Concerning Zers' digital behavior, our research supports our second proposition and drives to a threefold managerial implication: (a) the very high level of interconnectivity detected, together with the level of technology usage, allow managers to define the appropriate support for the maximization of Zers' performance; (b) the very high level of interconnectivity detected, in combination with the typology of technological device, allow organizations to (re)organize their structures; and (c) their high level of connectivity and their "social" digital behaviors will change the way organizations will manage individual and social capital, and the generation mix. This shift is already emerging when looking at the widespread of ICTs in formal and informal education [70].

Moreover, our study contributes to the advance in literature in several ways. Since the increasing older workforce and the influx of ICT into a wide variety of work settings is motivating a re-examination of the literature concerning ageing and work performance [71], this is the first study that examines the expectations and the behavior of the next generation of workers, jointly analyzing the role of ICTs. Secondly, given the limited nature of the few existent studies on generation Z, we contribute to the empirical research providing a universal profile from a heterogeneous sample. Accordingly, the discrimination between different countries, as well as the differentiation per gender, has been neglected until now. Finally, by improving our explorative analysis, we will bring significant advancements and insights to diversity management, which will have to be rethought and reformulated on the basis of changes that are taking place.

The major limitation of the study concerns its nature: it represents a first descriptive analysis that aims to address an emerging phenomenon. Clearly, the composition and the relatively small dimension of our sample, together with the lack of validate scales, limit the generalization of the results. For these reasons, future steps of the research will include a more detailed analysis aiming at validating the preliminarily identified profile. In detail, we plan to conduct the analysis through a larger sample and a comparison with previous generations, both in terms of personal characteristics and digital behaviors. Finally, measures of correlation and test of independence will be employed in order to validate the association between variables and the significance of group differences that exist according to demographic characteristics.

From a practical perspective, this kind of study will offer managers the opportunity to implement HR practices, knowledge management practices and interventions and new diversity management operations, aimed at overcoming limitations linked to generational differences within their organizations. At the same time, it will be possible to devise ways in which positively exploit these differences, through the promotion of diversity, in order to reach both an individual and organization growth [1–7, 17–20].

References

1. Barabino, M. C., Jacobs, B., & Maggio, M. A. (2001). Il diversity management. *Sviluppo & Organizzazione, 184*, 19–31.
2. Rumelt, R. P. (1984). Towards a strategic theory of the firm. In R. B. Lamb (Ed.), *Competitive strategic management*. Englewood Cliffs, NJ: Prentice Hall.
3. Keil, M., Amershi, B., Holmes, S., Jablonski, H., Lüthi, E., Matoba, K., et al. (2007). Manuale di Formazione sul Diversity Management. International Society for Diversity Management- idm. Antidiscrimination and Diversity Training VT/2006/009, pp 1–44. www. idm-diversity.org.
4. Cerrato, D. (2011). Natura e determinanti del vantaggio competitivo sostenibile nella prospettiva resource-based: Alcune riflessioni critiche. *Sinergie, 63*(03), 1–30.
5. Tardivo, G. (2011). L'evoluzione degli studi sul knowledge Management. *Sinergie, 76*(08), 1–22.
6. Vomberg, A. (2015). Talented people and strong brends: The contribution of human capital and brand equity to firm value. *Strategic Management Journal, 36*(13), 2122–2131.
7. Foss, N. J. (2016). Judgment, the Theory of the Firm, and the Economics of Institutions: My Contributions to the Entrepreneurship Field. In Prepared for D. Audretsch, & E. Lehman (Eds.), *Companion to makers of modern entrepreneurship*. Routledge.
8. Porter, M. E., & Kramer, M. R. (2011). The big idea. Creating shared value. How to reinvent capitalism: And unleash a wave of innovation and growth. *Harvard Business Review* (pp. 62–77).
9. McCrindle, M. (2015). An excerpt from the ABC of XYZ. Generations Defined. mccrindle.com.mau.
10. Holroyd, J. (2011). Talkin' 'bout my label. The Sidney Morning Herald. http://www.smh. com.au/lifestyle/diet-and-fitness/talkin-bout-my-label-20110720-lho7s.html.

11. Twenge, J. M. (2006). *Generation me: Why today's young Americans are more confident, assertive, entitled-and more miserable than ever before.* New-York: Free Press.
12. Withe, S. (2016). The Generation Z effect. Canadian University Report 2016, Special to The Globe and Mail.
13. Howe, N., & Strauss, W. (2007). The next 20 years: How customers and workforce attitudes will evolve. *Harvard Business Review* (pp. 41–52). Hbr.org.
14. Di Mauro, M. (2010). Organizzazioni e differenze. Pratiche, strumenti e percorsi formativi. FrancoAngeli s.r.l. (pp. 26–32).
15. Costa, G., & Giannecchini, M. (2009). *Risorse Umane. Persone, relazioni e valore.* McGraw-Hill, cap. 15 (pp. 505–540).
16. Frank, F. D., & Taylor, C. R. (2004). Talent management: Trends will shape the future. *Human Resource Planning, 27*(1), 33–41.
17. Cox, T. (1993). *Cultural diversity in organizations: Theory, research & practice* (8th ed.). San Francisco, CA: Berrett-Koehler.
18. Cox, T. (2001). *Creating the multicultural organization: A strategy for capturing the power of diversity.* San Francisco: Jossey-Bass.
19. Kemper, L. E., Bater, A. K., & Froese, F. J. (2016). Diversity management in aging society: A comparative study of Germany and Japan. *Management Revue, 27*(1/2), 29–49.
20. Renouard, Y. (1969). Il concetto di generazione nella storia. *In Studi salentini, 11,* 5–28.
21. Joshi, A., Dencker, J. C., & Franz, G. (2011). *Generations in organizations. Research in Organizational Behavior.* Elsevier Inc., (vol. 31, pp. 177–205). www.sciencedirect.com.
22. Howe, N., & Strauss, W. (2000). *Millenial rising the next great generation.* New York City: Vintage Books.
23. Limonta, T., Manzini, S., Nastri, A., Quaratino, L., & Searle, R. (2014). Yers ready for work around the world—Final Research Report. Fondazione ISTUD.
24. McIntosh-Elkins, J., McRitchie, K., & Scoones, M. (2007). From the silent generation to generation X, Y and Z: Strategies for Managing the Generation Mix. SIGUCCS'07 (pp. 240–246), October 7–10, 2007, Orlando, Florida, USA.
25. SHRM Generational Differences Survey Report. (2004). https://www.shrm.org/research/surveyfindings/documents/generational%20differences%20survey%20report.pdf.
26. Van Baviel, J., & Reher, D. (2013). The baby boom and its causes: What we know and what we need to know. *Population and Development Review, 39*(2), 257–288.
27. Eileen, C. T., & Cort, W. R. (2015). *Age Stereotypes in the Workplace* (pp. 1–8). Singapore: Springer Science+Business Media.
28. http://www.investopedia.com/video/play/baby-boomer/.
29. Howe, N., & Strauss, W. (2007). The next 20 years: How customer and workforce attitudes will evolve. *Harvard Business Review* (pp. 41–52).
30. Coupland, D. (1991). *Generation X: Tales for an accelerated culture.* St: Martin's Press.
31. Yu, H. C., & Miller, P. (2005). Leadership style-The X generation and baby boomers compared in different cultural contexts. *Leadership and Organization Development Journal, 26*(1), 35–50. doi:10.1108/01437730510575570.
32. Loomis, J. E. (2000). *Generation X.* Indianapolis: Rough Notes Co.
33. Morris, M. G., & Venkatesh, V. (2000). Age differences in technology adoption decisions: Implications for a changing work force. *Personnel Psychology, 53,* 375–403.
34. Egri, C. P., & Ralston, D. A. (2004). Generation cohorts and personal values: A comparison of China and the Unites States. *Organization Science, 15*(2), 210–220.
35. Gafni, R., & Geri, N. (2013). Generation Y versus Generation X: Differences in Smartphone Adaptation. In *Proceedings of the Chais conference on instructional technologies research 2013: Learning in the technological era.*
36. Cape, P. (2015). Engaging digital Boomers, Gen X and Millennials: Generational differences don't always match stereotypes. *Quirk's Marketing Research Review.*
37. Managing Generation X. Illinois Periodical Online. (IPO). http://www.lib.niu.edu/1998/il980118.html.
38. Durkin, D. (2008). Youth movement. *Communication World, 25,* 3–26.

39. La Marca, A. (2011). La "Generazione Y": giovani indecisi che sognano trionfi e vivono tra reale e virtuale. Dossier I Giovani. *Studiom Educationis. Anno XII, 3,* 73–96.
40. Martin, C., & Tulgan, B. (2001). *Managing Generation Y: Global citizens born in the late seventies and early eighties.* Amherst, MA: HRD Press.
41. Rietzschel, E. F., & Zacher, H. (2015). *Workplace creativity, innovation, and age* (pp. 1–8). Singapore: Springer Science+Business Media.
42. Eisner, S. P. (2005). Managing Generation Y. *Sam Advanced Management Journal.*
43. Myers, K. K., & Sadaghiani, K. (2010). Millennials in the workplace: A communication perspective on Millennials' organizational relationships and performance. *Journal of Business and Psychology, 25,* 225–238.
44. Johns, K. (2003). Managing generational diversity in the workforce. Trends & Tidbits. http:// www.workindex.com.
45. Dolezalek, H. (2007). X-Y vision. *Training, 44,* 22–27.
46. Reisenwitz, T. H., & Iyer, R. (2009). Differences in Generation X and Generation Y: Implications for the organization and marketers. *The Marketing Management Journal, 19*(2), 91–103.
47. Orrell, L. (2009). In economic crisis, think of the next generation. *Strategic Communication Management, 13,* 7.
48. Beldiman, D. (2013). *Access to information and knowledge: 21st century challenges in intellectual property and knowledge governance.* Cheltenham: Edward Elgar Publishing Inc.
49. Bannon, S., Ford, K., & Meltzer, L. (2011). Understanding millennials in the workplace. *The CPA Journal, 81*(11), 61–65.
50. Keeling, S. (2003). Advising the millennial generation. *NACADA Journal, 23*(1/2), 30–36.
51. Debard, R. D. (2004). Millennials coming to college. In R. D. Debard, & Coomes, M. D. (Eds.), *Serving the millennial generation: New directions for student services* (pp. 33–45).
52. Stone, D. L., Deadrick, D. L., Lukaszewski, K. M., & Johnson, R. (2015). The influence of technology on the future of human resource management. *Human Resource Management Review, 25,* 216–231.
53. SHRM. (2002). The future of HR Profession Eight Leading Consulting Firms Share Their Visions for the Future of Human Resources. http://www.shrm.org/pressroom/Documents/future_of_hr.pdf.
54. Perry, E., & Tyson, S. (2011). desired goals and actual outcomes of e-HRM. *Human Resource Management Journal, 21,* 335–354.
55. Lengnick-Hall, M. L., & Moritz, S. (2003). The impact of e-HR on the human resource management function. *Journal of Labour Research, 24*(3), 365–379.
56. Kiesler, S., Siegel, J., & McGuire, T. W. (1984). Social psychological aspects of computer-mediated communication. *American Psychologist, 39,* 1123.
57. Castells, M. (2011). *The rise of the network society: The information age: Economy, society and culture.* Hoboken: Wiley-Blackwell.
58. Venkatesh, V., Thong, Y. L. J., & Xu, X. L. (2012). Consumer acceptance and use of information technology: Extending the unified theory of acceptance and use of technology. *MIS Quarterly, 36*(1), 157–178.
59. Kumar, A., & Lim, H. (2008). Age differences in mobile service perceptions: Comparison of Generation Y and baby boomers. *Journal of Services Marketing, 27*(1), 1–23.
60. Morris, M. G., & Venkatesh, V. (2000). *Age differences in technology adoption decisions: implications for a changing work force* (vol. 53). Personnel Psychology Inc.
61. Dalton, G. W., & Thompson, P. H. (1971). Accelerating obsolescence of older engineers. *Harvard Business Review, 49*(5), 57–67.
62. Mitchell, V., Petrovici, D., Schlegelmilch, B. B., & Szocs, I. (2015). The influence of parents versus peers on Generation Y Internet ethical attitudes. *Electronic Commerce Research and Applications, Elsevier BV, 14,* 95–103.
63. Junco, R., & Mastrodicasa, J. (2007). *Connecting to the net.generation: What higher education professionals need to know about today's student.* National Association of Student Personnel Administrators (NASPA), Inc.

64. Hershatter, A., & Epstein, M. (2010). *Millennials and the world of work: An organization and management perspective* (Vol. 25 (2), pp. 211–223.). Springer Science+Business Media, LLC.
65. Apuzzo, R. (2015). Always Connected: Generation Z, the "Digitarians". http://randyapuzzo. com/blog/opinions/generation-z-the-digitarians/.
66. Levit, A. (2015). Make Way for Generation Z. The New York Times. http://www.nytimes. com/2015/03/29/jobs/make-way-for-generation-z.html.
67. Brisilin, R. (1970). Back-translation for cross-cultural research. *Journal of Cross-Cultural Psycology, 1*(3), 185–216.
68. Su, C. T., & Parham, L. D. (2002). Case Report—Generating a valid questionnaire translation for cross-cultural use. *American Journal of Occupational Terapy, 56,* 581–585.
69. Biernacki, P., & Waldorf, D. (1981). Snowball sampling. Problems and techniques of chain referral sampling. *Sociological Methods & Research, 10*(2), 141–163.
70. Iannotta, M., Gatti, M., & Giordani, F. (2014). Emerging models for corporate welfare and HR management in the service-dominant logic. In L. Mola, A. Carugati, A. Kokkinaki & N. Pouloudi (Eds.), *Proceedings of the 8th Mediterranean conference on information systems.*
71. Sharit, J., & Czaja, S. J. (1994). Aging, computer-based task performance, and stress: Issues and challenges. *Ergonomics, 37,* 559–577.

Initiatives Addressing Confidentiality in Electronic Health Records Architectural Consideration and Patient Engagement in Healthcare IT

Nabil Georges Badr

Abstract This paper reviews the literature on electronic health records and summarizes a few persistent challenges that electronic medical record (EMR) systems must address relating to security and safety of patients. A discussion on patient engagement and its connection with confidentiality in Health IT is followed by examples with an emphasis on the personal health record portal implementation at Kaiser Permanente. Next, through review of practitioner and architectural guideline documentation, a summary of concepts for electronic health records architectural considerations for privacy with the implementation of technologies such as access controls, encryption and data handling best practices. In this position paper, two major initiatives are revealed: (1) The premise of patient engagement and (2) the guidelines for a "Robust Health Data Infrastructure Architecture" platform for Health IT.

Keywords Health IT ecosystem · Electronic health record · Electronic medical record · Confidentiality

1 Introduction

Healthcare IT has been a subject of worldwide concern for more than a decade [1]. Healthcare is one of the largest segments of the US economy, approaching 20% of GDP (AHRQ pub. 14-0041-EF). Federal law requires all health insurance companies and healthcare providers to use electronic medical records (EHRs) by 2015. This paper narrows its focus on the discussion of privacy issues in healthcare IT (HIT) in the context of the United States.

Health information technology (HIT) is information technology applied to health and healthcare. It supports health information management across computerized systems and the secure exchange of health information between consumers, providers, payers, and quality monitors with the use of electronic medical record systems.

N.G. Badr (✉)
Grenoble Graduate School of Business, Grenoble, France
e-mail: nabil.badr@alumni.grenoble-em.com

© Springer International Publishing AG 2018 257
C. Rossignoli et al. (eds.), *Digital Technology and Organizational Change*,
Lecture Notes in Information Systems and Organisation 23,
https://doi.org/10.1007/978-3-319-62051-0_21

In a distinction made by HIMSS Analytics, "An electronic health record (EHR) focuses on the total health of the patient. In contrast, electronic medical records (EMR) contains the medical and treatment history of the patients in one practice" (HIMSS Analytics). An EMR is a digital version of a paper chart that contains all of a patient's medical history from one practice. An EMR is mostly used by providers for diagnosis and treatment. An EMR is a narrower view of a patient's medical history, while an EHR can be seen as a collection of EMR data as a more comprehensive report of the patient's overall health.

EMR adoption in the US is still in its launch: providers were found more likely to access EHR based information for higher-risk patients than for those who received less frequent care [2]. Partial implementations of EHR features such as closed loop medication administration (32% of US hospitals) have proven the most significant progress. Yet, to this date, less than 5% of US hospitals have reached full EMR implementations with cumulative capabilities supporting Continuity of Care Data (CCD) transactions across Emergency (ED), Ambulatory, and Pediatrics (OP); Kaiser Permanente hospitals are in the lead.[1]

U.S. Congress enacted the Health Insurance Portability and Accountability Act (HIPAA) in 1996 and followed it by the Health IT for Economic & Clinical Health Act (HITECH) in 2010. Extending its predecessor, policy makers intended HITECH to hold service providers and vendors with access to healthcare information accountable for compliance.

On March 23, 2010, President Obama signed the Patient Protection and Affordable Care Act (P.L. 111-148). The law puts in place comprehensive health insurance reforms applying new consumer protection regulation, improving quality of care and lowering cost in the objective of increasing access to affordable healthcare.

Privacy laws such as HITECH and HIPAA, typically consist of technical controls, a written information security plan, compliance with "Meaningful Use", and breach notification protocols. In addition to improving quality, safety and efficiency of healthcare, complying with "Meaningful Use" means maintaining privacy and security of patient health information, better clinical outcomes, and more robust research data on health systems. In order for physician to meet EHR Meaningful Use requirements and qualify for federal reimbursements through the American Recovery and Reinvestment Act (ARRA), organizations must protect their electronic health information by implementing proper controls, including encryption.

1.1 Motivation

Information collection, storage, and management is central to the practice of healthcare. With the advent of EHR, patient health information have an opportunity to become more widely available for providers and healthcare managers to broaden

---

[1]http://www.himssanalytics.org/stagesGraph.asp.

its potential use beyond individual patient care [3]. This is seen to trouble patients' and providers' expectations of privacy that kept medical records confidential between providers and patients.

Studies among patients have reported that 13% of respondents reported having withheld information from a provider because of privacy/security concerns [4]. The greatest perceived danger to patients is not that their EHR data might be misused, rather, that their data could be used not as intended.

Health Information Technology (HIT) owners and operators find a pressing need to focus their attention on creating and operating a solid electronic healthcare IT ecosystem. This ecosystem is founded on Digital Health Services that are transforming the way health IT data is created, digitized, collected, exchanged, analyzed, used and reported. Clinicians are encouraged to leverage the EHR's value in quality of care and discuss patients' privacy concerns during clinic visits, while policy makers consider how to address the real and perceived privacy and security risks of EHRs [5].

CAN HEALTHCARE IT ADDRESS THE SECURITY AND PRIVACY ISSUES IN ELECTRONIC HEALTHCARE RECORDS?

1.2 Approach

This position paper reviews the literature in EHR and summarizes a few persistent challenges that EMR and related HIT systems must address relating to confidentiality of patient data. A discussion on patient engagement and its connection with confidentiality in Health IT is followed by examples with an emphasis on the personal health record portal implementation at Kaiser Permanente.

This paper's contribution is staged from the perspective of information systems applied to the medical field of practice, we conducted the review to cover four threads:

1. Publications in the field of health informatics, namely the Journal of the American Medical Informatics Association and the International Journal of Medical Informatics;
2. A review of relevant practitioner publications such as Health Affairs, triangulated with federal agency publications concerned with the progress of innovations in health IT;
3. An overview of the implementation of EHR at Kaiser Permanente illustrating facts from their experience in patient engagement;
4. Finally, the witness of a few case studies performed by HIMMS[2]—The Healthcare Information and Management Systems Society (HIMSS is a global, cause-based, not-for-profit organization focused on better health through information technology (IT). HIMSS leads efforts to optimize health engagements and care outcomes using information technology).

---

[2]http://www.himss.org/.

In the next section, we review practitioner and architectural guideline documentation, and present a summary of concepts for EHR architectural considerations for privacy with the implementation of technologies such as access controls, encryption and data handling best practices.

2 Literature Review and Discussion

The flow of information in primary care practice has preoccupied practitioners since before the turn of the century. Substantial benefits through routine use of electronic medical records were touted to include improved quality, safety, and efficiency, along with increased ability to conduct education and research. Evidence of substantial and often unexpected related safety risks posed by the use of EHRs should be considered alongside the potential benefits of these systems [6].

Risk assessments are recommended with a focus on building the policies and procedures with the objective of establishing protection of consumer information. Interestingly enough, practitioners and lawmakers are now drawing parallel experiences from the banking industry for data privacy and protection. This includes the rigor of risk management tools such as STRIDE to identify, manage and protect against data security breaches [7].

Legislation such as the Federal Information Processing Standard 199 and the Federal Information Security Management Act (2002) defines information security measures of protecting information and information systems from unauthorized access, use, disclosure, disruption, modification, or destruction. These measures are codified as three essential attributes:

Integrity—guarding against improper information modification or destruction, and includes ensuring information non-repudiation and authenticity;

Confidentiality—preserving authorized restrictions on access and disclosure, including means for protecting personal privacy and proprietary information; and

Availability—ensuring timely and reliable access to and use of information.

For this paper, we adopt the definition of "Privacy" defined by the ONC (Office of the National Coordinator of Healthcare IT—U.S. Department of Health and Human Services) framework as an individual's interest in protecting his or her individually identifiable health information and the corresponding obligation of those persons and entities accessing, using, or disclosing that information to respect those interests through fair information practices [8]. This definition maps directly to the information confidentiality attribute of information security.

2.1 Patient Engagement Through Health IT

Patient engagement is about providers and patients working together to improve health. A patient's greater engagement in healthcare is known to practitioners to contribute to improved health outcomes.[3] HIMMS reports that "Patients want to be engaged in their healthcare decision-making process, and those who are engaged as decision-makers in their care tend to be healthier and have better outcomes". A current study agrees on the fact that patient engagement in healthcare could improve medication adherence [9] for example. Recently, a research conducted by Columbia University, stipulates that privacy (confidentiality) is an important by-product of patient engagement [10].

Patient engagement is an emerging concept in health IT. It is one of the five goals of the federal government's meaningful use program. Stage 3 of the "Meaningful Use" EHR incentive program requirements encourages patient engagement through various means, including the integration of patient-generated data into clinical care documentation and quality measures (see Footnote 1). The HIMSS patient engagement framework provides a five-milestone roadmap for health providers looking to support patients through the use of IT tools and resources: *inform me, engage me, empower me, partner with me*, and *support my e-Community*.

The significant growth in healthcare applications designed for consumer mobile devices provides a platform for individuals to collect, track, store, and transmit personal health information. These data could cover care experience surveys, symptom assessments, self-management diaries, demographics, etc. and integrated as patient-generated data in EHR. Boston Children's Hospital, for instance, implemented a Discharge Communication Platform (DisCo) which sends families either a text message or an email with 3 questions within 24 h of discharge to provide an additional layer of support for the discharged child and their caregivers —with real time follow up with a member of the medical team.[4] Another hospital (National Children's Hospital in Washington, DC) relied on handheld technology with Apps (Doc Journal) as means for patients and families to better engage with their care team through online health information entry, pharmaceutical references, journaling, etc (see Footnote 4).

Patient engagement is expanding into patient-generated health data (PGHD) where the patient captures the data and transfers it to the central system. Practitioners will then pick up the data, review it and authorized into the database. Marceglia et al. [11] developed a conceptual representation of the potential integration between a system centered on patient engagement and the clinical data captured in the electronic medical record (Fig. 1). Ideally, a real-time model of data acquisition and validation would place the patient at the controls of his or her personal health data and establish grounds from proper clinical use of this data [12].

---

[3]http://www.himss.org/library/patient-engagement-toolkit.
[4]http://www.himss.org/library.

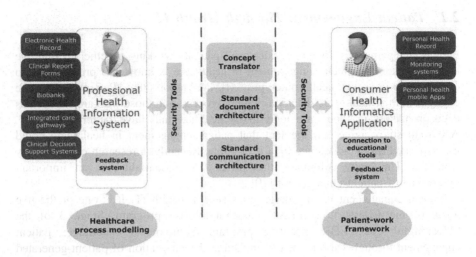

Fig. 1 Conceptual representation—Integration between a system centered on patient engagement and the clinical data captured in the medical record. *Source* Marceglia et al. [11]

Research on potential challenges of patient engagement in Health IT publications is still scarce. Studies have shown that patient collected clinical data are not always reliable [13]. Patient engagement could involve a plethora of data sources such as social media and online patient communities for information exchange, wearables and mobile apps [14]. Some approaches tend to use devices that may not be trusted as clinical devices such as mobile phone apps. Other approaches use clinical instruments, however, as they depend on the health literacy of the patient and sometimes on systems capacity [15], human or machine processing power [16]. From the practitioners' viewpoint, this increase in patient access to information may lead to potential conflicts with reluctant care providers aiming to protect health information for reasons of trust, territorialism or in the context of patient-physician confidentiality [17].

2.2 Patient Portals: Cornerstone for Patient Engagement

Patient portals are believed to be the gate to a wide scope of patient engagement [18]. Research is clear on the fact that IT platforms can enhance patient engagement and improve health outcomes [19]. For instance, patient portals have been shown to enhance adolescent healthcare quality and adolescents readily use a confidential portal [20]. However, "flexible, standardized, and interoperable solutions must be integrated with outcomes-based research to activate effectively patients as partners in their healthcare" [17]. Few studies address the potential connection between the usability of electronic health records and what features should be incorporated for data protection from errors and unauthorized access [19]. As an illustrative

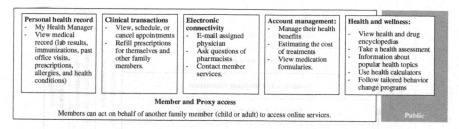

Personal health record	Clinical transactions	Electronic connectivity	Account management:	Health and wellness:
- My Health Manager - View medical record (lab results, immunizations, past office visits, prescriptions, allergies, and health conditions)	- View, schedule, or cancel appointments - Refill prescriptions for themselves and other family members.	- E-mail assigned physician - Ask questions of pharmacists - Contact member services.	- Manage their health benefits - Estimating the cost of treatments - View medication formularies.	- View health and drug encyclopedias - Take a health assessment - Information about popular health topics - Use health calculators - Follow tailored behavior change programs

Member and Proxy access

Members can act on behalf of another family member (child or adult) to access online services.

Public

Fig. 2 Representation by the author from information in Silvestre et al. [22]

evidence in patient engagement in healthcare, this paper presents Kaiser Permanente's (KP) patient portal's implementation of an online personal health record.

KP's Online Personal Health Record. Leading the US implementations of EMRs, with a primary focus on patient engagement,[5] Kaiser Permanente prioritises fostering patient engagement through a holistic strategy of care coordination, technological innovation, and community outreach.[6] Kaiser Permanente (KP), founded in 1945, aligned a vision of a *"Real-time, Personalized Healthcare"*, inspired by Dr. Sidney Garfield, MD co-founder, to offer online health services in 1996. In 2004, Kaiser Permanente launched an electronic health record online portal (EHR), *KP HealthConnect*™ [21]. KP has deployed mobile computer carts that allow doctors to maintain their patient contact. Physicians and nurses use the system in front of the patient engaging the latter in the healthcare process.[7]

With a focus on patient engagement, KP deployed a patient facing portal through which patients can enrol online, complete surveys, review their lab tests and receive recommendations from their primary care physician for continuity of care [22]. The online personal health record (PHR) includes a patient health record with comprehensive documentation across care settings inpatient and outpatient, clinical decision support, and complete, real-time connectivity to lab, pharmacy, radiology, and other ancillary systems. Members, who are also KP's health Insurance Plan subscribers, can use KP provided tools to manage their health benefits, including estimating the cost of treatments and viewing medication formularies. For Kaiser, blending traditional office visits with this modality of care has proven effective for this nationwide provider. The decrease in office visits in favor of scheduled telephone visits and secure e-mail messaging created operational efficiencies by offering nontraditional, patient-centered ways of providing care [23].

Designed with a bilingual interface (English and Spanish), KP serves 10.2 million members. This digitized health ecosystem offers member access to their

---

[5]http://mobihealthnews.com/29985/in-depth-a-brief-history-of-digital-patient-engagement-tools.

[6]https://store.healthleadersmedia.com/patient-engagement-for-population-health-the-kaiser-permanente-msha-models-1

[7]http://www.healthleadersmedia.com/content/MAG-88640/Behind-the-Wires.

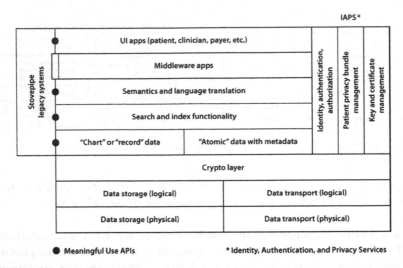

Fig. 3 JASON's proposed architecture for the exchange of health information *Source* "A Robust Health Data Infrastructure," publication number 14-0041-EF—figure

information, an option for proxy access for family members and a public portal for health management to the public (Fig. 2).

2.3 EHR Architectural Considerations for Privacy and Confidentiality

Architectural consideration in implementing a Digitized Health IT are specific to the ability of the data to be protected from unauthorized access, use and distribution. Prescriptions for cloud computing versus locally hosted solutions are contradicting in the way that they may or may not protect the confidentiality of the data [21]. Expanding on such infrastructure requirements, the next section of this paper addresses the fundamental components of a data architecture that aims at standardizing principles of confidentiality in Electronic Health Records, standards that would maintain confidentiality of the data across the digitized Health IT ecosystem.

On 4/09/2014, the Healthcare Research and Quality (AHRQ) released the JASON[8] report detailing a framework for a "Robust Health Data Infrastructure Architecture" (Fig. 3). In a nutshell, this framework introduces a common markup language for healthcare including controlled vocabularies referred to as the Fast Health Interoperable Resources (FHIR) being refined by the HL7 and the HIT Standards Committee. According to plans for an Interoperable Health IT

---

[8]JASON is an independent group of scientists who advise the United States government on matters of science and technology whose efforts are facilitated by the MITRE Corporation.

infrastructure published by the Office of the National Coordinator for Health IT in the US, one of the guiding principles for EHRs protect privacy and security in all aspects of interoperability.

Access Control. The target digitized healthcare IT ecosystem is comprised of many entities, all of which interact with the patient, including pharmacies, clinicians, payers, insurance, caregivers/family/friends, laboratories, data repositories, researchers, etc. All of these entities need to be connected to a secure IT infrastructure that provides technical and semantic interoperability and guarantees trust across healthcare environments. As healthcare data is stored, accessed and transferred in the healthcare environment, it is necessary to track its provenance, e.g., origin, across the continuum of care and lifespan of the data.[9]

Research has shown that EMR systems implementations should contain adequate safeguards for patient privacy and confidentiality [24]. Health Level 7 (HL7) standards activities contribute towards the goal of creating standardized digital services infrastructure by providing an information model, metadata and security and privacy mechanisms. Vendors building EMR software and devices and services for the HealthCare IT ecosystem, are encouraged to develop and publish APIs based on the JASON architecture for medical-records data that would enable their health records to be exchanged across the healthcare environment. These APIs must follow the "robustness principle" *(i.e. be liberal in what you accept and conservative in what you send)*. The architecture consolidates policy-related mechanisms into a well-defined access control system that, at a minimum, provides identity management, user authentication, and user authorization.

Encryption. The Robust Health Data Infrastructure Architecture suggests that all data be encrypted at rest and in motion, in accordance with the HIPPA rule of Meaningful Use. An encryption layer ensures the confidentiality of data, an authority is needed to control distribution of the cryptographic keys required to access the data, thus reinforcing the principle of separation of key management from data management addressed by Data Segmentation for Privacy standards in the HL7 and the Standards and Interoperability (S&I) frameworks. Measures for identity, authentication and privacy services are employed with the necessary key based encryption.

Encryption may not protect against data errors such as data that has been compromised, however it does provide safeguard for data breach [25]. Concepts such as patient controlled encryption schemes are being exploited to achieve secure and private medical records while maintaining the efficiency and functionality, including search-ability and delegation [26]. Encryption methods are investigated and proposed for record data, namely the attribute based encryption method, prescribed for a potentially cloud based data would provide the security to the database [27]. This encryption method would offer the opportunity for hosted application to offer hosted applications with *"reasonably"* good privacy.

---

[9]JASON. "A Robust Health Data Infrastructure," prepared for the Agency for Health Care Research and Quality, AHRQ publication number 14-0041-EF, Rockville, MD, 2014.

Data Provenance and Atomic Data. Recent studies show measurable benefits emerging from the adoption of health information technology; these benefits range from efficiency and effectiveness of care, provider and patient satisfaction, preventive care and patient safety [28]. Legislators, scientists, and information technology research and development in efforts to find measures that maintain privacy of patient data with the capability to serve public health [29] and clinical research Henry et al. [30].

In accordance with the HIPPA rule of *Meaningful Use*, the data provenance (source of the data) metadata is captured in EHRs typically include time/date stamps, authorship information, and contextual transactions information.

Additionally, EHR data is to be represented as discrete data elements (atomic data) with associated metadata, separating chart (data dissociated from the patient) and record data (patient data) for additional privacy, acknowledging the need to support clinical trials and clinical research while protecting patient privacy. This principle is manifested into efforts to separate clinical data from patient biographical data. The latter is protected to maintain patient privacy. The clinical data is hence available for use as atomic data to empower practitioners in diagnosis, fuel big data analytics tools for clinical research [31] and evidence based data for policy governance of general public health [32].

3 Conclusion

A foundational concept of information sharing in healthcare is to avail patient health and biography information to the providers of care. Despite extensive efforts in privacy legislation, patients still express great concern of privacy/security of their health related information. The greatest perceived danger to patients is not that their EHR data might be misused, rather, that their data could be used not as intended.

The discussion section of this paper has exposed approaches in theory and practice, through a foundation of a robust health data infrastructure architecture designed to achieve the balance between data availability and confidentiality. Guidelines were summarized that emphasize encryption of data at rest and in movement, data separation between clinical atomic data and health record private data, and the necessity of metadata on data provenance that include time/date stamps, authorship information, and contextual transactions information enabling the traceability of the information for validation and control over confidentiality.

Concerns of confidentiality may be seen to outweigh benefits of quality of care. In a look at the future, a vision of consumers in control of their information through Consumer Health Informatics (CHI) is paving the way for fully transparent health records [33]. These building blocks would facilitate the use of applications in a patient-centered medical home, patient decision aids and personal health management tools, and patient self-serve kiosks.

Patient engagement practices, enabled by secured portals, bring the control of who can have access to patient data. In our example, Kaiser's business model is a closed network model of insurance, hospitals, pharmacies and health professionals. The control over data capture, usage and preservation is an achievable objective. Challenges will prevail specifically in distributed health information systems with multiple providers with EMR system implementations and maturity levels. Legislators have been enthusiastic to maintain the balance between protecting private information and pertinent disclosure of that information to authorized points of care. Consequently, such access to data would demand the development of policies and procedures related to record management baring concerns of accuracy, integrity, and quality in patient records, especially in such situations where patient data entries are permitted and incorporated into the record.

References

1. Bates D. et al. (2003, Jan/Feb). A proposal for electronic medical records in U.S. Primary Care Journal of the American Medical Informatics Association *10*(1), 1.
2. Vest J. R. (2009). Health information exchange and healthcare utilization. *Journal of medical systems 33*(3), 223–31.
3. Caine K., & Tierney, W M. (2015, Jan, 30). *Journal of General Internal Medicine 1*, S38–41.
4. Campos-Castillo, C., & Anthony, D. L. (2015). The double-edged sword of electronic health records: Implications for patient disclosure. *Journal of the American Medical Informatics Association, 22*(e1), e130–e140.
5. Tucker, C. M., Arthur, T. M., Roncoroni, J., Wall, W., & Sanchez, J. (2015). Patient-centered, culturally sensitive healthcare. *Am. Journal of Lifestyle Medicine, 9*(1), 63–77.
6. Donaldson, L. (2015). *Patient safety and healthcare It* (p. 291). Mastering Informatics: A Healthcare Handbook for Success.
7. Xin, T., & Xiaofang, B. (2014). Online Banking Security Analysis based on STRIDE Threat Model. *International Journal of Security and Its Applications, 8*(2), 271–282.
8. Kotz, D., Avancha, S., & Baxi, A. (2009, November). A privacy framework for mobile health and home-care systems. In *Proceedings of the First ACM Workshop on Security and Privacy in Medical and Home-Care Systems* (pp. 1–12). ACM.
9. Oberlin, S. R., Parente, S. T., & Pruett, T. L. (2016). Improving medication adherence among kidney transplant recipients: Findings from other industries, patient engagement, and behavioral economics—scoping review. SAGE Open Medicine, *4*.
10. Higgins, T. (2016). The PACT of patient engagement: Unraveling the meaning of engagement with hybrid concept analysis.
11. Marceglia, S., Fontelo, P., & Ackerman, M. J. (2015). Transforming consumer health informatics: connecting CHI applications to the health-IT ecosystem. *Journal of the American Medical Informatics Association* ocu030.
12. Huerta, T. R., Walker, C., Murray, K. R., Hefner, J. L., McAlearney, A. S., & Moffatt-Bruce, S. (2016). Patient safety errors: Leveraging health information technology to facilitate patient reporting. *Journal for Healthcare Quality, 38*(1), 17–23.
13. Singh, K., Drouin, K., Newmark, L. P., Rozenblum, R., Lee, J., Landman, A., ... & Bates, D. W. (2016). Developing a framework for evaluating the patient engagement, quality, and safety of mobile health applications. *Issue Brief (Commonwealth Fund) 5*, 1–11.
14. Pavliscsak, H., Little, J. R., Poropatich, R. K., McVeigh, F. L., Tong, J., Tillman, J. S.,... & Fonda, S. J. (2016). Assessment of patient engagement with a mobile application among service members in transition. *JAMIA 23*(1), 110–118.
15. Garg, S. K., Lyles, C. R., Ackerman, S., Handley, M. A., Schillinger, D., Gourley, G., ... & Sarkar, U. (2016). Qualitative analysis of programmatic initiatives to text patients with mobile

devices in resource-limited health systems. *BMC Medical Informatics and Decision Making 16*(1), 1.

16. Shapiro, M., Johnston, D., Wald, J., & Mon, D. (2012, Apr). Patient-generated health data. In *White paper: Prepared for Office of Policy and Planning, Office of the National Coordinator for Health Information Technology. Research Triangle Park*, NC: RTI International.

17. Wiljer, D., Urowitz, S., Apatu, E., DeLenardo, C., Eysenbach, G., Harth, T., et al. (2008). Canadian committee for patient accessible health records c. patient accessible electronic health records: exploring recommendations for successful implementation strategies. *Journal of Medical Internet Research, 10*(4), e34.

18. Tulu, B., Trudel, J., Strong, D. M., Johnson, S. A., Sundaresan, D., & Garber, L. (2016). Patient portals: An underused resource for improving patient engagement. *Chest, 149*(1), 272–277.

19. Sawesi, S., Rashrash, M., Phalakornkule, K., Carpenter, J. S., & Jones, J. F. (2016). The impact of information technology on patient engagement and health behavior change: A systematic review of the literature. *JMIR Medical Informatics 4*(1).

20. Thompson, L. A., Martinko, T., Budd, P., Mercado, R., & Schentrup, A. M. (2016). Meaningful use of a confidential adolescent patient portal. *Journal of Adolescent Health, 58* (2), 134–140.

21. Chen, S. W., Chiang, D. L., Liu, C. H., Chen, T. S., Lai, F., Wang, H., et al. (2016). Confidentiality protection of digital health records in cloud computing. *Journal of Medical Systems, 40*(5), 1–12.

22. Silvestre, A., Sue, V. M., & Allen J. Y. (2009). If you build it, will they come? *The Kaiser Permanente Model Of Online Healthcare Health Affairs 28*(2), 334–344;.

23. Chen C, Garrido T, Chock D, Okawa G, Liang L. (2009, Mar-Apr). The Kaiser permanente electronic health record: Transforming and streamlining modalities of care. *Health Affairs (Millwood) 28*(2), 323–33.

24. Bayer, R. et al (2015) New challenges for electronic health records confidentiality and access to sensitive health information about parents and adolescents JAMA. *313*(1), 29–30.

25. Barkhuysen, P., deGrauw, W., et al. (2014). Is the quality of data in an electronic medical record sufficient for assessing the quality of primary care? *Journal of the American Medical Informatics Association, 21*, 692–698.

26. Benaloh, J., Chase, M., Horvitz, E. & Lauter K. (2009). *Patient controlled encryption: Ensuring privacy of electronic medical records.* ACM 978-1-60558-784-4/09/11.

27. Neetha X. and Chandrasekar V. (2015). Cloud computing data security for personal health record by using attribute based encryption. *International Journal of Information, Business and Management 7*(1), 209–214.

28. Buntin M. B., Burke, M. F., Hoaglin M. C. & Blumenthal D. (2011). The benefits of health information technology: A review of the recent literature shows predominantly positive. *Results Health Affairs 30*(3), 464–471.

29. Moody-Thomas, S., Nasuti, L., Yi, Y., Celestin, M. D., Jr., Horswell, R., & Land, T. G. (2015). Effect of systems change and use of electronic health records on quit rates among tobacco users in a public hospital system. *American Journal of Public Health, 105*(S2), e1–e7.

30. Henry, Y., Harkins, V., Ferrari, A., & Berger, P. B. (2015). Use of an electronic health record to optimize site performance in randomized clinical trials. *Journal of Clinical Trials, 5(208)*, 0870–2167.

31. Wang, Y., Kung, L., Ting, C., & Byrd, T. A. (2015, January). Beyond a technical perspective: understanding big data capabilities in healthcare. In Wang, Y., Kung, L., Ting, C.C. & Byrd, T.A. (Eds.), Beyond a technical perspective: understanding big data capabilities in healthcare. *Proceedings of 48th Annual Hawaii International Conference on System Sciences (HICSS)*, Kauai, Hawaii.

32. Greenes R A., (2014) Clinical decision support, the road to broad adoption. (2nd ed.), Academic Press. doi:10.1016/B978-0-12-398476-0.00032-4.

33. Walker, J., Darer, J. D., Elmore, J. G., et al. (2014). The road toward fully transparent medical records. *New England Journal of Medicine, 2014(370)*, 6–8.

Time Accounting System: Validating a Socio-Technical Solution for Service Exchange in Local Communities

Tunazzina Sultana, Angela Locoro and Flávio Soares Corrêa da Silva

Abstract This paper reports the first validation steps of the prototype of a Time Accounting System (TAS), which has been designed and developed to investigate how a technology that facilitates service exchanges using local currency can be accepted in a developing country, namely in Bangladesh. The paper describes the results of two Confirmatory Focus Groups (CFGs) that have been developed to assess the functionalities of the TAS. The main goal of these CFGs was to investigate how interactive and simple the system must be to be accepted by users, given that, based on some previous studies, the idea/concept of a TAS is expected to spread over in Bangladesh.

Keywords Time accounting system · Confirmatory focus groups · Qualitative prototype validation

1 Introduction

The impacts and consequences of Information Technology (IT) offers to designers and researchers a number of interesting aspects to study: on the one hand, technological innovation opens the opportunities for people to collaborate in "coordinated, efficient and reciprocal service transactions to improve the quality of life for all" [2]; on the other hand, a large number of developing countries, particularly

T. Sultana (✉) · A. Locoro
Dipartimento di Informatica, Sistemistica e Comunicazione, Università di Milano-Bicocca, Viale Sarca 336, 20126 Milan, Italy
e-mail: tunazzina.sultana@disco.unimib.it

A. Locoro
e-mail: angela.locoro@disco.unimib.it

F.S.C. da Silva
Instituto de Matemática E Estatística Da Universidade de São Paulo, Rua Do Matão – SP 1010, CEP 05508-090 São Paulo, Brazil
e-mail: correadasilva_f2001@yahoo.com.br

© Springer International Publishing AG 2018
C. Rossignoli et al. (eds.), *Digital Technology and Organizational Change*,
Lecture Notes in Information Systems and Organisation 23,
https://doi.org/10.1007/978-3-319-62051-0_22

low-income ones, failed in availing themselves of the benefits of ICT: this contributes to the "digital divide" between developed and developing countries.
Fortunately, the Internet growth rate in these countries, particularly from 2000 to
2013, is higher than in the developed countries,[1] raising the ground for different use
of ICT and the researchers' attention. This paper is a sequel of a work that aims to
shed light on a new way of using IT by combining western knowledge and local
needs to address the two following research questions: "Is a time-based service
exchange initiative (TAS) useful and appropriate for Bangladesh?"; and "In the
positive case, how can a time-based service exchange initiative (TAS), be introduced in Bangladesh?". The motivation to investigate the TAS concept in the
context of developing countries was based on the idea that such kind of systems can
bring a social and economic change in these countries in terms of addressing the
care of the elderly people, and the support to unemployed and low-income people
through ICT exploitation.

In this paper, we report the first phase of validation of the prototype of a TAS
that has been designed and developed based on the requirements that were elicited
considering social and technological aspects of the country and derived from an
exploratory survey [28] and two qualitative studies [5]. The design and development of the prototype of the TAS were conceived as a continuous process involving
both designers and users, and considering the requirements of the potential users in
order to make it more effective and efficient; and, from this perspective, we argue
that a TAS is as a socio-technical solution that can make service exchanges possible
through a system within a community.

In what follows, we first give some main motivations and background of this
research, and then describe the methodology adopted for this work. We then report
and discuss the main findings from two focus groups that are done to validate the
prototype. We then summarize the insights and the next step of our research in a
short conclusion.

2 Motivations and Background

Developed countries are presently passing the era of scarce governmental resources,
population ageing, and declining of social capital [9]. For these reasons, there are
initiatives trying to take advantage of technologies to tackle those problems and
help create and maintain the social network of interaction, trust, and exchange
among different units of the society [6]. One of these initiatives aim to develop
system like Timebanks, Community Exchanges, and Local Exchange Trading
Systems (LETS), where community members provide each other small services
according to their skills and availability and by relying on the reciprocity within the
whole network of members within the system by using local currencies. One

---

[1]ICT Facts & Figures, 2015.

particularly successful sort of local currency is Time Banking—which we call Time Accounting System or TAS—[5], spreading quickly in many developed countries within very short time [6]: for this reason it draws the attention of the researchers to better understand and support it as a worthy phenomenon.

TAS can be a suitable tool to tackle issues of social exclusion among the underprivileged people of a society, particularly elderly and low income groups [21–25], and to involve underemployed people who have a formal employment by connecting them through and within the network [3, 8–10, 18, 23]. A systematic survey of the literature [29] has shown that the use of technologies in support of local communities in developing countries is quite limited, especially when new forms of collaboration are involved. This fact, together with the increasing diffusion and adoption of ICT tools and devices (especially social network applications), create the conditions to investigate whether ICT based platforms can be used in developing countries beyond the simple aim of increasing socialization [27].

Our previous work has indicated that a TAS can be a useful and suitable tool to address the different problems mentioned in the previous paragraphs [5, 28] and is expected to spread over Bangladesh if it is well publicized and well understood by the receiving people. Hence, a prototype of a TAS has been designed and developed taking into account requirements that have been elicited through surveys and group discussions, and by involving potential users.

Since this research theme is new and there were no previous experiences to be leveraged in this effort, especially because every local conditions can determine different outcomes, our choice was to focus our research on a specific country, Bangladesh, that is interesting for its positive attitude towards innovation and could allow an easier research design since the author of this paper lives in Bangladesh and therefore has strong knowledge and personal motivations in this research. Moreover, since Bangladesh is experiencing the growing number of older populations [12, 15, 30] and now it is passing through the third stage of the demographic transition [13, 14], and it is going to face all of the associated challenges (health problem, social exclusion, mobility problem, unemployment, etc.), the very long run objective of this work is to promote and leverage the experience of use of TAS applications, to check their role in improving the elderly care and in offering new possibilities to the local people to reduce their unemployment and to improve the quality of their current socio-economic conditions. Hence, we are motivated to investigate the potential for the adoption of a TAS system in the Bangladesh urban domain, since the benefits of local exchange seem to be particularly fitting the urban social structure of Bangladesh [5].

3 The Methodology

We organized and moderated two Confirmatory Focus Group discussions in September 2015, within the community of Bangladeshi residents in Milan, with the aim of evaluating and refining the design of a TAS. This system should help them exchange ancillary services in their daily life. The group discussions were conducted by adopting the methodology proposed by [7] and used also by [4], since this method is extremely helpful to investigate new ideas for two reasons: (i) the refinement and improvements in the design which is done through exploratory focus groups (EFGs); (ii) the confirmation or evaluation of the utility of the design through confirmatory focus groups (CFGs) by involving actual and potential users. Moreover, this method was considered as the best one for this project since it will allow to go for a further rigorous investigation of the design in case of future development.

Usually, a focus group is a moderated discussion involving a relatively small group of participants (from six to twelve) who discuss freely about: (i) how promising and appealing they consider a prototype or an early version of a software artifact (Exploratory Focus Groups, from now on EFGs); (ii) the extent to which they consider that a refined prototype of an artifact is aligned with their desired requirements (Confirmatory Focus Groups, from now on CFGs). This discussion is usually held with the help of a moderator, who must be knowledgeable about the artifact under evaluation and stays in charge of supporting and guiding the discussion [17].

In our case, one of the authors, who is a member of the design team as well as member of the group of potential users of the TAS, played the role of a moderator. In these discussions, we pursued and ensured a relax sessions with potential users of the TAS application in a more informal manner so that we get frank opinions without hesitation or plain compliance [16]. Moreover, in order to encourage any kind of feedback, positive or negative, the moderator was highly receptive to criticisms and suggestions. Complying with the suggestions found in specialized literature [26], a person who has in-depth knowledge about the concept of a TAS was also enrolled as a silent observer of the focus groups, in order to take detailed notes of any exchange between the participants, particularly of non-verbal communications such as facial expressions. A typical focus group lasts about two hours and is usually recorded with the consent of the participants.

The CFGs involved twelve participants, lasting for four hours altogether. The participants in the CFGs were selected from the pool of participants in those EFGs whose outcome were the preliminary design guidelines for the development of the TAS prototype. A short report about these EFGs can be found in [5]. We also chose the members so as to maximize their variance with respect to education and income: as a result, the focus groups were comprised of service holders, retired service holders, businessmen, professionals, educated unemployed individuals, uneducated unemployed individuals, educated housewives, less-educated housewives, and students. The participants of the CFGs were selected and divided in 2 focus groups of 6 participants each, so that the groups were all homogeneous with respect to gender, age, use of smart phone and employment condition (the CFGs were configured as shown in Table 1). In this discussion, we deliberately exclude '65+' age group outcomes, as they were collected in another work as full requirements for an elderly-based TAS, where they could express their interest to get assistance and

Table 1 The composition of each CFG

Gender	1 M & 1 F	1 M & 1 F	1 M & 1 F
Age	<25	25–44	45–64
Smart phone user	User	User	User
Employment status	Unemployed	Employed	Employed/Unemployed

company at their old age as well as to change their role in the society from service receivers to service co-creators and providers [29].

We invited the participants to evaluate and discuss whether their previous requirements for the design of a TAS had been met and to evaluate if the sequences of steps to complete a task with the present prototype seemed sensible and reasonable. Discussions were done in a quiet room in which only the participants, the observer and the moderator were present.

We started our discussion by briefing about our objectives to the participants, and then we showed them a PowerPoint presentation. In that presentation, the slides contained different screenshots of the prototype. We displayed a total of twelve slides, representing the procedure of completing different tasks for making a transaction through our TAS.[2] In this case, we used the screenshots of tasks related to the issues which had been considered crucial during EFGs, and essential for the acceptance of a TAS.

We deliberately avoid allowing the participants to interact with the actual prototype of the software since our next phase of validation aimed at usability testing by the users to know how the users feel when they use the prototype of a TAS to identify the usability problem with the interface of the prototype. Moreover, the interaction with the actual prototype at this phase might bias them positively during the usability testing.

As previously observed, the respondents were initially wary of engaging into transactions with strangers through the system: they were concerned about the disclosure of identity of the TAS users, since they are likely to receive or provide a service through a TAS only if they can rely on the service receiver and/or the provider. Moreover, they were also interested in a system that would help them select their own zone of interest for a service. There were two main reasons for this requirement: (1) the members of a TAS are expected to be acquainted with each other and belong to the same community (which also addresses the identity issue) and (2) the help that they might be looking for through a TAS can be given mostly by their geographical neighbors. Additionally, users expressed interest in the possibility to book services in advance, in order to adjust their needs within routine

---

[2]In our TAS application a user (termed as Offerer) can declare her availability to offer any service (termed as Offer). A user (termed as Requester) can express his need (termed as Want). A Requester can have a Want for an Offer and the Offerer can accept the Want of the Requester. A Requester can reserve an Offer, and the Offerer can commit to provide that Offer. When the Offerer delivers the service to the Requester, a transaction is completed either by the Requester or the Offerer acknowledging the time received or used, respectively.

agendas of growing complexity. Therefore, we took the snapshots that were related to these particular issues and showed how those issues had been addressed in the prototype by answering any question about the information given in the slides. The discussions were organized according to specific questions for evaluating the prototype against the objectives mentioned above, leaving however room for the spontaneous questions. All the questions were phrased in an open-ended manner so that the participants could express their opinions freely.

The discussions were recorded with the permission of participants, and then two authors carried out affinity clustering with paper copies of their transcripts. We applied a hybrid approach [11], which combines inductive analysis to yield preliminary themes with deductive thematic analysis to reflect on the detected themes with respect to prior findings.

During the transcription, we assigned to each participant a unique identification number, e.g., P1, P2, etc. We then performed content analysis to identify themes and elements of interest. The detailed analysis of the discussions is reported in the next sections, where we group the relevant passages under three themes with supporting quotations and discuss them accordingly.

4 Analysis and Results of CFGs

Table 2 summarizes the main themes and their topics as they emerged from the analysis of the group conversations. The detailed analysis and description of all the identified themes and topics is reported in the next paragraphs.

4.1 Crucial Previous Requirements

All participants acknowledged that the prototype has complied with the previous requirements that were explored during EFGs; the sequences of steps to accomplish tasks are easy to follow and clear to understand. As the technological environment in Bangladesh is changing rapidly due to public and private initiatives in the ICT sectors [19, 31], recent changes in the technological environment of the country can accelerate the possibility of grasping the idea of TAS in its present form.

Table 2 The main theme with sub-topics emerging from the CFGs

Technical issues		Non technical issues
Crucial previous requirements — Informal tutorship for non tech-savvy people — Users identity/privacy — Zone Selection — Service Reservation	*New requirements* — Language concerns for acceptability — Time transfer capability — Mobile phones support — How-to for new users	*Reinforcement of previous concerns* — One hour equals one hour? — Promotion and motivation

P5: "Nowadays people are used to exploit online services for bus or train ticket or they pay their bill online [...] the procedure seems more similar to hotel booking [...] so I think it is easy to understand [...]"

People are getting more familiar with technology and digital devices. Indeed, the discussants raised with an assertive attitude the issue about not tech-savvy ones, considering that they could be supported by other people. In the EFGs we had already tackled this issue, and again this has been raised and solutions were proposed in the CFGs discussions.

P9: "They can ask to any family member [...] in the urban area it will not be a problem at all [...] but in the rural area, it may happen that the only mobile holder is out of home [...] in this case, if there is any nominated person by the coordinator, he could solve this problem"

Based on crucial previous requirements, we have also collected some new ideas to be considered as refining requirements. These are described in the "New requirements" section.

In our previous discussions, we have found that people were concerned about personal safety issues, which pushed them to admit their preference for TAS members of their same zone. CFGs discussions acknowledged that the present prototype is appropriate to reduce the wariness about this.

P5: "In fact, if I can check the user profile, it is ok for me [...] and if they are from my same area, I am more relaxed [...] and now we can check the area first [...] this makes my task easy [...]"

Although the discussants agreed that the present prototype covered the most part of the personal safety issues, interestingly they came up with new ideas about the selection of the service providers. These can be considered as new requirements.

4.2 The New Requirements

A second theme has emerged on 'personal safety issues' and 'ease of understanding' as optional or new requirements for a TAS adoption. As a part of their local culture, people usually consider a female and an old person to be less risky when they let them in their house.

P8: "[...] If the age and the gender can be seen from the user profile, it would be better; I can decide whether I will prefer to select a male or female for receiving help in cooking [...]"

This was explained by another participant as follows:

P12: "[...] Certainly, I will prefer a male when the service will not be provided in my house, and in case, if I need to allow someone to enter into my house, I would prefer someone of my father's age [...]"

While age is identified as a crucial factor for the personal safety issue (the older, the safer), it is also recognized that younger individuals are more suitable for specific tasks, as one of the participants put it:

P8: "[...] it would be better if I can see the age when I need to ask for such help that require physical labor, for example bring water or sack of rice from the shop [...]"

Some participants also expressed concerns about the language (either Bengali or English) and the alphabet (either Bengali or Roman) available in a TAS. In order to get more acceptability and popularity, their opinion was that the interface should be in both languages.

P12: "[...] I always prefer to read Bengali for better understanding, but I prefer to write in English on computer [...] because it takes me much time when I write in Bengali on computer, I get used to write in English"

These opinions could be explained in terms of socio-cultural and technological factors related to discomfort in typing using the Bengali alphabet. As expected, people are more comfortable with their mother tongue for speaking, reading or writing. However, if anyone wants to write using the Bengali alphabet on a mobile phone or computer, he/she needs specialized software to support the Bengali alphabet. Moreover, the peculiar pronunciation of the Bengali alphabet makes it more difficult to write [20]. As a consequence, users prefer to use the English alphabet for writing Bengali, e.g. AAMI, which means 'I', instead of writing the same word using the Bengali alphabet. There are evidences that this pattern of writing helps them express what they want to say in a better way than writing in English [1].

At present, the interface of the prototype is in English, as this was the preferred language of the EFGs participants, which has been also confirmed by the CFGs participants. However, considering the issue of acceptability of a TAS, the final choice will be an interface with the availability of both languages.

Participants reported that, although most of the TAS activities were simple and easy to understand, it would be better to have detailed information about a TAS and a video tutorial regarding how to use the system: this would imply a simpler understanding for visitors or first time users.

P2: "[...] It seems very easy to me, activities look like what we usually do for hotel booking [...] few days back, I used AirBnB for searching accommodation for personal reason [...] the procedure was the same [...] if you want to make the things easier, you can make a link for video tutorial for different task [...]"

The discussion then moved to the problem of the digital divide: what would happen to people who have limitations to or no internet access? Those who live in urban areas are in advantage compared with those who live in rural areas. The solution was proposed by the discussants themselves: as possessing a mobile phone in every household is no longer a new phenomenon, a TAS should provide a mobile notification of the required service. Since many people do not afford internet and a Smartphone, it is easy to understand why participants opt for mobile notifications.

An important point here is that the high diffusion of mobile phones can be relevant for the acceptability of TAS.

Last but not least, the most surprising and interesting idea raised by the discussants was about the transfer of 'time credit' to another area or another member. The groups were so enthusiastic about the concept that they discussed about the possibilities and necessities of using 'time balance' for their near and dear ones

> P5: "[...] I think there should be an option for using the points for our family members who are living in Bangladesh [...] you know, sometimes I feel very sad that am not in a position to help my parents in their work or to be with them in their need [...] I am earning money here [...] sending it to them [...] but I am not there [...] And they have some difficulties in their everyday needs [...] which cannot be solved by money [...] they look for someone who can help them go to town and visit a doctor [...] seek help from my relatives for this task [...] or they do shopping by themselves, it seems that I am doing nothing for them [...] there is no value of my money [...] I mean [...] if I can use my credit to receive help from someone in Bangladesh who can help my parents in their shopping [...] would be great [...]"

We consider this idea as one of the best outcomes of this phase, since this could help people keeping in touch even if they are distant from each other due to livelihood or other reasons. In fact, there are around 0.1 million Bangladeshi people living in Italy and they form one of the largest immigrant populations in this country.[3] Livelihood is considered as one of the main reasons for this migration. Most of these people are involved in formal and informal employment and they send money to their families back in Bangladesh. A TAS with the 'time transfer' capability is perceived as a bridge between these migrants and their relatives in their home country to keep and foster their relationship: they think that 'time transfer' can be as important as money transfer. Moreover, this idea shows the potential of a TAS as a tool for social capital development beyond the concept of "neighborhood".

4.3 Reinforcing Previous Concerns

Despite our effort to keep the discussion within the track of our TAS prototype acceptability, some of the participants raised their concern for the mentality of the Bangladeshi people in accepting the TAS principles, i.e., the evaluation of a service in the 'same unit of time' scale. This might raise some problems at the inception stage of the idea, since people are used to evaluate physical labor and mental labor differently.

> P5: "[...] If someone brings a bag of 20 kilos to my house in 15 minutes and someone else can fix a problem on my mobile phone in 15 minutes, how can you evaluate it in the same scale? People may not accept this easily"

---

[3]https://en.wikipedia.org/wiki/Bangladeshis_in_Italy, https://en.wikipedia.org/wiki/Bangladeshi_diaspora#Italy.

This wariness was also flanked by the fear of any abuse of the system by the users themselves:

P6: "[...] I think it is necessary to submit at least one paper document to the coordinator or to any specified person so that each person could be traced in case of any possible abuse [...]"

However, other participants were contrarian to this feeling of untrust:

P2: "I think in voluntary activities people will not do such immoral activities [...] because they will come voluntarily [...] no one will punish anyone who does not help others [...] anyway, in the worst case you can think for the photocopy of the ID [...] which is very unique"

Furthermore, the participants made a link between the voluntary attitude behind the participation in a TAS and religious viewpoints for negating the idea of abuse:

P2: "[...] Usually, when we come forward to help others voluntarily, religious view works within our brain, i.e., if we do something good for others, we will get a good return from Allah [...] so I think if someone gets involved in this system, he will not have that bad intention [...]"

Irrespective of its link with religion, the usefulness and the necessity of a TAS was discussed in regard to its acceptability in Bangladesh.

P7: "[...] In fact, religion came after society. In the primitive time, there was no religion, but there was society [...] people helped each other, this cooperation helped build the society [...] so [...] different people will join with different inspirations [...] it will give different types of utilities to different types of people [...]"

5   Discussion and Conclusion

In this paper, we have reported the evaluation of the prototype of a TAS as a proof of concept to be introduced in Bangladesh. The findings can be discussed considering two major dimensions: (i) effectiveness, i.e., to what extent the prototype seems sensible to complete a particular task on a TAS; (ii) and satisfaction, i.e., to what extent the prototype seems compatible with the requirements of the users. In general, both groups confirmed that the prototype seemed reasonable and sensible to complete a particular task for accomplishing a transaction through a TAS, and the requirements expressed in the EFGs were met. This showed a general satisfaction with the prototype.

Participants raised many issues regarding 'personal safety', 'comfort with technology' and 'ease to understand', among other issues. Despite the fact that the present prototype satisfies the participants in terms of achieving the goal of a TAS which was built with special attention to local socio-cultural and technological condition, they came up with new ideas and therefore show the direction for further work. Finally, the overall discussion indicates that the prototype has complied with the requirements elicited in the EFGs. There was a positive and constructive attitude among the participants towards the idea of a TAS. The participants were found very interested in a TAS and in the involvement in a TAS when there will be one available; they came up with the very visionary idea of transferring time credit between the areas and between the members of the system living in Bangladesh. They felt that this option would add extra value to the acceptance and use of a TAS in that country.

In the qualitative research that we have used for the evaluation of the present prototype to the aim of introducing it in developing countries, we have found a high level of acceptance from the users (focus groups participants). In this paper, we have also reported the participants' new requirements/requests for the system that could make it more user friendly and acceptable in the domain where it will be introduced. However, we take into account the limitations of this work: (i) not testing the usability of the current prototype; (ii) and validating the prototype in focus groups involving only the Bangladeshi people living in Milan.

The limitations of this study provide direction for future research: (i) test the usability of the current prototype in order to assess the user experience with a TAS, which would help us identify usability issues with the prototype interface; (ii) validate the prototype among the Bangladeshi people in Bangladesh, to unfold the functionalities of a TAS and help improve its design.

Despite the limited scope of validating the prototype in a different social context, i.e. not in Bangladesh, we emphasize that this research has the potential to identify a promising idea of TAS to be introduced as a socio-technical solution for the development of local communities. This work can then be seen as a contribution towards experimenting a system which plays an increasingly significant role in the western countries in alleviating the problems that these two different economies— developed and developing—are likely to share in the future, as a consequence of the economic crisis and of the aging of their population.

References

1. Aminuzzaman, S. (2005). Is mobile phone a sociocultural change agent? A study of the pattern of usage of mobile phones among university students in Bangladesh. In *International Conference on Mobile Communications and Asian Modernities II*. Beijing.
2. Bellotti, V., Carroll, J. M., & Han, K. (2013). Random acts of kindness: The intelligent and context-aware future of reciprocal altruism and community collaboration. In *Proceedings of IEEE CTS 2013: International Conference on Collaboration Technologies and Systems*. San Diego, CA, May 20–24. IEEE, 1–12.
3. Boyle, D. (2014). The potential of Time Banks to support social inclusion and employability. *EC JRC Scientific and Policy Reports, Report ER 26346 EN*.
4. Cabitza, F. (2015). On a QUESt for a web-based tool promoting knowledge-sharing in medical communities. *Behaviour & Information Technology, 34*(6), 598–612.
5. Cabitza, F., Locoro, A., Simone, C., & Sultana, T. (2016). Moving western neighbourliness to East? A study on local exchange in Bangladesh. In *Proceedings of the 19th ACM Conference*

on *Computer-Supported Cooperative Work and Social Computing, CSCW 2016*. San Francisco, USA.

6. Carroll, J. M. (2013). Co-production scenarios for mobile time banking. In *End-user development* (pp. 137–152). Berlin: Springer.

7. Chiarini Trembley, M., Hevner, A. R., & Berndt, D. J. (2010). Focus groups for artifact refinement and evaluation in design research. *Communications of the Association for Information Systems, 26*(27), 599–618.

8. Collom, E. (2007). The motivations, engagement, satisfaction, outcomes, and demographics of time bank participants: Survey findings from a US system. *International Journal of Community Currency Research, 11,* 36–83.

9. Collom, E. (2008). Banking time in an alternative market: A quantitative case study of a local currency system. In *103rd Annual Meeting of the American Sociological Association, Boston*.

10. Collom, E. (2008). Engagement of the elderly in time banking: The potential for social capital generation in an aging society. *Journal of Aging & Social Policy, 20*(4), 414–436.

11. Fereday, J., & Muir-Cochrane, E. (2008). Demonstrating rigor using thematic analysis: A hybrid approach of inductive and deductive coding and theme development. *International Journal of Qualitative Methods, 5*(1), 80–89.

12. Hossain, M. R. (2005). Aging in Bangladesh and its population projections. *Paki-stan Journal of Social Sciences, 3*(1), 62–67.

13. Islam, M. N., & Nath, D. C. (2012). A future journey to the elderly support in Bangladesh. *Journal of Anthropology*.

14. Khan, M., Mondal, M., Hoque, N., Islam, M., & Shahiduzzman, M. (2014). A study on quality of life of elderly population in Bangladesh. *American Journal of Health Research, 2* (4), 152–157.

15. Khanam, M. A., Streatfield, P. K., Kabir, Z. N., Qiu, C., Cornelius, C., & Wahlin, A. (2011). Prevalence and patterns of multimorbidity among elderly people in rural Bangladesh: A cross-sectional study. *Journal of Health, Pop-ulation, and Nutrition, 29*(4), 406.

16. Kitzinger, J. (1995). Qualitative research: Introducing focus groups. *Bmj, 311*(7000), 299–302.

17. Krueger, R. A., & Casey, M. A. (2009). *Focus groups: A practical guide for applied research*. Sage.

18. Lampinen, A., Lehtinen, V., Cheshire, C., & Suhonen, E. (2013). Indebtedness and reciprocity in local online exchange. In *Proceedings of the 2013 Conference on Computer supported cooperative work.* (pp. 661–672). ACM.

19. Rahman, A., Abdullah, M. N., Haroon, A., & Tooheen, R. B. (2013). ICT impact on socio-economic conditions of rural Bangladesh. *Journal of World Economic Research, 2,* 1–8.

20. Sarcar, S., Ghosh, S., Saha, P. K., & Samanta, D. (2010). Virtual keyboard design: State of the arts and research issues. In *Students' Technology Symposium (TechSym), 2010 IEEE*. (pp. 289–299). IEEE.

21. Seyfang, G. (2002). Tackling social exclusion with community currencies: Learning from LETS to time banks. *International Journal of Community Currency Research, 6*(1), 1–11.

22. Seyfang, G. (2003). Growing cohesive communities one favour at a time: Social exclusion, active citizenship and time banks. *International Journal of Urban and Regional Research, 27* (3), 699–706.

23. Seyfang, G. (2003). "With a little help from my friends". Evaluating time banks as a tool for community self-help. *Local Economy, 18*(3), 257–264.

24. Seyfang, G. (2004). Working outside the box: Community currencies, time banks and social inclusion. *Journal of Social Policy, 33*(01), 49–71.

25. Seyfang, G. (2005). Community currencies and social inclusion: A critical evaluation. CSERGE Working Paper EDM (2005).

26. Stewart, D. W., Shamdasani, P. N., & Rook, D. W. (2007). *Focus groups: Theory and practice*. Newbury Park, CA, USA: Sage.

27. Sultana, T. (2015). Social media in developing countries: A literature review and research direction. In *Procs of ItAIS2015: XII Conference of The Italian Chapter of AIS (ItAIS 2015)*. Rome, Italy.
28. Sultana, T., Locoro, A., & Cabitza, F. (2015). Investigating opportunities and obstacles for a community-oriented social media in Bangladesh. In *International Reports on Socio-informatics. 12*(1), 15–24. Limerick: IISI—International Institute for Socio-Informatics.
29. Sultana, T. & Locoro, A. (2016). No more throw-away 'elderly' people: Building a new image of ageing via a time accounting system. In *Symposium on Challenges and experiences in designing for an ageing society. Reflecting on concepts of age(ing) and communication practices, co-located with COOP 2016, Trento, Italy, IRSI Proceedings*.
30. Uddin, M. T., Islam, M. N., & Kabir, A. (2012). *Demographic dependency of aging process in Bangladesh*.
31. Walsh, C., & Power, T. (2011). Going digital on low-cost mobile phones in Bangladesh. In *Proceedings of the Annual International Conference on Education & e-Learning (EeL)*. 7–8 November 2011, Singapore, 151–156.

Author Index

Printed in the United States
By Bookmasters